Last Witness for
ROBERT LOUIS
STEVENSON

"Louis was the finest man I ever knew but it took me several years to come to this conclusion."

—Isobel Field.

Last Witness for
ROBERT LOUIS
STEVENSON

By Elsie Noble Caldwell

Norman : University of Oklahoma Press

9931

*The publication of this volume has been aided by a grant from
the* FORD FOUNDATION

Library of Congress Catalog Card Number: 60-7734

To the memory of
ISOBEL FIELD
who entrusted to me this last task

Preface

As a STUDENT of Polynesian lore and traditions I had long wished to portray the complete empathy that existed between this branch of the Caucasian race and Robert Louis Stevenson, especially the Samoans, with whom he said he had found "the end of the long, long trail." So I was very much pleased when his stepdaughter, Isobel Osbourne Field, whom I had then known for many years, said to me: "There are many things I wish to say about my stepfather before I go and you must say them for me. His character has been maligned by some, almost deified by others, until only we who knew him in everyday life saw a normal man of highest integrity and exceptional talents. Naturally what I have to say will be pungent with 'was nots' and 'did nots' in these my final words."

Once the project was launched, the Henry E. Huntington Library at San Marino, California, granted me full use of their extensive Stevensoniana, including their recently purchased W. H. Low collection. Also, I enjoyed the aid of the Los Angeles Public Library, the W. A. Clark Library of the University of California at Los Angeles, the Alexander Turnbull Library of Wellington, New Zealand, the Peabody Museum library of Salem, Massachusetts, the Bernice P. Bishop Museum library of Honolulu and the Hawaiian Historical Society, the *Daily Tribune* of Oakland, California, the *Scotsman* and *Scotland's Magazine*, of Edinburgh, Hon. Richard Powles, high commissioner at Apia, Western Samoa, and many friends in many lands. To all of these my sincere thanks.

The photographs used to illustrate this book are from Mrs.

Field's collection and my own except where credit is given to other sources.

Elsie Noble Caldwell

Los Angeles, California
August 27, 1959

Contents

Illustrations

xi

About Isobel Field

I FIRST MET Isobel Field in 1930 when I returned from one of my several visits to the South Pacific islands. I had written a news story about the Mau, a society organized in Western Samoa to resist the New Zealand government and since wholly discredited. Mrs. Field saw the article and, calling me on the telephone, deplored my lack of sympathy for the Samoans and asked me to come to see her.

Our meeting, beginning pleasantly enough, progressed to a pitch of ardor concerning who knew the Samoans better and liked them more. At last she said spiritedly, "You're a stupid woman!"

I shot back, "That makes us a pair!"

Ominous silence, her large eyes widened in astonishment. Then with a hearty laugh, "You told me you were Irish. Bravo for Ulster!" Upon which was built a long and firm friendship.

This was when she and Edward Salisbury Field were living in Los Angeles, and Ned, as she always called him, was a member of the Metro, Goldwyn, Mayer studio story staff. They had met in 1905 when Ned went to San Francisco to accept a position with a metropolitan daily newspaper. Before leaving Los Angeles, he had asked his mother for a letter of introduction to Mrs. Stevenson, the Fields and Van de Grifts having been neighbors in Indianapolis, where Edward Salisbury Field, Sr., had been a partner in a publishing business. Presenting himself at the Hyde and Lombard streets residence, he literally walked into the task of helping Mrs. Stevenson edit and catalog the huge accumulation of Louis's letters and manuscripts.

Following the San Francisco fire and earthquake in 1906, Mrs. Stevenson went to Santa Barbara, and there in the beautiful home of "Stonehedge" she died on February 18, 1914. On August 29 of that same year Isobel Osbourne Strong and Ned Field were married.

When the United States entered World War I, Ned Field joined the navy and served in naval intelligence for the duration, most of the time in London. Before he went overseas, however, he and Isobel took Mrs. Stevenson's ashes to Samoa, where with appropriate ceremony they were placed in the Stevenson tomb on the summit of Mount Vaea. Isobel never again visited Samoa.

Their happy home life at "Serena"—fourteen acres of Pacific Coast land nine miles south of Santa Barbara—was tragically ended when Ned died suddenly at their Zaca Lake cottage on September 20, 1936. Isobel—or "Teuila," as I always have known her—continued to share the wealth of the Field oil properties until her death, royalties on Stevenson's works having ceased with the expiration of copyrights.

In June of 1950 I returned from another of my frequent visits to Samoa, bringing to Teuila an *alofa* (greeting of affection) from Fauma-sina, who as a beautiful young girl had played tennis with Lloyd Osbourne at Vailima. Fauma-sina, then eighty, died in 1952—the last of my friends in Samoa who had been associated with the Vailima household. And Isobel Field herself died on June 26, 1953, leaving me to finish our joint project alone.

Elsie Noble Caldwell

Last Witness for
ROBERT LOUIS
STEVENSON

1. Fanny and Louis

WITH THE DEATH of Isobel Field in Santa Barbara, California, in 1953, there was stilled the last voice to speak authoritatively for Robert Louis Stevenson. Ever since the death of her mother in 1914, she had been a "swift witness" against the character assaults of the *chronique scandaleuse* and the calumniator who courted publicity through sensationalism to vitiate the memory of her famous stepfather and malign the character of her mother.

Often I have heard her say in her rich contralto voice, "Louis was the finest man I ever knew, but it took me several years to come to this conclusion." And if in a reminiscent mood, she would add, "I didn't value life in my early years and tried not to take anything seriously. But as I came to know Louis, I began to think of life as, indeed, he did—that it was a game to be played according to accepted ethics of human conduct. One could not be in his society without appreciating his example of the golden rule. Being human, he may not have been always thus!"

"First you will have a word about my mother—"

Frances Matilda Van de Grift came from fine Dutch-American stock with ancestors in this country as far back as pre-Revolutionary days. Her father, Jacob Van de Grift, went to Indianapolis from Philadelphia in 1836 and married the daughter of John Keen, who had fought in the War of Independence and was wounded in carrying a message to General George Washington. They had seven children, Frances Matilda the eldest, and their home on Michigan Avenue, next door to the

3

Second Presbyterian Church of Indianapolis, was considered rather pretentious. Henry Ward Beecher was called here as pastor in 1839, coming up from his first pastorate in Lawrenceburg, which was too near the Kentucky state line for his antislavery views. At the age of two, Frances Matilda was baptised in this church by the famous pulpit orator, who became a warm lifelong friend of Jacob Van de Grift.

Besides his lumber business and his interest in social and civic affairs, Jacob owned suburban property, and there he often went with his gay eldest daughter—now "Fanny" to family and schoolmates—to work in his vegetable and flower garden and to ride horseback. This was the joy that filled Fanny's life until there came to town a handsome young man from Kentucky, Samuel Osbourne, to act as secretary to the newly elected governor, Ashbell Parsons Willard.

Then, on December 4, 1857, in a home which had been prepared for them, Fanny at seventeen married Samuel Osbourne, the suave blonde southerner three years her senior. It was a wedding to fulfill the dream of any girl, with the Governor and his staff and other notables of the city in attendance.

At the outbreak of the Civil War the young husband, by that time a father, enlisted with the Union forces, along with George Marshall, who had married Josephine, Fannie's next younger sister. Both served for the duration of the war. George came home with tuberculosis, whereupon his doctor ordered him to California. Sam elected to go with him and the two young men sailed for Colón from New York, but George died as they were crossing the Isthmus of Panama. Sam continued to San Francisco, where he joined the stampede to the silver discoveries in Nevada. Heady with visions of quick riches, he wrote to Fanny to sell their home and join him. This was in 1865, and the primitive housing that Fanny faced would have daunted a less courageous woman.

With silver lodes, never rich in the Toyabee Range, showing

signs of petering out, Sam decided the family should move to Virginia City, where he obtained a good position as clerk in the Justice's Court. And here where family life might have been brighter, Sam violated his marital vows and Fanny suffered the first scar of heartbreak. She returned to San Francisco. Sam went to Montana and caused a rumor to be circulated that he had been killed by the Indians. Upon receiving this news, Fanny got work in a dressmaking shop. Then one day a tall man in a wide hat and high boots set the workroom into mild pandemonium by sweeping the quiet Fanny Osbourne into his arms.

During a year and a half in which Fanny was certain she had found security and happiness, a son, Samuel Lloyd, was born. But again her husband was guilty of infidelity. This time she took her two children and went back to her father's home— back to the house from which she had married so full of hope. At the end of a year Sam Osbourne gave his solemn promise of good behavior if she would return to him. Fanny accepted his word in good faith and, taking her sister Cora, returned to San Francisco.

To show his good faith, Sam bought a home at Eleventh Avenue and East Eighteenth Street in Oakland. This was in 1869. Here Fanny not only created a home of which any man might be proud but made for them a place in social and professional life on both sides of the Bay. She studied painting, doing creditable work, at the Virgil Williams School of Design, and in their home entertained among others such dignitaries as Judge Timothy Reardon and artists Raymond Dabb Yelland and Norton Bush. With Cora's help her dinners became famous among their intimate friends. Sam had a better than average salary as a court reporter and always was a gracious host. Into this serenity had come a third child—golden-haired Hervey, of such beauty and happy disposition that his father idolized him, as did all their friends.

Like the proverbial bomb bursting in their flower-garlanded cottage came the revelation of Sam Osbourne's love affair with a San Francisco woman. In complete disillusionment and humiliation Fanny left for Europe with her three children. She had done well with her art work, and Isobel, now entering her teens, had shown talent. Virgil Williams recommended an inexpensive art school in Antwerp.

Little Hervey, always frail, contracted a cold here. When it did not respond to treatment, they went on to Paris. Sunshine, care by the best doctors, and Fanny's devoted ministrations could not halt the ravages of glandular tuberculosis, however, and the beautiful baby was entombed in St. Germain Cemetery.

To avoid complete mental and physical collapse, Fanny resumed intensified study of both art and language, mother and daughter working together. Sammy Lloyd was put in a French school. They had no social life beyond occasional calls from other art students, when they would dine on sausages and French bread with black coffee while practicing conversational French. Even when their errors produced gales of laughter, Fanny never more than smiled.

Through the casual acquaintance of an American sculptor, Mr. Pardessus, Fanny heard about Grez, near the Fontainebleau Forest, where they could have good country air and excellent food at the inn and where there was a genial art instructor. When Fanny and the two children arrived, they found only one guest, Walter Palmer, an American art student. The place was ideal. There in the summer of 1876 with other guests drifting idly across Fontainebleau Forest came Robert Louis Stevenson.

Quoting Teuila anent that first meeting between Louis and Fanny, "It is romantic rubbish that Louis fell in love with my mother when he glimpsed her through a window, though she may have made an attractive picture in the lamplight. She simply was a foreigner from a country he never had seen. A

Zulu maid from South Africa would have been as attractive to him. And my mother, her life marred by infidelity, was immune to any amorous regard. Fact is, as their acquaintance progressed, she considered his stories of his travels with his donkey naïve as compared with her own adventures. And when he interrupted her sketching with questions about America and the Indians, he was a nuisance.

"My mother, naturally shy and reserved and feeling now more or less conspicious among masculine guests, took no part whatever in the diversions of the inn—promoted for the most part by the visiting Barbizon group—and permitted me very little participation. Mischievous Sammy Lloyd, spoiled by the equally mischievous attentions of the men, became oftentimes a disciplinary problem, resulting in many long evenings spent in the privacy of our own quarters. It was weeks after our arrival at Grez that I looked in surprise at my mother when I heard her laugh aloud. It was as if some dead part of her had suddenly come to life.

"I had a black alpaca bathing-suit that we had made ourselves. It had knee-length bloomers, a skirt discreetly longer, a neckline blouse, and sleeves below the elbows. With this I wore canvas shoes laced around the ankle, and I was permitted to splash with Sammy in the shallow stream while my mother sat on the bank sketching. This when we were quite alone, as we were much of the time."

It is logical that when they returned to Paris, their address should have been known to the guests at Grez. Quoting Teuila further: "Our apartments always consisted of a sitting room where Sammy slept on a couch when he was home from school, a tiny kitchen, and an ample bedroom with two single beds for my mother and me. There was no deviation at any time from the room that I occupied with my mother.

"Because girls studying art abroad were discreetly housed in private schools, most of the students we knew were young men in their early twenties—boys, to my mother, who was always prepared with ointment for a blistered heel or a bandage for a cut thumb, a dose of baking soda for a stomach upset, or a hot lemonade for a cold. Many, more transient than we, had their mail sent to our address, as did Louis, for he never lived in metropolitan Paris as far as I know.

"Life in a Paris apartment in those days was essentially intimate and gossip was our chief diversion. No one could remain isolated without raising the suspicion of his genuinely friendly neighbors, saying nothing of the sharp eyes and appraising deductions of the inquisitive concierge. It was known that my father, although unfaithful, was sending whatever money we needed; that my mother made her own pretty clothes and was not dressing beyond her means; that in this day of long multiple-ruffled and starched petticoats we sent our laundry out; that we spent many hours in the Louvre and Luxembourg galleries, and we only sketched in the parks and the Left Bank in groups of other students, and that my mother always chaperoned me to my dancing classes; our neighbors knew when we had guests and who they were; we exchanged recipes of American dishes for French and Italian—all of this in the quiet friendliness of middle-class folk who live decently and have an abiding conception of moral virtues. I want this brief picture of our daily life to refute categorically the absurd fiction built around our three years in France by pseudo biographers who would play questionable conduct against virtue in order to promote a quickening interest among readers, piling falsehood upon falsehood.

"My mother constantly carried the dread that some silly canard would get back to Oakland, where any tarradiddle would make a juicy topic of conservation, and where it would reach the ears of Sam Osbourne. So as Louis's visits became more frequent and he became an acknowledged suitor, I was thrown into the role of my mother's constant chaperone."[1]

[1] In a letter of January 24, 1957, Mrs. Lucy Orr Vahrenkamp (the

Because it was inexpensive, quiet, and homey, there was a second summer at Grez, then back to Paris for schooling, and a third unhappy summer at Grez when Fanny was grieved by news of her father's death. With spirit broken, she decided to return home and face the humiliation of divorce when she received word from Sam Osbourne that he had no intention of renouncing his inamorata. Louis declared he would follow her. She implored him not to, that it would make divorce proceedings even more embarrassing, as it did when he stubbornly defied her wishes.

He arrived ill and dangerously exhausted from his trip across the continent, so low in funds that he had to find the cheapest room in town. Fanny's friends and her family thought her little short of demented when she announced her intention of marrying him. Even Sam Osbourne had the gallantry to employ hindering delays in the divorce proceedings, hoping she would "come to her senses." With all his sins of infidelity he always had provided well for her comfort, except when he left her in Nevada and spent eighteen months in Montana—which waywardness he maintained he regretted.[2]

Teuila confessed that she "made no bones" about her resent-

daughter of Cora Van de Grift, who came west with Fanny from the parental home in Indianapolis after her first break with Sam Osbourne and lived in the Osbourne home in Oakland until she married Samuel Orr, friend of early Nevada days, prior to Fanny's departure for Europe) writes the author: . . . "Some things I do know. Sam Osbourne did not go to Europe when little Hervey was ill and died. I do not know what money he sent other than it would have been sufficient for their needs. My Aunt Fanny came home from Paris hoping for a reconciliation, but found it was impossible.

"One thing—*she never lived with Louis Stevenson until after they were married.* People thought of her as unconventional, but she was just the opposite. And both Lloyd and Teuila were always with her. She never would have left Sam Osbourne if she could have avoided it. So much has been written about Louis and Fanny— *and so little of it true.*"

[2] But Sam Osbourne's erratic behavior prevailed to the end of his life, when he completely disappeared between his courthouse office (he was still a court reporter) and his home.

ment of Louis's coming to Monterey. They were happily housed, with Fanny's younger sister Nellie adding gaiety, and Teuila believed her father would surely be joining them in his own good time, naïvely presuming upon her mother's continued grace of forgiveness. She had not the compassion to realize how much Louis, sick and weak and fighting utter discouragement in the constant rejection of his writing, depended on her mother's cheering society and her hearty midday meal—for him food for the mind and spirit even more than the body.

"Louis's conduct," Teuila recalled, "was not that of a romantic lover who had followed a sweetheart halfway around the world. Although he was gay and full of banter, he was almost coldly casual toward my mother—and hers [attitude] not much different toward him, except for her constant care in providing his preferences in food, such as hot baking-powder biscuits which he insisted upon calling little cakes.

"Maybe my mother saw in this contrast to my father the security from infidelity that had wrecked their marriage. At any rate she was happy when he was near, and I, standing in awe of her inflexible decisions, had no hopeful moments that she would not marry this penniless foreigner. At seventeen I would sit in judgment to be regretted in shame for the rest of my life!"

That Louis never alluded to her churlishness did not lessen her self-reproach in years to follow, and wryly she admitted that Louis's presence probably contributed toward her elopement with artist Joe Strong, *bon vivant* of Bohemian circles in San Francisco. She did not know then that only Louis saved a frantic mother from hurrying to the metropolis to retrieve an impulsive daughter. But they were too close for any hint of family rupture; yet each may have been as pleased as the other when Joe Strong was commissioned by the Spreckels Company in San Francisco to paint the Nuuanu Pali Oahu Island in Hawaii.

So two thousand miles of Pacific Ocean served as a philter potion when on May 19, 1880, Fanny and Louis were married at the home of Rev. and Mrs. Scott in San Francisco, with only Mrs. Virgil Williams as witness, Fanny marrying Louis so that she might nurse him through what doctors prophesied might be his final illness.[3]

Following Louis's miraculous recuperation at Silverado, with relaxation of strained parental relations and adequate financial assistance, they went to Davos, in Switzerland. Only then did Teuila fully appreciate her mother's devotion to Louis. It was here that the first accurate diagnosis of Louis's ailment was made. The popular fallacy was that he suffered a tuberculous condition of the lungs. His parents termed his malady consumption. Biographers have casually conceded this. But the high chiefs of Samoa knew that he did not have this dread disease that so recently had been brought to their islands by the *papalagi* (strangers).

Louis, Fanny, and thirteen-year-old Sammy Lloyd arrived in Davos on November 4, 1880, and scarcely were they settled in a comfortable Swiss hotel when Louis had one of his most severe hemorrhages. Fanny called Dr. Carl Ruedi, who at that time had just returned from Denver, Colorado, to take over the practice of his father, Dr. Luzius Ruedi, recognized throughout Europe as the foremost lung specialist.

Dr. Ruedi immediately diagnosed Louis's case as fibroidal.[4]

---

[3] Nellie Van de Grift Sanchez quotes a letter Louis wrote in 1881 to P. G. Hamerton: "It was not my bliss that I was interested in when I was married; it was a sort of marriage *in extremis;* and if I am where I am, it is thanks to the care of that lady, who married me when I was a mere complication of cough and bones, much fitter for an emblem of mortality than a bridegroom." (*The Life of Mrs. Robert Louis Stevenson* [New York, Scribner's, 1920], 77.)

[4] In corroboration of Dr. Ruedi's diagnosis, Dr. Edward N. Packard, of Saranac, New York, wrote to the author on May 12, 1952: "Dr. Hugh Kinghorn, president of the local Stevenson Society, which maintains the cottage in Saranac Lake where Stevenson lived and worked for a winter, tells me that Dr. E. L. Trudeau, who was consulted by Stevenson, was

He told Fanny frankly that there was no cure, only palliation. Louis must have complete rest and relaxation for two or three months, afterward only minor activity. Fanny wrote this verdict to her mother-in-law, but kept the unhappy news from Louis until it became necessary to quiet his restlessness by the doctor's warning.

But Louis's nerves were completely frazzled. He could neither rest nor work. Instead of lying, as directed, on the balcony, he was on the floor playing lead soldiers with Sammy and fooling with the Davos press. He did not care for the other guests at the inn. He did not like the food. He wrote to Charles Baxter: "I can not work, yet now I have fallen sick I have lost the capacity for idleness."

He dashed off poems, sharp and sarcastic, betraying his feverish state of mind:

> *A river that from morn to night*
> *Down all the valley plays the fool;*
> *Not once she pauses in her flight,*
> *Nor knows the comfort of a pool;*

---

never able to make a definite diagnosis of tuberculosis. Dr. Trudeau told Dr. Kinghorn that he never heard any abnormal physical sounds in Stevenson's chest and that he—Dr. Trudeau—thought it might have been a lung stone which eroded the blood vessels from time to time and caused the bleeding."

Dr. Lyman Cavanaugh, of Los Angeles, explains that fibronous bronchitis is a disease of the lung supportive tissue, not the lung air cells, and creates no secretion of mucus as in tuberculosis. The hemorrhages would occur as a result of tears in this supportive tissue, and these tears, scarred from the disease over a period of years, could come from various sources. They could result from deep breathing in the overstrenuous effort of walking or from nervous excitement under emotional strain or congestion from a cold in the bronchial passages—all because there is no elasticity in the supportive tissue to permit expansion under stress of deep breathing. And with each hemorrhage leaving its scar there is always the possibility of another to follow, plus the possibility of each succeeding attack's being more and more severe.

But still keeps up, by straight of bend
The selfsame pace she hath begun—
Still hurry, hurry to the end—
Good God, is that the way to run?

If I a river were, I hope
That I should better realize
The opportunities and scope
Of that romantic enterprise.

I should not ape the merely strange,
But aim besides at the divine,
And continuity and change
I still should labour to combine.

Here should I gallop down the race,
Here charge the sterling like a bull;
There, as a man might wipe his face,
Lie, pleased and panting, in a pool.[5]

Inability to breathe naturally and deeply prevents the blood from getting necessary oxygen and so is a hindrance to good health. This in the case of Louis created an avid desire for the out of doors. He craved oxygen. Yet physical exercise was impossible. Oxygen starvation prevented his putting on flesh, prevented recuperative rest with relaxation, made him a bundle of tense nerves, and, except for his innate courtliness and good breeding, would have made him intolerably irritable.

The recognized tendency toward excess in sexual indulgence attributed often to those suffering from tuberculosis of the lungs is caused by the increase of body temperature. This is in direct contrast to tendencies characteristic of those afflicted with fibrous bronchitis, which naturally lowers body temperature. Thus calumniators who have reveled in the sinful attractions of Edinburgh as having lured Louis from paths of

[5] Quoted by W. G. Lockett in *Robert Louis Stevenson at Davos* (London, Hurst and Blackett, 1934), 62.

virtue should have studied physiology. And it is wholly logical to presume that in instances of hypothetical surmise, each must write according to his own individual code of morals.

However, out of the restlessness of Davos and the confinement because of severe winter weather came *Treasure Island,* originally titled *The Sea Cook*—joy of three generations. The yarn, briefly sketched at Braemar, was begun orally over an imaginary map drawn to amuse young Lloyd, but Louis found himself intrigued by the characters he had invented and started writing them into a story. The first chapters went to London's *Weekly Budget,* which had a children's page, and to the author's surprise brought by return mail a check and a request for additional chapters. Working on the crested wave of success, he finished the story within three weeks, even with the bother of making a second map to replace the first one—lost—which Louis always declared was better than the second. Yet serial publication did not begin until October 1, 1881, in what by that time had become a separate magazine called *Young Folks.* In order to impress youthful readers with the story's authenticity, Louis used the nom de plume of "Captain George North."

One wonders if, when Fanny Osbourne became wife and nurse to this waywardly restless semi-invalid, she took into account the difficult role she was to play on the stage of publicity. And if at times she may have slipped from the high plane of cheerful serenity to be chided playfully by the invalid, did she realize that the world might read a sinister maliciousness or seek a hidden meaning in a momentary shift of temperament? Louis had a Puckish quality, but never for even a fleeting moment did he waver in chivalrous devotion to his "Stormy Petrel," a name referring to her March birth month.

Yet few wives of fact or fiction have been more maligned than Fanny Stevenson. The latest to add his iniquitous imputation is an English writer who attempts to account for her "moods of depression" by gallantly granting the probability that she suffered from epileptic fits! This is too absurd for comment. Teuila only laughed. Although she was never robust, Fanny's only illness of a serious nature was after Louis's death when Sir Frederick Treves operated for removal of gallstones. This famous physician to royalty declined to accept any fee, saying he deemed it a privilege to serve the wife of the man whose writings had afforded him so much pleasure. Fanny never used the word "widow" in reference to herself.

With the coming of spring Louis was glad to leave Davos and return to Braemar, where they had enjoyed a brief stay upon their arrival in Scotland. This health resort in the Grampian Hills near historic Balmoral Castle is pleasantly warm in summer but bleak and cold in winter. So, next, it was to the south of France, and after trying half a dozen places, they settled in Hyères, and Fanny—as the French say—again threw her petticoat over the back of a chair and made a home at "La Solitude." This wee model chalet of the Paris Exposition had been moved to a hillside site below the ruins of an ancient Saracen castle and near the famous rose gardens of Toulon, from which commercial attar comes.

Louis wrote to Jules Simoneau in Monterey: "Now I am in clover, only my health is a ruined temple . . . otherwise I have no wish that is not fulfilled; a beautiful garden, a fine view of plain, sea, and mountain; a wife that suits me down to the ground, and a barrel of good Beaujolais," the brand of Burgundy he particularly liked. He was happy with occasional visits from Bob Stevenson, Sidney Colvin, Charles Baxter, and W. E. Henley. These he found so stimulating, mentally and physically, that he dared to undertake an excursion to Nice, only to be brought down with pneumonia, which put Fanny through a night of horror when a doctor she called declared Louis was dying and there was little to be done. The following day she called another physician, who said Louis probably would live to be seventy.

Then he contracted an eye malady, ophthalmia, which kept him from using his eyes for several weeks. A siege of sciatica next; and to prevent further hemorrhages, the doctor bound his right arm to his side. Then Woggs (the beloved Skye terrier) got himself chewed up in a fight and had to be taken to a veterinarian.

With Fanny's devoted care and in spite of the handicap of constant moving from place to place, Louis wrote prodigiously turning out in two years *Prince Otto, Silverado Squatters, Dr. Jekyll and Mr. Hyde, Kidnapped,* the first draft of *The Black Arrow,* and collaborated with Sydney Colvin on *Deacon Brodie,* as well as with Fanny on her story, "The Dynamiter," one of the yarns Louis had admonished her to conceive on her daily walks.

By chance gossip on one of these walks Fanny learned of a cholera epidemic in near-by Toulon. With a minimum of commotion she packed Louis off for Nice, then made herself sick with worry when she could get no word for four days of his safe arrival. When he did write, it was a plea to come home to their lovely cottage in the suburbs of St. Marcel not far from Marseilles. Fanny wrote: "You are a dear creature and I love you, but I'm not going to say that I'm lonesome lest you come flying back to this den of death."

One of his letters, usually in humorous vein, is this acrostical jingle:

> *When my wife is far from me*
> *The undersigned feels all at sea.*
> —R. L. S.

> *I am as good as deaf*
> *When separate from F*

> *I am far from gay*
> *When separate from A*

> *I loathe the ways of men*
> *When separate from N*

Fanny and Louis

Life is a murky den
When separate from N

My sorrow rages high
When separate from Y

And all things seem uncanny
When separate from Fanny.

Where is my wife? Where is my Wogg?
I am alone, and life's a bog.

This nonsense warned Fanny of his restlessness, and she was in the midst of packing for a move to Royat when in he came. She wrote to her mother-in-law:

I don't wonder you ask me what Louis is doing in Marseilles. He became filled with the idea that it was shirking to leave me here to do all the work. He was a good deal hurt, poor boy, because I wasn't pleased.

Wasn't it delightful about the article in *Century*?[6] The person was evidently writing in such an ecstasy of joy at having found out Louis. I am so pleased that it was in the *Century*, for every friend and relation I have in the world will read it. I suppose you are even prouder of Louis than I am for he is only mine accidentally, and he is yours by birth and blood. Two or three times last night I woke up just from pure pleasure to think of all the people I know reading about Louis. . . .

He is incredibly better, and I suppose will just have to stay in Marseilles until I get done with things, for nothing will keep him away from me more than a week. It is so surprising, for I have never thought of Louis as a real domestic man, but now I find that all he wanted was a house of his own. Just the little time that we have been here has sufficed for him to form a

---

[6] An editorial review of *New Arabian Nights* in the *Century Magazine* of February, 1883.

quite passionate attachment for everything connected with the place, and it was like pulling up roots to get him away.

I am quite bewildered with all the letters I have to write and all the things I have to do. For the present I think we shall have to cling to the little circle of country around Nice, so when you come it must be somewhere there.

Consequently autumn found them settled in Hyères after a turbulent year of illnesses and Louis's threatened blindness, and at Christmas time Fanny wrote to her mother-in-law:

What a Christmas of thanksgiving this should be for us all, with Louis so well, his father so well, everything pointing to comfort and happiness. Louis is making such a success with his work, and doing better work every day. Dear mother and father of my beloved husband, I send you Christmas greetings from my heart of hearts. I mean to have a Merry Christmas and be as glad and thankful as possible for all the undeserved mercies that have been showered upon me.

It was here in La Solitude that Fanny, wishing to brighten their sitting room, painted Japanese scenes on the door panels. In a hilarious letter to Teuila she told of one picture of a woman yawning as she warmed herself over a brazier of glowing coals, from which she had to brush out the yawn because it set all their guests yawning and the house wasn't large enough to bed them all down.

Had these letters to Teuila been preserved, this voluminous correspondence switching from gaiety to gloom and from here to there with all degrees of anxiety, there would have been revealed a depth of feeling the world never will know. Fanny could abrogate all personal desires to Louis's whims and his needs, and she adored her father-in-law. Of her mother-in-law she once wrote, "We are poles apart and probably never will be close enough to really get acquainted." Yet with one exception she always spoke of her with filial regard. When they were living near by, Mrs. Stevenson came in one morning with a sniffling head cold. Fanny asked her not to go to Louis's room since he was peculiarly susceptible to colds and was particularly well at the moment. Nothing daunted, mother went in to visit her son. Consequence: Louis was in bed for two weeks with a severe cold. This written to Teuila in Honolulu was like writing a diary to relieve pent-up anger—not to be revealed publicly.

While Fanny seldom expressed resentment and never was given to noisy brabble, she never gave the impression of being in any degree a patient Griselda, and Teuila declares that in all their years together—daughter-in-law and mother-in-law—there never was a discourteous word spoken. The happy faculty of silence under stress and the fact that neither would jeopardize Louis's regard were their sole traits in common. It is to their everlasting credit that they remained friends to the end of their days, welded together at the last in mutual sorrow.

A very crucial situation developed in Royat when Louis announced that he never would live apart from his father. "So now," Fanny wrote when they had returned to Hyères, "it is to London we go to consult Dr. Clark about the possibility of Louis living in England."

Not long after came a letter from Bournemouth, both families having been advised to try the climate of the Channel city. And following this was the happiest news of all, that Father Stevenson had purchased a home for his daughter-in-law as a gift— a lovely cottage in a half-acre of garden. Both Fanny and Louis were giddy with happiness at having the first home of their nomad career, and they were alone in their little castle.

As usual the excitement of getting settled and the arrival of friends prostrated Louis. Unlike La Solitude, "Skerryvore," as they named their home, was near enough to London for friends to run down often, and while Louis found this exhilarating, it remained for Fanny to be rude to many who came unannounced. But always the door was open for Henry James, who immediately claimed priority of a big blue chair, the artist cousin Bob, Sidney Colvin, and most of all their neighbors, Sir Percy and Lady Shelley and Sir Henry[7] and Lady Taylor and their daughters.

Of their drawing room Louis said, "It is a place so beautiful it is like eating to sit in it. No other room is so lovely in the world; there I sit an Irish beggerman's cast-off bauchle in a palace throne-room. Incongruity never went so far. I blush for the figure I cut in such a bower."

It was here that John Singer Sargent came for two "sittings" when he painted the portrait which Louis never cared for: he did not like the striding on animated stilts and the tugging at his moustache. The original painting had Fanny in an East Indian costume as a bit of bright background. Since shoes seemed inappropriate with this dress, he painted her barefooted. Some sensation-seeking London reporters wrote that she was such a savage that she appeared at dinners and receptions without shoes. The family laughed this off as a good joke, but it was only one of many instances of ludicrous reporting that made Fanny wary of interviews.

Louis's rare trips to the Saville Club in London always left him invalided upon his return, and as a consequence he complained that he lived at Skerryvore "like a weevil in a biscuit."

Sir Percy Shelley, son of the poet, was his especial delight. Visiting informally, they discussed "everything agreeable and inviting," with always much talk of the sea and their common longing for a yacht.

During the three years here Louis did not equal the work done in the two years at Hyères. He was restless, was increasingly worried about his father's failing health, and was con-

[7] Sir Henry Taylor, poet and dramatist, died in 1886.

stantly entertaining or anticipating guests of his own ilk—a happiness which paid rich dividends of memories in years to come. They spent more money than was coming in, and once when the exchequer was lower than usual, Louis took one of Fanny's "Dynamiter" stories and whipped it into shape for publication.

Then there were depressing attacks of homesickness, for with all Louis's propensity for travel, his exuberant interest in discovering new places and strange peoples, and his easy adaptability to unusual environments, deep in his heart was the Scotsman's inherent love of the homeland. Even so near as Bournemouth one of these periods of nostalgia is portrayed in a bit of whimsey written as a charge to nurse "Cummie" in Edinburgh —most whimsical of all his whimseys. Perhaps he was subconsciously sensitive to the pendency of time.

Extract of his letter:

Some day climb as high as Halkerside for me (I am never likely to do it for myself) and sprinkle some of the well water on the turf. I am afraid it is a pagan rite, but quite harmless, and ye can sain it wi a bit prayer.

Tell the Peewies that I mind their forebears well. My heart is sometimes heavy, and sometimes glad, to mind it all. But for what we have recieved, the Lord make us truly thankful! Do not forget to sprinkle the water, and do it in my name. I feel a childish eagerness in this.

In the following poem it is presumed that she does so:

> *Aweel, my bairn, I'm no sae souple noo*
>   *As since I was. I cam pechin up yon brae*
> *Gey slow, gey slow.*
>   *A while I'll sit doon*
> *Ere I do your wull*
>   *Whit was it ye would hae?*
>   *Aye, here's your scrieve to say.*

Last Witness for Robert Louis Stevenson

An' thon's the wee bit burnie, soughin oot
    O moss an' heather, wi a sang sae sma
Had ye not writ sae clear where it sud rin
Hech sirs! I'd ne'er hae fund the pool ava.
    Hark to yon peewee's ca'!

The lums a Swanston wi their blawin reek
    Ablow me, whaur frae Halkerside ye may tell
The hale braw toun spreid endlang by its Frith;
Aye Lewie, fine ye'd like to be here yersel
    An' wark your ain cantrip spell.

I jalouse it's no just canny, yon same ploy,
    "Sprinkle the turf wi water" . . .
    Aye, with that same
Well-water from thon pool—gey cauld the drops!
Hech lad, yon's no a verra wiselike game
    "And do it in my name."

Weel, there's my nievefu' braidcast. "There's no harm"
    Quo he, "but ye can sain it wi a bit prayer."
Aye, that I wull.
    Mark not iniquity
O Lord, or who shall stand? Be Thy tender care
    Owre my bairn, where'er he fare.

How thae peewees skreagh an' skirl. . . . Guid
    keep us a' . . .
Like the sauls o the lost!
    "I mind your forebears weel,"
My daft lad bid me tell them.
    I'd best awa.
Ye've garred me play a gey wanchancy spiel
    The day, Lewie my chiel.[8]

[8] Published in *The Scotsman*, Edinburgh, August 11, 1956; used by permission of the author, A. V. Stuart.

Fanny and Louis

[Translation:]

Oh well, my baby, I'm not so active now
    As once I was. I come panting up the hill
Very slow, very slow,
       A while I'll sit down
    'Ere I do your will.
        What was it you would have?
        Yes, here's your note to say.

And that's the little stream trickling out
    Of moss and heather, with a song so small
Had you not written where it should run
Well sirs! I'd never found the pool at all.
       Hark to your wee birds' call!

The chimneys of Swanston, with their blowing smoke
    Ablow me, where Halkerside you may tell
The whole bright town spread endlong by its river;
Yes, Lewis, fine you'd like to be here yourself
      And work your own dreamy spell.
I suspect it's not just smooth, that same work,
    "Sprinkle the turf with water"
      Yes, with that same
Well-water from the pool—very cold the drops!
Hi lad, it's not a very sensible game.
    "And do it in my name."
Well, there's my handful of a broadcast. "There's
    no harm"
   Said he, "but you can settle it with a small prayer."
Yes, that I will.
    Mark not iniquity
O Lord, or who shall stand? Be thy tender care
    Over my child, wherever he is.
How those peewees scream and skirl. . . . The Lord
    keep us all . . .

23

> *Like the souls of the lost!*
>   *"I remember your forebears well,"*
> *My silly lad ask me to tell them.*
>   *I had better go.*
> *You've forced me to play a silly stunt*
>   *This day, Lewie my child.*

On May 16, only a few months after his parents had returned to their Edinburgh home, Louis received word of his father's critical illness. He left immediately but arrived too late for recognition—a regret that lasted through life.

Louis was free now to go where he wished. Both the local Bournemouth doctor and his uncle, Dr. George Balfour, recommended the mountains of Colorado, stubbornly refusing to accept Dr. Ruedi's positive diagnosis at Davos that climate had no effect on his malady, that his only need was pure outdoor air. So they prepared to rent Skerryvore for a year. Fanny, taking sad leave of her garden, left directions with her neighbor, Miss Adelaide Boodle, about management of the gardener and preservation of her precious plants, presuming only a temporary absence. Cryptically she wrote to Teuila, "Louis' mother is coming with us."

When they boarded the freighter *Ludgate Hill* at Southampton, Louis was completely exhausted and thoroughly discouraged about his health, though he had done little toward closing business and household affairs. The ship crossed the Channel to Havre and took on a shipment of horses. Before they sailed from the French port, Louis had improved as if by some miracle, and of the entire crossing he wrote to his cousin Bob:

I was so happy on board that ship I could not have believed it possible. We had the beastliest weather, and many discomforts, but the mere fact of its being a tramp-ship gave us many comforts; we could cut about with the men and officers, stay

in the wheel-house, discuss all manner of things, and really be
a little at sea. . . . I had literally forgotten what happiness was,
and the full mind—full of external and physical things, not full
of cares and labours and rot about a fellow's behaviour. My
heart literally sang; I truly care for nothing so much as for that.[9]

And still they failed to recognize the fact that it was the fresh
air, alive with oxygen, that made his heart sing.

Arriving in New York on the fallish day of September 7, 1887,
Fanny stood proudly but anxiously by while Louis was surrounded by reporters and greeted affectionately by his old
friend, Will Low; and was relieved when they were whisked
to a hotel to meet Mr. and Mrs. Charles Fairchild, then taken
the next day to their home at Newport. A cold in addition to
exhaustion from excitement put Louis in bed for most of the
fortnight they spent there.

Jekyll and Hyde was being discussed everywhere, and literary critics were leveling off with shafts of erudition that
made Louis's expressive eyes glow in pure mischief and wonder
at what he had done. All of which added materially to the
pleasure of meeting Charles Scribner and Mr. Burlingame and
Mr. McClure, and for the first meeting with Mr. St. Gaudens,
whose medallion of Louis is considered the best likeness ever
made aside from photographs.

Louis's condition was such that the cross-country trip to
Colorado was ruled out and Saranac was selected for the winter
—a more dismal choice could not be imagined. Fanny went on
first to find a house and make things as comfortable as possible for the family—Louis, his mother, Lloyd, and the French
maid, Valentine. Later she made a hurried trip to Canada and
bought fur coats for all, which prevented their freezing to death.
Isolated and with temperatures thirty and forty degrees below

[9] *Letters of R. L. S.*, ed. by Sidney Colvin (2 vols., New York, Scribner's, 1899), II, 77.

zero, no sanitary conveniences, water carried by the bucketful from down the hill, meager markets for provisions—the only word of cheer in Fanny's letters was that Louis seemed to mind it least of all.

It was here that Dr. Edward Livingstone Trudeau said he could detect no murmur in Louis's lungs, discounting the presence of tuberculosis.

The stimulus of success and the fabulous sums offered by rival New York publishers fairly swept Louis along in his writing at Saranac, and the result was twelve articles for *Scribner's* magazine, which included such essays as "The Lantern Bearers" and "A Chapter on Dreams." He revised *The Black Arrow*, which had plagued him with its mediocrity, and during the long evenings when the family sat around the huge log fire in the sitting room, turning to the meager warmth like so many spits on brackets, he helped Lloyd with his story, "The Wrong Box."

Here in the mental alacrity of creative work he conceived a plot for the characters of *Master of Ballantrae* that had lain dormant in his mind for several years, and he wrote the first chapters before they left in April. And adding to the *exaltation de l'esprit* was the notification from London that he was one of the nine persons in this year's annual selection for membership in the Athenaeum Club. His first comment was a regret that the honor could not have come during his father's lifetime.

It was in this mood of quiet exuberance that he had his last visits with Will Low before leaving New York for California. As usual, Fanny was the advance business agent. The rest of the family were at Union House in Manasquan on the New Jersey coast. Because it was off-season and there were no other guests, Mrs. Low went to the inn to be with the Stevensons. Mr. Low spent what time he could spare away from his studio. Also came Mr. St. Gaudens and John Sargent. Mostly there were short walks and boating, and at dinner one evening came the telegram from Fanny that she could secure the yacht *Casco* for a cruise.

"What will you do?" asked Mr. Low when he had read aloud the telegram that Louis had passed across the table to him.

"Accept, of course," replied Louis without a second's questioning of Fanny's judgment.

Louis was fond of recalling those evening walks and the intimate talks with Will Low. They argued about the values of art and literature and why wouldn't it have been better had they been bricklayers—as men do when they have attained a secure footing on the ladder of fame—and strangely they had kept almost an even climb to success. They laughed about the Barbizon days when the noon and evening meals at Siron's for five francs a day were a prime consideration.

Louis writes of Siron's, incidentally still maintained as Robert Louis Stevenson Inn:

I was for some time a consistent Barbizonian . . . and that noiseless hamlet lying close along the borders of the wood is for me, as for many others, a green spot in memory. The great Millet was just dead; the green shutters of his modest house were closed; his daughters were in mourning. . . .

Siron's inn, that excellent artists' barrack, was managed upon easy principles. At any hour of the night, when you returned from wandering in the forest, you went to the billiard-room and helped yourself to liquors, or descended to the cellar and returned laden with beer and wine. The Sirons were all locked in slumber; there was none to check your inroads; only at the week's end a computation was made, the gross sum was divided, and a varying share set down to every lodger's name under the rubric, *estrats*. At any hour of the morning, again, you could get your coffee or cold milk and set forth into the forest. . . . The whole of your accommodation, set aside that varying item of the *estrats*, cost you five francs a day . . . and if you were out of luck's way, you might depart for where you pleased and leave it pending.

Theoretically, the house was open to all comers; practically, it was a kind of club. The guests protected themselves, and, in so doing, they protected Siron. Formal manners being laid aside, essential courtesy was the more ridgedly exacted; the new arrival had to feel the pulse of the society; and a breach of its undefined observances was promptly punished. . . . I have seen people driven forth from Barbizon; it would be difficult to say in words what they had done, but they deserved their fate. They had shown themselves unworthy to enjoy these corporate freedoms; they had pushed themselves; they had "made their head"; they wanted tact to appreciate the "fine shades" of Barbizonian etiquette. And, once they were condemned, the process of extrusion was ruthless in its cruelty: after one evening with the formidable Bodmer, the Bailly of our commonwealth, the erring stranger was beheld no more; he rose exceedingly early the next day, and the first coach conveyed him from the scene of his discomfiture. . . .

Our society, thus purged and guarded, was full of high spirits, of laughter, and of the initiative of youth.[10]

In *A Chronicle of Friendships,* Will Low tells touchingly of another memory—his last evening's walk with Louis out toward the sea at Manasquan:

The tide was at its flow, the sea had turned once more to its ceaseless task, breaking in foam out upon the bar, foam of dim silver in the starlight, and rising ever nearer in circling shapes to die upon the sand at our feet. We had not spoken for a moment, and alone, we two, upon the beach, the world seemed very large, and the sea boundless and the sky without limit, when Louis broke the silence, speaking at first as though to himself.

[10] Graham Balfour, *Life of R. L. S.* (2 vols., New York, Scribner's, 1901), I, 154–56.

"England is over there," with a vague gesture seaward; "well, I bear her no grudge though she has cast me out. I cannot live there and—" turning to me almost fiercely—"Low, I wish to live! Life is better than art, to do things is better than to imagine them, yes, or to describe them. And God knows, I have not lived all these last years. No one knows, no one can know, the tedium of it. I've supported it as I could—I don't think that I am apt to whimper—but to be, even as I am now, is not to live. Yes, that's what art is good for, for without my work I suppose that I would have given up long ago, without my work and my friends and all those about me—I am not forgetting them; for, with all the courage I could summon, I would not be here to-day if all their loving care had not added to my courage and made it my duty to them to fight it out. As long as my father was there I would never think of leaving; all our old troubles were long ago forgotten, and these last years we were much to each other; but when he was laid at rest, I determined to make a new effort to live. Not as we lived at Fontainebleau, for youth was on my side then—remember how you never realized that I was less strong than the other men who were there with us—but to be the rest of my days a decent invalid gentleman. That's not a very wild ambition, is it? But it's a far cry from being bed-ridden. I'm willing to take care of myself, but to keep on my feet, to move about, to mix with other men, to ride a little, to swim a little, to be wary of my enemy but to get the better of him, that's what I call being a decent invalid gentleman and that, God willing, I mean to be.

"There's England over there and I've left it—perhaps I may never go back—and there on the other side of this big continent there's another sea rolling in. I loved the Pacific in the days when I was at Monterey, and perhaps now it will love me a little. I am going to meet it; ever since I was a boy the South Seas have laid a spell upon me and, though you have seen me all these weeks low enough in my mind, I begin to feel a dawn of hope. The voyage here, even with the bad weather off the banks, was life to me, and in a better climate on the Pacific, surely a better life awaits me."

He stopped for a moment and I was too moved to speak. Seldom had he spoken in other than in passing reference of his ailments, never to disclose the utter weariness that his voice, his gesture, and his words conveyed; at the same time that his slight figure, tense with his determination to conquer his ills, imparted a sense of hope, almost a latent certitude that on those far-off seas life as he desired it, awaited him.

After a pause he resumed in a lighter tone, "Yes, it will be horrid fun to be an invalid gentleman on board a yacht, to walk around with a spy-glass under your arm, to make landings and trade beads and chromos for cocoanuts, and have natives swim out to meet you. If this trip really sets me up I'll come back a regular Taffrail and never quit the sea. If it does all that I mean it to do, we will get some magazine to pay the shot and let us do a book together. The Ionian islands, the Greek archipelago, that's more your game. We, too, will live in Arcadia, and listen out for the sirens of Ulysses." I was used to this transition from grave to gay; and not ashamed, but seeking after the manner of our race to hide our emotions, we walked homeward gaily. . . . A few days after in New York, Louis said, "Don't see us off on the train. We can't lunch at Lavenue's, but we'll go to Martin's and drink a bottle of Beaujolais-Fleury to our *bon voyage.*" So this we did, and so parted.[11]

[11] (New York, Scribner's, 1908), 427–29; used by permission.

2. The Sailing of the *Casco*

THE FANNY whom Teuila met in San Francisco was far from the worried and harried mother she had last seen eight years before, and the tinkling laugh she had heard so seldom was music to the family, who had looked with dire apprehension upon her marriage to Louis. Away now from exacting responsibilities she was so much a girl that Dr. Merritt was reluctant to discuss with her the proposed charter of his luxury yacht, *Casco*. When final details were concluded, insurance, upkeep, payment of $500 per month rental, etc., he said rather grumpily, "And now, little lady, I hope you are satisfied."

To which she replied, "Yes, big man, and I hope you are."

That it was a bare-boat charter which she had negotiated did not in the least daunt the "little lady." Dr. Merritt had stipulated that Captain Otis should remain as master, so Fanny delegated him to secure a crew of four that would meet with her approval, thus eliminating landlubber applicants, already coming in, who were merely bent on adventure.

Then Fanny began calculations for provisions. Five in the crew, five in the family—three meals a day for ten people besides endless "mug-ups" for the crew and morning and afternoon tea for the family—six months away from markets—a daily schedule multiplied by seven—a weekly schedule multiplied by four and one-half, and the whole to six months. It was no haphazard estimate.

Frank Unger, friend of Louis's in San Francisco days, dashed about for hard-to-find items; elegant Charley Stoddard, who had been to Tahiti, gave advice;[1] while Fanny quietly ordered barrels of flour and sugar, sacks of rice and beans, buckets of butter and lard and syrup, kegs of dried beef, dozens of hams and sides of bacon, crates of dried and canned fruits, cartons of cigarette materials, cases of beverages of all kinds, coal for cooking, kerosene for lighting, and reams of reading matter hopefully designed to please different tastes. Then when she went to Sacramento to meet the family, she had to borrow Isobel's hat. She had forgotten to buy herself a spring bonnet.

Dr. Merritt had not been enthusiastic about chartering the *Casco* to the Stevenson party and was less so when he saw Louis, gaunt and pale from the tiring trip across country. Captain Otis shared the Doctor's qualms and secretly made preparations for a burial at sea. As usual, a brief acquaintance changed their minds.

In order to avoid the confusion in the small flat that Isobel had rented, Louis had a room in the near-by Occidental Hotel. Alas, without Fanny's protective guard there came a constant stream of callers, so as soon as the *Casco* was sufficiently provisioned, he and Lloyd went aboard as she lay at an Oakland pier.

However, before he left the hotel, Louis went to the room of an Australian writer who he heard was ill there and alone.

[1] From their brief acquaintance in Monterey and in San Francisco prior to the sailing of the *Casco,* Teuila had the impression that Charles Warren Stoddard was rather patronizing toward Louis. This impression is belied, however, by his tribute to Louis in his *Exits and Entrances* (Boston, Lothrop, 1903), in which he says: "I found Stevenson a man of frailest physique, though most unaccountably tenacious of life; a man whose pen was indefatigable, whose brain was never at rest; who, as far as I am able to judge, looked upon everybody and everything from a supremely intellectual point of view. His was a superior organization that seems never to have been tainted by things common or unclean; one more likely to be revolted than appealed to by carnality in any form. A man unfleshly to the verge of emaciation, and, in this connection, I am not unmindful of a market in fleshpots not beneath the consideration of sanctimonious speculators; but here was a man whose sympathies were literary and artistic; whose intimacies were born and bred above the ears."

Because he himself had known loneliness and stint in San Francisco, he sensed the young man might be low in funds, so with an apology of "one writer to another" he gave him a sum of money.

Mrs. Field says she remembers the incident but knew nothing about the loan of money until seven years later, after Louis's death, there appeared in the *London Times* of December 18, 1894, over the signature of "H," the following tribute: "Stevenson, who knew me slightly, came to my bedside and said, 'I suppose you are like all of us, you don't keep your money. Now if a little loan, as one man of letters to another—eh?' This to a lad writing rubbish for a vulgar sheet in California." Whether the gift was twenty dollars or a hundred, one can imagine the pleasure Louis felt in making it.

As he boarded the elegantly fitted *Casco*, there must have gone through Louis's mind the jingle he wrote at Hyères:

> *My wife and I in one romantic cot,*
> *The world forgetting, by the world forgot,*
> *High as the gods upon Olympus dwell,*
> *Pleased with the things we have, and pleased as well*
> *To wait in hopes for those which we have not.*
> *She vows an ardour for a horse to trot;*
> *I pledge my votive powers upon a yacht;*
> *Which shall be first remembered, who can tell,—*
>   *My wife or I?*

Certain it is that no "horse to trot" went through Fanny's tired mind as she, Aunt Maggie, and Valentine Roch joined Louis and Lloyd on board the *Casco* on the evening of June 26. The following morning the tug *Katie* towed the yacht across the bay to an anchorage under Telegraph Hill in San Francisco. And the next morning, June 28, 1888, with dawn breaking over hill-rimmed San Francisco Bay, Louis might have said with Whittier, "This day we fashion destiny, our web of Fate we spin," as he saw for the last time the green Marin County hills of his Silverado honeymoon days.

But no celestial sphere was his instrument of destiny; instead it was the *Pelican,* a rakish tug of low freeboard that clank-clanked alongside the trim yacht, belching coal smoke from her stubby stack as she reversed her engine in a noisy backwash. The captains exchanged greetings, a deck hand threw a line to the *Casco,* anchors were hove up, and the Stars and Stripes went fluttering to the masthead. Teuila and a group of friends waved good-bye. Yachting friends had wanted to escort the voyagers through the Golden Gate, but Louis had said no. A few ships in the harbor ran up the flag signals "B R D" in nautical farewell. The *Casco* signaled "Thank you" in reply.

On the front page of the *Oakland Daily Evening Tribune,* the only Bay area newspaper carrying the story, was this account of the sailing:

STEVENSON'S VOYAGE
The Novelist Sets Sail for the South Seas

Robert Louis Stevenson, the author, sailed to-day for the islands of the South Pacific. The yacht Casco, which Mr. Stevenson had chartered, was towed out of the estuary yesterday afternoon and anchored alongside the seawall on the other side of the bay last night, sailing with the ebb tide this morning. The party consists of Mr. Stevenson, his wife, and mother, and his step-son, Lloyd Osbourne. A crew of five men, who will navigate the yacht, is commanded by Captain S. H. Otis. The cruise will last at least six months, the first objective point being the Marquesas group. The Society islands will then be visited, and afterward they will touch at Samoa, explore the Cook islands, and sail northward to Fiji and the Sandwich islands, returning to San Francisco from Honolulu. The prime object of the voyage is to recuperate Mr. Stevenson's health. During the past ten years he has been an invalid, confined to his room most of the time by serious lung troubles. His physicians are of the opinion that the cavity known to exist in his lungs has been healed, but he is likely to remain weak, and may always be incapacited for more than the slightest exertion or exposure, unless a radical change of climate such as would result from a long sea voyage in the tropics effects a permanent cure. Aside from the rejuvenation of his health, Mr. Stevenson will gather material for literary work of every character, which has been contracted for by Scribner's sons. The reading public will look forward with deep interest to the return of this most popular of writers, knowing full well that he will bring back a rich store of literary treasure.

At a safe offing beyond the Golden Gate the *Casco* set her sails and cast loose the *Pelican's* tow line hanging in a bight. The yacht sheered the blue water, rising and falling to the long Pacific Coast swells as she heeled to a brisk northwesterly breeze on her starboard beam. On board it was not so happy. Fanny, Lloyd, and Valentine took to their berths without delay. Aunt Maggie, as Teuila always spoke of Louis's mother, wrote in her book, *From Saranac to the Marquesas:*

Sunday, July 1 [*1888*]
This is our fourth day at sea, and all goes well, I am thankful to say. Everybody was at lunch to-day except Fanny: she and Lloyd and Valentine spent most of their time during the first three days in bed, and even the captain did not appear at meals for two days, so that Louis and I had them all by ourselves....[2]

In the ecstasy of sailing, Louis's mind must have flown back

[2] (London, Methuen and Co., 1903), 62.

to a June night in Edinburgh in 1875 when William Seed came to see his father about building lighthouses along the ragged coast of New Zealand. Incidentally, Mr. Seed was not premier as Sidney Colvin tagged him in commenting editorially upon Louis's letter telling of this visit: "Awfully nice man here to-night. Public servant—New Zealand. Telling us all about the South Sea Islands till I was sick with desire to go there; beautiful shapes, green for ever; perfect climate; perfect shapes of men and women, with red flowers in their hair; and nothing to do but study oratory and etiquette, sit in the sun, and pick up the fruits as they fall. Navigator's Island is the place; absolute balm for the weary."

William Seed's son, Arthur, tells of his father's visit in a recent New Zealand *Listener* interview: ". . . My father conferred with Stevenson, senior, and spent some months with him drawing up plans for the lighting of the New Zealand coast. He became intimate with the family and met R. L. S. as a young man of twenty-five already suffering with consumption. Very little was known of the disease at that time and the general thought was that a warm climate would alleviate it. Hence my father suggested to Stevenson, senior, that R. L. S. should settle in Samoa."

Louis wrote to Charles Baxter: "I have found a yacht, and we are going the full pitch for seven months. If I can not get my health back (more or less), 'tis madness; but of course there is hope, and I will play big. . . . If this business fails to set me up, £2,000 is gone, and I know I can't get better."[3]

And to Henry James he wrote: ". . . It seems too good to be true, and is a very good way of getting through the green-sickness of maturity, which, with all its accompanying ills, is now declaring itself in my mind and life. They tell me it is not

[3] From Union House, Manasquan, N. J., May 11, 1888. (*Letters of R. L. S.*, ed. by Colvin, II, 125.)

so severe as that of youth; If I (and the *Casco*) are spared, I shall tell you more exactly, as I am one of the few people in the world who do not forget their own lives."[4]

[4] *Ibid.*, II, 127.

3. Sailing into a New World

STEVENSON WROTE in his book *"In the South Seas"*:

To cross the Channel is, for a boy of twelve, to change heavens; to cross the Atlantic, for a man of twenty-four, is hardly to modify his diet. But I was now escaped from the shadow of the Roman Empire, under whose toppling monuments we were all cradled, whose laws and letters are on every hand of us, constraining and preventing. I was now to see what men might be whose fathers had never studied Virgil, had never been conquered by Caesar, and never been ruled by the wisdom of Gaius or Papinian. By the same step I had journeyed forth out of that comfortable zone of kindred languages, where the curse of Babel is so easy to be remedied . . . .[1]

Captain Otis, who had frankly disapproved of Louis when he saw him bundled up in coat and shawl in San Francisco, changed his mind when he found him an excellent sailor and affable companion, and as they sailed southward into the mellowness of tropical breezes, life on the *Casco* was not only pleasant but luxurious. Except for sudden squalls which sent everyone scurrying for shelter, there was an atmosphere of complete serenity. Even Fanny, who disliked the sea, was serenely happy in the improvement in Louis's health.

One day when the *Casco*'s sails were flapping like tired wings and she was drifting along at about two knots an hour, Louis was leaning far out over the bow dangling a fishing line.

[1] (London, Chatto and Windus, 1900), 7-8.

Fanny, watching his precarious perch, remarked proudly to Aunt Maggie, "Now I am justified. I never thought I'd see him looking so well!"

He had gained considerable weight; his bones had a good covering of flesh which was tanned and smooth; his eyes, always his most striking feature, had lost their expression of smoldering coals and were bright with relaxation and fun.

The warmth of tropical latitudes brought complete mental and physical lassitude. The swish of spray as the schooner's bow cut the waves, the slap-slap, slap-slap of top seas on the sides, the steady rise and fall in the eternal rhythm of the sea— day and night, day and night—intoxicate the senses to the point of hypnosis. Several times Louis roused himself and tried to work on *The Master of Ballantrae*. The story was to begin in *Scribner's* December issue. December was four and one-half months away, and the editors already had enough for four numbers. His mind was as blank as the sheet of yellow paper on his writing pad. He felt much like the little boy in the poem, "that time had fallen asleep."

Under date of July 15, 1888, he wrote:

"Schooner yacht *Casco*, seventy-two tons register, ninety-five feet long; eleven souls, all told; steward, a much travelled Japanese; four deck hands—three Swedes and the inevitable Finn; captain and five lumberers in the cabin; all the human trumpery, like so many barnacles upon a piece of wreck, seventeen days out of San Francisco. Since on the fifth day, we were left ignominiously behind a certain full-rigged English ship, our quondam comrade, bound around the Horn, we have not spied a sail, nor a land bird, nor a shred of seaweed. In impudent isolation, the toy schooner has plowed her path of [now] across the empty deep, far from all track of commerce, far from any hand of help; now to the sound of slatting sails and stomping of sheet-blocks, staggering in the turmoil of that

Two Brothers Re

MARSHALL ISLANDS
Brown Group

Gaspar Rico

RADACK CHAIN

RALICK CHAIN

Arecifes

Johnston Is.

June 1889, Schooner "Equator"

Majuro Is.
Jaluit
Namorik
Kili
Ebon

Aur Is.

Mulgrave Is.

Little Makin
Big Makin

GILBERT ISLANDS

Butaritari
Apaiang
Maiana
Kuria
Aranuka
Nonuti
Tapituea
Onoatoa
Tamana

Maraki
Tarawa
Apemama

Peru

Nukunau

Arorae

Howland Is.
Baker Is.

Pleasant Is.
Ocean Is.

Arthur Is.
PHOENIX IS.
Gardner Is.

Enderbury Is.
Phoenix Is.

SOLOMON
ISLANDS

MALAYTA

SANCRISTOVAL
Vanikoro
Pandora Reef
Torres Is.

Motuiti Is.

SANTA
CRUZ IS.
Nitendi

ELLICE IS.

Gran Coca
Nanumango
Nui
Nukufetau
Funafuti

Nanomea
Niutao
Vaitupu

TOKELAU (UNION)
ISLANDS
Atafu
Nukunona
Fakaofo

S.S. Janet Nicoll

Aneuda
Tukopia
Banks Is.

Sophia Is.

Rotumah
Horne (Futuna)

Olosenga
(Swain)

SAMOA (NAVIGATOR) IS
Savaii
Apia
Uea (Wallis)
Upolu

Equator
1889

Manu
Tutuila
Rose Is

Espiritu Santo
Mallicollo
NEW
HEBRIDES

Astrolabe
Belep Is.
Cape

NEW
CALEDONIA
Pt. St. Vincent
Noumea

Aurora
Pentecost Is.
Ambrym
Api (Tamaho)
Shepherd Is.

Tanna
Aniwa
Uea
Lifu
LOYALTY IS.
Mare
Kunie
(Isle of Pines)

Erromango
Aneitium

VANUA
LEVU
Yasawa
Group
VITI
LEVU

Niua

Exploring Is.

Keppel Is.
TONGA (FRIENDLY)

Vavau
Group

Kandavu

Suva

Lau
(Eastern)
Group
Tafoa

FIJI
ISLANDS

Nukualofa

Pylstaart

Namuka
Tongatabu
Eua

Haapai Group

Niue (Savage)

to Sydney

from Sydney & Auckland
S.S. Janet Nicoll 1890

Scale in Miles

0   100 200 300 400 500   1000

Necker Is.   Bird Is.
KAUAI   OAHU   MOLOKAI
Niihau   MAUI
Honolulu   Mauna Kea (13,955)
LANAI   Hilo
Mauna Loa   Kilauea
(13,700)   HAWAII (OWHYHEE)
HAWAIIAN (SANDWICH) ISLANDS

"Casco" 1889

from San Francisco 1888 Schooner Yacht "Casco"

Palmyra
Fanning Is.
CENTRAL POLYNESIAN SPORADES
Christmas Is.   Equator

Malden Is.
Starbuck Is.
MARQUESAS IS.
Victoria Is.
Nukuhiva
Uahuka
Penrhyn Is.   Uapu   Hiva-oa
(Tongarewa)   Tahuata   Motane
Flint Is.   Fatuhiva
ukapuka
(danger Is)
Jassau Is.   Manihiki (Humphrey Is)   PAUMOTU (LOW)
ARCHIPELAGO
Suwarrow Is.   Arutua   Ahii
Tikehau   Aratica
SOCIETY IS.   Makatea   Raraka
Tubai   Katiu   Takaroa
Borabora   Huahine   Teau   Raroia
Raiatea   Fakarava
Mooréa Channel   Anaa   Amanu
Taiarapu   Marutea   Hau
Tahiti   Maitea
Aitutaki   Atiu   (Otaheita)
COOK (HERVEY) ISLANDS   Hereheretue   Parnoa   Tureia
Duke of Gloucester Is.   Vanavana
Rarotonga   Tematangi
Mangaia

Robert Louis Stevenson's Cruises in the South Seas

business falsely called a calm, now in the assault of squalls, bringing her lee-rail in the sea. To the limit of N.E. Trades we carried some attendant pilot birds, silent, brown-suited, quackish fellows, infinitely graceful on the wing, dropping at times in comfortable sheltered hollows of the swell and running a while in the snowy footmarks on the water before they rise again in flight. Scarce had these dropped us, ere the Boatswains took their place, birds of ungainly shape but beautiful against the heavens in their white plummage . . . a turtle fast asleep in the early morning sunshine . . . .

The Southern Cross hung athwart in the fore-rigging like the frame of a wrecked kite . . . the pole star and the familiar plough dropping ever lower in the wake. These build up thus far the history of our voyage. It is singular to come so far and see so infinitely little. But our own ship, our own poor eleven selves, have been the main feature of these endless hungry solitudes; where it strikes one with surprise to see the pilot bird squatter down upon the swells and greedily drink brine, and almost with pain to see him wing stalwartly day after day with no more considerable hope than now and then a piece of orange peel and now and then a pot of floating grease. . . .

16th—Or was it really for orange peel and grease that the pilot bird pursued us all these hundreds of sea miles? and not rather for esoteric comradeship and the sense of the picturesque.[2]

Apathy lifted perceptibly as observations revealed toward the end of the third week that Nuku Hiva (Marchand Island) was not far off. Anticipation was like mercury in a fair-weather barometer. Any shore line would be welcome after the monotony of only sea and sky. But this is one instance in which anticipation is not the better part of realization, for the uninitiated cannot conjure up the gemlike quality of South Sea

[2] From a manuscript in the archives of the Henry E. Huntington Library, San Marino, California.

islands. They are forested tips of sunken mountains extending two or three thousand feet above restless ocean currents that constantly change from turquoise to sapphire by day, and from cobalt in the moonlight to indigo on a stormy night. Louis with his vivid imagination was not prepared for the emotional appeal of his first glimpse of this outpost of the Marquesas group, for he reveals graphically his first enraptured moments:

The first experience can never be repeated. The first love, the first sunrise, the first South Sea Island, are memories apart and touched by the virginity of sense.

Our mark of anchorage was a blow-hole in the rocks, near the south-easterly corner of the bay. Punctually to our use, the blow-hole spouted; the schooner turned upon her heel; the anchor plunged. It was a small sound, a great event; my soul went down with these moorings whence no windlass may extract nor any diver fish it up; and I, and some part of my ship's company, were from that hour the bondslaves of the isles of Vivien.[3]

This bit of description bears the date of July 28, but in his diary he writes on July 22:

No language can express the pleasure of this spot—It is not alone the forms of the mountains, the square cut cliffs, the pinnacled buttresses—the razor edge against the heavens, even that roughened and greened with climbing forest. It is not the greenness of the dales and hollows, nor yet the palms so ungainly yet so pleasing. It is not the incredible generous smoothness of the air, not the cleanness and lightness of the perfumes. It is not the perpetual songs of the birds, nor yet the bleating of the thousand sheep which are now being driven along a shoreside hill, thick as an army of marching ants, the lads pur-

[3] *Ibid.*

43

suing them with singular and birdlike cries—it is not one, nor yet all of them together; the spring of delight, I think, is mainly in the colours. About an hour ago before the sun was up I stood and gazed on our two mountains as they overhung the port with every variety of surface and verdure, pinnacle and cliff and grassy mound, cotton patch and forest and the clusters of palms; not one of these, nor one square inch of one of them, nor the least variety of indication in the ground but wore its proper tint.[4]

On August 3 there is this note in his diary: "Tropical night thoughts: I woke this morning about three; the night was heavenly with scent and temperature, the long swell brimmed into the bay and filled it full and then subsided, silently, gently and deeply, the *Casco* rolled; only at times a block piped like a bird . . . ."

Nuku Hiva, or Marchand Island, principal of the Marquesas group, with a length of fourteen miles and a width of ten miles is fairly large as South Sea islands go; and it ranks second in beauty only to Mooréa of the Tahitian group, which is known as the "Belle of the Pacific." Diminutive, however, as compared with Nuku Hiva, since it is only about eight miles each way, yet with Mount Tohivea 3,975 feet high as compared with Nuku Hiva's highest peak of 3,890 feet above sea level. Two other Nuku Hiva peaks reach heights of 2,000 and 3,000 feet respectively; all are steep-to from the sea, giving the effect of medieval escarpments, and the naked tors piercing the junglelike green of the forest create this startling beauty. The only beaches are the mouths of narrow valleys, and even these slip into the sea to great depths.

Before leaving San Francisco, all except Louis had been vaccinated against smallpox and the doctor had given Fanny some vaccine to use in event of necessity. It had been twenty years since Nuku Hiva had experienced its fearful smallpox scourge

[4] In the W. H. Low collection in the Henry E. Huntington Library.

and the population had dropped from two thousand to a few hundreds in the years 1864–65. Since the population had grown to five hundred by 1919, it is believed that there were between three and four hundred when the *Casco* party arrived, and no cases of the disease had been found in fifteen years. The vaccine was not used, but at what a risk!

It is probable that the *Casco* party found little to admire in the people as they were at that time, yet one hundred years earlier they would have seen one of the finest specimens of people in the world: handsome, built like Greek gods and goddesses, healthy and proud, and the men with the courage of a paladin. They were fighters for the glory of fighting, and it was this trait, not the necessity for food, that instigated cannibalism. In deeply recessed valleys, cut off from neighbors by steep mountains impassable except for the very rugged, clans lived quite isolated from each other. When young men felt the urge for excitement, they negotiated these mountain ridges or skirted the island in canoes for the age-old game of conquest. Capturing, not killing, was the object, and the higher the victim's rank the greater their glory; and these rivalries, not hatreds, were passed down from generation to generation.

A vivid description of the sacrificial rites is given by Rev. I. R. Dordillon: "Captives who were taken alive to the tribal feast place to be sacrificed were called *tinaka*. Those destined for the tribal god were taken to the temple, where they were killed and sacrificed with the reciting of the chant called *haihai heana;* the body was suspended in a coconut tree, left there for three days, then cut up and buried in the ground. . . . Those victims that were destined to be eaten were killed on the feast place and there cut up and distributed."[5]

Although there was no record of cannibalism since 1880—and

[5] Quoted by E. S. Craighill Handy in "Native Culture of the Marquesas," *Bulletin* 9 (1923) of the Bishop Museum library, Honolulu. Original Dordillon manuscript in possession of the Roman Catholic mission in the Marquesas.

never any record of their having killed strangers—Louis in 1884, unfamiliar with the rules of their game, might be pardoned for his concern for the safety of the *Casco* party when he expressed fear for the women folk.

And perhaps the Marquesans had forgiven the incident of 1813 when Captain David Porter discovered a few remote islands of the Marquesas not yet claimed by Europeans, took possession of them in the name of the United States of America, named them the Washington group, and proceeded by a display of the might of four ships to subdue the whole thoroughly frightened native population of an estimated 100,000 in the three great valleys of what he named Madison Island, in honor (?) of President James Madison. Then he went pirating for further conquests, leaving three contraband ships and crews to guard the island. It was not long before the natives, under an Englishman named Wilson, revolted, and only one ship got away to flee to Hawaii.

Thirty years later France took possession of the island group, and it was about this time that the scourge of disease and crime almost decimated the population, leaving those remaining in a state of apathy and degeneration from which they have never fully recovered. This is what greeted the *Casco* party, and in contrast to the beauty of the islands, the state of the inhabitants must have left them sadly disillusioned. Yet Louis found traits to admire, and his friendship with them was genuine. He liked their foods and had Fanny learn how to make *kaku,* which is baked breadfruit mixed with a sauce of soft coconut pulp and thoroughly beaten.

To the Marquesans this beautiful ship which had sailed so silently into their sheltered bay was like a bird from heaven. Only one who has lived in such isolation can understand their happy surprise. Men, women, and children ran to the beach as older men of rank manned the outriggers and paddled out to board the guest ship. This was their tribute of welcome as well

as their pleasure, not a little mixed with curiosity and wonder.
They leaped over the side and on the *Casco's* deck, Polynesian
etiquette requiring that they sit down immediately as a gesture of gracious reception. Standing would indicate defiance
bordering on insult. To them smiles sufficed for words of a
common tongue, as they ranged their swarthy, tattooed bodies
cross-legged on every available deck space.

Louis interpreted this procedure as rudeness, and since the
art of tattooing was strange to him, he looked upon it as abhorrent, failing to appreciate at that time his fine art of Polynesia. Fanny and Aunt Maggie served their best sweets of jam
and preserves, not knowing that a salty hardtack would have
been the guests' choice of a real treat. Only the presence of Mr.
Regler, a trader, and the chief, Paipi-Kikino, gave the visitors
assurance against harm.

Louis wrote:

I own I was inspired with sensible repugnance; even with
alarm. The ship was manifestly in their power; we had women
on board; I knew nothing of my guests beyond the fact that
they were cannibals. . . . Later in the day, as I sat writing up
my journal, the cabin was filled from end to end with Marquesans; three brown-skinned generations, squatted cross-legged
on the floor, and regarding me in silence with embarrassing
eyes. The eyes of all Polynesians are large, luminous and melt-
ing . . . . A kind of despair came over me, to sit there helpless
under all these staring orbs, and be thus blocked in a corner
of my cabin by this speechless crowd; and a kind of rage to
think they were beyond the reach of articulate communication,
like furred animals, or folk born deaf, or the dwellers of some
alien planet. . . . I had journeyed forth out of that comfortable
zone of kindred languages, where the curse of Babel is so easy
to be remedied; and my fellow creatures sat before me dumb
like images. . . . I even questioned if my travels should be much

47

prolonged; perhaps they were destined to a speedy end; perhaps . . . Kauanui, whom I remarked there, sitting silent with the rest, for a man of some authority, might leap from his hams with an ear-splitting signal, the ship be carried at a rush, and the ship's company butchered for the table.[6]

And all the while the Marquesans were paying him the greatest respect they knew, even if one man, as Louis said, "wore only a handkerchief badly adjusted."

There is no record of how long this impasse lasted—it may have been for one or two hours—or by what means it was terminated. Doubtless the islanders were waiting for an invitation to initiate their ceremony of welcome expressed in a chant or dance. And Louis, unwittingly discourteous in continuing his writing, should have seated himself on the floor with them and by clapping his hands signaled the opening song.

Schopenhauer said a century ago, "Ignorance is degrading only when found in company of riches," but for one of such acknowledged charm, as we know R. L. S. to have been, to be placed in this embarrassing position must have provided an excellent example of confusion of tongues. However, on shore visits of the entire company during subsequent days, the incident did not mitigate against their hospitable reception in feasting, entertainment, and bestowal of gifts. Then when Louis, upon departure, made gifts in return and saw them left untouched on the beach, he felt humiliated and resentful, not knowing that he had offended by failing to make formal presentation to the ranking chief, as the occasion demanded. A few generations earlier an incident such as this could have spelled death to the donor.

It is of more than passing interest that fifty-five years before, in 1833, Rev. Hiram Bingham, grandfather of the late United States Senator Bingham and dean of Hawaiian ministers, made

[6] Manuscript in the archives of the Henry E. Huntington Library.

an unsuccessful attempt to establish and maintain missionaries in the Marquesas—this after thirteen years of successful work in Hawaii.[7]

It is a credit to the Marquesans, although due in part to lack of acquaintance with Rev. Bingham's book, that the Stevenson party strolled the Anaho beach of Nuku Hiva in perfect safety for the fifteen days before they moved to their second anchorage in Taiohae Bay on the southern side of the island. This is the locale of Herman Melville's *Typee*, which had fascinated Louis in San Francisco when it was lent to him by Charles Stoddard. And because it is the seat of government for the islands, there was a tiring round of social affairs, with the Marquesans as well as the European residents, which over-taxed Louis's strength.

A sailing vessel, where there are no towing facilities, must anchor offshore in order to get a breeze in her canvas for departure. Consequently going ashore meant getting over the side into a rowboat, which was bobbing and usually wet, and being

[7] Rev. Bingham said: "The London Missionary Society failed in the Marquesas because of a lack of an adequate number of laborers to man the field so as to make a strong impression. . . . In accordance with the wishes of the American Board and their own, Messrs Alexander, Armstrong, and Parker, with their wives, were intrusted with the important service of attempting to preach the gospel, and translate and publish the Bible of the Marquesas. The faith and courage with which the ladies, two of them with tender babes in their arms, set off in this new enterprise, were highly commendable, and their unshrinking heroism too admirable to be soon forgotten.

"This detachment from our mission sailed from Honolulu on July 2nd, 1833 . . . and reached Nuku Hiva on August 10th. They were welcomed on shore by the aged Hape on August 15th. . . . On the 21st they were left by the Captain (Bancroft) in their novel and untried situation." (*A Residence of Twenty-one Years in the Sandwich Islands* [Hartford, Conn., and New York, 1847].

"Novel and untried" proved feeble words, indeed. After experiencing threats to personal safety, thievery of household goods and clothing, of humiliating inattention and all manner of rudeness during the brief religious services, of defiance of any suggestions of education in crafts and sanitation, the three families gave up hope at the end of eight months and asked to be returned to Hawaii.

carried up on the beach, the men going like frogs on a swarthy giant's back, the women quite ladylike in armchair fashion of crossed brown hands, or those of lighter weight carried like infants in arms.

So their stay at Taiohae was brief, and they went a day's sailing farther south by east to Taa Huku Bay on Hiva Oa Island. It was a rough trip, and everyone except Aunt Maggie was seasick, even Louis and the Captain and the new Chinese cook, who had replaced the Japanese who had gone on a spree at Anaho. It is well that just once Louis should have known why Fanny preferred "a horse to trot."

This island of Hiva Oa was in the news at this time because a man by the name of McCallum had gone there and acquired riches within a few years by raising cotton and marketing copra from his five thousand coconut trees. The island is five miles wide and twenty-two miles long, with wide, fertile valleys; and exposed as it is to the southeast Trades, has a remarkably equable climate. Who knows but that Louis, when he went on a day's horseback ride with Brother Michel, was not dreaming of a South Sea plantation? Yet it was this excursion that brought the sad consequence of one of his worst illnesses.

Under date of August 27, Louis wrote of the previous day:

I made a more extended circuit in the vale with Brother Michel. We were mounted on a pair of sober nags, suitable to these rude paths; the weather was exquisite, and the company in which I found myself no less agreeable than the scenes through which I passed. We mounted at first by a steep grade along the summit of one of those twisted spurs that, from a distance, mark out provinces of sun and shade upon the mountain-side. The ground fell away on either hand with an extreme declivity. From either hand, out of profound ravines, mounted the song of falling water and the smoke of household fires. Here and there the hills of foliage would divide, and our eyes would

This is the way Louis looked when Fanny Osbourne first
met him at Grez. Fanny made the sketch in charcoal, and
Theodore Blake Wirgman, one of the Barbizon-Grez
group, copied it in ink.

Louis (right) with Fanny and Lloyd Osbourne and Sport (the dog) on the veranda at Saranac in the fur coats Fanny had purchased in Canada.

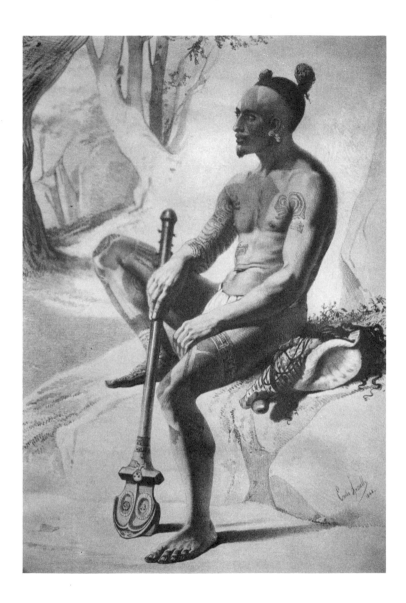

A Marquesas Island chief of one hundred years ago. L. R. Dordillon, missionary, writes that this man was probably six feet, eight inches in height.

Courtesy Bernice P. Bishop Museum, Honolulu

Teuila (center, right) demonstrates "one finger poi" at a luau in Honolulu.

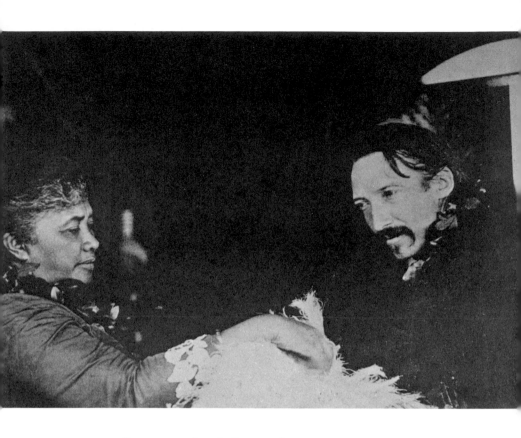

Princess Liliuokalani and R. L. S.

King Kalakaua

Beautiful Princess Kaiulani, "the island rose."

Fanny Stevenson weighted down with the furbelows of the nineties.

plunge down upon one of those deep-nested habitations. And still, high in front, arose the precipitous barrier of the mountain, greened over where it seemed that scarce a harebell could find root, barred with the zigzags of a human road where it seemed that not a goat could scramble. And in truth for all the labour that it cost, the road is regarded even by the Marquesans as impassable. They will not risk a horse on that ascent; and those who lie to the westward come and go in their canoes.

I never knew a hill to lose so little on near approach: a consequence, I must suppose, of its surprising steepness. When we turned about, I was amazed to behold so deep a view behind, and so high a shoulder of blue sea, crowned by the whale-like island of Motane. And yet the wall of mountain had not visibly dwindled, and I could even have fancied, as I raised my eyes to measure it, that it loomed higher than before.

We struck now into covert paths, crossed and heard more near at hand the bickering of the streams, and tasted the coolness of those recesses where the houses stood. The birds sang about us as we descended. All along our path my guide was being hailed by voices: "Mikaël—Kaoha, Mikaël!" From the doorstep, from the cotton-patch, or out of the deep grove of island chestnuts, these friendly cries arose, and were cheerily answered as we passed. In a sharp angle of a glen, on a rushing brook and under fathoms of cool foliage, we struck a house upon a well-built *paepae,* the fire brightly burning under the *popoi-*shed against the evening meal; and here the cries became a chorus and the house folk running out, obliged us to dismount and breathe.

It seemed a numerous family: we saw eight at least; and one of these honoured me with a particular attention. This was the mother, naked to the waist, of an aged countenance, but with hair still copious and black, and breasts still erect and youthful. On our arrival I could see she remarked me, but instead of offering and greeting, disappeared at once into the bush.

Thence she returned with two crimson flowers. "Good-bye!" was her salutation, uttered not without coquetry; and as she said it she pressed the flowers into my hand—"Good-bye! I speak Inglis." It was from a whaler-man, who (she informed me) was "a plenty good chap," that she had learned my language; and I could not but think how handsome she must have been in these times of her youth, and could not but guess that some memories of the dandy whaler-man prompted her attentions to myself. Nor could I refrain from wondering what had befallen her lover; in the rain and mire of what sea-ports he had tramped since then; in what close and garish drinking-dens had found his pleasure; and in the ward of what infirmary dreamed his last of the Marquesas. But she, the more fortunate, lived on in her green island.

The talk, in this lost house upon the mountains, ran chiefly upon Mapiao and his visits to the *Casco:* the news of which had probably gone abroad by then to all the island, so that there was no *paepae* in Hiva-oa where they did not make the subject of excited comment.

Not much beyond we came upon a high place in the foot of the ravine. Two roads divided it, and met in the midst. Save for this intersection the amphitheatre was strangely perfect, and had a certain ruder air of things Roman. Depths of foliage and the bulk of the mountain kept it in grateful shadow. On the benches several young folk sat clustered or apart. One of these, a girl perhaps fourteen years of age, buxom and comely, caught the eye of Brother Michel. Why was she not at school? —she was done with school now. What was she doing here?— she lived here now. Why so?—no answer but a deepening blush. There was no severity in Brother Michel's manner; the girl's own confusion told her story. "*Elle a honte,*" was the missionary's comment as we rode away.

Near by in the stream, a grown girl was bathing naked in a goyle between two stepping-stones; and it amused me to see

with what alacrity and real alarm she bounded on her many-
coloured under-clothes. Even in these daughters of cannibals
shame was eloquent.[8]

"Underwear, me eye!" a South Seas veteran once exclaimed.
But Louis in that age of multiple petticoats could be pardoned
for this reference to the young lady's attire, and no doubt he
was so dazzled by her nymphlike beauty that he would not have
seen her whip her *pareau* around her loins, for it would have
been her only garment, as it is still today—one and one-half
yards of cotton goods or *tapa* knotted tightly around her waist;
and if strangers were present, she would pull the front upward
over her breasts.

That the girl's blush drew from Brother Michel the remark
that she was ashamed does not imply that she was a bad girl
morally, but rather that she had been guilty of some trifling
misbehavior and was self-consciously shy in the presence of
the priest. These Polynesian girls fairly crinkle with embarrassment, and in their natural habitat have not learned the dubious
art of shrugging off an offense of good manners. To them
nothing is more humiliating than to be dubbed "*le tatau*" by
their elders and considered unfit for association with others.

From the pleasure of this horseback ride when he was mentally traveling with Louis Becke in his book, *By Reef and Palm,*
and whom in a letter to Sydney Colvin he called a "Howling
cheese," Louis returned to the *Casco* utterly exhausted. It had
been hot in the sun and he had become overheated; in the cool
of the ravines he had become chilled; he developed a fever and
his hacking cough returned. He remained in bed while Fanny,
Aunt Maggie, and Lloyd paid farewell calls in the village.[9]

[8] *In the South Seas* (vol. XVII of Pentland edition of Stevenson's
Works [20 vols., London, Cassell and Co., 1906–1907]), 126–28.

[9] It was to the solace of this superbly beautiful Atuona valley on Hiva
Oa Island that Paul Gauguin, ill and disillusioned fled in November, 1901.
Cruelly cheated of his funds by those in Paris to whom he had entrusted

Calling Captain Otis for a conference, Louis asked him to steer for the Paumotus, "some place a little more remote," but the Captain shook his head. The Low Archipelago is no place for a sailing vessel. Indeed, if ever Louis had flown over this thousand-mile-long desolate stretch of miniature islets and gigantic rings of atolls, as I have, he would have shared the Captain's caution. Islets and atolls are simply reefs of live coral, many exposed at low tide, and appear from the air to be a submerged range of mountains. The Lost Continent of Mu becomes more than hypothetical conjecture. Blue and green and turquoise currents swirl around undersea pinnacles, twisting masses of seaweed to shelter multi-hued fish as well as sharks that dart and slither through the clear depths.

But yielding to Louis's persuasion and to Fanny's deepening anxiety for her husband's health as a result of his exploring venture, Captain Otis accepted the grave responsibility of setting a course leading directly into the midst of this maze of isles and atolls, with Fakarava as their destination. It was the time of the year, early September, for fairly dependable good weather; the sea was calm, the breeze light but steady.

On the morning of the fifth day of sailing they passed the uninhabited island of Tikei of the Pernicious group. That evening found them cautiously threading their way through tortuous reef passages. To anchor anywhere and wait for daylight seems out of the range of possibility; yet Stevenson's own description runs counter to this liability of imminent danger:

---

disposition of his paintings, he was humbled to penury in Tahiti, even denied hospital care. Yet he worked on, driven to finish the task he felt destiny had imposed on him. Scarcely able to hold his palette, he painted the Marquesans who had given him a house in which to live and were providing him with food. Venerable old Tioka ministered to him as father to son, and when on the morning of May 8, 1903, he found him unconscious and near death he ran for Father Vernier. And through the priest's slow aneling he wept a parent's tears. They buried Paul Gauguin in their own cemetery on the sun-swept hillside above the village of Taahanku and lovingly cairned the grave with stones.

The night fell lovely in the extreme. After the moon went down, the heaven was a thing to wonder at for stars. And as I lay in the cockpit and looked upon the steersman I was haunted by Emerson's verses:

> *And the lone seaman all the night*
> *Sails astonished among the stars.*

By this glittering and imperfect brightness, about four bells in the first watch we made our third atoll, Raraka. The low line of the isle lay straight along the sky; so that I was at first reminded of a towpath, and we seemed to be mounting some engineered and navigable stream. . . . Here and there, but rarely faint tree-tops broke the level. And the sound of the surf accompanied us, now in a drowsy monotone, now with a menacing swing.

The isle lay nearly east and west, barring our advance on Fakarava. We must, therefore, hug the coast until we gained the western end, where, through a passage eight miles wide, we might sail southward between Raraka and the next isle, Kauehi. We had the wind free, a lightish air; but clouds of an inky blackness were beginning to arise, and at times it lightened—without thunder. Something, I know not what, continually set us upon the island. We lay more and more to the nor'ard; and you would have thought the shore copied our maneuver and outsailed us. Once and twice Raraka headed us again—again, in the sea fashion, the quite innocent steersman was abused—and again the *Casco* kept away. . . .

We had but just repeated our maneuver and kept away . . . when I was aware of land again, not only on the weather bow, but dead ahead. I played the part of the judicious landsman, holding my peace till the last moment; and presently my mariners preceived it for themselves.

"Land ahead!" said the steersman.

"By God, it's Kauehi!" cried the mate.

55

And so it was. And with that I began to be sorry for cartographers. We were scarce doing three and a half; and they asked me to believe that (in five minutes) we had dropped an island, passed eight miles of open water, and run almost high and dry upon the next. But my captain was more sorry for himself to be afloat in such a labyrinth; laid the *Casco* to, with the log line up and down, and sat on the stern rail and watched it till morning. He had enough of night in the Paumotus.[10]

To take issue with one so highly skilled as a chronicler of facts may be presumptuous, but heaving-to in a sailing vessel with no auxiliary engine by which to maneuver out of tight spots is palpably to court disaster. And Captain Otis sitting on the stern rail through the night watching the log line is no doubt a bit of intentional humor. Knowing the sea and its potential savagery, one rather could picture Captain Otis and the first mate continually checking their charted course and, no doubt, praying in that trenchant profanity which more often than not is the seaman's substitute for the landlubber's more conventional phrasing of divine supplication.

At the wheel the helmsman constantly would be receiving the quiet orders of Captain Otis, while keenly alert to the night's varying windage in the sails and to the shifting swirl of currents conveyed to his sailor's "feel" through the tug and jerk of the helm. The crew would be standing ready to trim the sails at a second's notice as the vessel negotiated passage after narrow passage . . . bow to port! . . . bow hard to starboard! . . . now steady ahead . . . reduce sail! . . . add sail! So on throughout the dark night as the Captain would have expertly conned the sturdy *Casco*.

Apropos of this doubt about strict adherence to fact, Isobel Field told of a dinner conversation at the Edinburgh home of Dr. George Balfour when this austere uncle took his nephew

[10] *In the South Seas*, 145–46.

to task for saying in his *St. Ives* that Swanston Cottage could be seen from Edinburgh Castle.

"But Louis never took liberties with fact," defended Isobel, who had acted as amanuensis during the writing of *St. Ives*.

The Doctor was not convinced and a wager was made, he pledging a bottle of sloe gin against her dozen fine men's hand-kerchiefs. Isobel remembered the scene in the book where Flora takes St. Ives, imprisoned in the castle and planning escape, to a place where she could point out Swanston Cottage, where she lived with her brother and their aunt. "Come," the author had her say, "I believe I can show you the very smoke out of our chimney." Then, St. Ives speaking,

So saying, she carried me round the battlements toward the opposite or southern side of the fortress, and indeed to a bastion almost immediately overlooking the place of our projected flight. Thence we had a view of some fore-shortened suburbs at our feet, and beyond of a green, open, and irregular country rising toward the Pentland Hills. The face of one of these summits (say two leagues from where we stood) is marked with a procession of white scars. And to this she directed my attention.

"You see those marks?" she said. "We call them the Seven Sisters. Follow a little lower with your eye, and you will see a fold of the hill, the tops of some trees, and a tail of smoke out of the midst of them. That is Swanston Cottage, where my brother and I are living with my aunt. If it gives you pleasure to see it, I am glad. We, too, can see the castle from a corner in the garden, and we go there in the morning often . . . and we think of you, M. de Saint-Yves; but I am afraid it does not altogether make us glad."[11]

So to the Castle the next morning went Isobel and one of the handsome Balfour sons. They found their way along the narrow

[11] *St. Ives* (vol. XIX, Pentland ed. of *Works*), 56, 356.

seldom-used gallery to the southern side and there looked down on the roof of Swanston Cottage as Flora and St. Ives had done in the story. That evening at dinner Dr. Balfour forfeited one of his precious bottles of properly aged sloe gin.

Mrs. Field maintained that Louis could not have been in error regarding the *Casco* incident, and since there is no one to adjudicate a wager, the matter must stand as a respectful difference of opinion. Providence may have provided a quiet spot between turbulent currents. And with his apparent fearlessness of the sea Louis may never have realized their peril or the capriciousness of a schooner under sail.

Aside from the question of veracity, it was a foolhardy venture, and it was not until mid-morning that the *Casco*, on a rising tide, entered the narrow southeast opening of the great Fakarava Lagoon. This inner sea is thirty-five miles long and thirteen miles wide, circled by a rim of palm-fringed coral which is only one-fourth to one-half mile in width—an amazing ocean phenomenon. The water is clear to a depth of many fathoms and surged only by the ebb and flow of tides that race through these narrow openings.

The *Casco's* passengers were breathless with its beauty. To the weary Captain and his crew there was infinitely more than mere beauty. The land, if it may be designated as such, is scarcely fifteen feet above sea level except at the upper end of the lagoon, where the village of Rotoava boasts a possible twenty feet. And the coconut tree demonstrates its remarkable adaptability to hardship by finding sufficient rootage to fringe almost the entire length of this narrow rim. There is no soil, only decayed coral, sand, and seaweed washed up through countless centuries and snagged on the ragged coral formation, which also has caught the coconuts floating on the sea.

While the name Paumotus, or Submissive Islands, had been in use since the Tahitians conquered the sparsely populated Low Archipelago, and was still in use when R. L. S. was there, the people subsequently were permitted to resume their true name of Tuamotus, meaning Distant Islands. The Tuamotuans are not considered pure Polynesian and never have spoken the language of their conquerors; and although it is thought that they have Melanesian blood, their language is not Fijian.

Much has been made, mostly by fictionists, of the many ships and their crews which have mysteriously disappeared in this vast archipelago—of a blonde white woman seen by traders, of a white man's hand sticking up out of a mound of sand—most of which can be written off as traders' tales.

History records the people as exceptionally honest and agreeable, living quietly among themselves, happy and reasonably healthy, and fortunately not sufficiently wealthy in natural resources to attract traders who would disrupt their primitive economy, built solely upon pearl shell and copra, or beachcombers who would corrupt their morals by drink and licentiousness. Their diet is rich in fish, shellfish, breadfruit, bananas, taro, and the inevitable coconut which provides both cream and oil; never have incidents of cannabalism been reported, or such sectional rivalries as characterized the Marquesans.

It is a strange sensation to lie quietly at anchor in the middle of a turbulent ocean; but with no movement of the schooner the nights were stuffy on board and Louis could not sleep, so they went ashore in this little village of one hundred people and were given the only available house by a man they presumed to be the owner. Stipulation for rental payment was shrugged off as of no concern. Aunt Maggie describes their quarters under date of September 12, 1888:

. . . here we are in a dear little wooden erection of three rooms, with a verandah front and back. It is one of the best houses on the island after the Residency. The sitting-room is quite large and very airy, with two doors opening on the verandahs, two windows to the front, one to the back, and one at the far end;

the two bedrooms open off the other end, and all are painted white, with the doors and windows panelled in blue. In the sitting-room there are two rocking-chairs, four round-backed chairs, and a table. . . . There are also two brackets on the wall, three framed pictures, a small mirror, and a gun. There are wooden bedsteads in the bedrooms, small wardrobes, basin-stands, and so on, and actually a copy of David Wilkie's "Village School" framed and hanging up in one. We were rather afraid of the wooden beds, so we brought ashore our mattresses from the *Casco,* keep them in the bedrooms through the day, and at night bring them out and spread them where we please. Usually Louis and Fanny take the front verandah, Lloyd the back, and Valentine and I retire to different corners of the sitting-room, leaving both doors wide open, so that there is plenty of air. . . . the sun wakes us up soon after six, and we make breakfast with the help of a paraffin cooking-stove; we have coffee, soup, bread-and-butter, and marmalade. For lunch and dinner we return to the *Casco.*

There is quite a large piece of ground around our house, with a nice white fence in front and a wall of coral on the other sides; there are a great many cocoa-nut palms in it, but from the gate to the house there is an avenue of bananas, and that is a very fine thing here, as the soil for them has all to be brought from Tahiti. There are two fig-trees also that are said to bear splendid fruit.[12]

That there was a house of this type in a place so remote from modern civilization seems not to have impressed Mrs. Stevenson beyond the fact that they were surprisingly comfortable. It was the home of people who were away for the time being. The man, Taniera, who was giving his ready consent for its use, was the local catechist and general factotum for the vice-regent of the Tuamotus when administration headquarters were still in

[12] *From Saranac to the Marquesas,* 148–50.

Rotoava. Later the French government moved them to Apataki, the present site. Brother Taniera had been banished to Fakarava from Tahiti for spending the tax money he had collected in a bit of high living in Papeete, a matter which did not in the least lessen the respect and affection the Tuamotuans had for him. He was thoroughly likable, an excellent carpenter and boat-builder, and a genial friend. They universally regretted that his banishment would last only five years.

While anthropologists and ethnologists wrestle with the study of the origins of mankind, the divisions of races, and their relations to each other, a passing incident oftentimes will afford a singularly enlightening insight into the nature and disposition of a people. This house so casually possessed by the Stevensons belonged to M. François, a French Tahitian, and his Tuamotuan wife. They had one small child. François had taken his family with him to another island, there to cut copra and gather pearl shell, and to register their outlying land according to a new edict from the French government in Papeete. There was no "for rent" sign on their house. Strangers were rare in Rotoava. The family might be away for a few days or a few weeks. As Taniera by implication assumed ownership, the Stevensons could not have known about François and his family.

On the second evening of their occupancy, when Fanny and Louis were spending a few quiet hours by themselves, the others of the party having remained on the *Casco* following dinner so, as Aunt Maggie says, they could leave Fanny and Louis in peace, the following incident occurred. Louis relates it after describing the setting:

I must tell, instead, of our house, where, toward seven at night, the catechist came suddenly in with his pleased air of being welcome; armed besides with a considerable bunch of keys. These he proceeded to try on the sea-chests, drawing each in turn from its place against the wall. Heads of strangers appeared in the doorway and volunteered suggestions. All in vain. Either they were the wrong keys or the wrong boxes, or the wrong man was trying them. For a little Taniera fumed and fretted; then had recourse to the more summary method of the hatchet; one of the chests was broken open, and an armful of clothing, male and female, baled out and handed to the strangers on the verandah.

These were François, his wife, and their child. About eight A. M. in the midst of the lagoon, their cutter had capsized in jibbing. They got her righted and though she was still full of water put the child on board. The mainsail had been carried away, but the jib still drew her sluggishly along, and François and the woman swam astern and worked the rudder with their hands. The cold was cruel; the fatigue, as time went on, became excessive; and in that preserve of sharks, fear haunted them. Again and again, François, the half-breed, would have desisted and gone down; but the woman, whole blood of an amphibious race, still supported him with cheerful words. . . .

It was about five in the evening, after nine hours' swimming, that François and his wife reached land at Rotoava. . . . They had supped and told and retold their story, dripping as they came; the flesh of the woman, whom Mrs. Stevenson helped to shift, was cold as stone; and François, having changed to a dry cotton shirt and trousers, passed the remainder of the evening on my floor and between open doorways, in a thorough draught. Yet François, the son of a French father, speaks excellent French himself and seems intelligent.

It was our first idea that the catechist, true to his evangelical vocation, was clothing the naked from his superfluity. Then it came out that François was but dealing with his own. The clothes were his, so was the chest, so was the house. . . . Yet you observe he had hung back on the verandah while Taniera tried his 'prentice hand upon the locks; and even now, when his true character appeared, the only use he made of the estate was to leave the clothes of his family drying on the fence. Taniera was still the friend of the house, still fed the poultry, still came about on his daily visits, François, during the remainder of his stay, holding bashfully aloof.

And there was stranger matter. Since François had lost the whole of his cutter, the half ton of copra, an axe, bowls, knives, and clothes . . . . I proposed to advance him what he needed on the rent. To my enduring amazement he refused, and the reason he gave—if that can be called a reason which but darkens counsel—was that Taniera was his friend. His friend, you observe; not his creditor. I inquired into that and was assured that Taniera, an exile in a strange isle, might possibly be in debt himself, but certainly was no man's creditor. . . .

. . . when the time came for me to leave . . . I duly paid my rent to Taniera. He was satisfied and so was I. But what had he to do with it? Mr. Donat, acting magistrate and a man of kindred blood, could throw no light upon the mystery; a plain private person, with a taste for letters, cannot be expected to do more.[13]

Louis learned later that money is not a medium of exchange in Polynesia, or was not at that time. If he had taken his departure without any payment and had sent gifts back from Papeete to compensate for his landlord's loss, these would have been wholly acceptable and profoundly appreciated. It is the gift that devalues currency. This is the reason traders used to go to the islands loaded with gaudy jewelry, showy patterns of calico, cheap knives, and hatchets and get in exchange thousands of dollars' worth of copra, pearl shell, and *bêche-de-mer*. Louis had not yet learned the art of Polynesian giving, nor fathomed the traditional complexities of their polite reciprocal courtesies. The catechist, as we have seen, had become money conscious.

[13] *In the South Seas*, 169.

With all the serene quiet of Rotoava, complete idleness and relaxation, pure balmy air, and good food, Louis was not able to throw off the cold he had contracted at Hiva Oa. Even with sleeping on the open veranda his breathing became more and more difficult, and Fanny knew that congestion threatened. She wished desperately for a doctor, but as always she concealed her worry from her husband and patiently—at least outwardly so—waited for Louis to make the decision to leave for Papeete.

Mrs. Field declared unequivocally that in matters of this kind her mother deferred to Louis's pleasure with never a hint of assuming the initiative except when this responsibility was imposed upon her by sheer necessity of circumstances. It is a pity, and a tendency to be deeply regretted, that many writers of Stevenson biography have for some strange reason, or no reason at all, indulged in ungallant Henleyisms regarding Fanny. Each follows the other in much the same manner as sheep jumping over the pasture fence led by a renegade ram, and apparently with as little thought.

Fanny and Louis were deeply in love, and no intelligent woman is foolish enough to forfeit the esteem of a devoted husband by offending the one she holds most dear. Troublesome problems come to everyone whose life thrusts him into an executive role. Fanny accepted this trust when she married the man whose state of health was the prime concern of both. Louis had a repugnance to discord of any description, amounting almost to a phobia, and when Fanny's patience would be near the breaking point, he would make a joke of the situation, unless it was something too serious to be accepted lightly; and Mrs. Field declared this rarely failed to alleviate the umbrage and restore good humor.

Fanny herself writes, during one of Louis's critical illnesses, that she "went into another room and 'gloomed'" because she did not wish to reveal her despair to her husband.

Yet it was two weeks before the *Casco* sailed out of the

Fakarava Lagoon like a great white gull and left the tree-shaded village of Rotoava to its timeless monotony of daily living—a monotony that never seems monotonous, if one can be forgiven for a superbly ambiguous statement.

Arrival at Papeete, capital of Tahiti, was delayed by slack winds, and a two days' sailing was drawn out to three. Louis was exhausted and burning with fever. He and Fanny went immediately to the Hotel de France, which is squarely in the middle of the little town. Papeete is not what one would term noisy, yet it is never quiet. Day and night people saunter along the narrow crooked streets and byroads, talking, laughing, and singing. Constantly there is the musical, half-plaintive, long-drawn-out "I—a—o— ra—na!" in greetings of men, women, and children, accompanied by the incessant jingle-jangle, jingle-jangle of bicycle bells of every possible tonal quality and reverberation, together with the muffled undertone of the rhythmic pad, pad, pad of horses' feet, the whir of buggy wheels, and the gritty grind of harsh steel tires on the loose gravel. After the sublime quiet it was like Bedlam to Louis.

Papeete at this time had a population of about four thousand; approximately one-half of these were French, the other half were the usual mixture of Occidental and Oriental. The Tahitians, except for a few well-to-do and socially prominent citizens who had semi-European homes in the town, lived in small villages along the seashore. The shrewd Cantonese, with their inherent predilection for organizing commercially in foreign lands, already were in possession of small business, with the usual diversion of gambling; with the passing of years when population doubled and trebled, they gradually increased their commercial grasp to become bankers, money changers, and property owners.

Papeete always has been the least formal of South Pacific capitals—to use the more moderate of qualifying adjectives applied by those of strictly conventional preferences. French colonization has always been of the laissez-faire type and never has imposed a code of moral behavior beyond the optional discretion of the indigenous peoples. The supreme art of happy indolence by which the Tahitians fascinated the first Europeans was their downfall as far as observance of their traditional customs and social etiquette was concerned. This gave license to indulgences of unscrupulous adventurers and traders and invented the word "beachcomber."

The Stevensons sensed this laxity after enjoying the shy primitive formalities of the Marquesans and the Tuamotuans. This gracious hovering between naïveté and sophistication, which could be charmingly disarming or utterly confusing, and apparently without guide or precept, save whim of the moment, left them uncertain what to expect of themselves or from those who loitered past the cottage with cordial salutations and unabashed peeps through the scrim curtains hanging at doorway and windows.

Following the absolute quiet of Fakarava, Louis found it impossible to sleep, even after they left the hotel for the cottage back under the trees. Without essential rest his condition was becoming more and more alarming each day. He sent for Captain Otis and gave him minute instructions about procedure in the event of his death. Fanny sent for a doctor, although she herself was his best doctor. All the physician could do was administer a sedative. That he predicted a hemorrhage during the night, as some chroniclers state, is regarded as absurd by other members of the profession. The fact that none occurred bears out their contention.

During these first few days Fanny and Louis had but one thought, to get rid of the lung congestion, the hacking cough, and the fever. Then, within the next few days, Louis improved sufficiently to receive the local dignitaries who had been waiting to call, to go to the hotel for his meals, and in general to enjoy the life which he at first had found irksome. He enjoyed the pleasant greetings and surely could not have missed the occasional *"Iaorana oe!"* as it was flung over a bare brown shoulder by a shyly daring coquette, a saluation innocently playful or amorously tender.

He tried to settle down to write. *The Master of Ballantrae* was beginning to plague all his waking thoughts. And perhaps in the mail he received was a letter from *Scribner's* reminding him that the opening number in December was not far off. It was no use. Idleness had become a habit in this *dolce far niente* land. He had sailed into such mental and spiritual enchantment that the story was crowded from his mind. Efforts to concentrate sufficiently to create new scenes and characters were only tantalizing. And he had the comfort of knowing that in each issue of *Scribner's* was appearing an article or essay written before he left Saranac.

Published consecutively through January to December were: "A Chapter on Dreams," "The Lantern Bearers," "Beggars," "Pulvis et Umbra," "Gentlemen," "Some Gentlemen in Fiction," "Popular Authors," "Epilogue to an Inland Voyage," "Letter to a Young Gentleman Who Proposes to Embrace the Career of Art," "Contributions to the History of Fife," "The Education of an Engineer," and "A Christmas Sermon." For these *Scribner's* paid $3,500, which, together with royalties from *Dr. Jekyll and Mr. Hyde* and the inheritance from his father's estate, made this thousand-dollar-a-month cruise possible. Yet, Mrs. Field said, with all his generosity he never lost the caution in spending that he had learned so gallingly in his early years.

In contemplating still "some place more remote," he discussed with Captain Otis the advisability of going to Huahiné, the easternmost island of the Leeward group of the Society Islands. While the surrounding reefs are dangerous and night sailing is out of the question, once inside the northern barrier there is excellent anchorage and an adequate pier. But they decided against it when told of the excessive rainfall.

Then Taravao was suggested. This village, beautiful and picturesque from the sea, is on the tiny isthmus that very nearly cuts the island of Tahiti in two, with the smaller or southern portion being known as Taiarapu. Wedged in between two mountains seven thousand feet high and scarcely one hundred feet above sea level, Taravao sacrifices comfort to beauty. Surrounded by a dense forest of enormous trees and tangled mat of undergrowth it is hot and muggy, with never enough breeze to keep mosquitoes away.

The sailing from Papeete had been rough and perilous and even Louis had had enough of the *Casco* for the time being. One wonders if he thought back to when he declared that he "loved a ship as a man loves Burgundy or daybreak." It had taken thirty hours to negotiate the sixty miles around the north end of the island from Papeete, and now when they decided to go back to Tautira, they chose to make the trip by land. Aunt Maggie says it was sixteen miles; more likely sixteen kilometers, which would be about twelve miles—a long drive for a team of horses in the tropics, and an even longer drive through the heat of the day for a frail man.

Fanny would endure anything to get away from the schooner. It was on this rough trip from Papeete to Taravao through turbulent Mooréa channel that she is credited with the remark, when danger threatened and a boat was lowered, "Isn't that nice? We shall soon be ashore!" Louis adding, "Thus does the female mind unconsciously skirt along the verge of eternity."

No one mentions the children of these villages, but it must have warmed the hearts of all to see the youngsters of all ages running along the shore, jumping up and down and waving their arms and shouting at the tops of their voices, *"Te pathi! Te pathi!"* ("A ship! A ship!"), and standing in curious circles during the process of disembarking. All the little fellows would be stark naked, and many of the older ones, lacking anything else to wave, would have ripped off their *pareaus* in their excitement.

Fanny found a Chinaman with two horses and a small vehicle, probably a light wagon which we in California in early days called a buckboard. It would have had a canopy top and, equipped with substantial leaf springs, would not be an uncomfortable conveyance. The rear seat could have been removed and a bed contrived of mattress and pillows.

And never in all the world could one find greater beauty along the way, following the sea on one side and the deep forest on the other, the air filled with the smells of surf and dank mould of ages, the rich perfume of blossoming frangipani trees half smothered under wide-limbed breadfruit and feathery casuarina, every now and again passing pools literally surfaced with blue, purple, and lavender water hyacinths with their stronger fragrance undertoning the frangipani.

Many shallow streams rippling to the sea had to be crossed, the horses wading in, stopping to quench their thirst in the cool mountain water, staggering over the rocky bed and pulling the resisting wheels crunchingly to emerge dripping on the opposite bank. Louis was ill, and weary to the point of exhaustion, yet when they paused for the horses to rest and for him to sip a cup of cocoa, he must have thought back to the time when he wrote in "Forest Notes": "The air penetrates through your clothes, and nestles to your living body. . . . You forget all your scruples and live awhile in peace and freedom, and for the moment only. For here, all is absent that can stimulate to moral feeling. . . . You forget the grim contrariety of interests. You forget the narrow lane where all men jostle together in unchivalrous contention, and the kennel, deep and unclean, that gapes on either hand for the defeated."[14]

From those they met on the narrow, winding road there were many softly spoken salutations and many songs of *"Vine Mau,"* with children and younger people running to the road with

[14] In *Juvenilia and Other Papers, etc.* (vol. XX, Pentland ed. of *Works*), 185.

their family's invitation to stop and eat with them. A refusal would bring gifts of baked breadfruit and green *fei* (banana) or a fresh ripe papaya. One can mentally picture the wan smile on the sick man's face in appreciation of these impulsively generous ministrations.

Because of the heat the horses could not travel beyond a walk except in the shade and on bits of good road, so the day must have seemed interminable to all three—Louis, Fanny, and Valentine. The transcendent beauty of Tautira's evening time meant nothing. As quickly as possible Fanny bargained for a semi-European house and got Louis to bed. He was too tired to know or care where he laid his head. This is a trick of the tropics, where energy is lower than in colder zones and one may be reduced to a state of utter collapse without being near death; then with rest and sleep nature restores with pure balmy air and the tranquility of noiselessness.

Tautira is like a miniature park—an open stretch of grassy land, level as a golf course, with a quiet, shallow river of cool clear water trickling down from Haavini Valley between two ridges of high mountains. It is one of the beauty spots of beautiful Tahiti, where, as in the old missionary hymn,

> . . . *every prospect pleases,*
> *And only man is vile.*

Tahitian houses, unlike others in the South Seas, have outside walls of split bamboo as a concession to privacy, yet affording the necessary circulation of air. Even with wide doorways and long French windows, wooden-walled houses are stuffy and unhealthy and have contributed materially to the decline of health among the more ambitious Polynesians who adopted this mode of building a hundred or so years ago.

A semi-European house usually consisted of a fairly large board-walled room with one or two bamboo-walled rooms adjacent, and customarily established the owner as a person of importance. Evidently it was a house of this type to which the Chinese driver took the Stevensons. In defense of the man who asked the exorbitant rental, of which Aunt Maggie speaks, he probably did not realize the difference between five francs and fifty francs per week. More than likely it was the first time he ever had been asked to set a price on his house. In the end he would have been happy with a small gift and would have felt complimented that strangers had lived in his house.

When Moé of the royal House of Fa'a'a, who at that time held the hereditary title of Matea of Tautira heard of the Stevensons' arrival, she hurried home from a visit in Papeete to act in her official capacity as hostess, or matriarch, of her village. She was of the thirty-eighth generation of this ancient lineage and was married to a brother of King Pomare. The exploits of King Moé of Taiarapu, warrior of centuries past who subjugated this portion of the island of Tahiti, have been told and retold through the ages until legend has enshrined him as one of the great Polynesian gods.

So it was the Matea, royal woman of culture and refinement, whose tact saved an embarrassing situation for the guests who, unwittingly, had arrived without being invited—quite as if a Polynesian had invaded one of Britain's royal estates, for these villages are on the same basis of royal domain. Ori, a chief of nobility, had acted as host but without authority in the matter of housing the strangers. So it was the Matea who moved Louis and Fanny into Ori's *faré* (house), leaving him only one room for his personal belongings and finding another *faré* for him and his family.

It was the Matea who sent men to spear the gaily colored little fish they eat raw, and other men to pick fresh coconuts, grate the meat, and squeeze out the cream; then she herself cut the tender white meat of the fish into the cream and carried it to the Stevenson *faré*. Fanny declared that she believed this food, deliciously sweet and easily digested, saved Louis's life.

Certainly it could have helped. Shortly after the *Casco* was brought around from Taravao, there was talk of putting off for Honolulu. Then came the dramatic moment when Captain Otis struck the mainmast in a gesture of disgust that prayers for their safe sailing to Hawaii would aid his ability as a navigator and found his fist sinking into dry rot. At that moment he must have thought back to that near disastrous trip from Papeete to Taravao, or back still farther to that night in the Tuamotus, and given an ear to divine providence. There was nothing to do but return to Papeete and get a new mainmast.

4. *Master of Ballantrae* and Another Departure

LOUIS, RECOVERING REMARKABLY, got out his notes on the unfinished manuscript that had plagued him all these fourteen weeks since they had left San Francisco. Out came the tarboard pad and the long yellow sheets of lined paper, and surrounded by such elemental happiness as would purge the soul of all malice, Louis was obliged to bring into his primitive quarters the greeds and cruelties of men he had gloried in fashioning in the harshness of Saranac. To carry the theme of a story through months of idleness, through such new scenes as present a world hitherto unknown, and to retain the logical sequence of events and the dramatic unity of action is a triumph for any writer. To do this through illness is almost a superhuman feat of creative writing.

Fanny stood guard, not altogether figuratively, at the door of the *faré* to turn away callers with all the graciousness she could blend with stern intent, while inside the bamboo walls with the thickly thatched roof, like a prisoner in chains, Louis mentally returned to Scotland. He walked again, as he had some years before, along the low roads of southern Scotland from Borgue in Kirkcudbrightshire, through the braes of Maxwelltown to Dumfries and the shire of Durrisdeer, back to Wigtown and up the coast to Ballantrae and Girvan and on to Ayr.

Only the name Ballantrae (pronounced in Gaelic *Bail-antraigh* and meaning Houses by the Sea) has a place in the story, yet the author does not speak of his visit there. Borgue on Wigtown Bay is the Scots' idea of the most likely site of Durrisdeer Castle, located as it is at the entrance to Solway Firth, remote and stormy.

It was shortly after Christmas, and it must have been easy for the wanderer to imagine festivities in the many castles that still are maintained throughout the countryside. He thought of the many homecomings as he himself remained at the small village of Ballantrae. Certainly his mind was not idle as he walked leisurely from farm to farm or village to village, visiting with the friendly people to whom a stranger is a tonic and topic of conversation for days and weeks to come. The walk was with a friend, probably Walter Simpson, with whom he made the canoe trip from Antwerp to Grez.

Ballantrae is now a village of five hundred, with a parish of eleven hundred, probably about what it was in 1876. A quiet fishing village of comfortable homes where many seafaring men like to retire to spend the last years of their lives within sight and hearing of the blue wastes of the Atlantic that roll in across the Irish Sea. Louis, always a good listener, heard here the stories of the countryside, the rivalries between families, between friends, the feuds of blood kin that come down through centuries when generation after generation live and die on the place where they were born.

The Durrisdeers, for example, had been extinct for three generations. There had been romance and jealousies in their ranks and the old castle held memories of feuds; yet there was no definite application of these tales in Louis's mind at the time —that is, of the Ballantrae type. He was merely vagabonding, consciously or unconsciously seeking health in the open air because of that insistent call of starving lungs.

Later he walked from Edinburgh northward to Stirling and as far as Pitlochry on the Garry River. In the cold winds and rain and the chilling mists of evening time he pondered the austerities of the days of Scottish kings, the Murrays and the Stewarts, the vain revolt of the Jacobites, and the prevailing custom of the seventeenth century of sending one son out with the Forty-fives and keeping a younger son at home to inherit the title in event the older was killed. He pondered the justice of the courts of that day when evidence presented condemned a defendant who too often had no counsel and was too frightened or ignorant of his rights to speak against a possible false accusation.

At Falkirk and Stirling he literally traveled over the battlefields of James, Fifth High Stewart, who was with young Sir William Wallace in 1297 when they fought against Edward I of England; and the horror of the fate of the Scottish patriot when at last he was captured by the English and taken to London, there to be hanged, beheaded, disemboweled, and quartered to satisfy their glory of conquest. Could the Marquesans have been more savage?

Thus he thought back through history—James, Fifth High Stewart, had four sons and one daughter. The fourth son was Sir James of Durrisdeer, who died without issue. He remembered having walked through the village of Durrisdeer in Dumfrieshire which is just north of Thornhill.

He thought of the Murrays, Earls of Tullibardine. Sir John Murray, Lord Murray of Tullibardine, was ancestor of the Duke of Atholl. His eldest son, William, the second Earl, married the heiress of John, Earl of Atholl; on expectation of succeeding to that earldom at the death of James, the last (Stewart) Earl of Atholl, he initiated, with the consent of his only son, resignation of his Tullibardine titles and estates in favor of his younger brother, Sir Patrick Murray.

Sir Patrick's eldest son died childless, and his titles and estate went to kinsman John, second (Murray) Earl of Atholl. So John Murray, eldest son of John, first Marquess of Atholl, received the title of Earl of Tullibardine and Lord Murray for his lifetime. When he succeeded his father, he became second Marquess of Atholl, later raised to dukedom. Upon his death his life dignities became extinct, but his hereditary honors devolved on his son James, second duke of Atholl. In 1724 the

Earl of Tullibardine in the family of Murray became extinct.

So out of this rehearsal of Scottish history the family of Durrisdeer was built into fiction, through the veil of Pitlochry mists, by the wayfarer who walked the highroads of Scotland with the smell of heather and bog moss to sweeten the rain and wind along the winding Garry River.

Mrs. Field said, "If Louis had one particular pride, it was in his knowledge of Scottish history, and he knew the peerage like a Burke." As a consequence, when Louis wrote the preface to *The Master of Ballantrae* (which was not, however, to be published until the appearance of the last volume of the Edinburgh edition of Stevenson's works, appendix, in 1898), he wove history and fiction in a most convincing manner in describing his interview with "Mr. Thomson," really Charles Baxter, in a scene laid in the latter's home at No. 7, Tothesay Place, Edinburgh, Scotland:

"You remember my predecessor's, old Peter M'Brair's business?" [asked Mr. Thomson].

"I remember him acutely; he could not look at me without a pang of reprobation, and he could not feel the pang without betraying it. He was to me a man of great historical interest, but the interest was not returned."

"Ah, well, we go beyond him," said Mr. Thomson. "I daresay old Peter knew as little about this as I do. You see, I succeeded to a prodigious accumulation of the old law-papers and old tin boxes, some of them of Peter's hoarding, some of his father's, John, first of the dynasty, a great man in his day. Among other collections, were all the papers of the Durrisdeers."

"The Durrisdeers!" cried I. "My dear fellow, these may be of the greatest interest. One of them was out in the '45; one had some strange passages with the devil—you will find a note of it in Law's *Memorials*, I think; and there was an unexplained tragedy, I know not what, much later, about a hundred years ago—"

76

"More than a hundred years ago," said Mr. Thomson. "In 1783."

"How do you know that? I mean some death."

"Yes the lamentable deaths of my Lord Durrisdeer and his brother, the Master of Ballantrae (attainted in the troubles)," said Mr. Thomson with something the tone of a man quoting. "Is that it?"

"To say the truth," said I, "I have only seen some dim reference to the things in memoirs; and heard some traditions dimmer still, through my uncle (whom I think you knew). My uncle lived when he was a boy in the neighbourhood of St. Bride's; he has often told me of the avenue closed up and grown over with grass; the great gates never opened, the last lord and his old-maid sister who lived in the back parts of the house, a quiet, plain, poor, humdrum couple it would seem—but pathetic too, as the last of that stirring and brave house—and, to the country folk, faintly terrible from some deformed traditions."

"Yes," said Mr. Thomson. "Henry Graeme Durie, the last lord, died in 1820; his sister, the Honourable Miss Katherine Durie, in '27; so much I know; and by what I have been going over the last few days, they were what you say, decent, quiet people and not rich. To say truth, it was a letter of my lord's that put me on the search for the packet we are going to open this evening. Some papers could not be found; and he wrote to Jack M'Brair suggesting they might be among those sealed up by Mr. Mackellar. M'Brair answered, that the papers in question were all in Mackellar's own hand, all (as the writer understood) of a purely narrative character; and besides, said he, 'I am bound not to open them before the year 1889.' You may fancy if these words struck me: I instituted a hunt through all the M'Brair repositories; and at last hit upon that packet which (if you have had enough wine) I propose to show you at once."

In the smoking-room, to which my host now led me, was a

packet, fastened with many seals and enclosed in a single sheet
of strong paper thus endorsed:

"Papers relating to the lives and lamentable deaths of the
late Lord Durrisdeer, and his elder brother James, commonly
called Master of Ballantrae, attainted in the troubles: entrusted
into the hands of John M'Brair, in the Lawnmarket of Edinburgh, W. S.; this 20th day of September Anno Domini 1789;
by him to be kept secret until the revolution of one hundred
years complete, or until the 20th day of September 1889: the
same compiled and written by me,

EPHRAIM MACKELLAR
*For nearly forty years Land Steward on
the estates of his Lordship."*

As Mr. Thomson is a married man, I will not say what hour
had struck when we laid down the last of the following pages;
but I will give a few words of what ensued.

"Here," said Mr. Thomson, "is a novel ready to your hand:
all you have to do is to work up the scenery, develop the characters, and improve the style."

"My dear fellow," said I, "they are just the three things that
I would rather die than set my hand to. It shall be published
as it stands."

"But it's so bald," objected Mr. Thomson.

"I believe there is nothing so noble as baldness," replied I,
"and I am sure there is nothing so interesting. I would have all
literature bald, and all authors (if you like) but one."

"Well, well," said Mr. Thomson, "we shall see."

Johnstone Thomson, W. S., is Charles Baxter, W. S. (afterward the author's executor), with whom, as Thomson Johnstone, Louis carried on a correspondence in the broadest of
broad Scots. And Louis himself vouched for some fact in the

dialog with "Mr. Thomson" by writing to Mr. Baxter some time later for further information from the papers they had examined. In addition, Stevenson wrote what he called a "Genesis" of the story, also published posthumously:[1]

I was walking one night in the verandah of a small house in which I lived, outside the hamlet of Saranac. It was winter; the night was very dark; the air extraordinary clear and cold, and sweet with the purity of forests. From a good way below, the river was heard contending with ice and boulders: a few lights appeared, scattered unevenly among the darkness, but so far away as not to lessen the sense of isolation. For the making of a story here were fine conditions. I was besides moved with the spirit of emulation, for I had just finished my third or fourth perusal of *The Phantom Ship*. "Come," said I to my engine, "let us make a tale, a story of many years and countries, of the sea and the land, savagery and civilisation; a story that shall have the same large features and may be treated in the same summary elliptic method as the book you have been reading and admiring." I was here brought up with a reflection exceedingly just in itself, but which, as the sequel shows, I failed to profit by. I saw that Marryat, not less than Homer, Milton, and Virgil, profited by the choice of a familiar and legendary subject; so that he prepared his readers on the very title-page; and this set me cudgelling my brains, if by any chance I could hit upon some similar belief to be the centre-piece of my own meditated fiction. In the course of this vain search there cropped in my memory a singular case of a buried and resuscitated fakir, which I had often been told of by an uncle of mine, then lately dead, Inspector-General John Balfour. On such a fine frosty night, with no wind and the thermom-

---

[1] In 1896, in vol. XXI of the Edinburgh edition of his works (London, Chatto and Windus, etc.) and in vol. XXII of the Thistle edition (New York, Scribner's, 1902), and many times since.

eter below zero, the brain works with much vivacity; and the next moment I had seen the circumstance transplanted from India and the tropics to the Adirondack wilderness and the stringent cold of the Canadian border. Here then, almost before I had begun my story, I had two countries, two of the ends of the earth involved: and thus though the notion of the resuscitated man failed entirely on the score of general acceptation, or even (as I have since found) acceptability, it fitted at once with my design of a tale of many lands; and this decided me to consider further of its possibilities. The man who should thus be buried was the first question: a good man whose return to life would be hailed by the reader and the other characters with gladness? This trenched upon the Christian picture and was dismissed. If the idea, then, was to be of any use at all for me, I had to create a kind of evil genius to his friends and family, take him through many disappearances, and make this final restoration from the pit of death, in the icy American wilderness, the last and grimmest of the series. I need not tell my brothers of the craft that I was now in the most interesting moment of an author's life; the hours that followed that night upon the balcony, and the following nights and days, whether walking abroad or lying wakeful in my bed, were hours of unadulterated joy. My mother, who was then living with me alone, perhaps had less enjoyment; for in the absence of my wife, who is my usual helper in these times of parturition, I must spur her up at all seasons to hear me relate and try to clarify my unformed fancies.

And while I was groping for the fable and the characters required, behold, I found them lying ready and nine years old in my memory. Pease porridge hot, pease porridge cold, pease porridge in the pot, nine years old. Was there ever a more complete justification of the rule of Horace? Here, thinking of quite other things, I had stumbled on the solution, or perhaps I should rather say (in stagewright phrase) the Curtain or final Tableau of a story conceived long before on the moors between Pitlochry and Strathardle, conceived in the Highland rain, in the blend of the smell of heather and bog-plants, and with a mind full of the Athole correspondence and the memories of the dumlicide justice.[2] So long ago, so far away it was, that I had first evoked the faces and the mutual tragic situation of the men of Durrisdeer.

My story was now world-wide enough: Scotland, India, and America being all obligatory scenes. But of these India was strange to me except in books;[3] I had never known any living Indian save a Parsee, a member of my club in London, equally civilised and (to all seeing) equally occidental with myself. It was plain, thus far, that I should have to get into India and out of it again upon a foot of fairy lightness; and I believe this first suggested to me the idea of the Chevalier Burke for a narrator. It was at first intended that he should be Scottish, and I was then filled with fears that he might prove only the degraded shadow of my own Alan Breck. Presently, however, it began to occur to me it would be like my Master to curry favor with the Prince's Irishmen; and that an Irish refugee would have a particular reason to find himself in India with his countryman, the unfortunate Lally. Irish, therefore, I decided he should be, and then, all of a sudden, I was aware of a tall shadow of Barry Lyndon. No man (in Lord Foppington's phrase) of a nice morality could go very deep with my Master: in the original idea of this story conceived in Scotland, this companion had been besides intended to be worse than the bad elder son with whom (as it was then meant) he was to visit Scotland; if I took an Irishman, and a very bad Irishman, in the midst of the eight-

[2] In some later editions "dumlicide justice" has been deleted and "Chevalier de Johnstone" substituted; see, for example, Skerryvore edition (London, Heinemann, 1924).

[3] During all his youthful years Louis had listened to tales of Indian life from his maternal uncle, Dr. John Balfour, who had been the last man to flee Delhi at the time of the famous mutiny in 1857.

eenth century, how was I to evade Barry Lyndon? The wretch besieged me, offering his services; he gave me excellent references; he proved that he was highly fitted for the work I had to do; he, or my own evil heart, suggested it was easy to disguise his ancient livery with a little lace and a few frogs and buttons, so that Thackeray himself should hardly recognise him. And then of a sudden there came to me memories of a young Irishman, with whom I was once intimate, and had spent long nights walking and talking with, upon a very desolate coast in a bleak autumn: I recalled him as a youth of an extraordinary moral simplicity—almost vacancy; plastic to any influence, the creature of his admirations: and putting such a youth in fancy into the career of a soldier of fortune, it occurred to me that he would serve my turn as well as Mr. Lyndon, and in place of entering into competition with the Master, would afford a slight though a distinct relief. I know not if I have done him well, though his moral dissertations always highly entertained me: but I own I have been surprised to find that he reminded some critics of Barry Lyndon after all. . . .

These were the first four chapters he wrote at Saranac, from Christmas through to the middle of April. Edmond Gosse says Louis confessed that he was written out and had to lay the story aside. At any rate, it was during this period of intensive work that he distressed himself by signing a second contract with *McClure's* magazine after having given exclusive rights to *Scribner's*. And by the same token, during this period he neglected to procure American copyright to protect *Jekyll and Hyde*.

The conclusion of chapter four is a doleful picture. Henry is telling Mackellar the hopelessness of his place in the esteem of his own immediate family of Durie, as well as the regard commensurate with his position by the countryside folk of Durrisdeer; How the agony of his mind was torturing; yet like a trapped man he could not reveal these invisible fetters of his brother's intrigue, so he must continue to live in cringing humiliation while his heart is sick with the resentment he dare not express.

So it was this gloomy ending of chapter four that Louis carried with him through the first months of his discovery of a new world and a strange people. Now it was November in Tautira before he resumed the story. Here behind the bamboo walls of the *faré* of Chief Ori, he tuned his mind again to the cruel taunting of defenseless Henry by the satanic Master until the younger brother, goaded to fury, struck his tormentor across his blasphemous mouth.

With gentle breezes blowing across his pad Louis wrote of the duel by candlelight in the dead of night; he created further suffering of Henry, who thought he had killed his brother and would be despised and condemned even more by his father and his wife, Katherine, of whose affections he always had been in doubt, the wife whom Louis called "Clementina" in the manuscript.

Here in the story he made an error that caused him considerable embarrassment by having Katherine thrust the bloody sword up to its hilt in the frozen ground in order to efface the bloodstain. In the soft rain-soaked sward of Tautira this would have been easy enough. Later when he heard that Marcel Schwob proposed to translate one of his books, Louis wrote to him, "Should you choose [*The Master*], pray do not let Mrs. Henry thrust the sword up to the hilt in the frozen ground—one of my inconceivable blunders, an exaggeration to stagger Hugo. Say 'she sought to thrust it into the ground.' "[4]

In spite of some anxiety about the time it was taking to repair the mast at Papeete and the rather alarming diminishing of their supply of coffee and butter and wines, blissful days passed at Tautira, and with all the shy deference of formality,

[4] Sidney, January 19, 1891. *Letters of R. L. S.*, ed. by Colvin, II, 259.

village life centered around the strangers. Each morning children and young men brought baskets of mangoes and papayas, whole stems of wild mountain *fei* (bananas), fish cleaned and dripping from the sea, or a calabash of freshly caught mullet cut into small pieces and sprinkled with lime juice for eating raw with baked taro or breadfruit—a real South Sea delicacy preferable to raw oysters.

All this while, Louis, hidden behind the bamboo walls yet able to observe the goings on about the *faré,* was busy with his hates and miseries, and when he would tire of his quarreling characters, he and Fanny would go for a stroll along the river into the deep shade of the forest. Never, however, could they walk far before they would hear the coaxing greeting of *"Iaorana! Haere mai amu!"* ("Greeting! Come eat with us!") It is a serious affront to ignore these invitations, so proudly extended, to share the family *ahima'a.* Nor had guests any desire to refuse as the food would be lifted from the *umu* (ground oven), boys sent scurrying up trees to pick coconuts for cool drinks, and girls sent to cut and clean sections of banana leaves for plates. Consequently, strolling usually was limited in range of miles or kilometers, but fascinatingly distant in the matter of human relations.

Against this constant tide of kindnesses and amid incomparable beauties of nature—red dawns and golden sunsets, cloud banks and storm, eerie moonlight trailing silver beams across dark waters, the surge of the sea in one's ears, the slow rustle of broad-leafed breadfruit trees, the sharp, harsh swish of palm fronds, nesting calls of wild pigeons like muted notes of dryads' flutes, and between these sounds, like rests in a music score, a beatified silence. It can be a spell so poignantly compelling that, once it has been experienced, one need never ask why a man forsakes "civilization."

On November 22, when the return of the *Casco* seemed reasonably certain, Louis and Fanny arranged a feast in return for the many courtesies they had received from the people of Tautira—not alone the immediate village but the entire district, which is one of the most fertile in Tahiti. Four huge pigs were purchased and men hired to roast them in the big *umus;* boys were sent into the forest to gather hundreds of breadfruit and dozens of stems of ripe and green bananas; taro, pineapple, and yam patches were denuded; coconuts were piled pyramid-fashion higher than a man's head, and fleets of boats were sent out for deep-sea fishing.

Formal invitations were sent to the school teacher and his pupils, to the Protestant minister and his flock, to the Roman Catholic priest and his following, and to all the chiefs and their subordinates. A small group of Mormons inadvertently were overlooked, but they came anyway, with no thought of having been slighted or conscious of any chagrin. Indeed, they would have been guilty of offense in not coming.

When all the cooked food had been spread on the shady lawn in front of Arii Ori's *faré,* Louis came out on the veranda, and, standing with his family and Moé, the Matea, he made a speech of presentation in French which Ori translated into Tahitian.

Aunt Maggie records that since only four pigs had been purchased and now the Mormons made five distinct groups, they feared there might be some embarrassment in an even distribution of the formal cuts of pork. Not so with Arii Ori. High chiefs are masters of tact and above reproach in honesty whether in dispensing food or land or titulary honors. He would not hold his title if he were not capable of executing without criticism all the delicate formalities of a ruler.

Aunt Maggie speaks, too, of the fact that the feast cost Louis seventeen pounds—in those days of sterling currency this would be about seventy dollars—probably the most bountiful ever given. But the guests brought gifts, as is their custom, which must have canceled a greater part of the cost to Louis— "ten little pigs, twenty-three fowls, and countless coconuts,

85

bananas, breadfruits, bundles of taro and pineapples, not to speak of cotton-silk pillows. One man brought two hen's eggs for hatching when we should return to our home far away, and 'when they sing it will remind you of Tautira.'"

It would not require any singing hens to remind the Tautira people of this event. For a generation they would reckon time from this occasion: not in memory of the generous supply of food, not the days of intensive preparation, but the complaisance of the donor, the genuine expression of friendship.

But the *Casco* did not come. It became a refrain with everyone, " '*E ita pahi! 'E ita pahi!*" ("No ship! No ship!") Louis worked steadily within the bamboo walls which afforded him seclusion without shutting off fresh air. Aunt Maggie says she never saw so much flesh on his bones. He usually wore nothing more than a suit of pajamas. Tautira is sheltered from both northwest and southeast winds and probably has the balmiest climate anywhere in the South Pacific. Following his custom of working on more than one composition, Louis wrote "The Song of Ra-héro" probably as a relief from *The Master of Ballantrae*. And he dedicated this saga of ancient Polynesia to Ori-a-Ori:

> *Ori, my brother in the island mode,*
> *In every tongue and meaning much my friend,*
> *This story of your country and your clan,*
> *In your loved house, your too much honored guest,*
> *I made in English. Take it, being done;*
> *And let me sign it with the name you gave.*
> *Teriitera.*

It is scarcely possible that Louis had at that time any written account of the Ohatutira (ancient name for Tautira) hero Arii Ra-héro (Red-sun); although the French government had in its possession the extensive records of Tahitian history and legends compiled by the Reverend John Muggridge Orsmond, missionary to Tahiti in 1774–76, upon which he had worked for nearly thirty years. It was from her grandfather's notes that Teuira Henry wrote her valuable book, *Ancient Tahiti,* published by the Bernice Pauahi Bishop Museum Library in 1928.

Therefore it came from listening to the stories of the Matea of Tautira, or of Arii Ori, both of whom would have had a comprehensive knowledge of all the legends and historical events of Tahiti and especially of this southern peninsula of Taiarapu. Mrs. Field said that one of Louis's chief charms was his intent listening and the gracious manner he had in putting any talker at ease. And while he took the recognized poet's license in depicting some of the events in the long story of "Redsun," there may have been many differences in the recital by different people; even the Matea and Ori, in telling the same story, may have stressed different details.

Having written this saga, Louis did not write further of Tahiti in *In the South Seas,* but skipped from the Tuamotus to the Gilbert Islands. And there must have been a degree of malevolence in "Song of Ra-héro" which was a mild counterpart to that in *Master of Ballantrae,* so in fretting to sustain the vicious persecution of Mr. Henry by the Master, Louis may have found the poetic composition of "Ra-héro" a mental emancipation. The poem has a fluency that comes with the joy of writing and the fluidity of thought that springs from depths of understanding. Read "Ra-héro" and one lives in the agony of the mother whose beloved son, Tamatea, was so wantonly betrayed and killed and one feels her cry for vengeance:

But the mother of Tamatea arose with death in her eyes.
All night long, and the next, Taiarapu rang with her cries.
As when a babe in the wood turns with a chill of doubt
And perceives nor home, nor friends, for the trees have
closed about,

87

Last Witness for Robert Louis Stevenson

The mountain rings and her breast is torn with the
voice of despair:
So the lion-like woman idly wearied the air
For a while, and pierced men's hearing in vain, and
wounded their hearts.
But as when the weather changes, in dangerous parts,
And sudden the hurricane wrack unrolls up the front of sky,
At once the ship lies idle, the sails hang silent on high,
The breath of the wind that blew is blown out like the
flame of a lamp
And the silent armies of death draw near with inaudible
tramp:
So sudden, the voice of her weeping ceased; in silence she rose
And passed from the house of her sorrow, a woman clothed
with repose,
Carrying death in her breast and sharpening death with
her hand.

Then at long, long last when she had grown old in her campaign to bring punishment to Ra-héro:

But the mother of Tamatea threw her arms abroad,
"Pyre of my son," she shouted, "debited vengeance of God,
Late, late, I behold you, yet I behold you at last,
And glory, beholding! For now are the days of my agony past,
The lust that famished my soul now eats and drinks its desire,
And they that encompassed my son shrivel alive in the fire.
Tenfold precious the vengeance that comes after lingering
years!
Ye quenched the voice of my singer?—hark, in your
dying ears,
The song of the conflagration! Ye left me a widow alone?
—Behold, the whole of your race consumes, sinew and bone
And tortured flesh together: man, mother, and maid

*Heaped in a common shambles; and already borne by
the trade,
The smoke of your dissolution darkens the stars of night.*"[5]

Ra-héro alone escaped from the funeral pyre and was doomed to further suffering by wandering alone in the forest and along the beaches, his great handsome body now scarred and ugly from burns, until at last he captured a woman whose husband he had killed and fled again to his mountain retreat.

Louis, the true egalitarian with a passionate belief in the equality of men, had not the slightest desire to play down the drama of this age-old legend, told and retold through countless centuries by simple word of mouth, and he must have known he was contributing richly to Polynesian lore in recording the story in this form—the oral recital to which he listened in the droning hush of those enchanted dusks of evening time.

Hubert G. Woodford, lecturer in English literature, Manchester University, comments in reply to an adverse criticism of Stevenson's works:

Tastes differ so widely that when readers confess that they find Dickens or Scott or the Brontës boring, it is as difficult to argue against them as it is to argue against those who say that they cannot enjoy fish or onions or a green Chartreuse.

In a long teaching-life in literature, this is the first time I have met some one who finds Stevenson boring. We may criticize Stevenson on many other grounds, but his life and writings are so free from dullness and so crammed with colour and adventure, that one still discovers the young protesting against bedtime whilst devouring *Treasure Island, Kidnapped,* and *A Child's Garden of Verses,* and the children of a larger growth held captive by one of the greatest story-tellers of all time.

The revived interest in Stevenson to-day is doubtless due

[5] First published in *Ballads* (1891).

to the fact that the modern reading public is finding so much modern fiction unsatisfying and insipid, and is turning to this most versatile of writers, whose vision of life was so vivid and exciting, and whose style was so much the man himself, that he seldom fails to communicate to the reader his own abounding zest for life.[6]

When November slipped into December with discouraging news of the *Casco*, the Stevenson household cast anxious eyes at their dwindling stores. Captain Otis had written that a second spar required repairs. Each remembered with a thankful heart their stormy thirty-hour sail from Papeete to Taravao, when they should have made the twenty-five miles in six or seven hours. Otis wrote that he had salvaged a mainmast from a harbor derelict, but that he had no skilled labor, so that to upstep the *Casco's* rotten one and step the replacement, heeling it through the deck and making it fast to the keelson, was proving a slow and tedious task. Men work a few hours in the early morning, he said, and unless attracted by some diversion, consent to work a few hours in the late afternoon.

Arii Ori touchingly declared that he and Louis were brothers and everything he had was theirs. He was honored to share with them. The Matea gave a feast to prove her subordinate's statement. Yet out of consideration for his guests Ori offered to go to Papeete in his canoe and fetch provisions from the *Casco*. Louis hesitated. It meant thirty-five miles of rowing with only a few yards of primitive sail. But they did want coffee and wine, butter, jam, and flour. So on December 3 they waved good-bye as he paddled down the river, was tossed by the waves as he crossed the reef, and faded into a speck against the horizon. He was to return in three days. It was evening of the eighth before a lookout spied a bobbing dot on the blue

[6] *John o'London's Weekly*, 1951.

water. Men hurried to meet their chief and relieve his tired arms at the paddle.

Still bad news of the work on the *Casco*. Louis and Fanny became acutely concerned about finances. Paying a thousand dollars a month for an idle schooner, plus the expense of repairs, went beyond their calculations. On November 10, Louis had written to Charles Baxter:

Our mainmast is dry-rotten, and we are all to the devil; I shall lie in a debtor's jail. Never mind, Tautira is first chop. I am so besotted that I shall put on the back of this my attempt at words to *Wandering Willie;* if you can conceive at all the difficulty, you will also conceive the vanity with which I regard any kind of result; and whatever mine is like, it has some sense, and Burns's has none.

Home no more home to me, whither must I wander?
Hunger my driver, I go where I must.
Cold blows the winter wind over hill and heather;
Thick drives the rain, and my roof is in the dust.
Loved of wise men was the shade of my roof-tree,
The true word of welcome was spoken at the door—
Dear days of old with faces in the firelight,
Kind folks of old, you come again no more.

Home was home then, my dear, full of kindly faces,
Home was home then, my dear, happy for the child.
Fire and the windows bright glittered on the moorland;
Song, tuneful song, built a palace in the wild.
Now, when day dawns on the brow of the moorland,
Lone stands the house, and the chimney-stone is cold.
Lone let it stand, now the friends are all departed,
The kind hearts, the true hearts, that loved the place
of old.[7]

[7] *Letters of R. L. S.*, ed. by Colvin, II, 145-46.

It is an interesting glimpse inside those bamboo walls to find that simultaneously with the letter to Charles Baxter with this homely poem the author put the same lines into the mouth of the Master as he and Mackellar rode away from Durrisdeer to Glasgow, their port of embarkation for a new world, as if to wring from that hardened heart a hint of human warmth in his remark; "Ah, Mackellar, do you think I have never a regret?"

"I do not think you could be so bad a man," said I, "if you had not all the machinery to be a good one."

"No, not all," says he: "Not all. You are there in error. The malady of not wanting, my evangelist." But methought he sighed as he mounted again into the chaise.

This is the opening of chapter eight, which probably was completed with chapters five, six, and seven during the nine weeks at Tautira; and chapter eight ends with their arrival in New York harbor after Mackellar had made the unsuccessful attempt en route to push the Master overboard and was humiliated by the forgiveness of this fantastic character.

In another November letter to Charles Baxter Louis wrote:

> Tautira (The Garden of the world),
> otherwise called Hans-Christian-
> Andersen-ville.

My dear Charles,—Whether I have a penny left in the wide world, I know not, nor shall know, till I get to Honolulu, where I anticipate a devil of an awakening. It will be from a mighty pleasant dream at least: Tautira being mere Heaven. But suppose, for the sake of argument, any money to be left in the hands of my painful doer, what is to be done with it? Save us from exile would be the wise man's choice, I suppose; for the exile threatens to be eternal. But yet I am of opinion—in case there should be *some* dibs in the hand of the P. D., *i. e.* painful doer; because if there be none, I shall take to my flageolet on the high-road, and work home the best way I can, having previously made away with my family—I am of opinion that if—and his are in the customary state, and you are thinking of an offering, and there should be still some funds over, you would be a real good P. D. to put some in with yours and tak' the credit o't, like a wee man! I know it's a beastly thing to ask; but it, after all, does no earthly harm, only that much good. And besides, like enough there's nothing in the till, and there is an end. Yet I live here in the full lustre of millions; it is thought I am the richest son of man that has yet been to Tautira: I!—and I am secretly eaten with the fear of lying in pawn, perhaps for the remainder of my days, in San Francisco. As usual, my colds have much hashed my finances . . . .[8]

But that Louis was supremely happy in Tautira is attested by his letter to John Addington Symonds, which he reserved the right to use as the introduction to *In The South Seas:*

One November night, in the village of Tautira, we sat at the high table in the hall of assembly, hearing the natives sing. It was dark in the hall and very warm; though at times the land wind blew a little shrewdly through the chinks, and at times, through the larger openings, we could see the moonlight on the lawn. As the songs arose in the rattling Tahitian chorus, the chief translated here and there a verse. Farther along in the volume you shall read the songs themselves; and I am in hopes that not only you only, but all who can find a savour in the ancient poetry of places, will read them with some pleasure. You are to conceive us, therefore, in strange circumstances and very pleasing; in a strange land and climate, the most beautiful on earth; surrounded by a foreign race that all

[8] *Ibid.*, 144–45.

travellers have agreed to be the most engaging; and taking a double interest in two foreign arts.

We came forth at last, in a cloudy moonlight, on the forest lawn which is the street of Tautira. The Pacific roared outside upon the reef. Here and there one of the scattered palm-built lodges shone out under the shadow of the wood, the lamplight bursting through the crannies of the wall. We went homeward slowly, Ori a Ori carrying behind us the lantern and the chairs, properties with which we had just been enacting our part of the distinguished visitor. It was one of those moments in which minds not altogether churlish recall the names and deplore the absence of congenial friends; and it was your name that first rose from my lips. "How Symonds would have enjoyed this evening!" said one, and then another. The word caught in my mind; I went to bed, and it was still there. The glittering, frosty solitudes in which your days are cast, arose before me: I seemed to see you walking there in the late night, under the pine-trees and the stars; and I received the image with something like remorse.

There is a modern attitude toward fortune; in this place I will not use a graver name. Staunchly to withstand her buffets and to enjoy with equanimity her favours was the code of the virtuous of old. Our fathers, it would seem, wondered and doubted how they had merited their misfortunes: we, rather how we have deserved our happiness. And we stand often abashed, and sometimes revolted, at those partialities of fate by which we profit most. It was so with me on that November night: I felt that our positions should be changed. It was you, dear Symonds, who should have gone upon that voyage and written this account. With your rich stores of knowledge, you could have remarked and understood a thousand things of interest and beauty that escaped my ignorance; and the brilliant colours of your style would have carried into a thousand sickrooms the sea air and the strong sun of tropic islands. It was otherwise decreed. But suffer me at least to connect you, if only in name and only in the fondness of imagination, with the voyage of the "Silver Ship."

Robert Louis Stevenson.

[In a postscript]:

Dear Symonds,—I send you this (November 11th), the morning of its completion. If I ever write an account of this voyage, may I place this letter at the beginning? It represents— I need not tell you, for you too are an artist—a most genuine feeling, which kept me long awake last night; and though perhaps a little elaborate, I think it a good piece of writing. We are *in heaven here.* Do not forget.—*R. L. S.*

Please keep this: I have no perfect copy.

Tautira, on the peninsula of Tahiti.[9]

Not until December 22 did the *Casco* arrive. Early in the morning the children of the village were shouting, "'*E pahi!* '*E pahi!*'" but the Stevensons had to remain in suspense until midday, when the schooner, jockeying cautiously, had worked in close enough for them to discern the Stars and Stripes flying at the masthead, with the red ensign below indicating a British charter. This was Saturday. Eager as they were to be on their way, the family could have packed their belongings and left immediately, but that would have been rude. A Sunday sailing would have been equally bad form. And Monday should be given over to a feast of farewell with appropriate speeches. So it was Tuesday, Christmas Day, before they were northward bound across that pudding-string of the universe that we call the Equator.

Louis was in better health than at any time in his life. Even the anxiety over a "debtor's cell" and the unfinished manuscript of *Master of Ballantrae* had not weighed him down or hindered his eating like a Teva, the clan to which he now belonged by

[9] *Ibid.*, 146–48.

95

virtue of having exchanged names with Ori. But he dreaded the conventional social amenities of Honolulu and wrote of the place to Sydney Colvin as "that boiling pot of disagreeables which I constantly expect."

Looking back on their nine weeks, Louis declared: "But the best fortune of our stay in Tautira was my knowledge of Ori himself, one of the finest creatures extant. The day of our parting was a sad one. We deduced from it a rule for travellers: not to stay two months in one place—which is to cultivate regrets."

And he might have made this statement with a hundred times the intensity of feeling on behalf of those left behind. He was going to new scenes. Ori and his people had only the shadow sketches that Fanny had drawn on the wall of his *faré*. Of Ori's farewell letter, Louis wrote to Henry James: ". . . it is a strange thing for a tough, sick middle-aged scrivener like R.L.S. to receive a letter so conceived from a man fifty years old, a leading politician, a crack orator, and the great wit of his village: boldly say, 'the highly popular M.P. of Tautira.' My nineteenth century strikes here, and lies alongside of something beautiful and ancient. I think the receipt of such a letter might humble, shall I say even——? and for me, I would rather have received it than written *Redgauntlet* or the Sixth *Æneid*."

Ori's letter:

I make you to know my great affection. At the hour when you left us, I was filled with tears; my wife, Rui Telime, also, and all of my household. When you embarked I felt a great sorrow. It is for this that I went upon the road, and you looked from that ship, and I looked at you on the ship with great grief until you had raised the anchor and hoisted the sails. When the ship started I ran along the beach to see you still; and when you were on the open sea I cried out to you, "Farewell, Louis"; and when I was coming back to my house I seemed to hear your voice crying, "Rui, farewell." Afterwards I watched the ship as long as I could until the night fell; and when it was dark I said to myself, "If I had wings I should fly to the ship to meet you and to sleep amongst you, so that I might be able to come back to shore and to tell Rui Telime, "I have slept upon the ship of Teriitera."

After that we passed that night in the impatience of grief. Towards eight o'clock I seemed to hear your voice, "Teriitera— Rui— here is the hour for *putter* and *tiro*" [cheese and syrup]. I did not sleep that night, thinking continually of you, my very dear friend, until the morning; being then still awake, I went to see Tapina Tutu on her bed, and alas, she was not there. Afterwards I looked into your rooms; they did not please me as they used to do. I did not hear your voice saying, "Hail Rui"; I thought then that you had gone, and that you had left me.

Rising up I went to the beach to see your ship, and I could not see it. I wept then until the night, telling myself continually, "Teriitera returns into his own country and leaves his dear Rui in grief, so that I suffer for him, and weep for him." I will not forget you in my memory. Here is the thought: I desire to meet you again. It is my dear Teriitera makes the only riches I desire in this world. It is your eyes that I desire to see again. It must be that your body and my body shall eat together at one table: there is what would make my heart content. But now we are separated. May God be with you all. May His word and His mercy go with you, so that you may be well and we also, according to the words of Paul.

Ori a Ori, that is to say, Rui.[10]

A hundred years ago Ori's ancestor would have expressed his grief by cutting his upper lip just below the nostrils with a shark's tooth, held a cloth to catch the blood, then dried the cloth and given it to Louis as a manifestation of his grief. Now

[10] *Ibid.,* 168–69.

Ori writes this beautiful letter to his *Teriitera,* "Splendor of the Sky."

Because of the delay at Tautira, anticipated visits to the islands of Bora Bora and Eimeo (old name for Mooréa) of the Tahitian group had to be abandoned, which was a pity.

But, like all travelers on the last leg of a journey, the Stevensons were impatient to get to Honolulu. A few days of good sailing put them all in high spirits; then came squalls, calms, and days of drifting, when tacking against what little breeze was coming on the northwest Trades slowed them to only sixty and seventy miles a day. They were practically riding on the Equator. The deck was too hot to sit outside, the brass railings blistering to the touch. The quantities of vegetables and fruit that Ori had given them were spoiling and their own rations were perilously low. Spirits were falling like a barometer before a storm. Only Louis remained cheerful, and when Ah Fu was reduced to serving meals of such scanty portions that he was in danger of collapsing from mortification, Louis remarked, "It seems then, that we are between the devil and the salt horse, and the deep green sea." Captain Otis did not think it was funny, but then he had an earache.

To lighten the tedium, Fanny suggested that each one write a story of some specific incident of the cruise, then draw for the turn to have his story read after dinner. Captain Otis declared this was the most blood-curdling proposition he had ever faced, and it left him trembling with fear. Unfortunately for the poor skipper, Louis drew first place, and his story was so clever that the Captain fell ill and begged off—a fortunate illness, he confessed later.

Not until January 13 did they cross the line into the Northern Hemisphere—nineteen days out of Tautira. And not until a few days later did they pick up a creditable breeze that sent them along 170 miles in twenty-four hours. This proved to be preliminary to a gale, and the question was whether to lay to and play safe, or "run for it" with full sail and face the hazard of high seas. Louis agreed to the latter course, and Captain Otis sent the schooner racing ahead "under double-reefed fore and main sails, with the bonnet off the jib, flying from a gale that swept her like a toy across the sea," as Arthur Johnstone describes it.[11]

The Stevensons, battened in the cabin, were knocked about until voluntary and controlled movements were impossible. Starting in one direction meant being catapulted in another, sideways, backward, or forward, or up or down, all dignity forfeited to wind and sea. Waves continually climbed across the bow and occasionally over the superstructure. None of the crew ventured out unless with secure lashings against being washed overboard. The *Casco* was now averaging 230 miles a day with rain and thunder and lightning adding misery upon misery.

Fanny solemnly declared that this was her last sea voyage, that she was going ashore in Honolulu and stay there. Valentine lost her temper in vain effort to tidy the cabin. Poor skinny little Ah Fu was hurled headlong into the cabin every time he appeared with a platter of food. Louis, with his persistent good humor, whether genuine or assumed to allay the fears of his family, irritated Captain Otis to the point of profanity when he said he was enjoying the experience and would use it in a story—and thus "The Wrecker" was enriched, plus one or two broken spars and a torn sail. In spite of fiddles on the table and the tablecloth and pad carefully kept wet by Ah Fu, dishes plunged over the edge unless held down, and a bowl of soup or a cup of coffee had to be held in one's hand and the contents drunk with all possible haste in order to avoid a drenching.

There were ten days of this exhausting knocking about before they sighted the southern tip of the island of Hawaii and

[11] Arthur Johnstone, *Robert Louis Stevenson in the Pacific* (London, Chatto and Windus, 1905), 46.

ran under its protecting lee. Then, with 200 miles of comparatively smooth sailing past Maui, Lanai, and Molokai, they sighted the bold tor of Diamond Head on Oahu Island and got their first faint glimpse of Honolulu; here to stand becalmed for twelve long hours, dining on "bully" beef while their mouths watered for the fresh fruits and vegetables within an hour's sailing.

But Diamond Head light had flashed the news of the arrival of the long overdue schooner, and at nine o'clock the next morning when she picked up a good breeze and came past Waikiki at the rate of an express train, Isobel and Joe Strong and their small son, Austin, were in a tiny skiff in the roadstead to meet her, escaping being run down by the veriest miracle and sending Louis and Captain Otis into an eloquent duet of profanity while the pilot madly maneuvered the helm to avoid them.

Captain Otis comments: "There was not much difficulty in getting the gentleman aboard but when it came to his wife, it was perhaps as lively and exciting an adventure as the lady ever participated in, and I imagine that Mrs. Strong must retain a vivid recollection of the scuffle that ensued." Indeed she did, for the rest of her life! In an era of high collars and tight corsets, with skirt and petticoat six yards around reaching to the instep, and the exposure of an ankle shockingly unladylike, it was a performance that might have been hilariously funny, but it only contributed to the *Casco* passengers' irritability. The meager fare of the past few days when sea-whetted appetites faced imminent famine had stunted their appreciation of comedy.

Without his customary early tea and toast Louis was bristling with more or less refined profanity, so when Miss Valentine Roch, equally bristling with petulance, gave him a particularly saucy response, he said sternly, "One more word like that out of you and I'll open your boxes." Thus on this sour note she was booked on the next steamer for San Francisco and faded from the Stevenson picture, with the exception of an occasion four years later when she was interviewed by a newspaper reporter and related that Fanny condemned the original draft of *Dr. Jekyll and Mr. Hyde* so vehemently that Louis threw the manuscript in the fireplace.

Her account was correct as far as it went. Louis, in sending the story by Valentine to Fanny early in the morning while she was still in her dressing room, added a note asking, "How do you think this will go in *Cornhill's?*" Fanny sent the script back with a note and it *did* go in the fireplace, but her note read: "No, no; not *Cornhill's*. It is much too good and you must make it into a novel." Valentine was innocent of misrepresentation, for she had seen Louis toss the script into the fire.

Before dismissing the *Casco*, Louis entertained at several small dinner parties on board. Then he gave a *luau* on shore for Captain Otis and the crew, including in this courtesy gesture King Kalakaua and Queen Kapiolani and Princess (later Queen) Liliuokalani, who had received them with royal cordiality, and Mrs. Caroline Bush, who had taken them into her home until they had found permanent quarters. When the list of guests went up to fifty, quite outgrowing the Stevenson cottage, Louis appealed to Henry Poor for the use of the spacious *lanai* of his home, which was practically next door.

With the bountiful feast at Tautira as a criterion they had two roast pigs stuffed with vegetables and roast whole fowls, besides long rice cooked with chicken, great platters of delicate raw fish, huge bowls of *poi*, individual bowls of salmon *lomi*, and dozens of individual *laulaus;* while stacked down the center of each long table were piles of baked yams and breadfruit, both cooked and raw bananas, pineapples and coconuts, and champagne served like water.

Joe Strong declared afterward that never before in all his

life had he opened so many bottles for a single occasion. It was an extravagance that amazed the guests and so impressed Henry's little half-sister, ten-year-old Delilah Poor, that she still thinks it was her big brother's *luau* for the Stevensons. Here again Mrs. Field put us right.

5. Hawaii

Unfortunately Louis went to Honolulu with a preconceived dislike for the place. About what prompted him to designate it as "a boiling pot of disagreeables" in a letter to Sydney Colvin written on the *Casco* en route from Tautira, even Isobel Field could not hazard a guess, unless it was adverse reports brought back by San Francisco friends who had found life in the infant Pacific metropolis irritatingly provincial.

If there was one word that was anathema to Louis it was "pretense." A phrase used by John F. Genung is apropos of Louis's sentiments: "If he had the framing of an ideal for us, his first counsel, I imagine, would be, Do not assume an *attitude* toward life, but just live; do not be a spectator or critic of the business of living, but throw yourself into the heart of it, and say no more about it."

Coming from nine weeks of delightful association with the graciousness and the simple, natural poise of the Matea of Tautira and the noble dignity of Arii Ori, he was immediately conscious of a disharmony, probably the dissension and rivalry of which he had been forewarned. Social veneer was thin, revealing the assumptions of cultural status which always prevail in a new order. Yet the social register carried many of the names of the proud New England families who had gone out as missionaries in 1820.

There was Rev. Samuel W. Parker, who, together with Rev. Alexander and Rev. Armstrong, was sent by Rev. Hiram Bingham to the Marquesas in 1833, where they remained for only eight months and were obliged to return to the mission fields of Hawaii because of fear for their lives among the Marquesans. Other names now equally well known in social and commercial circles are those of early missionaries whose work earned for them such comments as this: "Influence of some kind was the law of native development. Had not the missionaries and their friends among the foreign merchants and professional men been in the ascendant, these islands would have presented only the usual history of a handful of foreigners exacting everything from a people who denied their right to anything. As it is, in no place in the world that I have visited, are the rules which control vice and regulate amusement so strict, yet so reasonably and fairly enforced."[1]

This was in 1866; the first missionaries had gone out in 1820; it was now 1889 when Louis with his penetrating candor was appraising the third generation of these hardy folk who had set themselves up as sugarcane and pineapple aristocracy and had drifted considerably away from the strict teachings of their fathers. He was seeing with astounding clarity the crushing beginnings of an end to a proud branch of Polynesian people, which ultimately was to leave them in the category of delightfully pleasant nondescripts.

It is true that when the Kamehamehas abandoned the old royal palace at Kailua on Hawaii Island and built the present palace in Honolulu, the social status of the commercial capital was elevated according to accepted standards of royalty. But the Kamehamehas, including the capable and saintly Queen Emma, had the moral backing of the then active missionaries which aided them in opposing political moves by foreigners.

Kalakaua, born in 1836, succeeded Kamehameha-Lunalilo in 1874 and launched forth on a political career for which he was ill trained, making a trip to the United States with the vague aim of building more secure relations and acquainting himself

[1] Manley Hopkins, *Hawaii* (London, Longmans, Green and Co., 1866), 386.

with foreign methods of diplomacy. Later he went to Samoa, accompanied again by Henry Poor, who had gone with him to the United States, to lay before the Samoan rulers a plan for them to join Hawaii in a federated self-governing principality with himself as king. While Kalakaua's ancestry springs from Upolu, the Samoans have other royal *ali'i* of higher rank than his family, and they declined to consider recognition of him as supreme sovereign.

Had this idea been promulgated a half-century earlier by one of the more virile and forceful Kamehamehas, whose royal roots also are in Samoa on the island of Savaii (once called Chatham Island), both the Hawaiians and the Samoans might have been spared the indignities of a foreign government and permitted to function as an independent principality with a British or United States protectorate, as does the kingdom of Toga today.

Fearing further moves toward foreign alliances by Kalakaua, who was being coached by his strong-minded sister, Liliuokalani, married to John O. Dominis, formerly of Boston, Massachusetts, the commercial interests of Honolulu forced the King in 1887 to grant a new constitution with royal prerogatives so curtailed that he was reduced to a mere figurehead.

Defeated and disillusioned, criticized by his sister for not fighting for his rights, Kalakaua settled down to enjoy what was left of his due as king and ward off as long as possible the plainly impending fate of being completely assimilated by American commercial interests. It was into this open play of sinister disregard for the Hawaiian people and their native land and the political machinations to unseat the monarchy that Louis came. He saw as never before the cruel bite of the clamping jaws of greed. He liked Kalakaua, liked the cheer and good humor with which he sat on his shaky throne, and most of all liked his stint of visible symptoms of grandeur.

Already Joe and Isobel Strong had identified themselves with the royal social set, generally termed the drinking (not drunken) crowd. While Joe's parents had gone to Hawaii as missionaries, they had voluntarily retired from the work, and since their son had gone on a commission from the Spreckels Sugar Company of San Francisco to paint a huge canvas of the Oahu Pali, he and Isobel quite naturally fell in with the more Bohemian group, a designation rather illusory considering the environment. Kalakaua was a Christian and supported the churches, but was more liberal in his conception of Christianity than the Kamehamehas and had lifted the ban on the hula which had been imposed by them at the behest of the missionaries. Consequently, by the time Louis arrived, traditional gaiety again prevailed among the Hawaiians and Kalakaua's reputation for piousness had suffered accordingly with the church folk.

Cliques, pretense, intrigues, all these irritated Louis like a rash or a slow poison; so after a few days in Honolulu with Joe and Isobel, they moved to a small cottage with the romantic name of "Manuia Lanai" on Waikiki Beach, not far from the more ample residence of Henry Poor. Waikiki, three miles from Honolulu, was at this time a quiet country beach. The Manuia Lanai lawn ran right to the sea, where waves broke over the reef and lapped the shore line in spitting little curls.

Best of all was a small guest house to the rear of the cottage, well hidden with shrubbery, meagerly but comfortably furnished with bed, table, and chairs, with the usual pandanus matting on the floor. Louis called it filthy. It probably was only discolored from the sea air, for filth of any kind is not usual among the Polynesians. Louis took exclusive possession of this primitive abode, and with Ah Fu's ministrations of toast and tea at daybreak, he began again the plaguing final chapters of *The Master of Ballantrae.*

This was the first of February. Already three installments had appeared in *Scribner's* magazine. A fourth was due this month, which would use all the copy he had left with Mr. Burlingame.

Instead of forwarding the work done in Tautira, he sent only three more installments, finding parts he did not like, so there was rewriting to do, a thing rarely necessary.

It was Fanny who, as usual, had to bear the brunt of fending off guests while Louis worked in his hideaway. To those who merely came to call on a famous author, she and Aunt Maggie served cool drinks and as tactfully as possible mitigated their disappointment. About those she knew Louis would wish to meet, and except for work this would include almost everyone, she must use her judgment concerning interruptions, the while placating the guests. It was a difficult role. Some declared she was keeping him at work because she wanted the money he would earn, while in reality her greatest concern was that he should not work too hard. His health was better than it had ever been. She determined to keep it so if humanly possible. Financial worries, which never had been too vexing, were lifted by the arrival of a check for a thousand dollars from Mr. Burlingame, and while it was not acknowledged until April, it probably arrived in March. Mail was not too frequent at this time.

Louis had gone through the usual apprehensions of one in a foreign land whose funds are running low, and immediately upon arrival in Honolulu he had written to Mr. Burlingame:

. . . Not one word of business have I received either from the States or England, nor anything in the shape of coin; which leaves me in a fine uncertainty and quite penniless on these islands. H. M. [His Majesty, King Kalakaua] (who is a gentleman of courtly order and much tinctured with letters) is very polite; I may possibly ask for the position of palace doorkeeper. . . .

To resume my desultory song . . . in my present state of benighted ignorance as to my affairs for the last seven months—I know not whether my house or my mother's house have been let—I desire to see something definite in front of me—outside the lot of palace doorkeeper. . . . I may also be deceived as to the numbers of *The Master* now going and already gone; but to me they seem First Chop, sir, First Chop. I hope I shall pull off that damed ending; but it still depresses me: this is your doing, Mr. Burlingame: you would have it there and then, and I fear it—I fear that ending.

R. L. S.[2]

A week or so later, on February 8, he wrote to Charles Baxter:

Here we are at Honolulu, and have dismissed the yacht, and lie here till April anyway, in a fine state of haze, which I am yet in hopes some letter of yours (still on the way) may dissipate. No money, and not one word as to money! However, I have got the yacht paid off in triumph, I think; and though we stay here impignorate, it should not be for long, even if you bring us no extra help from home. The cruise has been a great success, both as to matter, fun, and health; and yet, Lord, man! we're pleased to be ashore. . . . Altogether, this foolhardy venture is achieved; and if I have but nine months of life and any kind of health, I shall have both eaten my cake and got it back again with usury. But, man, there have been days when I felt guilty, and thought I was in no position for the head of a house. . . . My wife is no great shakes; she is the one who has suf-fered most. My mother has had a Huge Old Time; Lloyd is first chop; I so well that I do not know myself—sea-bathing, if you please, and what is far more dangerous, entertaining and being entertained by His Majesty here, who is a very fine intelligent fellow, but, O, Charles! what a crop for the drink! He carries it too like a mountain with a sparrow on its shoulders. . . .

The extraordinary health I enjoy and variety of interests I find among these islands would tempt me to remain here; only for Lloyd, who is not well placed in such countries for a per-

[2] *Letters of R. L. S.*, ed. by Colvin, II, 156.

manency; and a little for Colvin, to whom I feel I owe a sort
of filial duty. And these two considerations will no doubt bring
be back—to go to bed again—in England.—   Yours ever
affectionately,

R. L. S.[3]

Again on March 8 he wrote to Charles Baxter:

". . . Lloyd and I have finished a story, *The Wrong Box*. If it
is not funny, I am sure I do not know what is. I have split
over writing it. Since I have been here, I have been toiling
like a galley slave: three numbers of *The Master* to rewrite,
five chapters of *The Wrong Box* to write and rewrite, and
about five hundred lines of a narrative poem to write, rewrite,
and re-rewrite. Now I have *The Master* waiting for me for
its continuation, two numbers more; when that's done, I shall
breathe. This spasm of activity has been chequered with champagne parties: Happy and Glorious Hawaii Ponoi paua: kou
moi—(Native Hawaiians, dote upon your monarch!) Hawaiian
God save the King. (In addition to my other labours, I am
learning the language with a native moonshee.) Kalakaua is
a terrible companion; a bottle of fizz is like a glass of sherry
to him; he thinks nothing of five or six in an afternoon as a whet
for dinner. You should see a photograph of our party after an
afternoon with H. H. M.: my! what a crew!—
                    Yours ever affectionately,
                                        R. L. S.[4]

And still again in April he wrote:

"My dear Burlingame,—This is to announce the most prodigious
change of programme. I have seen so much of the South Seas
that I desire to see more, and I get so much health here that

[3] *Ibid.*, 159.
[4] *Ibid.*, 166.

I dread a return to our vile climates. I have applied accordingly to the missionary folk to let me go round in the *Morning Star;* and if the Boston Board should refuse, I shall get somehow to Fiji, hire a trading schooner, and see the Fijis and Friendlies and Samoa. . . .

Before I sail, I shall make out to let you have the last of *The Master:* though I tell you it sticks! . . . I am quite worked out, and this cursed end of *The Master* hangs over me like the arm of the gallows; but it is always darkest before dawn, and no doubt the clouds will soon rise; but it is a difficult thing to write, above all in Mackellarese; and I can not yet see my way clear. If I pull this off, *The Master* will be a pretty good novel or I am the more deceived; and even if I don't pull it off, it'll still have some stuff in it.

. . . I will let you know my next address, which will probably be Sydney. If we get on the *Morning Star,* I propose at present to get marooned on Ponape, and take my chance of getting a passage to Australia. . . .

R. L. S.[5]

It is not known certainly to whom Louis applied for passage on the *Morning Star,* but it most likely was Dr. Hyde; or on his call on this dignitary he may have taken his mother for a social visit with this top man of missionary affairs. Aunt Maggie must have missed the church circles, in which she particularly delighted. And she, with the family, must have been aware of the intended slights of the sugarcane and pineapple aristocracy, who looked with open disfavor on those who were accepted in the royal Kalakaua group, and whose absence at the Wednesday afternoon salons at Manuia Lanai was noticeable.

Dr. Hyde was not a uniformly pleasant man. Former U. S. Senator Hiram Bingham was in his Sunday school class in Honolulu and remembers him as somewhat lacking in the graces

[5] *Ibid.,* 172–73.

ordinarily associated with his calling, yet a man of highest integrity and the strictest principles of conduct. However it may have been, we know Louis did call on Dr. Hyde at his residence in Beretania Street, a missionary manse, no doubt maintained by the Boston headquarters. Dr. Hyde was not one of those who had invested in lands.

And the matter of the *Morning Star* was settled quickly—we presume pleasantly—for on April 6, Louis wrote to Miss Boodle that they had decided against the missionary ship in favor of the trading schooner *Equator*, which was due from San Francisco in June. "A far preferable idea," he wrote, "giving us more time and a thousandfold more liberty; so we determined to cut off the missionaries with a shilling. The Sandwich Islands do not interest us very much; we live here, oppressed with civilisation, and look for good things in the future."[6]

In further comment about Honolulu Louis wrote to Charles Baxter on May 10:

. . . I have just been a week away alone on the lee coast of Hawaii, the only white creature in many miles, riding five and a half hours one day, living with a native, seeing four lepers shipped off to Molokai, hearing native causes, and giving my opinion as *amicus curiae* as to the interpretation of a statute in English; a lovely week among God's best—at least God's sweetest works—Polynesians. It has bettered me greatly. If I could only stay there the time that remains, I could get my work done and be happy; but the care of my family keeps me in vile Honolulu, where I am always out of sorts, amidst heat and cold and cesspools and beastly *haoles*. What is a *haole?* You are one; and so, I am sorry to say, am I. After so long a dose of whites, it was a blessing to get among Polynesians again even for a week. . . .[7]

[6] *Ibid.,* 175.   [7] *Ibid.,* 180.

Holidaying on the lee coast of the big island of Hawaii—ancient stronghold of the Kamehamehas—took Louis to the realm of nobles of the race who had been made kings for untold centuries. Aside from the spectacular beauty of Kauai, this Kona coast is one of the beauty areas of the islands with its bay-indented shore line, rank shrubbery of wild fruits and flowers, and background of brooding Mauna Loa and sister peak of Mauna Kea thrusting their shoulders thirteen thousand feet into the clouds. The old royal palace at Kailua would have been opened for Louis's coming, for Kalakaua still maintained it as a country residence and Liliuokalani was especially fond of staying here for months at a time.

Traveling on the inter-island freight and passenger boat, Louis must have seen but does not mention the cruelty inflicted upon cattle and horses in the primitive method of loading for shipment, especially at the deep-water port of Lahaina on Maui Island, which he would have touched either going or coming. In his compassion for suffering animals he may have made protest for cruelties were practiced by Europeans[8] as well as Hawaiians, and scarcely less today.

Much as Louis disliked Honolulu, he carried away one of the sweetest memories of his life—sweet and sad memories of little Princess Kaiulani, daughter of his Scottish friend, Archibald Scott Cleghorn, wealthy merchant and later governor, and Princess Lilelike. From his cottage Louis often walked along the beach to the quietly secluded Cleghorn garden to visit with his compatriot, and he became deeply attached to Kaiulani, then in her early teens. Exceptionally intelligent and with swanlike grace, she was, in his words, "more beautiful than the fairest flower."

Because of her high position in the royal line, her father,

[8] To avoid clumsy locutions, I have used "Europeans" as an all-inclusive term to refer to persons with European backgrounds, including North Americans.

after her mother's death, decided she must go to England for advanced schooling. Louis entreated against this plan, that she could not stand the climate—arguing in vain, however. It was then he expressed his sad *aloha:*

Written in April to Kaiulani in the April of her age; and at Waikiki, within easy walk of Kaiulani's banyan! When she comes to my land and her father's, and the rain beats upon the window (as I fear it will), let her look at this page; it will be like a weed gathered and pressed at home; and she will remember her own islands, and the shadow of the mighty tree; and she will hear the peacocks screaming in the dusk and the wind blowing in the palms; and she will think of her father sitting there alone.

R. L. S.[9]

Ever after that, as when at Vailima he heard of her recurring attacks of influenza in that harsh climate, Teuila says he longed for the time when her father would call her home. Alas, he received no such word. Not until nearly four years after Louis died did her father send for her; then, broken in health, she lived only a year in her beloved homeland and died in March, 1899.

[9] From a letter to Will Low in New York, May 20, 1889: ". . . see my little Kaiulani, as she goes through—but she is gone already. . . . I wear the colours of that little royal maiden, *Nous allons chanter à la ronde, si vous voulez!* only she is not blonde by several chalks, though she is but a half-blood, and the wrong half Edinburgh Scots like mysel'. . . . I love the Polynesian: This civilisation of ours is a dingy ungentlemanly business; it drops out too much of man, and too much of that the very beauty of the poor beast; who has his beauties in spite of Zola and Co." (*Letters of R. L. S.,* ed. by Colvin, II, 182.)

6. More About *Master of Ballantrae*

EVIDENTLY LOUIS finished the final chapters of the trouble-some *Master* before he went on his holiday but delayed send-ing it off until his return, and perhaps the hate woven into the ending was not so difficult considering the circumstances under which he labored to climax the depravity of ill feeling between the two brothers. Both beginning and ending had been ridden by the specter of unpleasantness: first the controversy with Henley, and now these unhappy months in Honolulu. Only Tautira provided a serene interlude.

That he should have preserved any degree of dramatic unity and logical sequence of events is remarkable since he worked entirely without notes, and when critics complain, let them con-sider the candor with which he himself faced this difficulty. The story has been praised as one of his best and condemned as one of the worst; certainly it has not been one of the most popular with the reading public.

Why one likes or dislikes a story matters little unless he is able to identify these opinions, and Louis boldly invited con-troversy both in choice of characters and in style of telling, to say nothing of plot and theme. Having braved the critics of *Dr. Jekyll and Mr. Hyde* and (smilingly, no doubt) survived their attempts to analyze himself as well as the story, he evi-dently felt the desire to venture further as a paladin of the unusual in fiction. Certainly no more cruel or sinister manifes-tation of human behavior could have been conjured forth to dwell in an author's mind, and only the consummate art in telling from a most difficult angle saves *The Master* from the

114

ignominy of such unreality as to leave the reader completely unmoved.

One wonders if the hint of possible saintliness under the satanic exterior of the Master reveals Louis the Celt's sub-conscious understanding of that peculiar Celtic heritage which swings the pendulum of emotions from pride to depravity, from love and tenderness to blasphemy, and makes him the thoroughbred of fiction, the romanticist of fact. Yet no one could say that Louis had by birth and training other than the kindliest of natures, abhorring cruelty in any form, either to man or beast, as illustrated in most of his writings.

In the Francis Peabody collection of Stevensoniana now at Yale University Library are the author's own manuscript notes regarding the story:

Surely, beyond the worsted lace of his gentility, and a trick of Celtic boastfulness, my poor chevalier, eminently proud of his degradation, unaffectedly unconscious of his genuine merit, is a creature utterly distinct, in the essential part of him, from the brute whom Thackeray disinterred out of Newgate Cal-endar and set re-existing, for the time of the duration of the English language.

The need of a confidant for Mr. Henry led to the introduc-tion of Mackellar, for it was only to a servant that a man such as I conceived Mr. Henry, could unbosom; and no sooner had he begun to take on lineament, than I perceived the uses of the character, and was at once tempted to intrust to him the part of spokesman.

Nothing more pleases me than for one of my puppets to dis-play himself in his own language; in no other way than this of the dramatic monologue, are humorous and incongruous traits so persuasively presented. The narration, put in the mouth of the land steward, would supply, as if by the way and accidently, a certain subdued element of comedy, much to be desired, and scarce otherwise, except by violence, to be introduced. Besides which, the device enabled me to view my heroine from the outside, which was doubly desirable. First, and generally, because I am always afraid of my women, which are not admired in my home circle; second, and particularly, because I should be thus enabled to pass over without realization an ugly and delicate business,—the master's courtship of his brother's wife.

Accordingly, and perfectly satisfied with myself, I hastily wrote and rewrote the first half of my story, down to the end of the duel, through the eyes and in the words of the good Ephraim. Cowardice is always punished; I have no sooner got this length, I had no sooner learned to appreciate the advantages of my method, than I was brought face to face with its defects and fell into a panic fear of the conclusion.

How, with a narrator like Mackellar, should I transact the melodrama in the wilderness. How with his style, so full of disabilities, attack a passage which must be either altogether seizing or altogether silly and absurd? The first half was already in type, when I made up my mind to have it thus done, and recommence the tale in the third person. Friends advised, one this way, one that; indolence had doubtless a voice; I had besides a natural love for the documentary method of narration; and I ended by committing myself to the impersonation of Mackellar, and suffering the publication to proceed.

I was doubtless right and wrong; the book has suffered and gained in consequence; gained in relief and verisimilitude, suffered in fire, force, and (as one of my critics has well said) in "large dramatic rhythm." The same astute and kindly judge complains of "the dredging machine of Mr. Mackellar's memory, shooting out the facts bucketful by bucketful"; and I understand the ground of his complaint, although my sense is otherwise. The realism I love is that of method; not only that all in a story may possibly have come to pass, but that all might naturally be recorded—a realism that justifies the book itself as well as the fable it commemorates.

In the archives of the Henry E. Huntington Library at San Marino, California, are two pages of yellow foolscap manuscript marked 7 and 8 which might be a continuation of this candid dissertation of the Master and his associate characters. The query "known that?" carried over from the previous page suggests the maze of pitfalls he had to avoid:

known that? is a captious question that has often marred my pleasure in fine scenes of fiction. I must confess, however, that my choice of the first person made this Master of Ballantrae, before I was done with it, a burthen and a nightmare. I never thought of the business in the Wilderness but I fell back aghast; and when the remainder of the book, down to the departure from New York, had been finished in the adorable island of Tahiti, and I found myself after another voyage face to face in the suburbs of Honolulu with the first page of my conclusion, I came near to confessing a defeat. Months passed before I could see how to attack the problem, how the pen of Mackellar was to relate a series of incidents so highly coloured, so excessive, and so tragic; the magazine was already on my heels, when desperation helped me; and in a few days of furious industry the novel was, for good or evil rushed to its last word. Some violence was done; Mackellar would scarcely have so written, yet I think that on the whole and in view of the extreme difficulty of the passage, I shall be thought to have preserved the note beyond expectation.

With James Durie himself I never had a moment's stick; I had no model in my eye, whatever, he rose before me, and took shape, and justification, as when a whistler unconsciously and note by note recalls a melody. I have been at school and college with Mackellar and with Henry; the chronicle, as I have said, was drawn from the possibilities of a callow youth who went long since to the bad; my old Durrisdeer was founded on the face of an old gentleman whom I once loved, although I scarcely knew him, but for the Master I had no original, which is perhaps another way of confessing that the original was no other than myself. We have all a certain attitude toward our own character and part in life; we desire more or less identity between the essence and the seeming; we put the two in different relations of cause and effect, some living up to the appearance, others trimming the appearance to the life; and the secret of the Master is principally this, that he is indifferent to that problem. A live man, a full man, in every other point a human man, he has this one element of inhumanity. Abjectly fond of admiration, he is careless, how or for what he is admired in error; whether for a fact or for a lie, or (whether by different people) for incongruous pretensions. An unveracious [error for *avaricious?* M S clearly *unveracious*] vanity, monstrous in its exactions, and unusual, although far from unparalleled, in its unveracity. Of such are the persons (one of whom was known to me) who pass themselves off as authors of other people's books. It is in short a very ordinary and despicable character magnified. But if the question were put to me, I should have to own that this magnitude improves even on myself. It is my only ground with Mr. Hole, whose illustrations convey other points I can't find language to [commend?], that his Master is not my Master; mine had a more slender body, a larger, a finer and darker countenance, attitudes more precise and more theatrical; and more of the fairy prince, and more of Satan; and the black mole on his cheek (I could not tell you why) was an essential part of him.

The story told to Mackellar on board the *Nonesuch* was, it may amuse the reader to learn, a dream I had in Papeete, when I supposed myself to be reading a tale of Edgar Allan Poe's; it was only in the [?—word undecipherable] of the next day that I perceived its suitability to its present purpose.

I have said very little about Clementina,[1] because I have said so little of her in the text. She was one of my ungrateful children, for I am rarely on a fond [sound?] footing with my daughters. I had a model for her; dull people think they can do wonders with a model, it is a fine illusion; this is my model, and she has not been drawn—and this is my heroine, and she has never been entirely animate. A certain correspondent wrote to protest against a copying blunder in the original text; I had made Clementina thrust a sword "up to the hilt" in the frosty ground; the folly of the statement, equal to the worst in Victor Hugo, shows that I was regarding her modestly from the outside. When a character lives, when the writer feels and reveals him from within, such flights are quite impossible; the author is conscious of, he receives [?] every effort, he feels, he estimates the resistance; the thing done, is done by him; and he is brought to a pause by a physical impossibility even as if it were he himself, and not his puppet, that had emerged to violate the laws of nature.

One can imagine with what happy relief he dedicated the story to Sir Percy Florence and Lady Shelley, whom the Stevensons had known in Bournemouth:

Here is a tale which extends over many years and travels into many countries. By a peculiar fitness of circumstance the writer began, continued it, and concluded it among distant and diverse

---

[1] Clementina was the original name of the heroine. It is not known when or by whom the name was changed to Alison. The name Clementina most likely was for the daughter of Ardshiel of the Forty-fives, who was born in the poverty of exile. Louis was especially partial to this period of Scottish history and held in high regard the Jacobites who, in the words of Burns, "shook hands with ruin for what they esteemed the cause of King and Country."

scenes. Above all, he was much at sea. The character and fortune of the fraternal enemies, the hall and shrubbery of Durrisdeer, the problem of Mackellar's homespun and how to shape
it for superior flights; these were his company on deck in many
star-reflecting harbors, ran often in his mind at sea to the tune
of slatting canvas, and were dismissed (something of the sud-
denest) on approach of squalls. It is my hope that these surroundings of its manufacture may to some degree find favor for
my story with sea-farers and sea-lovers like yourselves.

And at least here is a dedication from a great way off; written by the loud shores of a subtropical island near upon ten
thousand miles from Boscombe Chine and Manor; scenes which
rise before me as I write, along with the faces and voices of
my friends.

Well, I am for the sea once more; no doubt Sir Percy also.
Let us make the signal B. R. D.!²

Waikiki, May 17, 1889.   R. L. S.

By the author's instructions Ballantrae is pronounced with
a long *a* in the first syllable, and by a Scottish authority, as said
earlier, the Gaelic spelling is *Bail-an-traigh,* meaning "houses
by the sea"; but the people of this small village on the south-
western coast of Scotland use the broad *a* since it is a kindred
word to "Baltimore," the title of the Calvert family in the Irish
peerage. The Scots claim that it is the English who have de-
moralized the ancient name by the short *a* of the first syllable.

Whether or not these comments of Louis's regarding his problems in writing *The Master* were published and saved him from
what he feared might be adverse criticism, they may have
tempered the blasts of professional reviewers following the

² At that time B. R. D. was the International Code signal for *adieu,*
according to Mr. Charles H. P. Copeland, curator of maritime history at
East India Marine Hall, Salem, Mass.

publication of the book by Cassell and Company of London in 1890. *The Critic,* weekly review of literature and arts, New York, on February 8, reprinted the following from *The Scots Observer:*

The Master of Ballantrae is one of the gloomiest, or rather the grimiest, of stories. There is not a noble or a lovable character in the book; the narrator is a poltroon; the hero is a devil in human shape, while his arch-enemy sinks into a vindictive dullard; the one woman in the story is morbidly enamored of her husband's brother; the chief scene is a scene of fratricidal strife; The supernumeries are a choice assortment of smugglers, pirates, murderers, and mutineers; than the plot there is nothing uglier in Balzac; and the whole thing is a triumph of imagination and literary art. But it is not pleasant reading.

There is wit, but it is cold, cruel, even brutal; there is humor, but it is black, corrosive, bitter as gall. The story, which turns on the unnatural hatred of two brothers, would in the hands of a weaker writer simply shock and repel. Told as Mr. Stevenson tells it, it throws a sombre fascination over the reader from the first, and holds him enchained to the close. The author has done nothing cleverer; he has never before gone so deep; his narrative has never been more masterly in its concision, vividness, and energy. Every situation is boldly faced; every incident fitted with consummate skill into the framework of the plot; not a single descriptive touch is wasted. The book shows how thorough a Scot Mr. Stevenson is: beneath all that fascinating, many-colored web which he has woven of wild romance and capricious fancy and extravagant fun, the hard, gloomy, uncompromising side of the Scottish intellect asserts itself.

In *The Master of Ballantrae* the spirit which animated the old Scottish theologians and preachers and soldiers—the severe, unflinching, pleasure-hating spirit to which the race owes so many of its defects and so much of its fibre—seems to have entered into the Kingdom of Romance, and made part of that Kingdom its own. But *The Master of Ballantrae* is a romance which differs from the romances of Sir Walter as a black marble vault differs from a radiant palace.

And Noah Brooks wrote in *The Book Buyer*, 1889: "In his latest romance *The Master of Ballantrae* Stevenson seems to have touched high-water mark. I am tempted to go beyond this and say no modern work of fiction in the English language rises higher in the scale of literary merit than this."

7. Molokai and Aftermath

Louis wished to get away from Honolulu while waiting for the schooner *Equator* to arrive from San Francisco, and the short trip of a few hours across Kaiwi Channel to Molokai Island presented an opportune escape. Considering subsequent involvements, it is regrettable that he had only a fleeting glimpse of the leper settlement on Makanalua Peninsula. He had seen four lepers "condemned" to the settlement when he was on the island of Hawaii. The sympathy that stirred his heart then should have been a warning, for with his sensitive temperament he was vicariously sharing their exile.

Far from any remote intention to minimize the mental and physical tragedy of the disease and the handicap of isolation, it was an interesting and revealing experience, personally, to sit in the office of a director of public health and see a middle-aged man "sentenced" to the settlement when leprosy spots were found on the soles of his feet; and to watch his middle-aged wife ask and receive permission to go with him. There was no wailing and weeping, only their mutual sad concern for the strong brown feet that supposedly had picked up the germ on a Japanese fishing boat.

"What about your children?" asked the doctor of the wife.

"My sister and her husband will adopt them. We have raised our families together. They understand it is their father who needs me." Turning, she added, "It is better that we go to Molokai than that he should hide in the bush like a hunted animal and have his food flung to him as did our grandfathers many years ago. We have friends in the settlement and God is

123

there as well as here." She turned back again to exchange tender smiles with her stricken husband. They were not the ones who were shedding tears.

While still on Molokai, Louis wrote to Fanny of the happy faces of those able to walk about and the air of complacent resignation of those beyond the hope of more than a few years of life. At this time there were, and had been for nearly fifty years, two Protestant churches on the island whose ministers regularly visited the settlement. There were schools for study and recreation and doctors and nurses on continual duty in the small hospital; there were flowers everywhere—hibiscus, plumieria, ginger, ilima, bougainvillea, and pink and white shower trees—and above all there was that ever present Polynesian friendliness which shines through tragedy and suffering.

Molokai Island is about thirty-five miles long and about seven miles wide, with the leper settlement approximately midway on the north shore where the Makanalua Peninsula extends two and one-half miles outward from cliffs a few hundred feet high. On the west shore of this point of land is the tree-shaded village of Kalaupapa, where the hospital, church, store, and offices of the settlement are located, and where boats stand offshore about a quarter of a mile while rowboats take off and bring in passengers across the reef. Open to the Trades, the area always has a delightfully cool breeze, windswept only when storms whip up out of the Pacific to ravage all the islands equally. The words "barren" and "desolate" are applied only by those unfamiliar with the place.

There is no fence around the settlement, only a guard stationed where the path leads up over the *pali*, although only a few of the most rugged and the most restless would have cared to negotiate the steep incline, either ascending or descending. The only dreary aspect of the settlement is the stigma of isolation, and Louis quite naturally—as would we all—endowed each patient with the agony of his own feelings, not realizing that they by their dispositions saw infinitely more than he the pleasures of each passing day. Ambition to do, or to be, does not figure largely in their consciousness. Men fish or work in the gardens, women sew, and girls weave mats and hats, and everyone laughs and sings.

Father Damien, the controversial Belgian priest of the Roman Catholic church, was by the same token of calculative sentiment cloaked by Louis with his own conception of heroism and saintliness. Louis heard much discussion of the priest, then only two years dead, and his sixteen years of work in the settlement, as after a generation or more one still does. However fervent he was in his ministrations, it is not reasonable to assume that he was a victim of his endeavors. Yet if he did contract the disease through an impulsive inadvertence, it should not lessen the good he accomplished in his effort toward maintaining spiritual welfare.

Consecration to duty does not essentially carry the emotions of sympathy and compassion with which Louis would have had him canonized, and it is extremely doubtful that the rugged priest looked upon himself as a martyr. Until stricken with leprosy, which apparently is contracted only through continued and close contact, he went to Honolulu or anywhere else at will. He was brusque and intolerant of any interference, which probably was why he selected this particular field for his self-assigned mission.

It is a recognized fact that any number of doctors and nurses, even laymen, work all their adult lives among lepers without contracting the disease. Dr. Mildred E. Staley, who was born in Hawaii and died in 1947 on Molokai at the age of eighty-two, spent her entire medical career as a specialist in early diagnosis of leprosy. For twenty-five years she went among the outcasts of India, then of Malaya and Fiji, and though retired from active practice when she returned to spend her well-earned leisure in Hawaii, she remained a consultant in leper cases.

Last Witness for Robert Louis Stevenson

After his return to Honolulu Louis wrote to Sidney Colvin:

I am just home after twelve days' journey to Molokai, seven of them at the leper settlement, where I can only say that the sight of so much courage, cheerfulness, and devotion strung me too high to mind the infinite pity and horror of the sights. I used to ride over from Kalawao to Kalaupapa (about three miles across the promontory, the cliff-wall, ivied with forest and yet inaccessible from steepness, on my left), go to the Sisters' home, which is a miracle of neatness, play a game of croquet with seven leper girls (90° in the shade), get a little old-maid meal served me by the Sisters, and ride home again, tired enough, but not too tired. The girls have all dolls, and love dressing them. You who know so many ladies delicately clad, and they who know so many dressmakers, please make it known it would be an acceptable gift to send scraps for doll dress-making to the Reverend Sister Maryanne, Bishop Home, Kalaupapa, Molokai, Hawaiian Islands.

I have seen sights that cannot be told, and heard stories that cannot be repeated; yet I never have admired my poor race so much, nor (strange as it may seem) loved life more than in the settlement. A horror of moral beauty broods over the place: that's like bad Victor Hugo, but it is the only way I can express the sense that lived with me all these days. And this even though it was in great part Catholic, and my sympathies flew never with so much difficulty as towards Catholic virtues. The pass-book kept with heaven stirs me to anger and laughter. One of the sisters calls the place "the ticket office to heaven." Well, what is the odds? They do their darg, and do it with kindness and efficiency incredible; and we must take folk's virtue as we find them, and love the better part. Of old Damien, whose weaknesses and worse perhaps I heard fully, I think only the more. It was a European peasant: dirty, bigotted, untruthful, unwise, tricky, but superb with generosity, residual candour and fun-

126

damental good-humour: convince him he had done wrong (it might take hours of insult) and he would undo what he had done and like his corrector better. A man, with all the grime and paltriness of mankind, but a saint and hero all the more for that. . . .[1]

This depressing visit to Molokai and the unhappy months in Honolulu must certainly have formed the basis, consciously or unconsciously, for Louis's famous vitriolic open letter to the Reverend C. M. Hyde of Honolulu a year later which shocked Stevenson lovers everywhere. One cannot think that it was wholly in defense of Father Damien that he wrote in criticism of Dr. Hyde, but rather that the cleric served as whipping boy for the "beastly haoles" whom he had found irritating and unendurable during his stay in Honolulu. In characteristic generosity and in the spirit of the gentleman, Louis confessed later his regret at having written and published the letter.

It was in Sydney, Australia, that Louis read in *The Presbyterian* (for October 26, 1889), published there, a letter written by Dr. Hyde, presumably in confidence, to a fellow churchman, Rev. H. B. Gage, of California, in reply to one telling of the plan in England to erect a monument in memory of Father Damien's work in Molokai. The letter read:

Dear Brother, — In answer to your inquiries about Father Damien, I can only reply that we who knew the man are surprised at the extravagant newspaper laudations, as if he was a most saintly philanthropist. The simple truth is, he was a coarse, dirty man, headstrong and bigoted. He was not sent to Molokai, but went there without orders; did not stay at the leper settlement (before he became one himself), but circulated freely over the whole island (less than half the island is

[1] *Letters of R. L. S.*, ed. by Colvin, II, 187–88. Written from Honolulu in May or June, 1889.

devoted to the lepers), and he came often to Honolulu. He had no hand in the reforms and improvements inaugurated, which were the work of our Board of Health, as occasion required and means were provided. He was not a pure man in his relations with women, and the leprosy of which he died should be attributed to his vices and carelessness. Others have done much for the lepers, our own ministers, the government physicians, and so forth, but never with the Catholic idea of meriting eternal life. Yours, etc.,

C. M. Hyde

This is the letter that roused Louis to pen what has become a classic in denunciation and sarcasm to relieve a burning resentment and now erupt in Aetna-like fury. He begins:

To deal fitly with a letter so extraordinary, I must draw at the outset on my private knowledge of the signatory and his sect. It may offend others; scarcely you, who have been so busy to collect, so bold to publish, gossip on your rivals. And this is perhaps the moment when I may best explain to you the character of what you are to read: I conceive you as a man quite beyond and below the reticences of civility: and what measure you mete, with that shall it be measured you again; with you, at last, I rejoice to feel the button off the foil and to plunge home. And if in aught that I shall say I should offend others, your colleagues, whom I respect and remember with affection, I can but offer them my regret; I am not free, I am inspired by the consideration of interests far more large; and such pain as can be inflicted by anything from me must be indeed trifling when compared with the pain with which they read your letter. It is not the hangman, but the criminal, that brings dishonour on the house.

You belong, sir, to a sect—I believe my sect, and that in which my ancestors laboured—which has enjoyed, and partly failed to

utilise, an exceptional advantage in the islands of Hawaii. The
first missionaries came; they found the land already self-purged
of its old and bloody faith; they were embraced, almost on their
arrival, with enthusiasm; what troubles they supported came
far more from whites than from Hawaiians; and to these last
they stood (in a rough figure) in the shoes of God. This is not
a place to enter into the degree or causes of their failure, such
as it is. One element alone is pertinent, and must here be plainly
dealt with. In the course of their evangelical calling, they—or
too many of them—grew rich. It may be news to you that the
houses of missionaries are a cause of mocking on the streets of
Honolulu. It will at least be news to you, that when I returned
your civil visit, the driver of my cab commented on the size,
the taste, and the comfort of your home. It would have been
news certainly to myself, had any one told me that afternoon
that I should live to drag such matter into print. But you see,
sir, how you degrade better men to your own level; and it is
needful that those who are to judge betwixt you and me, betwixt Damien and the devil's advocate, should understand your
letter to have been penned in a house which could raise, and
that very justly, the envy and the comments of the passers-by.
I think (to employ a phrase of yours which I admire) it "should
be attributed" to you that you have never visited the scene of
Damien's life and death. If you had, and had recalled it, and
looked about your pleasant rooms, even your pen perhaps
would have been stayed.

Your sect (and remember, as far as any sect avows me, it
is mine) has not done ill in a worldly sense in the Hawaiian
Kingdom. When calamity befell their innocent parishioners,
when leprosy descended and took root in the Eight Islands, a
quid pro quo was to be looked for. To that prosperous mission,
and to you, as one of its adornments, God has sent at last an
opportunity. I know I am touching here upon a nerve acutely
sensitive. I know that others of your colleagues look back on

the inertia of your Church, and the intrusive and decisive heroism of Damien, with something almost to be called remorse. I am sure it is so with yourself; I am persuaded your letter was inspired by a certain envy, not essentially ignoble, and the one human trait to be espied in that performance.

You were thinking of the lost chance, the past day; of that which should have been conceived and was not; of the service due and not rendered. *Time was,* said a voice in your ear, in your pleasant room, and as you sat raging and writing; and if the words written were base beyond parallel, the rage, I am happy to repeat—it is the only compliment I shall pay you—the rage was almost virtuous. But, sir, when we have failed, and another has succeeded; when we have stood by and another has stepped in; when we sit and grow bulky in our charming mansions, and a plain, uncouth peasant steps into the battle, under the eyes of God, and succours the afflicted, and consoles the dying, and is himself afflicted in his turn, and dies upon the field of honour—the battle cannot be retrieved as your unhappy irritation has suggested. It is a lost battle, and lost forever. One thing remained to you in your defeat—some rags of common honour; and these you have made haste to cast away.

Common honour; not the honour of having done anything right, but the honour of not having done aught conspicuously foul; the honour of the inert: that was what remained to you. We are not all expected to be Damiens; a man may conceive his duty more narrowly, he may love his comforts better; and none will cast a stone at him for that. But will a gentleman of your reverend profession allow me an example from the fields of gallantry? When two gentlemen compete for the favour of a lady, and the one succeeds and the other is rejected, and (as will sometimes happen) matter damaging to the successful rival's credit reaches the ear of the defeated, it is held by plain men of no pretensions that his mouth is, in the circumstance, almost necessarily closed. Your church and Damien's were in

Hawaii upon a rivalry to do well: to help, to edify, to set divine examples. You having (in one huge instance) failed, and Damien succeeded, I marvel it should not have occurred to you that you were doomed to silence; that you had been outstripped in that high rivalry, and sat inglorious in the midst of your well-being, in your pleasant room—and Damien, crowned with glories and horrors, toiled and rotted in that pigstye of his under the cliffs of Kalawao—you, the elect, who would not, were the last man on earth to collect and propagate gossip on the volunteer who would and did.

I think I see you—for I try to see you in the flesh as I write these sentences—I think I see you leap at the word pigstye, a hyperbolical expression at best. "He had no hand in the reforms," he was "a coarse, dirty man"; these were your own words; and you may think it possible that I am come to support you with fresh evidence. In a sense, it is even so. Damien has been too much depicted with a convential halo and conventional features; so drawn by men who perhaps had not the eye to remark or the pen to express the individual; or who perhaps were only blinded and silenced by generous admiration, such as I partly envy for myself—such as you, if your soul were enlightened, would envy on your bended knees. It is not the least defect of such a method of portraiture that it makes the path easy for the devil's advocate, and leaves for the misuse of the slanderer a considerable field of truth. For the truth that is suppressed by friends is the readiest weapon of the enemy. The world in your despite, may perhaps owe you something, if your letter be the means of substituting once for all a credible likeness for a wax abstraction. For, if that world at all remember you, on the day when Damien of Molokai shall be named Saint, it will be in virtue of one work: your letter to the Reverend H. B. Gage.

You may ask upon what authority I speak. It was my inclement destiny to become acquainted, not with Damien, but with

Dr. Hyde. When I visited the lazaretto Damien was already in his resting grave. But such information as I have, I gathered on the spot in conversation with those who knew him well and long: some indeed who revered his memory; but others who had sparred and wrangled with him, who beheld him with no halo, who perhaps regarded him with small respect, and through whose unprepared and scarcely partial communications the plain, human features of the man shone on me convincingly. These gave me what knowledge I possess; and I learnt it in that scene where it could be most completely and sensitively understood—Kalawao, which you have never visited, about which you have never so much as endeavoured to inform yourself: for, brief as your letter is, you have found the means to stumble into that confession.

"Less than one-half of the island," you say, "is devoted to the lepers." Molokai—"Molokai ahina,"— the "grey," lofty, and most desolate island—along all its northern side plunges a front of precipice into a sea of unusual profundity. This range of cliff is, from east to west, the true end and frontier of the island. Only in one spot there projects into the ocean a certain triangular and rugged down, grassy, stony, windy, and rising in the midst into a hill with a dead crater: the whole bearing to the cliff that overhangs it somewhat the same relation as a bracket to a wall. With this hint you will not be able to pick out the leper station on a map; you will be able to judge how much of Molokai is thus cut off between the surf and precipice, whether less than half, or less than a quarter, or a fifth, or a tenth—or say, a twentieth; and the next time you burst into print you will be in a position to share with us the issue of your calculations.

I imagine you to be one of those persons who talk with cheerfulness of that place which oxen and wainropes could not drag you to behold. You, who do not even know its situation on the map, probably denounce sensational descriptions, stretching

132

your limbs the while in your pleasant parlour on Beretania Street. When I was pulled ashore there one early morning, there sat with me in the boat two sisters, bidding farewell (in humble imitation of Damien) to the lights and joys of human life. One of these wept silently; I could not withhold myself from joining her. Had you been there, it is my belief that nature would have triumphed even in you; and as the boat drew a little nearer, and you beheld the stairs crowded with abominable deformations of our common manhood, and saw yourself landing in the midst of such a population as only now and then surrounds us in the horror of a nightmare—what a haggard eye you would have rolled over your reluctant shoulder towards the house on Beretania Street! Had you gone on; had you found every fourth face a blot upon the landscape; had you visited the hospital and seen the butt-ends of human beings lying there almost unrecognizable, but still breathing, still thinking, still remembering; you would have understood that life in the lazaretto is an ordeal from which the nerves of a man's spirit shrink, even as his eye quails under the brightness of the sun; you would have felt it was (even to-day) a pitiful place to visit and a hell to dwell in. It is not the fear of possible infection. That seems a little thing when compared with the pain, the pity, and the disgust of the visitor's surroundings, and the atmosphere of affliction, disease, and physical disgrace in which he breathes. I do not think I am a man more than usually timid; but I never recall the days and night I spent upon that island promontory (eight days and seven nights), without heartfelt thankfulness that I am somewhere else. I find in my diary that I speak of my stay as a "grinding experience"; I have once jotted in the margin, "Harrowing is the word"; and when the *Mokolii* bore me at last towards the outer world, I kept repeating to myself, with a new conception of their pregnancy, those simple words of the song—" 'Tis the most distressful country that ever yet was seen."

And observe: that which I saw and suffered from was a settlement purged, bettered, beautified; the new village built, the hospital and the Bishop-Home excellently arranged; the sisters, the doctor, and the missionaries, all indefatigable in their noble tasks. It was a different place when Damien came there, and made his great renunciation, and slept that first night under a tree amidst rotting brethren: alone with pestilence; and looking forward (with what courage, with what pitiful sinkings of dread, God only knows) to a lifetime of dressing sores and stumps.

You will say, perhaps, that I am too sensitive that sights as painful abound in cancer hospitals and are confronted daily by doctors and nurses. I have long learned to admire and envy doctors and nurses. But there is no cancer hospital so large and populous as Kalawao and Kalaupapa; and in such a matter every fresh case, like every inch of length in the pipe of an organ, deepens the note of the impression; for what daunts the onlooker is that monstrous sum of human suffering by which he stands surrounded. Lastly, no doctor or nurse is called upon to enter once for all the doors of that gehenna; they do not say farewell, they need not abandon hope, on its sad threshold; they but go for a time to their high calling, and can look forward as they go to relief, to recreation, and to rest. But Damien shut to with his own hand the doors of his own sepulchre.

I shall now extract three passages from my diary at Kalawao.

A. "Damien is dead and already somewhat ungratefully remembered in the field of his labours and sufferings. 'He was a good man, but very officious,' says one. Another tells me he had fallen (as other priests so easily do) into something of the ways and habits of a Kanaka; but he had the wit to recognise the fact, and the good sense to laugh at [over] it. A plain man it seems he was; I cannot find he was a popular."

B. "After Ragsdale's death [Ragsdale was a famous *Luna*,

or overseer, of the unruly settlement] there followed a brief term of office by Father Damien which served only to publish the weakness of that noble man. He was rough in his ways, and he had no control. Authority was relaxed; Damien's life was threatened, and he was soon eager to resign."

C. "Of Damien I begin to have an idea. He seems to have been a man of the peasant class, certainly of the peasant type: shrewd; ignorant and bigoted, yet with an open mind, and capable of receiving and digesting a reproof if it is bluntly administered; superbly generous in the least thing as well as in the greatest, and as ready to give his last shirt (although not without human grumbling) as he had been to sacrifice his life; essentially indiscreet and officious, which made him a troublesome colleague; domineering in all his ways, which made him incurably unpopular with the Kanakas, but yet destitute of real authority, so that his boys laughed at him and he must carry out his wishes by means of bribes. He learned to have a mania for doctoring; and set up the Kanakas against the remedies of his regular rivals; perhaps (if any-thing matter at all in the treatment of such a disease) the worst that he did, and certainly the easiest. The best and the worst of the man appear very plainly in his dealings with Mr. Chapman's money; he had originally laid it out (intended to lay it out) "entirely for the benefit of Catholics," and even so not wisely; but after a long, plain talk, he admitted his error fully and revised the list.

"The sad state of the boys' home is in part the result of this lack of control; in part of his own slovenly ways and false ideas of hygiene. Brother officials used to call it 'Damien's Chinatown.' 'Well,' they would say, 'your Chinatown keeps growing.' And he would laugh with perfect good nature, and adhere to his errors with perfect obstinacy. So much I have gathered of truth about this plain, noble human brother and father of ours; his imperfections are the traits of his race, by which we know him for our fellow; his martyrdom and his example nothing can lessen or annul; and only a person here on the spot can properly appreciate their greatness."

I have set down these private passages, as you perceive, without correction; thanks to you, the public has them in their bluntness. They are almost a list of the man's faults, for it is rather these that I am seeking: with his virtues, with the heroic profile of his life, I and the world were already sufficiently acquainted. I was besides a little suspicious of Catholic testimony; in no ill sense, but merely because Damien's admirers and disciples were the least likely to be critical. I know you will be more suspicious still; and the facts set down above were one and all collected from the lips of Protestants who had opposed the father in his life. Yet I am strangely deceived, or they build up the image of a man, with all his weaknesses, essentially heroic, and alive with rugged honesty, generosity, and mirth.

Take it for what it is, rough private jottings of the worst side of Damien's character, collected from the lips of those who had laboured with and (in your own phrase) "knew the man";— though I question whether Damien would have said that he knew you. Take it, and observe with wonder how well you were served by your gossips, how ill by your intelligence and sympathy; in how many points of fact we are at one, and how widely our appreciations vary. There is something wrong here; either with you or me. It is possible, for instance, that you, who seem to have so many ears in Kalawao, had heard of the affair of Mr. Chapman's money, and were singly struck by Damien's intended wrong-doing. I was struck with that also, and set it fairly down; but I was struck much more by the fact that he had the honesty of mind to be convinced.

I may here tell you that it was a long business; that one of his colleagues sat with him late into the night, multiplying arguments and accusations: that the father listened as usual with "perfect good-nature and perfect obstinacy"; but at the last when he was persuaded—"Yes," said he, "I am very much obliged to you; you have done me a service; it would have been a theft." There are many (not Catholics merely) who require their heroes and saints to be infallible; to these the story will be painful; not to the true lovers, patrons, and servants of mankind.

And I take it, this is the type of our division; that you are one of those who have an eye for faults and failures; that you take a pleasure to find and publish them; and that, having found them, you make haste to forget the overveiling virtues and the real success which had alone introduced them to your knowledge. It is a dangerous frame of mind. That you may understand how dangerous, and into what a situation it has already brought you, we will (if you please) go hand-in-hand through the different phases of your letter, and candidly examine each from the point of view of its truth, its appositeness and its charity.

Damien was coarse.

It is very possible. You make us sorry for the lepers who had only a coarse old peasant for their friend and father. But you, who were so refined, why were you not there, to cheer them with the lights of culture? Or may I remind you that we have some reason to doubt if John the Baptist were genteel; and in the case of Peter, on whose career you doubtless dwell approvingly in your pulpit, no doubt at all he was a "coarse, headstrong" fisherman! Yet even in our Protestant Bibles Peter is called Saint.

Damien was dirty.

He was. Think of the poor lepers annoyed with this dirty comrade! But the clean Dr. Hyde was at his food in a fine house.

Damien was headstrong.

137

I believe you are right again; and I thank God for his strong head and heart.

Damien was bigoted.

I am not fond of bigots myself, because they are not fond of me. But what is meant by bigotry, that we should regard it as a blemish in a priest? Damien believed his own religion with the simplicity of a peasant or a child; as I would I could suppose that you do. For this I wonder at him some way off; and had that been his only character, should have avoided him in life. But the point of interest in Damien, which has caused him to be so much talked about and made him at last the subject of your pen and mine, was that, in him, his bigotry, his intense and narrow faith, wrought potently for good, and strengthened him to be one of the world's heroes and exemplars.

Damien was not sent to Molokai, but went there without orders.

Is this a misreading? or do you really mean the words for blame? I have heard Christ, in the pulpits of our church, held up for imitation on the ground that His sacrifice was voluntary. Does Dr. Hyde think otherwise?

Damien did not stay at the settlement, etc.

It is true he was allowed many indulgences. Am I to understand that you blame the father for profiting by these, or the offices for granting them? In either case, it is a mighty Spartan standard to issue from the house on Beretania Street; and I am convinced you will find yourself with few supporters.

Damien had no hand in the reforms, etc.

I think even you will admit that I have already been frank in my description of the man I am defending; but before I take you up upon this head, I will be franker still, and tell you that perhaps nowhere in the world can a man taste a more pleasurable sense of contrast than when he passes from Damien's "Chinatown" at Kalawao to the beautiful Bishop Home at Kalaupapa. At this point, in my desire to make all fair for you, I will break my rule and adduce Catholic testimony.

Here is a passage from my diary about my visit to the Chinatown, from which you will see how it is (even now) regarded by its own officials: "We went round all the dormitories, refectories, etc.—dark and dingy enough, with a superficial cleanliness, which he [Mr. Dutton, the lay brother] did not seek to defend. 'It is almost decent,' said he; 'the sisters will make that all right when we get them here.' " And yet I gathered it was already better since Damien was dead and far better than when he was there alone and had his own (not always excellent) way. I have now come far enough to meet you on a common ground of fact; and I tell you that, to my mind not prejudiced by jealousy, all the reforms of the lazaretto, and even those he most vigorously opposed, are properly the work of Damien. They are the evidence of his success; they are what his heroism provoked from the reluctant and the careless.

Many were before him in the field; Mr. Meyer, for instance, of whose faithful work we hear too little: there have been many since; and some had more worldly wisdom, though none had more devotion, than our saint. Before his day, even you will confess, they had effected little. It was his part, by one striking act of martyrdom, to direct all men's eyes on that distressful country. At a blow, and at the price of his life, he made the place illustrious and public. And that, if you will consider largely, was the one reform needful; pregnant of all that should succeed. It brought money; it brought (best individual addition of them all) the sisters; it brought supervision, for public opinion and public interest landed with the man at Kalawao. If ever a man brought reforms, and died to bring them, it was he. There is not a clean cup or towel in the Bishop Home, but dirty Damien washed it.

Damien was not a pure man in his relations with women, etc.

How do you know that? Is this the nature of the conversation in that house on Beretania Street which the cabman envied, driving past?—racy details of the misconduct of the poor peasant priest, toiling under the cliffs of Molokai?

Many have visited the station before me; they seem not to have heard the rumour. When I was there I heard many shocking tales, for my informants were men speaking with the plainness of the laity; and I heard plenty of complaints of Damien. Why was this never mentioned? and how came it to you in the retirement of your clerical parlour?

But I must not even seem to deceive you. This scandal, when I read it in your letter, was not new to me. I had heard it once before; and I must tell you how. There came to Samoa a man from Honolulu; he, in a public-house on the beach volunteered the statement that Damien had "contracted the disease from having connection with the female lepers"; and I find a joy in telling you how the report was welcomed in a public-house. A man sprang to his feet; I am not at liberty to give his name, but from what I heard I doubt if you would care to have him to dinner in Beretania Street. "You miserable little —— [here is a word I dare not print, it would so shock your ears]. You miserable little ——," he cried, "if the story were a thousand times true can't you see you are a million times a lower —— for daring to repeat it?"

I wish it could be told of you that when the report reached you in your house, perhaps after family worship, you had found in your soul enough holy anger to receive it with the same expressions: ay, even with that one which I dare not print; it would not need to have been blotted away, like Uncle Toby's oath, by the tears of the recording angel; it would have been counted to you for your brightest righteousness. But you have deliberately chosen the part of the man from Honolulu, and you have played it with improvements of your own. The

140

man from Honolulu — miserable leering creature — communi-
cated the tale to a rude knot of beach-combing drinkers in a
public-house, where (I will so far agree with your temperance
opinions) man is not always at his noblest; and the man from
Honolulu had himself been drinking—drinking, we may char-
itably fancy, to excess.

It was to your "Dear Brother, the Reverend H. B. Gage," that
you chose to communicate the sickening story; and the blue
ribbon which adorns your portly bosom forbids me to allow
you the extenuating plea that you were drunk when it was
done. Your "dear brother"—a brother indeed—made haste to
deliver up your letter (as a means of grace, perhaps) to the
religious papers; where, after many months, I found and read
and wondered at it; and whence I have now reproduced it for
the wonder of others. And you and your dear brother have,
by this cycle of operations, built up a contrast very edifying to
examine in detail. The man whom you would not care to have
to dinner, on the one side; on the other, the Reverend Dr. Hyde
and the Reverend H. B. Gage: the Apia bar-room, the Honolulu manse.

But I fear you scarce appreciate how you appear to your fellow-men; and to bring it home to you, I will suppose your story
to be true. I will suppose—and God forgive me for supposing
it—that Damien faltered and stumbled in his narrow path of
duty; I will suppose that, in the horror of his isolation, perhaps
in the fever of the incipient disease, he, who was doing so much
more than he had sworn, failed in the letter of his priestly oath
—he, who was so much a better man than either you or me,
who did what we have never dreamed of daring—he too tasted
our common frailty. "O, Iago, the pity of it!" The least tender
should be moved to tears; the most incredulous to prayer. And
all that you could do was to pen your letter to the Reverend
H. B. Gage!

Is it growing at all clear to you what a picture you have drawn of your own heart? I will try yet once again to make it clearer. You had a father: suppose this tale were about him, and some informant brought it to you, proof in hand: I am not making too high an estimate of your emotional nature when I suppose you would regret the circumstance? that you would feel the tale of frailty the more keenly since it shamed the author of your days? and that the last thing you would do would be to publish it in the religious press? Well, the man who tried to do what Damien did, is my father, and the father of the man in the Apia bar, and the father of all who love goodness; and he was your father too, if God has given you the grace to see it.

There it is—cruelly vindictive and mean, boringly repetitious, shamelessly titled "An Open Letter to the Reverend Dr. Hyde of Honolulu from Robert Louis Stevenson. Sidney, 1890." The pendulum of Celtic temperament swung the full arc of cold and calculated ruthlessness to reveal a Stevenson hitherto unknown. Exaggeration and reiteration of detail, with one serious misstatement of fact, betray the turbulence of his thoughts as he belabored a man with unfair accusations to vent his spleen upon a community and a situation he had found intolerable. This is not the Stevenson we know and love. That he regretted his act did not soften the blow that crushed the career of Dr. Hyde, who, to his death, maintained a dignified and absolute silence. The misstatement is that Dr. Hyde "rushed into print" with his remarks regarding Father Damien, when, as a matter of strictest fact, the letter never was intended for publication.

Former Senator Hiram Bingham wrote an interesting letter about the incident, dated March 17, 1952:

Dear Mrs. Caldwell:

With regard to the Father Damien incident, it certainly was most unfortunate that Dr. Hyde's correspondent in Australia should have published his private letter without getting Dr. Hyde's permission. Furthermore, it is also most unfortunate that R. L. S. did not seem to know that quite a number of Protestant Hawaiians, including one or two ministers of the gospel, were living at Molokai at that time, although they did not have leprosy, and never acquired it.

I visited the leper settlement with the Reverend Theodore Richards in the spring of 1899. We talked with some of the lepers, and Mr. Richards talked with some of the Catholic priests who were helping to look after the lepers. They were not very keen about Father Damien; so Mr. Richards told me at the time.

Mrs. Hyde was, for many years, my Sunday School teacher, and one of her sons was a schoolmate of mine. Naturally I saw a good deal of the Hydes, although I was never fond of Dr. Hyde. It is too bad that his one claim to fame should be that he was the recipient of that letter which has become a classic.

. . . My father was a friend and associate of Dr. Hyde and sympathized with his attitude toward Father Damien, although not approving of the letter which was published in a Sydney paper without the knowledge or consent of Dr. Hyde, leading as it did to the writing and publishing of one of the most striking pieces of invective in the English language. Poor Dr. Hyde never recovered from it.

My father was a very conscientious, old-fashioned Calvinist. My mother was a lovely old-fashioned New England Puritan. They disapproved of most of the games, pleasures, and social amenities which come so naturally to us today. They spent their lives trying to raise the Gilbert Islanders from the depths of heathenism and ignorance. They disapproved of the habits of the King of the Hawaiian Islands. They regretted that he had favored the reintroduction of hula dancing which had been abolished at the court during the days of my grandfather, the first missionary to Honolulu.

Sincerely yours,
Hiram Bingham

The strangest aspect of the whole Hyde case is that Louis, with his knowledge of law, knew he was playing with libel. George Mackaness, writing for *Amateur Book Collector,* December, 1951, quotes Dr. Scot-Skirving as saying that he met Stevenson one day on a Sydney street early in February, 1890, and asked him what he was doing with himself. "Well," said he, "I propose to devote myself to writing libel, but it will be a justified and righteous one."

Louis asked and received the consent of his family to publish the letter, warning them that it might mean the loss of all his wealth if Dr. Hyde should bring suit for defamation of character. Publishing the open letter, as was done, without the imprint of the printer might possibly have occurred to him as a technical defense; yet newspapers soon carried it prominently. First *The Elele* of Honolulu ran a supplement to their issue of May 10; then *The Australian Star* printed it on May 24 after Louis had concluded his stay in Sydney. From that time the letter began to appear in different parts of the world, fifteen times in all, and was even reprinted in pamphlet form, after the original, by Constable and Company, Edinburgh; Thomas B. Mosher, Portland, Maine, designated as the eleventh edition; Alfred Bartlett, Boston; Chatto and Windus, London; and Scribner's, New York, in 1916.

8. The *Equator*

DURING THE MONTHS between leaving Honolulu and arriving at Sydney, there was intended to be sufficient diversion and new experience to purge the heart and mind of every unpleasantness. Louis was in high spirits, writing to all his friends that he was again off to sea. There was no unfinished story or a deadline hanging over his head like Damocles' sword; there was plenty of money in the exchequer; *The Wrong Box* was to be published in London, as well as the book form of *Master of Ballantrae*. His health was remarkably improved.

There was no expensive charter on the *Equator*, but the seventy-foot schooner of sixty-two tons capacity was a drab craft compared with the *Casco* and its luxurious appointments. The captain's cabin had been fitted with an extra berth for occupancy by Louis and Fanny, and two berths had been built in the trade-room for Lloyd Osbourne and Joe Strong. Isobel and young Austin were to proceed to Sydney by trans-Pacific Matson Navigation Company steamer and await the arrival of the wandering *Equator*. Louis expressed relief that his mother was on her way to Edinburgh. Not that she was troublesome. Mrs. Field says quite the reverse, except that she had not the disposition to enjoy unconventional living. As for Fanny, only one who shares equally with her a dislike for the sea can appreciate her courage and her devotion to her husband in embarking upon another cruise of indefinite length and undetermined destinations.

The most consoling feature was that Ah Fu, accepted first as a passenger, was later commandeered as cook when it was demonstrated that the *Equator's* cook, who had signed on at San Francisco, was a rank pretender to the realm of the galley. The pseudo cook was then demoted to table and cabin steward. This pretender, Thomson Murray MacCallum, now a man in his eighties, lives at Inglewood, California, and laughs about his good fortune in being relieved from a burning conscience, since he knew he was not a qualified cook when he signed on, and knew that he scarcely could conceal his incompetence until they were at sea.[1] He figured that any way was legitimate for a youth of seventeen to get passage back to the South Seas.

And it is the naïve observation of this young man that put a discerning finger on a matter that has puzzled many Stevenson readers when he said simply that "Mr. Strong didn't seem to fit in." Others said that Joe Strong was taken on as a passenger on the *Equator* in order to get him away from his drinking companions in Honolulu, but Louis never once mentions his presence, speaking only of Lloyd Osbourne besides his wife. Anyone—man, woman, or child—who does not "fit in" on a cruise of this kind is fatal to serenity. It creates a mental fungus that grows and hardens by the hour, that no kindness can kill.

Mr. MacCallum tells that on the first morning out from Honolulu he went in the Stevenson cabin to "make it up" while Louis was still in his berth. In an attempt at genial conversation the boy mentioned that there was a copy of *Dr. Jekyll and Mr. Hyde* in the ship's library. At Louis's desire to see it, he hurried to bring it up from the main cabin. One glance and Louis was out of his berth with a rumble of burring profanity —much appreciated by a Scotch New Zealander. Slapping the book cover with his slender fingers, he said angrily, "Look! my name spelled with a *ph!* A *ph* indeed!"

In pajamas and bare feet he stormed out to Fanny, still ranting imprecations upon the offending *ph,* quite disregarding

[1] Mr. MacCallum died in 1957.

the fact that it was a pirated edition against which he had no recourse since he had neglected to protect the story by American copyright.

Mr. MacCallum remembers with what haste he made up the berths and cleared out before Louis returned.

Louis had expressed a particular desire to visit Ponape (Ascension) Island of the Caroline group, and it can be im- agined what might have come from the pen of the romancer if that wish could have been fulfilled, for this beautiful little island is one of the rare exceptions among the thousands of atolls. In the practically unexplored and heavily timbered interior are tracings of a previous civilization not yet accounted for by scientists. Some declare that they date back to the Lost Continent of Mu, others say they probably are the remnants of sixteenth-century Spanish or Portuguese fortifications built as a refuge against possible savage attacks of the then unknown native inhabitants whose strange appearance gave them a certain protection in their ferocious aspects.

But copra trading schooners go where there is cargo to be picked up; and Fanny's arrangement with Carpenter and Company, the owners, was that they would make no demands upon the itinerary. So it was to the Gilbert Islands that young Captain Reid, aged twenty-three, set a direct course—a straight line of 2,084 nautical miles.

Copra schooners of this type are particularly valuable in seeking out small villages where no trading posts are maintained and there pick up any amount, large or small, that the natives would have ready for shipment. The quality of this copra is usually above the average, having been dried in small quantities, the coconut meat uniformly cut, turned by hand according to the hours of sunshine; and protected from rain, it is of an even slate color with the maximum oil content.

A village apparently without life springs to activity with the first glimpse of a white sail against the horizon; some men rush to launch their row boats, others carry sacks of copra on their shoulders, each group racing to be the first to meet the schooner that is probably standing off beyond the reef. Once on board, the copra is carefully weighed in full view of the shipper, then the Captain invites him, usually accompanied by his wife, into the trade-room. Here he displays his stock of merchandise—gaily colored prints, fancy combs, a piece or two of jewelry for the missus; for the man shirts and dungarees, bush knives, axes, shovels, etc., until the shipper finds he has bought more than he has copra to pay for—which makes any captain a good trader. It is part of his business to keep his customers in debt to him, for then he is certain of a cargo upon his next call.

Mr. MacCallum tells of Louis's expressing a desire to own a schooner like the *Equator* and have a captain like Dennis Reid, skilled in navigation and with high personal charm, but after witnessing a few trading operations, he showed no further interest in such a project.

It was three weeks before Greater Makin, first of the Gilberts, was sighted. They were down in the intense heat only three degrees north of the Equator—that shimmering, blinding heat of a sun directly overhead—and if the passage had proved a bit on the somber side, the arrival at Butaritari could be nothing less. All the Line Islands are merely low atolls of coral, and this island of Taritari, or Greater Makin, is only a few feet above sea level without even so much as a hummock to break the monotony of the sky line. Louis said later that he longed for an island with a profile. Of the going ashore he wrote:

. . . The tide being out, we waded for some quarter of a mile in tepid shallows, and stepped ashore at last into a fragrant stagnancy of sun and heat. The lee side of a line island after noon is indeed a breathless place; on the ocean beach the trade will be still blowing, boisterous and cool; out in the lagoon it will be blowing also, speeding the canoes; but the screen of bush completely intercepts it from the shore, and sleep and silence and companies of mosquitoes brood upon the towns.

. . . A few inhabitants were still abroad in the north end, at which we landed. As we advanced we were soon done with encounter, and seemed to explore a city of the dead. Only between the posts of the open houses, we could see the townsfolk stretched in the siesta, sometimes a family together veiled in a mosquito net, sometimes a single sleeper on a platform like a corpse on a bier.[2]

They learned soon enough that they had landed in the wake of one of the rare drinking sprees when Chief Tebureimoa raised the *tapu* against the traders' selling liquor to the natives, and it was discovered that the entire populace was sleeping off a binge. He comments further: "It was a serious question that night if we should sleep ashore. But we were travellers, folk that had come far in quest of the adventurous; on the first sign of an adventure it would have been a singular inconsistency to have withdrawn; and we sent on board instead for our revolvers. . . . Captain Reid of the *Equator* stayed on shore with us to be at hand in case of trouble, and we retired to bed at the accustomed hour, agreeably excited by the day's events."

They were occupying the home of the Hawaiian missionary, who was away on calls to other atolls, and were comparatively safe within the compound of the trader, Mr. Rick, one of the three traders on the island. Yet the houses, built high above the walls of the compound, left the family in the lamplight a clean target for stones to be thrown in on their dinner table, frightening poor Ah Fu out of his wits. Caution would have been the better part of valor on this occasion, and other islands more attractive would have offered equal opportunity for adventure. We cannot but presume that this putting ashore at

[2] *In the South Seas* (vol. XVII, Pentland ed. of *Works*), 209.

the first island they touched was to escape the sticky heat on the *Equator,* and that danger was preferable. And, of course, they had no idea that their stay would be drawn out to six weeks.

Louis had studied the Polynesian language both in Tautira and Honolulu, and he must have been disappointed that this effort did not avail as a linguistic medium in Butaritari. The origin of the Micronesians ("People of the Many Little Islands") is in doubt, but they themselves regard the Samoan Island of Upolu as the center of the world and declare this the source of their migrations to the scattered groups of Ellice, Phoenix, Union, and Tokelau many centuries ago; yet their speech is closer to the Tahitian than the Samoan, though not sufficient to give them a lingual understanding. Sir Arthur Grimble, for seven years—1926 to 1933—administrator in the Gilberts and knighted for his research there, traces their ancestry to Malaya through the study of words, family names and places, and their myths and legends. His collected evidence shows their origin in Gilolo and neighboring islands of the East Indies and indicates that these migrants to Micronesia destroyed a previous population with a comparatively high culture.

The Reverend Hiram Bingham spent a quarter of a century in missionary work in the Gilberts. Besides writing a dictionary of the Gilbertese language, he translated the Bible. During World War II, when U. S. forces at last drove the Japanese off the island of Tarawa, they heard many expressions of fond appreciation of Rev. Bingham's work from the descendants of those who had known the heroic missionary of half a century ago.

How infinitely richer Louis's visit to the Gilberts would have been had the copra trader's schedule permitted him to stay on the island of Apaiang where Rev. Bingham had his residence. He writes of the missionary: "The plaited palms were what we recognized. We had seen them before on Apaiang, the most Christianized of all the islands; where excellent Mr. Bingham lived and laboured and has left golden memories; whence all the education in the northern Gilberts traces its descent; and where we were bordered by little native Sunday-school misses in clean frocks, with demure faces, and singing hymns as to the manner born.[3]

Later Louis made the following observation regarding missionaries in general: "Those who have a taste for hearing missions, Protestants or Catholics, decried, must seek their pleasure elsewhere than in my pages. Whether Catholic or Protestant, with all their gross blots, with all their deficiency of candour, of humour, and of common sense, the missionaries are the best and most useful whites in the Pacific."

In writing of the Gilbertese, Louis dwelled more than usual on the sordid and sensational—as most men do, and indeed, many women—and while the beauty of living is not to be found in an environment so utterly plain, where nature provides no vistas to exalt the senses, yet there is beauty and quiet pathos in a little girl of ten dramatizing the sunset by holding two sticks at arm's length to measure the time of the slowly sinking golden orb into the sea horizon, then staring as if transfixed at the effulgence of rose and crimson, purple and mauve and delicate blue that paints the sky halfway to the zenith.

[3] *Ibid.*, 323.

9. Samoa

It was not until December 2, 1889, after leaving Honolulu in June, that Louis wrote to Sidney Colvin from on board the *Equator*, 190 miles off Samoa:

We are just nearing the end of our long cruise. Rain, calms, squalls, bang—there's the foretopmast gone; rain, calm, squalls, away with the staysail; more rain, more calm, more squalls; a prodigious heavy sea all the time, and the *Equator* staggering and hovering like a swallow in a storm; and the cabin, a great square, crowded with wet human beings, and the rain avalanching on the deck, and the leaks dripping everywhere: Fanny, in the midst of fifteen males, bearing up wonderfully. But such voyages are at the best a trial. We had one particularity: coming down on Winslow Reef, p. d. [position doubtful]: two positions in the directory, a third (if you cared to count that) on the chart; heavy sea running, and the night due. The boats were cleared, bread put on board, and we made up our packets for a boat voyage of four or five hundred miles, and turned in, expectant of a crash. Needless to say it did not come, and no doubt we were far to leeward. If we only had twopenceworth of wind, we might be at dinner in Apia to-morrow evening; but no such luck: here we roll, dead before a light air—and that is no point of sailing at all for a fore and aft schooner—the sun blazing overhead, thermometer 88°, four degrees above what I have learned to call South Sea temperature; but for all that, land so near and so much grief being happily astern, we are

152

all pretty gay on board, and have been photographing and draught-playing and sky-larking like anything.

I am minded to stay not very long in Samoa and confine my studies there (as far as any one can forecast) to the history of the late war. My book is now practically modelled: if I can execute what is designed, there are few better books now extant on this globe, bar the epics, and the big tragedies, and histories, and the choice lyric poetics and a novel or so—none. But it is not executed yet; and let not him that putteth on his armour, vaunt himself. At least, nobody has had such stuff; such wild stories, such beautiful scenes, such singular intimacies, such manners and traditions, so incredible a mixture of the beautiful and horrible, the savage and civilised. I will give you here some idea of the table of contents, which ought to make your mouth water. I propose to call the book *The South Seas:* it is rather a large title, but not many people have seen more of them than I, perhaps no one—certainly no one capable of using the material. . . .

. . . Samoa has yet to be accounted for: I think it will be all history, and I shall work in observations on Samoan manners, under the similar heads in other Polynesian islands. It is still possible, though unlikely, that I may add a passing visit to Fiji or Tonga, or even both; but I am growing impatient to see yourself, and I do not want to be later than June of coming to England. . . . We shall return, God willing, by Sydney, Ceylon, Suez and, I guess, Marseilles the many-masted (copyright epithet). I shall likely pause a day or two in Paris, but all that is too far ahead—although now it begins to look near— so near, and I can hear the rattle of the hansom up Endell Street, and see the gates swing back, and feel myself jump out upon the Monument steps—Hosanna!—home again.[1]

Two days later, on December 4, Louis wrote to E. L. Bur-

[1] *Letters of R. L. S.,* ed. by Colvin, II, 197–201.

lingame: "We are now about to rise, like whales, from this long dive."[2]

But it was not until December 7 that they sighted the north shore of the Samoan island of Upolu and the softly rounded deep green hills back of the open harbor of Apia. They had expected scenery comparable to that of the Marquesas and Tahiti and were frankly disappointed. Nature has no harsh contrasts in Samoa, although at the time of the Stevensons' arrival the serene majesty of the hills had been betrayed by the evils of man in the half-submerged hulls of the four warships sunk in the hurricane of the previous March.

Beyond an occasional rocky shore there are few places where the contour of the hills is even slightly visible through the dense forest. Mount Vaea dominates the center sky line back of the harbor, with the Mulinuu, the long finger of land that has been the official meeting place of the *ali'i* (rulers) for countless centuries, on the right, palm fringed to the sea, and the curving beach of Mulifanua on the left.

There was no eagerly curious crowd awaiting their arrival. Apia was sophisticated. The *Equator's* crew rowed them ashore from their anchorage just inside the reef and piled their assorted luggage of bags, baskets, wooden food bowls, spears, paddles, and pandanus hats on the stubby wharf; and they themselves were scarcely less nondescript after their months of rough travel. As they walked along the waterfront—the only street in the town—toward the primitive Tivoli Hotel, they warmed to the dignified yet cordial and smiling *"talofa"* from the men whom they met, and the same greeting softly spoken and shy from the women and children.

Among the three hundred European residents the arrival of a visitor always was an auspicious occasion, and Rev. W. E. Clarke, pastor of the London Missionary Society church, hurried to the Tivoli with an invitation to Mission House for tea.

[2] *Ibid.*, 203.

Louis accepted readily. Perhaps his prejudices had mellowed during his long months away from civilization, although he confessed to Fanny that he "liked the man."

Among other guests at tea was a Scotsman, Rev. James Chalmers, on leave from missionary work among the still savage Melanesians of New Guinea. Immediately Celtic spirits sparked and soared, Scottish stories burred gleefully until the climax that Violet Roch records from the notes of her uncle, William Cooper, New Zealand magistrate in Apia at that time: ". . . with Rev. Chalmers demonstrating some variations of the Highland fling. The performance was perilously like a desecration of a missionary verandah at that time and for a while the other two missionaries and their wives regarded the proceedings with mild but silent horror. The manifest enjoyment of the two Scots was so infectious, however, that disapproval finally yielded to vocal appreciation and hearty applause."[3]

This Scottish missionary set Louis's heart tingling with such a friendship as he never before had known, and how much it influenced his decision to make a permanent home in Samoa no one can tell, but a year later he wrote to Sidney Colvin: "Two favours I want to ask of you. First I wish you to get 'Pioneering in New Guinea,' by J. Chalmers. It's a missionary book, and has less pretensions to be literature than Spurgeon's sermons. Yet I think even through that, you will see some of the traits of the hero that wrote it; a man that took me fairly by storm for the most attractive simple, brave, and interesting man in the whole Pacific. He is away now to go up the Fly river; a desperate venture, it is thought; he is quite a Livingstone card."[4]

Alas, it was this venture into the wildest regions of New Guinea's hinterland from which this "most attractive, simple, brave, and interesting man" never returned. He was wantonly

[3] Wellington, N. Z., *Evening Post*, December 13, 1950.
[4] *Vailima Letters* (New York, Scribner's, 1896), ed. by Sidney Colvin, 34.

murdered by savages as he sat in what was presumably a peaceful conclave of chiefs. One wonders at the extravagance of the Creator that He would sacrifice a man of supreme talent and superb personality, so infinitely rich in potential service to mankind, to a people with no conception of life above animal standards. As far as it is possible to reckon the exact date, James Chalmers met his death on April 8, 1891, on Goaribari Island, Fly River, Papau, together with his associate missionary, Oliver Tompkins. Chalmers had been sent to New Guinea by the London Missionary Society in 1877, at his own request given a difficult assignment, and this was the sad ending of fourteen years of devoted service.

Louis had seen him the previous year when under date of November 5, 1890, he wrote from his new home at Vailima:

My dear Tamate,

I wish I could tell you how pleased I was to get your note. I shall never cease to rejoice I had the good fortune to meet you; and whatever you are good enough to think of me, be sure it is returned with interest. I cannot come on the Richmond; our presence here is very needful; our work pressing; the most I can do (and in that I do not mean to fail) is to go by the next Wainui and meet you—and remain about the same time with you—in Auckland.

My wife who is tired and dirty and rheumatic and embittered by bad yeast—and yet (like myself) interested beyond measure by our hard and busy life here on the mountain, bids me send all things nice—"I can't think of anything nice enough," quo' she—to Tamate and his wife. The same from

your affectionate friend,
Robert Louis Stevenson[5]

Besides the *Pioneering in New Guinea* which Louis requested,

[5] Original in the Henry E. Huntington Library.

James Chalmers wrote *Send Me Among Savages* and *Work and Adventure in New Guinea* in collaboration with William Wyatt Gill, who was for twenty-two years a missionary in the Hervey group of the South Pacific. Louis, in innocently stating that he had more material than any other writer from his few months in the South Seas, was only bearing out the literary paradox that still prevails: that he who knows the most realizes he knows the least.

But to return to the Stevenson party's arrival at Apia—Joe Strong had gone to Samoa the previous year with Henry Poor, emissary of King Kalakaua, and had met the shrewd Michigan trader, Harry J. Moors, who was sufficiently astute to compete in business with the powerful German firm of Deutsche Handels und Plantagen Gesellschaft, shortened locally to D. H. & P. G. Strong was proud to be able to introduce Louis to Mr. Moors, and the latter was quick to recognize financial gain as well as social elevation.

Mr. Moors had married a beautiful and refined Samoan woman and had a family of fine children, yet with character- istic European superiority he denied her the status of equality, hence he himself sat on the border line of Apia society. Friend- ship with the Stevensons would be an advantage.

Thus Harry Moors became Louis's business agent and gen- eral informant on Samoan affairs. He invited him to use his upper balcony as a cool and quiet place for writing. Louis, working on *A Footnote to History,* was highly pleased with this arrangement, although the family had rented a small cottage a few blocks away where Ah Fu was installed as cook and which Fanny, with her serene adaptability, had quickly made into an attractive home.

When Fanny knew that Louis was writing to the point of mental and physical exhaustion, she would summon him home to rest. And Louis, realizing he owed everything to her care, would answer her summons promptly and smilingly. It was from this situation that there developed the mild antagonism between Harry Moors and Fanny, which did not decrease with the years, though she always was mindful of the many services he rendered to Louis during their first months in Apia. It was this first experience that led Moors to observe that Louis was dominated too much by his wife and would be better off without her.

Christmas of 1889 was a social triumph for Harry Moors with Louis and Fanny as dinner guests. Louis reported to Sidney Colvin on December 27:

. . . Christmas Day I wish you could have seen our party at table. H. J. Moors at one end with my wife, I at the other with Mrs. M., between us two native women, Carruthers the lawyer, Moors' two shop boys—Walters and A. M. the quadroon —and the guests of the evening, Shirley Baker, the defamed and much accused man of Tonga, and his son with the artificial joint to his arm—where the assassins shot him in shooting at his father. . . . After dinner it was quite pretty to see our Christmas party, it was so easily pleased and prettily behaved. In the morning I should say I had been to lunch at the German consulate, where I had as usual a very pleasant time. I shall miss Dr. Stuebel much when he leaves, and when Adams and Lafarge go also, it will be a great blow. I am getting spoiled with all this good society.[6]

Louis learned that a piece of partially cleared land owned by Thomas Trood (sometimes spelled "Trude") was for sale. There were 314.5 acres on a slight rise eight hundred feet above sea level and only three miles from the town of Apia—the price, approximately five dollars an acre. He was aghast when Fanny advised him to buy it.

"What do we want with three hundred acres of bush and timber?" he demanded.

[6] *Vailima Letters,* 35.

"We want a home. The climate here is perfect for you, and within a year I can make our living off the land. Even with our makeshift home you are happier here than I've ever seen you."

In this mood Fanny was not to be brooked, and so the bold venture was on. The only drawback: Louis was desperately homesick for Scotland. But Fanny knew that there must be an anchor some place, and she knew that she must make him contented away from a climate that had very nearly cost him his life. So before they left for Sydney on board the steamer *Lubeck* in February, 1890, the land then known as "Fuiono Tuluina," under Land Claims 2035 and 2036, was in the name of Robert Louis Stevenson. It would be his to return to after the visit with friends in England and Scotland. He was happy, but Fanny was more than happy: she had a deep sense of security for the first time in her married life. During their absence additional land was to be cleared and a cottage of four rooms, two below and two above, with an outside stairway, was to be built.

In the early autumn month of March the Sydney climate, with wind and rain, can be exceedingly disagreeable. Almost immediately Louis was taken ill. He worked himself into a fever with the Damien letter. He was sick with disappointment that he could not continue his journey to Europe as he had planned. This was when Fanny, against all rules and regulations, got herself taken on the trader *Janet Nichol* because Louis was so low that she feared for his life if they had to remain in what he jocularly termed the "New South Pole" for the proud state of New South Wales.

Rough as a crossing of the Tasman Sea can be in bad weather, Louis was almost immediately improved. His letter to Sidney Colvin is richly descriptive:

SS. "Janet Nicoll," off Upolu [*Spring, 1890*].
My dearest Colvin,—I was sharply ill at Sydney, cut off, right out of bed, in this steamer on a fresh island cruise, and have

already reaped the benefit. We are excellently found this time, on a spacious vessel, with an excellent table; the captain, super-cargo, our one fellow passenger, etc., very nice; and the char-terer, Mr. Henderson, the very man I could have chosen. The truth is, I fear, this life is the only one that suits me; so long as I cruise in the South Seas, I shall be well and happy—alas, no, I do not mean that, and *absit omen!*—I mean that, so soon as I cease from cruising, the nerves are strained, the decline com-mences, and I steer slowly but surely back to bedward. We left Sydney, had a cruel rough passage to Auckland, for the *Janet* is the worst roller I was ever aboard of. I was confined to my cabin, ports closed, self shied out of the berth, stomach (pampared till the day I left on a diet of perpetual egg-nog) revolted at ship's food and ship eating, in a frowsy bunk, cling-ing with one hand to the plate, with the other to the glass, and using the knife and fork (except at intervals) with the eyelid. No matter: I picked up hand over hand. After a day in Auck-land, we set sail again; were blown up in the main cabin with calcium fires, as we left the bay. Let no man say I am unscien-tific: when I ran, on the alert, out of my state-room, and found the main cabin incarnadined with the glow of the last scene of a pantomime, I stopped dead: "What is this?" said I. "This ship is on fire, I see that; but why a pantomime?" And I stood and reasoned the point, until my head was so muddled with the fumes that I could not find the companion. A few seconds later, the captain had to enter crawling on his belly, and took days to recover (if he has recovered) from the fumes. By singular good fortune, we got the hose down in time and saved the ship, but Lloyd lost most of his clothes and a great part of our pho-tographs was destroyed. Fanny saw the native sailors tossing overboard a blazing trunk; she stopped them in time, and be-hold, it contained my manuscripts. Thereafter we had three (or two) days fine weather: then got into a gale of wind, with rain and a vexatious sea. As we drew into our anchorage in a bight of Savage Island, a man ashore told me afterwards the sight of the *Janet Nicoll* made him sick; and indeed it was rough play, though nothing to the night before. All through this gale I worked four to six hours per diem, spearing the ink-bottle like a flying fish, and holding my papers together as I might. For of all things, what I was at was history—the Samoan business —and I had to turn from one to another of these piles of manuscript notes, and from one page to another in each, until I should have found employment for the hands of Briareus. All the same, this history is a godsend for a voyage; I can put in time getting events co-ordinated and the narrative distributed, when my much-heaving numskull would be incapable of finish or fine style. . . .[7]

It was on this cruise that they stopped at the controversial island of Mothe, calling at the tiny village of Nassau, the principal one of three villages on this exceptionally beautiful island in a vast and lonely sea. It is only a bit more than two miles across, with a peak six hundred feet high in the center, wooded as if planted by a landscape artist. It was owned by a European and was for sale—probably still is. For one thing it is five hundred miles northeast from Apia and is surrounded by some of the most dangerous shoals in the South Pacific, some seven miles in width. The immediate area is well named, Danger Islands. Captain Hird advised against Fanny's going ashore, but Louis and Lloyd went with Mr. Henderson, although they had been told there was not sufficient copra to make a shipment. The owner of the island had not been there for two years, which tells the story of "no copra." But certainly one never could find a more perfect Eden set down in a vast ocean. There is every kind of fruit, and many European vegetables; good pigs and fowls, and an ample supply of water from the high mountain —and the island is sparsely populated.

[7] *Letters of R. L. S.*, ed. by Colvin, II, 220–22.

Its nearest neighbor is Swain's Island, which is about five hundred miles directly west, another island privately owned, to which the *Janet* probably went in the swing north and west from Niue (Savage) Island. In contrast to Mothe Island, it is a low atoll, the highest point not twenty feet above sea level, with no aspects of beauty. But it has a resident owner who lives there with 82 relatives among a population of 140. It is interesting because it represents the final stages of an era that prevailed when the Stevensons arrived.

It was in the late 1840's that Eli Hutchinson Jennings left his home in New York bound for the Antarctic on a whaler. At Apia he jumped ship, later married the daughter of the chief who had hid him in the bush, and got a job with the German trading company of J. C. Godeffroy and Son, later the famous D. H. & P. G. Company mentioned earlier. Having some knowledge of navigation, Jennings was put in charge of one of the company's small sailing ships for picking up copra. Admiralty charts marked tiny Swain's Island "uninhabited," but using glasses as they cruised by one clear day, Jennings saw a lone figure on the beach. They hove to, and he went ashore, to be welcomed by a fellow American. Aided by eight or ten Micronesian men from Tokelau he had one hundred casks of fine coconut oil he wished to ship. The Tokelauns called him "Bulu," which is the only name recorded by young Captain Jennings. It is thought now that it might have been Bullock.

However, when it came time for the next semiannual trip, young Jennings went as a passenger for Swain's Island with his Samoan wife and young son. He took materials for a house, together with yams, taro, and bananas for planting. Records show that they arrived on October 13, 1856. He invited Toke-launs to bring their families and take up residence on the atoll so that they could assist with the work he planned. A few came.

Then "Bulu," or Bullock, disappeared. There is no record of his having left the island; no record of a quarrel with Jennings;

there is no marked burial place on the island. And what is strange in regions of isolated men—there are no known descendants. Only the huge iron kettles, shoulder high, in which he rendered coconut oil in the burning equatorial sun are still there, black and scaly with rust. After all, no one knows how "Bulu" reached the island in the first place, or how long he had been there. Crimes among pirates were frequent at that time, but murder among law-conscious men never has been generally patterned in the warp and weft of South Pacific life. So to this day no one has ever challenged Jennings' right of ownership of Swain's Island, known to the Micronesians as "Olosega."

When Louis, Fanny, and Lloyd went ashore, they found the entire island, two and one-half miles long by half a mile wide, a thriving plantation of coconut trees, from which was dried annually nearly one hundred tons of copra. The owner then was the son who had been taken as a baby to the new island home, but who had been educated in the United States and New Zealand. The present owner is the grandson of the first Jennings.

Fanny tells in her book *Cruise of the "Janet Nichol"* that young Eli Hutchinson Jennings went to Swain's in a miff because the Samoan government declined to sponsor a side-wheel steamer he had built at Apia.[8] There is no record either in D. H. & P. G. books or in family gossip among the Jennings, and Carruthers' to substantiate this tale. One must suppose it is one of those fantastic stories that start from nowhere in this land of strange stories.

At Apia again the Stevensons went ashore only long enough to appraise the progress of work on their cottage, which was to be a temporary home, and the clearing for the big house, reckoning they could complete the cruise, return to Sydney, and be back in Apia before the cottage was completed. Louis

[8] (New York, Scribner's, 1914), 33.

had not yet regained the strength lost during his illness in Australia. However, after weeks more on the *Janet,* feeling health returning with each passing day, writing constantly, through buffeting seas, on the preliminary draft of *Footnote to History,* he decided on a stopover at the beautiful town of Noumea in New Caledonia, leaving Fanny and Lloyd to continue with the *Janet.* Perhaps Fanny, knowing she was a sufferance passenger on a ship that barred women, feared to relinquish her status quo and risk being marooned in Noumea, even with all its beauty and comparative sophistication. And she was eager to join Isobel and her family, who had endured two periods of anxious waiting with no word whatever from the wanderers since they had left Apia.

This stay at Noumea was the only acquaintance Louis had with the Melanesians, although he expressed the desire many times to visit Fiji and know something of the Fijians—a lack of knowledge to be regretted in both quarters, for the Fijians are the highest type of Melanesians and among the finest of the South Pacific people. One recent author, emboldened by ignorance, moved the Fijians to Samoa and had Louis speaking the Fijian language, one more instance of South Pacific loose statement. The few Melanesians brought to Samoa by the D. H. & P. G. Company were from the Solomon Islands, and being indentured laborers would have no opportunity to know or be known by Louis, except for the boy who sought refuge at Vailima with his back in welts from an overseer's lash.

Louis's return to Sydney was filled with apprehension concerning his health, and the visit lasted only until the family could get transportation back to Apia and get Lloyd off to Skerryvore for the furnishings of the Stevenson home. By good fortune they discovered an "islander," Mr. Arthur Aris King, who was en route to London on holiday, and Louis employed him to assist Lloyd on this mission, which was rather too exacting for a young man scarcely out of his teens. Later they decided to sell Skerryvore and use the money to finance the building of the big house, to be called "Vailima," and which was to be recorded in Fanny's name. The latter was not done, however, until after Louis's death.

Louis deplored the necessity of assigning these important business missions to Lloyd. He was constantly irritated and baffled by the boy's bluff and boasting and called him a "Rodomonte." The lure of Cambridge halls of learning had not thus far prevailed against the decks of sailing ships and seamen's tales of adventure. Yet Louis's own health and lack of physical endurance made the risk imperative, and he had not yet, in spite of misgivings, found the gangling youth unworthy of trust.

When the two returned, Mr. King stayed on for a while at Vailima. It didn't work. Masculinity cannot bear being relegated to second place, and Fanny was the major-domo of Vailima, which brought Mr. King to Louis with the plaint: "The women are too much for any man."

Which in turn brought Louis's classical appraisal of femininity: "Show me the man who understands their ways!"

Despite Mr. King's objection to a woman-dominated household, it was this very feature that had won the high regard of the Samoans, especially since Fanny was older than Louis. Perhaps the Vailima family was never aware of this particular form of esteem. But it is traditional among Samoans that a man assumes an exalted place in deliberations of the *fono* if he is married to a woman older than himself who has, or is presumed to have, the astuteness to advise him prior to the sharp political debates which more often than not are features of legislative assemblies, where the most eloquent and persuasive *tulafale sili* (orators) are among the *fonotia* (those attending the *fono*).

After weeks in the cramped quarters of the trading schooners *Equator* and *Janet Nichol* and the barely tenable housing at Butaritari and Apamama—to say nothing of the crude little miner's cabin at Silverado—the four-room cottage must have seemed heavenly to the wanderers. Located in a quiet, wooded area of "Fuiono Tuluina," it was clean and new, with two rooms below and two above and a railed balcony and outside stairs.

A deal table, two chairs, and a kerosene lamp comprised the furniture brought up from Apia. Fanny spread *laufala* rugs on the pine floors, tacked huge pieces of *siapo* (tapa) on the bare walls, and curtained the windows with bright-patterned calico. With Louis's books on a shelf and two boards nailed on a brace in the corner of the sitting room for a couch, the effect need not have been so shocking to the fastidious Henry Adams and his friend John La Farge. Unfortunately, Louis and Fanny, with Simele's help, were fitting pipe on a stove in the adjacent cook house when the august callers arrived. They were streaked with soot, Louis was in his unmatched socks (an item of attire noted by the visitors), and Fanny was barefooted. Making the most of an embarrassing situation, the host and hostess confessed to a scarcity of food—an avocado and some hard biscuits—not mentioning that their boy was even then on his way home from market, and made a joke of their predicament, which later afforded them much merriment, as it did to the Vailima household when the famous historian's comments anent the famous author's deplorable existence came out in print.

Hardships such as are known in temperate or frigid zones do not exist in the South Seas. Rain is the most frequent unpleasant feature of the weather, with a normal downfall of two hundred inches—not a cold, dreary rain, but a deluge of warm water like a tempered shower turned on full force. Garden seeds may be washed out completely or pounded into the ground so deep they cannot sprout; delicate plants are flattened and bruised. The soft, wet earth is no place for shoes, and the weather is too hot for galoshes; hence the luxury of going barefooted, a health-giving practice denied the sophisticated whose soles are sensitive to stones and stubble. The Samoans are as meticulous about grooming their feet as the *papalagi* is in keeping his nails well manicured. Small feet and hands being a mark of distinction among high-class Samoan women, Fanny qualified for this honor with her dainty feet, on which a size four shoe was large.

Nature's cruel element is wind. Vicious and wicked, it tears at everything. Loose boards, young trees, roofs of houses all go flying through the air when it attains hurricane velocity. Birds with feathers drenched and soggy are even blown from their perches in the trees and become prey to rats and wild hogs. Louis expressed a baleful dislike of wind on the land, and many persons share his aversion to this turbulence with its prodigious unseen power for destruction. So when the cottage tilted one night Fanny and Louis sought the safer sanctuary of the stable, where the two gray horses, Eadie and Donald, and the former circus pony, Jack, gave them manger room until morning, when the cottage was seen to be quite upright and steady. Imagination is a potent factor in fear.

Difficulties attending those first months in their cottage would have been quite unnecessary had they not been obliged to work their way through barriers set up by the *papalagi* against true Samoan traditional friendliness, which, of course, they did eventually. Just as the chief of Apamama in the Gilberts built a group of thatched *fales* which the Stevensons named "Equator City," a group of Samoan young men would have made them free of Apia markets and the former German steward from the *Lubeck* whom Louis declared was "born with two left hands."

These young men, perhaps six, armed with axe, shovel, and knives, plus songs and laughter, would have in a matter of hours dug an ample *umu* (cooking pit) and prepared a feast. One stalwart would have gone into the forest for the low, stocky *Maota* tree (*Dysoxylon Sp.*), the wood of which burns readily with a smoke that fills the air like incense in a Buddhist temple; and because wild *lupe* (pigeons) feed on this fruit, he would have approached stealthily and snared two or three young cocks.

167

Another "boy" would have gone to spear fish on the reef; another to gather round, porous stones for heating in the *umu;* one to hunt tender fresh-water shrimp; one to climb a breadfruit tree and select some fruit just ripe for cooking; others to bring in stems of green bananas for cooking and ripe ones for *poi;* and still others going for mangoes and avocados and *maume* fruit (papayas) and climbing tall trees for coconuts ripe enough that the cream could be squeezed out of the grated meat.

When the wood has been burned out of the *umu* and the stones are hot, then each item of food, carefully wrapped in a fragrant plantain leaf, is dropped cautiously amid the stones; mats and heavy pieces of siapo are placed over it, and the pit filled with the earth that was removed. In the two hours or so of waiting there is time to grate the coconut meat and squeeze the cream into individual *ipu* (polished half-shells of the coconut); and when the *umu* is opened, small porous stones, heated again if necessary, are lifted out with forked sticks, whirled around in the *ipus,* and one has a cream to compare in delicacy of flavor with Marguery's once famous *Sauce à la Béchamel.* Dessert would be crushed ripe bananas mixed with the coconut cream and flavored with just a drop of the oil from lime leaves, and drunk from *ipus.* Other foods would be served on clean, fresh sections of stiff banana leaves, which when discarded would be thrown into the *tafuna'i* (pit for burning rubbish).

Only coffee and wine would have been lacking, and 'ava never is served with food; but Louis could have had his *ipu* of red wine, and sitting cross-legged in the wide-spreading shade of a breadfruit tree with his beloved Fanny, he could have been a second Omar Khayyam.

Traditionally the firing of the *umu* establishes title to the land with undisputed validity as long as the *umu* is not allowed to grow cold. Many *umus* date back for centuries. This establishes the owner as a *Matai* of a *Faoa'a'ai,* master of an estate, with the privilege of participating in Samoan political affairs and a voice in the *fono* of chiefs.

All of which Louis achieved in spite of the merchants and advisers of Apia who imposed what they deemed European necessities when the newcomers would have fared infinitely better with the produce of nature's storehouse, which was to be had for the simple effort of gathering. *Maume* apples, sweet and juicy, grow everywhere; also bananas, and boys are ready to climb trees for breadfruit, mangoes, coconuts, and the spicy *vi* fruit (*Spondias dulcis*) which grows tantalizingly on a tree of enormous size.

So Fanny took her European domesticity into the wilderness and baked bread on a cookstove and made beef stew with little help from the few European servants available, the while directing the Samoan men in work they knew nothing whatever about, for Samoans know little of planting and less than nothing about animal husbandry, the minus quality bordering on cruelty, which, of course, neither Fanny nor Louis would countenance.

Louis writes of the time their two faithful work horses, Eadie and Donald, were driven up the steep trail from Apia at such a rate that they arrived near death from exhaustion, with blood running from the mare's nostrils. Fortunately it was in the era of petticoats; each snatched one from a pile of fresh laundry and rubbed the horses down with cool water. He tells of their relief when the two grays finally began to nibble grass. For untold centuries there were no four-footed animals in Polynesia, and the natives still have no conception of humane treatment of them. Half the cases coming up for prosecution before the court in Apia are for cruelty to animals.

Along with the problem of bringing food each day from the markets of Apia, Fanny and Louis had this serious matter of personally looking after their stock. Fanny had an idea she could make stock raising pay, and with adequate aid she could have realized this aim. Compared with the miniature islands they had visited previously, Upolu was a small continent and their own three hundred acres a generous plantation. Upolu Island is more than forty miles in length and averages about twenty miles in width. Clearing off the timber is a Herculean task, and keeping the cleared area from growing up in weeds is a constant one. Less than twenty acres was cleared at Vailima during the time of the Stevensons' residence there.

Problems and small anxieties are in proportion to the pleasures of one's environment. To one unfamiliar with the South Seas it might seem that pioneering was an ordeal for Louis and Fanny, but it is doubtful that either ever spent happier months than those filled to overflowing with plans for their first securely permanent future.

Although deploring the lack of time and appropriate quiet for working on *The Wrecker*, Louis wrote to Mr. Burlingame:

I am a mere farmer: my talk, which would scarce interest you on Broadway, is all of *fuafua* and *tuitui*,[9] and black boys, and planting and weeding, and axes and cutlasses; my hands are covered with blisters and full of thorns; letters are, doubtless, a fine thing, so are beer and skittles, but give me farming in the tropics for real interest. Life goes in enchantment; I come home to find I am late for dinner; and when I go to bed at night, I could cry for the weariness of my loins and thighs. Do not speak to me of vexation, the life brims with it, but with living interest fairly.[10]

Later he wrote to Henry James:

Work? work is now arrested, but I have written, I should think, about thirty chapters of the South Sea book; they will

[9] *Fuafua*, raising fruit; *tuitui*, a pestiferous weed.
[10] *Letters of R. L. S.*, ed. by Colvin, II, 253.

all want rehandling, I dare say. Gracious what a strain is a long book! The time it took me to design this volume, before I could dream of putting pen to paper, was excessive; and then think of writing a book of travels on the spot, when I am continually extending my information, revising my opinions, and seeing the most finely finished portions of my work come part by part in pieces. Very soon I shall have no opinions left. And without an opinion, how to string artistically vast accumulations of fact? Darwin said no one could observe without a theory; I suppose he was right; 'tis a fine point of metaphysic; but I take my oath, no man can write without one—at least the way he would like to—and my theories melt, melt, melt, and as they melt the thaw-waters wash down my writing, and leave unideal tracts— wastes instead of cultivated farms.[11]

Louis had not yet met the high chiefs, Mata'afa and Malietoa, and the lesser chiefs Tamasese and Tuimaleali'ifano. The information he was using for *South Sea Letters* and *Footnote to History* was coming from Europeans—Germans and British— and Americans, with each slanting his stories of Samoan political affairs according to his own interests. And if this were confusion worse confounded, it grew to confusion compounded when he came to know the ruling *ali'i* (chiefs).

Samoa had had a long line of powerful rulers dating back to her rebellion against the oppression of Tongan kings, who were demanding unfair tribute of Samoan superior art craft. Reckoning by generations, this was somewhere between the thirteenth and fourteenth centuries and marked the beginning of the Malietoa dynasty which ruled all the islands of Samoa, with the exception of the Manua group of Tau, Ofu and Olosega, until the title became vacant and was taken over by the powerful house of A'ana.

At the turn of the nineteenth century, during the reign of

[11] *Ibid.,* 255–56.

Ali'i Safa-o-Fafine, foreigners began to arrive more and more frequently, and the benign chief, fearing for his people, sought to bring the islands of Tutuila, Upolu, Savaii, Manono, and Apolima into closer protective relationship, appealing eloquently for unity against any *papalagi*, friend or foe. During this campaign the chief died. Tamafaiga succeeded him, and in endeavoring to carry out the plans of his predecessor, assumed a dictatorial attitude and elevated himself to a deity. As a consequence he was assassinated in 1829. This ended the centuries-old unified rule. The title of Malietoa was revived on the island of Savaii, but it was not strong enough to prevail against the other claimants, and it was this weakness that brought on the rivalries which the European invaders promoted into civil warfare in order to gain supremacy over the entire group, barring Manua.

The Berlin Treaty, concluded by the Three Powers—England, Germany, and the United States—on June 14, 1889, gave to the United States all territory east of the 171st degree of west longitude, Germany all west of it, and England received Germany's islands in the Bismarck Archipelago as a reward for withdrawing all claims in Samoa. Historians cite this as one of the most cold-blooded instances of international disposition of a helpless people the civilized world has ever seen. President Cleveland in his message to Congress deplored our part in the intrigue, calling it "most reprehensible." This was in June, 1889, following the great hurricane of the previous March and prior to the first arrival of the Stevensons in December.

A treaty made in and by foreign countries did not mean that the Samoans were going to cease their national rivalries and meekly pay homage to their conquerors; instead, it intensified their hatred of the Germans. Plantation managers went about in twos and threes for mutual protection against ambushed warriors armed with clubs and stones, and often they fled to British-owned plantations for overnight safety.

For some reason, which may have been based purely upon personality, Louis favored the cause of the man who at that time held the title of Mata'afa. The then Malietoa, he thought, lacked the necessary force of character in this turbulence; yet his title gave him preference over Mata'afa, and his quiet dignity and calm courage appealed more to the Samoans than the fiery, stubborn Mata'afa, who defied the Germans when they ordered him to leave his home on the historic Mulinuu, the royal residence of chiefs, because they wanted the site for their own buildings.

Titles are not bestowed on a strictly hereditary basis, but by selection within the family of a man deemed best qualified for the position by virtue of potential kingly attributes, the name then being submitted to the *fono* for ratification. Then, by the very nature of heavy responsibilities and devoted homage, he develops, by grace of his own pride, a character of justice and benignity by which he hopes to earn for himself a place among the illustrious rulers of past centuries.

The Germans added insult by promoting the lesser title of Tamasese and intensifying the rivalry by the third aspirant, even though they knew he would be but a puppet ruler under German dominance. Small wonder that Louis found himself constantly rewriting yesterday's observations.

With characteristic fairness he delved into study of the Samoan language in order to get firsthand stories from these venerable chiefs. Fortunately the young man who first presented himself as interpreter was from a royal family of Savaii, since the royal dialect has a vocabulary quite different from the common language. It is an affront to royalty to use commoners' words or expressions, and in equally bad taste to address a commoner in royal words and phrases.

The Samoan alphabet has fourteen letters, the same as the Tahitian and two more than the Hawaiian. The Tahitian *r* is replaced in Samoan by *l*; and the Hawaiian *k* is usually replaced in Samoan by *t*. Louis already had some knowledge of both these tongues and he was naturally a linguist, but the glottal stop indicated by the hamzah and the accent placed on different syllables of a word to mean different things make the language exceedingly difficult orally, yet quite easy to read and write. The glottal stop and its essential rhythm are what give the language its lilt and save it from bordering on the guttural monotony of many tongues. Louis's sense of word rhythm would have aided him immeasurably in speaking as well as listening, for the weight of the accent depends upon a careful tuning of the ear to word harmony.

From these fourteen letters—*a, e, i, o, u, f, g, l, m, n, p, s, t, v*— (the hamzah is reckoned as the fifteenth by ethnologists for its essential contribution to both speaking and writing) is built a poetic and eloquent language, with beauties of expression and phrasing that defy literal translation. The missionaries gave the Polynesians their first written language, using this Arabic symbol indicated by the inverted comma to fill in the missing consonant between two vowels as expressed in the glottal stop.

In addition to two or three hamzahs that may trip lightly through a single word, the *papalagi* often is plagued and baffled by the tonal quality and duration in the pronunciation of a vowel. A staccato vowel means one thing, a prolonged vowel another, and a soft-spoken unaccented vowel still another—all in words with exactly the same spelling. The beginner often embarrasses his listeners by innocently lingering too long on a vowel or cutting it a fraction too short.

In words in which the same vowel follows in succession of twos or threes, it is the hamzah that gives the musical phonetic value, as in the word *maʻamaʻa*, meaning stony; or *faʻavaʻaʻasaga*, to be treated as a conquered person, although this is sometimes written *faʻavaʻaasaga*, with a bit of the beauty lost without the final hamzah.

In the word *fa'a'ala,* to make the opening speech of a *fono,* the three *a's* are divided by the hamzah; while the same word, meaning to rouse from sleep, has but one mark—*fa'aala.* The same thing happens in the words *fa'a'ata,* to provoke laughter, and *fa'aata,* to refuse a request respectfully.

The glottal stop at the beginning of a word is the most difficult for the foreigner. Only the Samoan can put his tongue in the roof of his mouth and give the word the lift indicated by the hamzah. Try it with the word *'amata'aga,* meaning the beginning; or the word *'uputu'u,* a tradition; or *'o'osa,* to be old yet seeking a wife. This last word, properly pronounced, has one of the richest onomatopoeic values found in any language to express forlorn loneliness.

Another element in Samoan speech which the *papalagi* abuses in as many ways as is possible in the space of two letters is the consonantal diphthong *ng.* The letter *n* never is written, yet all *g's* carry the *n* sound as a soft tonal prefix. Even if the word begins with a *g,* the *n* sound still precedes it. Practice is required to shade the *n* into *Goigoi* without smothering the *G* and making this beautiful feminine name into plain *Noinoi,* instead of *Ngoingoi.* Which accounts for the murderous assaults upon the lovely name, Pago Pago. When the *papalagi* graduates beyond *Pa-go Pa-go* and puts the *n* before the *g,* he smugly says *Pan-go Pan-go,* instead of the honeyed softness of *Pang-o Pang-o,* which is one of the most beautiful geographical names in the world. This diphthong also is a prefix to some verbs to denote the neuter gender.

Plurals are indicated by the letter *o* preceding the noun, as *o 'ula* instead of *'ulas* when one means wreaths around the neck. However, occasionally a plural has another spelling, as in English. For example, the plural of *fa'a'ai,* food paid by the loser of a game, is *fa'a'a'ai.* And all numerals are preceded by the letter *e,* that is *e fa* (four), *e lima* (five).

It was the missionaries to the South Seas—in Hawaii in 1820

and Samoa in 1830—who recognized the culture of the Polynesians and gave them their first written language; and books by such godly men as John Williams, William Wyatt Gill, George Archibald Lundie, George Turner, and J. B. Stair, all published from ten to thirty years before the Stevensons went to Samoa, stimulated prominent ethnologists of Australia and New Zealand to intensify their previous rather desultory research on the origins of the race.

The result was that men of the caliber of Stephenson Percy Smith and MacMillan Brown devoted half a lifetime to tracing by legends, myths, poetry, and crafts the paths of migrations across southern Asia. Back, back, back they went, step by step, year after year until Stephenson Smith writes in an appendix to his book, *Hawaiki*:[12]

Since the foregoing was sent to the printer, further information has been received bearing on the Indian origin of the Polynesians. In the last number of the *Memoirs of the Asiatic Society of Bengal*, Vol. *vii*, No. 3, is to be found a long and interesting paper by Mr. James Hornall, Director of Fisheries, Madras Government, on the subject of "The Origins and Ethnological Signification of Indian Boat Designs," in which the author deals exhaustively with his subject.

The matter that most interests us is that the author claims the Polynesians to have been living on the coasts of India in very early times, indeed, in Pre-Dravidian times, and that these same Polynesians introduced the use of the out-rigger canoe to coastal India. Though not stating so definitely, Mr. Hornall seems to think that these Polynesians came to India from Indonesia, whereas we think the people were a branch of the Proto-Aryans, or Gangetic race of Logan.

The author gives an illustration of one of the "Parawa fishermen" of the Indian coast of the present day, and this picture

[12] London, Whitcombe and Tombs, 1921.

might easily be taken for a Maori, Rarotongan, Tahitian, Hawaiian, or Samoan, except that the hair is slightly too crispy.

In another paper appearing in the *Geographical Review*, the organ of the American Geographical Society, Dr. Griffiths Taylor of the Sydney University, describing the various migrations of mankind from the very earliest dates, includes our Polynesians in the Aryan branch of mankind. This is very satisfactory to those of us who have contended for this connection of the Polynesians for many years past.

These men were speaking of the dim era of 475 to 65 B. C. and on down through the Christian centuries with dates approximated from oral Polynesian records of myths and legends. Only Colonel James Churchward dared to hazard a theory on the lost civilization of Mu. Untold centuries of isolation, when the Polynesians believed they were the only people in the world and their scattered islands constituted the world, gave them their word *papalagi*. *Papa* means bursting forth, or explosion, and *lagi* (pronounced *lang-i*) is heaven; so the first foreigners were thought to have come from heaven through a bursting of the clouds. Subsequent years of tribulation brought realizazation to the Samoans that they had miscalculated the direction from which the foreigners arrived. The other name is *fafa* with a prolonged final *a* rich in denunciatory inflection. All *a*'s are very broad.

The coming of the missionaries was a blessing that all recognized, and the village of Sapalili on the eastern coast of Savaii Island is held in reverence because it was there that John Williams, first of the London missionaries, landed on August 20, 1830. He was accompanied by the Samoan chief, Fauea, who had been visiting in Rarotonga and asked to come along as a representative of Malietoa in order to make proper presentation of the newcomers—a matter of courtesy still acknowledged by the Samoans. This was only ten or twelve days after the assassination of the war priest, Tamafaiga, and when Fauea heard the good news, he exclaimed with great glee: *"Ua mate le tiapolo! Ua mate le tiapolo!"* "The devil is dead! The devil is dead!" and explained to Rev. Williams that he had feared for their lives if Tamafaiga still ruled, but he knew Malietoa would receive them kindly. As a matter of actual date, the war priest had been killed six or eight months earlier. Such a discrepancy can arise easily when dates are kept only orally and time means little, as it does to the South Sea people, who dwell in the hypnotic aura of *dolce far niente.*

Fourteen years later the Germans established their first trading post at Apia—in 1854—the beginning of an era of trouble which Louis looked in upon thirty-five years later, when a generation of resentment had been built into the Samoan character—sweetened, to be sure, by the presence of men like W. E. Clarke and James Chalmers, together with men in judicatory and administrative capacities like William Cooper of New Zealand, municipal magistrate in Apia, and Henry Clay Ide, appointed first as land commissioner by Grover Cleveland and later as chief justice and consul for the United States; also S. J. Foster, who served as U. S. consul during 1875–76. And in this category belongs Thomas Trood, British vice-consul, from whom Louis purchased the Vailima acres. Trood had purchased the land from a Scot named W. Johnston, but the first official recording is in Trood's name.

So far as character is concerned, the Samoans are no more virtuous, and no less, than men everywhere throughout the world. Perhaps their chief point of commendation is that they do not aspire to set standards of moral behavior for the strangers who come to their shores, yet are quick to sense, and respect, those who conform to their ideas of moral conduct. If one should attempt to cite a prime principle as a basis for their love of Tusitala, is would be this matter of sincere regard on his part for their conventions.

". . . and here is a guinea piece. Will you stand by the toss of the coin?"

"I will stand and fall by it," said Mr. Henry. "Heads, I go; shield I stay."

The coin was spun, and it fell shield. "So there is a lesson for Jacob," says the Master.

From an illustration by William Hole for *The Master of Ballantrae* in *Scribner's Magazine*. Stevenson had requested that Hole illustrate the novel because of his knowledge of the architecture of the period.

"Louis was a wonderful listener; whether to a planter's tale or a queen's lament for her people, he gave his full attention."—Isobel Field.

A card game. It is evident from the facial expressions that Teuila (front, center) holds the winning hand. Others in the game are (l. to r.) Joe Strong, R. L. S., Lloyd Osbourne (standing), and Fanny Stevenson.

Lloyd Osbourne caught this smile, half-impudent, that
Teuila said was characteristic of Louis's lighter moods.

Courtesy Lucy Orr Vahrenkamp

When young Lloyd with his new camera opened the door of Louis's room, he was greeted with stern "*O-U-T!*" But he snapped an excellent picture before his hasty retreat.

Top: The first house at Vailima, known later as "Pineapple Cottage." Cookhouse at right is where Louis and Fanny were helping to put up a stove when Henry Adams and John LaFarge called. Bottom: Vailima with the addition (left) that was larger than the original house.

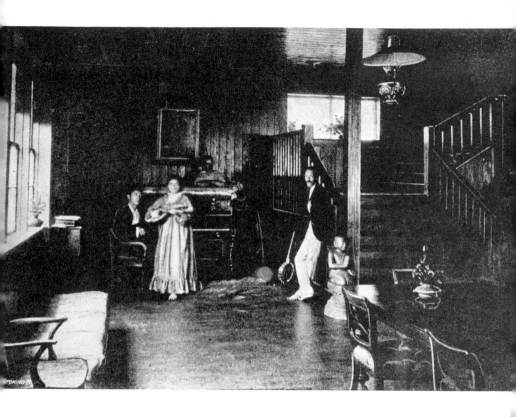

The staircase at Vailima. Both staircase and hall remain
the same today.

The great hall at Vailima.

It is a safe surmise, in which Samoan chiefs of a generation just past have concurred, that if to Tusitala, with the sympathetic and appreciative understanding which he so quickly acquired with acquaintance, could have been delegated the work of co-ordinating the rival factions, all the war and bloodshed might have been avoided. Louis was an eloquent and forceful speaker, and Samoan *tulafale sili* (orators) appreciated this, for they have been famous for their power to sway a populace as well as a *fono* of chiefs; as in the case of Lauaki, who still is spoken of as the "King Maker," yet was only a commoner and had no title. Present-day orators still begin their formal addresses before the assembled great *fono* with his dramatic declaration: "From the dawn of Saua to the setting sun of Falialupo, Samoa is one!" Boomed forth in his low-pitched resonant voice before a hushed circle of men sitting cross-legged on the floor of a royal *fale,* or to a populace sitting on the grassy Mulinuu, this statement, chiefs have said, stirred them to such patriotic heights that their political differences appeared paltry.

There are five traditional age-old districts in Samoa, each with an *ali'i* who rules, or did rule, even with the powers of life or death. A culprit reaching the sanctuary of his chief's *fale* could not be taken by his pursuers unless his culpability, judged by the chief and his *fono,* was such as to forfeit protection. While Samoans have a consummate pride in leadership, there is pride that amounts almost to a fetish in their loyalty to a chosen leader—a *chosen* leader, not a usurper. In ancient times the chiefs from the five districts would meet in a great *fono* with all the lesser chiefs in attendance, and here in peaceful parley a supreme chief, or king, would be selected, and out of traditional courtesy—for which the Polynesians are noted—the choice would be from the oldest lineage, presuming he was the most worthy.

There were interisland raids as demonstrations of bravery. Every *ali'i* had his warriors. Armed with short clubs, they fought their battles more as a display of dexterity than triumph by bloodshed. And more often than not, especially among the young men of the 'Aumaga, there was a beautiful *taupou* (village maiden of highest rank) at the root of the fray, with pride as an incentive. Hate was introduced by the Europeans.

But Louis did not acquire his place of esteem in the minds and hearts of the Samoans without having served a probationary period during those first six months while the big house was being built. Altruism could not prevail when European carpenters were being paid a dollar for a day's work and the Samoans fifty cents. And because he had not at that time learned to dissociate himself from the Europeans, he was looked upon merely as another *papalagi*.

It was when he moved into the big house and the family arrived—Lloyd Osbourne and Aunt Maggie from Scotland, Isobel and Joe Strong and their little son, Austin, from Australia—and life settled him into the role of a *matai* of a *faoa'a'ai* (lord of the manor) that they began to look upon him as one who was not there to exploit their resources: a strange *papalagi*, indeed. However, Aunt Maggie fled the still primitive home and went back to Sydney on the *Lubeck*. Trips on this steamship of 1,815 tons, with thirty days each way to Sydney, were regarded as a luxury. It was spick and span, with only four years of service, good food, airy deck space, efficient stewards, and courteous officers. Even Fanny, who disliked the sea, vied with the others of the family for valid excuses for visits to New Zealand, Fiji, or Australia.

It was one of these recreational trips to Australia that the family prescribed for Louis following receipt of a gift of two pistols from Lady Jane Shelley. He had felt keenly the death of Sir Percy a year and a half before, for the happiest memories of Bournemouth were of those hours spent with Sir Percy as the two, plagued alike with frail health, sat on the seashore and talked of yachts and sailing and far ports. Louis's day dreams had come true in Samoa. Sir Percy's had not. On January 15, 1890, Louis had written to Lady Shelley:

Apia, Samoa.

My dear Lady Shelley:

I have known now for some days the loss that has befallen you; the news came to me in a letter from California in a simple newspaper cutting without detail or even date; the more I think of it the less I can imagine the greatness of your bereavement. He was so kind, so bright, so natural, had as much of all that is most beautiful and pleasant in youth, he endeared himself so swiftly even to strangers, he was so full of innocent interests, so full of strange, interesting, simple thoughts; I can not think how you are to endure the loss of that companion.

Late as we knew him, it seems like a great hole made, and bursts another link with England, that we shall see him no more, enjoy no more that quaint wit of his, his ready laughter, his delight in all romance, the delightful sweetness of his nature. I pray God support you in this loss; none could be heavier; you have but one single consolation that he died young—or so at least he was when we last saw him and if there was any change, it can have been but through sickness.

I feel that I have made my wife old; depend upon it, if a husband is still young in all good senses, his wife has been a blessing; and when our dear ones go there is no consolation possible, but that we have not altogether failed on our part, and it was for us to have been there with them. No one could ever think of him as old; he had the morning dew upon his spirit; a boy and a poet—so a poet's son—until the last. What he was when he was young in years also, we do not know; what we saw of him, so near the end, is beautiful to recall.

Do you remember coming once to call on us, you two together, on a day of high wind? And how, as you drove, he made a romance that you were driving through a forest, and would come presently to an old ruined abbey like one of Mrs. Radcliffe's and go in through courts and corridors and cloisters, till you came at last to a huge stone hall partly unroofed, and there in the chimney find a great bonfire blazing in the wind—and no one near? What a deal of his father there was in that! And how much of the best of his grandfather! and how much of the perennial boy! You must have many of the like to remember; alas, that pleasant fancy will no longer delight you. But you have a sure hope that separation will not be for long as not forever.

I write for myself and for my wife, who is down with a little fever. We can but say one thing; we pray God to support you. Accept our love and sympathy.

Your affectionate
Robert Louis Stevenson

And now the second letter, dated only 1892:

S. S. Lubeck,
Between Sydney and Samoa.

My dear Lady Shelley

I have long been wishing to write you a decent letter, and like the most of such wishes, in my case at least—it will very likely never be fulfilled. I can't think of anything that would have given me greater pleasure than the revolvers from the *Oceana* [a yacht of Sir Percy's]. Lloyd has had them all marked with my name *and the name of the donors;* they shall stand in my house I hope forever, and as long as any of us continue to go in and out, they will call to mind far away places and loved faces.

I was glad to get your letter, and to see how faithfully and wisely you have borne your loss. These survivals are not, after all, for so long. You ask me to visit you, dear lady, it is still a race between us for the goal; but if I prove the laggard and do by any chance ever return to England, the visit shall be paid. It is more likely that I shall die, as I shall live, in Upolu, farther from the inviolate island than even Shelley; the farthest, I suppose, of all that ever blackened paper with printed English words.—I would like exceedingly to visit you to-day at Boscombe, come into the long drawing-room, go up the stairs in the conservatory and sit awhile to speak with you in the shrine; but I would not stop for lunch; for then I should see the empty place to which I have not yet become the least accustomed— and when lunch was over, how could I go into the green room alone? No, it is perhaps better to stay where I am, and look at my pistols where both names are engraved, and think of you, as I have known you, undivided.

I am so glad Sir Percy saw the Master [*The Master of Ballantrae,* dedicated to Sir Percy Florence and Lady Shelley]. I little thought what a strange second sense, B R D would come to bear; well we all fly it, and the night is at hand. I have just had an acute attack in Sydney and got off with some difficulty for my own congenial island, there I trust to be all right again— for a while. Our place promises to be most beautiful, six hundred feet above the sea, part on the slope of a steep mountain, part on a kind of table land cut through by the deep bed of streams. All is in forest. We can see the ships entering and leaving the port of Apia at our feet; if they lie far out and have tall spars, we can even see them rolling at anchor in the roads; some fifty miles of blue Pacific lies outspread in front of us; and on the left the view is inclosed by some green mountains six or eight miles to the eastward.

When I left, my wife and I had been for months toiling very hard and living very meagerly in a sort of shanty; a very resonant place in rains, and a very draughty one in wind, of both of which we had plenty. (I should say the ship is rolling very hard, which must explain my handwriting; I dare not set the ink-pot on the table—and my pen describes some singular evolutions in which I have no share; the letter was begun some days ago when it was smooth.) I was glad to hear of the

Shelley memorial [at University College, Oxford]. An idea strikes me; how would it be to put upon it for epigraph [*sic*] the splendid verse; "The inheritors of unfulfilled renown"— I forget how the phrase finishes, but I know it is apposite and beautiful, and means something like "arose to greet him." I do not like to put my oar in; but I shall make an alternative suggestion from the same poem, the stanza about life and death and the grass being trampled. Either of these would be excellent; but give me "the inheritors."

This dreadful ink so runs [?] and sticks, I doubt if one word will be legible by the time it reaches you. I hope enough will remain to testify to the warm affection with which I sign myself

Your friend

Robert Louis Stevenson[13]

During Louis's absence, and fortunately before the return of Aunt Maggie, the entire household was reorganized. European servants—and even Fanny's East Indian cook she had brought from Suva—did not fit into the necessarily primitive housekeeping pattern from which Fanny was trying to evolve European standards of service, not having discovered that Samoan boys learn the art of cooking as a masculine accomplishment. So it was Teuila who installed Samoan "boys" as helpers—not servants—and set the household on an even keel of daily routine by appointing each to specific tasks. To herself she assigned cleaning lamp chimneys, filling bowls with kerosene, and trimming wicks.

Although Isobel and Joe Strong and Austin lived in the cottage, Louis and Fanny scarcely had settled in the big house when they realized it was too small and decided to build a wing; and the wing became larger than the original house. A

---

[13] Text from Boscombe MMS. A. Printed by permission of Lloyd Osbourne in R. Glynn Grylls, *Mary Shelley* (New York and London, Oxford University Press, 1938).

special room was built for Aunt Maggie and furnished with things brought from Skerryvore. There she had the privacy that older folk crave. Mrs. Field said she did not remember ever having been in Aunt Maggie's room, simply because the entire family respected her unspoken desire for privacy. She had brought a maid with her from Australia who proved more of a cumbrance than a help, so she was returned by the next steamer.

It was about this time that marital difficulties arose for Isobel. Joe Strong did not fit into the life generally. He did not like any form of manual labor. An early morning hour spent in clearing the bush or helping Fanny with her vegetable beds left him spent and exhausted for the day, and between him and Louis, never congenial, there was an ever deepening animosity. Isobel recognized this latent enmity and foresaw difficulties when, in Sydney, she demurred about their coming to Vailima. But Louis had insisted he wanted his family with him, that Fanny's family was all he had and he needed them to make life complete at Vailima.

Mrs. Field told dramatically of the break with her husband:

"I was sewing in the cottage when Joe came hurrying up the steps with his two traveling bags. 'Looks like you were going some place,' I said half-facetiously.

" 'I'm leaving,' he snapped as he began snatching his clothes off the hooks and throwing them into his bags.

" 'Leaving me, or leaving Samoa?' I asked.

" 'Both' he growled.

" 'You might tell me what has happened.'

" 'Ask Louis,' was all he would say, and kept repeating it, disdaining even a civil good-bye as he called two of the Samoan boys to carry his bags on a shoulder-pole.

"Scarcely had he disappeared when Louis came striding across the lawn and up the stairs. He was more angry than I'd ever seen him, and he was breathing with alarming intensity. I literally pushed him into a chair.

" 'I came to tell you that you will have to divorce Joe. He has outraged the principles of decent behavior. I'll assume all responsibility for both you and Austin—for Austin's schooling —and your home is here with us. We can't spare you. Your home is here. We need you,' he kept saying over and over.

"I was too concerned for him to think of myself, and I must have stood there like a dummy before I thought to pour a glass of cool limeade. Before he left, he could laugh at my one-man fire brigade. But I never learned what took place between the two men, nor do I believe my mother knew. However, an entry in her diary December 23, 1892—subsequently deleted—reveals what must have been a stormy scene":

My diary has been long neglected. About the time I stopped writing we found Joe Strong out in various misdeeds, robbing the cellar and store-room at night with false keys; in revenge, when he found that he was discovered, he went round to all our friends in Apia and spread slanders about Belle. We turned him away, and applied for a divorce for Belle, which was got with no difficulty, as he had been living with a native woman of Apia as his wife ever since he came here—an old affair begun when he was here before, also he had been engaged in an intrigue with Fanua.

He came up here late one night to beg forgiveness and asked to be taken back. I was so shocked at seeing him that I had an attack of angina, which seems to remain with me. Louis was made sole guardian of Austin, who has been sent to Nelly[14] to school.[15]

[14] Nelly Sanchez, Fanny's sister, in Oakland, California.
[15] This deletion was made first by Fanny, later by Teuila, out of consideration for Joe Strong's sister, and although I saw the diary in 1938 at Serena, I was not told the contents or the reason for deletion until after the sister's death. The diary was given to the Robert Louis Stevenson House in Monterey, California, in 1949.

Immediately the atmosphere had cleared from the domestic blow-up, a lack of restraint was noticeable in Louis. Desultory arrival at meals irritated him, so with the family assembled promptly and in proper dress there were no barbs lurking behind an apparently casual remark, for though Louis deplored this type of table talk, he was no slouch (Teuila's expression) at leveling a rapier thrust at any Achilles heel exposed by a Gascon or a braggadocio.

It was at this time that Louis cut Joe out of a picture recently taken with himself, Lloyd, and the two gray horses, Donald and Eadie. Then, after painstakingly matching the two edges with the foliage of the trees in the background, he had a new negative made and the original destroyed.

With all Louis's fascination with the elemental life of the South Seas, it did not extend to laxity in dress. He deplored the slovenly appearance of many European men who apparently had forgotten the niceties of attire, a laziness that breeds a lessening of moral fiber and becomes a curse anywhere in the tropics. Therefore, when the family had moved into the big house, he instituted by precept a rule, unspoken and delitescent as it was imperative, that everyone should dress for dinner in the evening. He was proud of his table, his family, and the "boys" in their fresh white *lavalavas* who served the food with their easy, smiling grace.

He, himself, contrary to some reports, bordered on the fastidious, and he looked the traditional landed baron when he would come downstairs in evening dress—sometimes in black trousers with white dress-jacket; in all white if the weather should be stifling and muggy; in all black with short dress-jacket, white tie, and perhaps light-colored cummerbund for a formal occasion. These cummerbunds were the Oriental style of sash, two yards and more in length and six or eight inches in width, tailored of heavy silk, faille, or grosgrain, and lined with white satin. Maroon and midnight blue were favorite colors, but with black he often wore a deep cream and sometimes with white he wore what he called thistle-red if in a gay mood. Adjustment of these sashes required help, and if Fanny were not handy, he would come to Teuila to hold one end while he whirled himself into the thing to avoid slack and wrinkles.

This dress-up campaign gave Teuila courage to agitate for a shorter hair cut. Louis remonstrated, "I'll only look hungrier and leaner." But after inspecting work done on Lloyd and Austin, he reluctantly consented. Given a mirror and viewing the result with slow and critical appraisal, he admitted, "I can't see that is makes me look any worse."

Louis seldom issued a command or gave an order at Vailima, but he had a manner in making a simple request that effectively put it into this category. One particular rule which everyone recognized as imperative and absolute was that family meals should be attended promptly and should be times of good cheer with stimulating conversation. He usually led off himself with a challenge to wit and intelligence that put every member on his mettle. It might be poetry, history, philosophy, or a bit of his typical, ever lurking nonsense which never failed to create an hour or two of hilarious fun.

Mrs. Field told of the lift, mentally and spiritually, that these meal-time sessions of happiness gave to her, following her break with Joe Strong; and how, like an infection, the spirit of them took hold of the Samoan help (not servants) and was carried outside to the boys' families. It literally set the tenor of Vailima life. Louis, with nerves relaxed, would return to his writing, or perhaps have an hour with Simile for their exchange of lessons in Samoan and English.

The business of fun is meat and drink to the Samoans, and woe is the *papalagi* who becomes the butt of one of their jokes and goes serenely on unconscious of the sport they are having at his expense. Teuila confessed to a prank played on her when

she asked one of the boys to take a pitcher of water to the upstairs room of the cottage and the boy climbed one of the posts
instead of going up the stairs. If she had chided him, he would
have replied with a perfectly innocent expression that he didn't
know what the stairs was for and he supposed that this was the
way she went to her upstairs rooms.

Even Louis was the victim of a joke by the people of Tau
Island when he visited the Manua group. Chronologically this
episode does not belong at this particular place in this account,
but the subject matter does. It was in June, 1894, that the officers
of the British man o'war *Curaçao* invited Louis for a short cruise
to American Samoa. Later, on July 7, he wrote to Henry James
of this trip:

I am going to try and dictate to you a letter or note, and
begin the same without any spark of hope, my mind being
entirely in abeyance. This malady is very bitter on a literary
man. I have it now coming on for a month, and it seems to get
worse instead of better. If it should prove to be softening of
the brain, a melancholy interest will attach to the present document. I heard a great deal about you from my mother and Graham Balfour; the latter declares that you could take a First in
any Samoan subject. If that be so, I should like to hear you on
the theory of the constitution. Also to consult you on the force
of the particles *o lo'o* and *ua,* which are the subject of dispute
among local pundits. You might, if you ever answer this, give
me your opinion on the origin of the Samoan race, just to complete the favour. . . .

We have at present in port the model warship of Great Britain. She is called the *Curaçao,* and has the nicest set of officers
and men conceivable. They, the officers, are all very intimate
with us, and the front verandah is known as the Curaçao Club,
and the road up to Vailima is known as the Curaçao Track. It
was rather a surprise to me; many naval officers have I known,

and somehow had not learned to think entirely well of them, and perhaps sometimes ask myself a little uneasily how that kind of men could do great actions? and behold! the answer comes to me, and I see a ship that I would guarantee to go anywhere it was possible for men to go, and accomplish anything it was permitted man to attempt. I had a cruise on board of her not long ago to Manu'a, and was delighted. . . . We stayed two days at the island, and had, in addition, a very picturesque snapshot at the native life. The three islands of Manu'a are independent and are ruled over by a little slip of a half-caste girl about twenty, who sits all day in a pink gown, in a little white European house with about a quarter of an acre of roses in front of it, looking at the palm-trees on the village street, and listening to the surf. This, so far as I could discover, was all she had to do. "This is a very dull place," she said. It appears she could go to no other village for fear of raising the jealousy of her own people in the capital. And as for going about "*tapa-tafaoing*," as we say here, its cost was too enormous. A strong able-bodied native must walk in front of her and blow the conch shell continuously from the moment she leaves one house until the moment she enters another. Did you ever blow the conch shell? I presume not; but the sweat literally hailed off that man, and I expected every moment to see him burst a blood-vessel. We were entertained to kava in the guest-house with some very original features. The young men who run for the kava have a right to misconduct themselves *ad libitum* on the way back; and though they were told to restrain themselves on the occasion of our visit, there was a strange hurly-burly at their return, when they came beating the trees and the posts of the houses, leaping, shouting, and yelling like Bacchants.

I tasted on that occasion what it is to be great. My name was called next after the captain's, and several chiefs (a thing quite new to me, and not at all Samoan practice) drank to me by name.[16]

The Samoans were simply putting on a burlesque for the benefit of the ship's officers and the famous Tusitala, and throwing
in a great story about their half-caste ruler. True, the girl was
the granddaughter of the ruler, Tui Manu'a; but even a man
could not have been an *ali'i* with European blood in his veins.
And a girl, even if pure Samoan, could not have held this high
position. The Manua group at that time was ruled by Tufele-
Moeveo as supreme *ali'i* of the three islands of Tau, Ofu, and
Olosega.

The white European house with the rose garden in front
where this girl, Makerita (Marguerita), was sitting is still there
and her family still are vainly contending their eligibility to
the title of Tui Manu'a, in defiance of all Samoan traditions.
So far as her going from house to house following a man blowing
a conch shell and not going to neighboring villages because of
arousing jealousy is concerned, this is just a fable for the *papalagi* guests.

As for the riotous behavior of the men fetching the *'ava*—this
solemn ceremony usually is burlesqued for the stranger. If
Louis had gone alone, with proper introduction from an *ali'i* of
Upolu Island, with formal announcement of his coming, he
would have received the *'ava* with all its traditional ceremony,
and the young men would have paid him every respect of
dignified silence and courteous deportment. The *ali'i* of Manua
are so highly regarded by other *ali'i* in all the islands of Samoa
that they are addressed as "Tui Manu'a, thou art my lord!" But
the title of Tui Manu'a was declared vacant at the death of Tui
Manu'a-Elisara in 1880, there being no male heirs to continue
the line.

However, the Manua people were repaid in prankish values
by the people of Tutuila some years later. A woman writer was
visiting in Pago Pago and expressed a desire to go to Manua
when the navy cruiser went across the sixty-odd miles with the

16 *Letters of R. L. S.*, ed. by Colvin, II, 402–405.

mail. It was not explained that this was a regular fortnightly trip; instead, she was told in hushed awe that the Manuans were such a savage people that the navy seldom called there and that she must not risk her life by going ashore. This got into a book she wrote, and it was thought a good joke until Tufele-Fa'toi'a, then *ali'i sili* and *to'o to'o* (supreme chief and orator) of Manua saw it, when he was ready to demonstrate the savagery she had portrayed to the world.

Fa'atoi'a had been called home from school in Hawaii, where he was being groomed as a prospective contender for the pentathlon in the Olympic games, to assume this high office upon the death of his father, Tufele-Moeveo. This aristocratic patriarch was known as the "Iron Man" of Samoa because he refused to cede his island kingdom when Ali'i Mauga of Tutuila bowed to the terms of the Berlin Treaty and gave to the United States his portion of "all Samoa east of the 171st meridian. Yet economic conditions forced him to make this concession in 1904.

A few years ago the Tutuila people played another prank on a foreigner. This man wanted a *matai* title, something to boast about when he returned home, as if *matai* titles were free for the asking. The chiefs conferred solemnly and agreed that there was a vacant title in a village across the island—over the mountains, a good four hours' walk. They would have a great feast for him. Of course, he would furnish the food: two kegs of New Zealand beef; men hired to fish and dig taro—maybe a hundred dollars it would cost. The *papalagi* agreed. It was a great feast. He returned weary but happy. And if he found out before he left that he had been given a girl's name as a title, he did not betray his chagrin.

The stock prank in Apia is to look blank and puzzled when a stranger inquires about the location of Stevenson's burial place. When the stranger adds, "The writer—Robert Louis Stevenson," the Samoans then ask in assumed innoncence, "Was he with Morris, Hedstrom or Burns, Philp [two of the largest trading companies]?"

A British writer recently deplored the ignorance of the young Samoans about their Tusitala! He thought their lack of reverence for his memory was shocking. One cannot wholly approve this attitude of the Samoans even when it is adopted for pure fun; yet Louis with his sense of humor probably would have been the last to condemn it.

News correspondents during World War II were constantly being made the butt of jokes and innocently sending their absurd observations to be broadcast to the world. One such incident occurred just before Christmas. The Samoans recruited as stevedores at Pago Pago to unload and load transports concocted the idea of kneeling and clasping their hands in an attitude of prayer at every mention of the word Christmas. This was broadcast over a nationwide network as a sober fact to demonstrate the piety of the men.

It is more than likely that Louis never would have come as close to the Samoans as he did without a sense of humor in addition to his other qualities that they admired. Early in Vailima days before they had moved into the big house, he visited Tutuila Island with the then new United States consul, Harold Sewall. It was an exploring trip for both, and there is no records of any pranks. Graham Balfour quotes from a diary that Louis kept during what must have been one of his most delightful adventures and which gave him his first contact with real Samoan life.

Of Pago Pago harbor, which geologists say is a submerged volcanic crater, he wrote in his diary:

The island at its highest point is nearly severed in two by the long-elbowed harbour, about half a mile in width, cased everywhere in abrupt mountain-sides. The tongue of water sleeps in perfect quiet, and laps around its continent with the flapping wavelets of a lake. . . . its colour is green like a forest pool, bright in the shallows, dark in the midst with the reflected sides of woody mountains. At times a flicker of silver breaks the uniformity, miniature whitecaps flashing and disappearing on the sombre ground; to see it, you might think the wind was treading on and toeing the flat water, but not so—the harbour lies unshaken, and the flickering is that of fishes.

Right in the wind's eye, and right athwart the dawn, a conspicuous mountain stands, designed like an old fort or castle, with naked cliffy sides and a green head. In the peep of the day the mass is outlined dimly; as the east fires, the sharpness of the silhouette grows indefinite, and through all the chinks of the high wood the red looks through, like coals through a grate. From the other end of the harbour, and at the extreme of the bay, when the sun is down and the night beginning, and colours and shapes at the sea-level are already confounded in the greyness of the dusk, the same peak retains for some time a tinge of phantom rose.[17]

This description of Mount Pioa, called the "Rainmaker" by the Samoans, was continued in a night view, when he wakened before midnight:

I went to the water's edge; the moon was at its zenith; vast fleecy clouds were travelling overhead, their borders frayed and extended as usual in fantastic arms and promontories. The level of their flight is not really high, it only seems so; the trade-wind, although so strong in current, is but a shallow stream, and it is common to see, beyond and above its carry, other clouds faring on other and higher winds. As I looked, the skirt of a cloud touched upon the summit of Pioa, and seemed to hang and gather there, and darken as it hung. I knew the climate, fled to shelter, and was scarce laid down again upon the mat, before the squall burst. . . . All night long the flaws con-

[17] Quoted from Graham Balfour's *The Life of Robert Louis Stevenson,* II, 115–16.

tinued at brief intervals. Morning came, and showed mists on
all the mountain-tops, a grey and yellow dawn, a fresh accumulation of rain imminent on the summit of Pioa, and the whole
harbour scene stripped of its tropic colouring and wearing the
appearance of a Scottish loch.[18]

During their three weeks' stay they made a trip in what Louis
calls a whale-boat to the Bay of Oa, with eight men rowing.
This is probably Aoa Bay, which is at the northeastern tip of
fifteen-mile-long Tutuila Island, which meant a rowing excursion of six or seven miles. But what Louis calls a whale-boat is
not the usual high-sided craft we know as such; it is what the
Samoans term a "long boat," perhaps twenty or thirty feet long,
slender and low in the water, pointed at each end, and easy to
maneuver through rough water. Such boats are of the same
design as the racing craft, or *fautasi,* which are forty and fifty
feet long, with thwarts for fifty or sixty oarsmen. Louis says
they rowed "to the sound of song." These "*ole pesi,*" rowing
songs, are Samoan classics; distances are measured by the
number of verses sung from one point to another as calculated
from "the place where the surf breaks over a hidden rock," or
"where a coconut tree leans far out and drops its fruit into the
sea"—twelve verses to one place, twenty to the next, and so on.
Louis wrote:

No road leads along this coast; we scarce saw a house; these
delectable inlets lay quite desert, inviting seizure, and there was
none like Keats's Endymion to hear our snowlight cadences.
On a sudden we began to open the bay of Oa. At the first sight
my mind was made up—the bay of Oa was the place for me.
We could not enter it, we were assured; and being entered,
we could not land; both statements plainly fictive; both easily
resolved into the fact that there was no guest-house, and no

18 *Ibid.,* 116–17.

girls to make the kava for our boatmen and admire their singing. A little gentle insistence produced a smiling acquiescence, and the eight oars began to urge us slowly into a bay of the *Aeneid*. Right overhead a conical hill arises; its top is all sheer cliff of a rosy yellow, stained with orange and purple, bristled and ivied with individual climbing trees; lower down the woods are massed; lower again the rock crops out in a steep buttress, which divides the arc of beach. The boat was eased in, we landed and turned this way and that like fools in a perplexity of pleasures; now some way into the wood toward the spire, but the woods had soon strangled the path—in the Samoan phrase, the way was dead—and we began to flounder in impenetrable bush, still far from the foot of the ascent, although already the greater trees began to throw out arms dripping with lianas, and to accept us in the margin of their shadows. Now along the beach; it was grown upon with crooked, thick-leaved trees down to the water's edge. Immediately behind there once had been a clearing; it was all choked with the mummy-apple, which in this country springs up at once at the heels of the axeman, and among this were intermingled the coco-palm and the banana. Our landing and the bay itself had nearly turned my head. "Here are the works of all the poets *passim*," I said, and just then my companion stopped. "Behold an omen," said he, and pointed. It was a sight I had heard of before in the islands, but not seen: a little tree such as grow sometimes in infinitesimal islets on the reef, almost stripped of its leaves, and covered instead with feasting butterflies. These, as we drew near, arose and hovered in a cloud of lilac and silver-grey. . . .

All night the crickets sang with a clear trill of silver; all night sea filled the hollow of the bay with varying utterances; now sounding continuously like a mill-weir, now (perhaps from further off) with swells and silences. I went wandering on the beach, when the tide was low. I went round the tree before our boys had stirred. It was the first clear grey of the morning; and I could see them lie, each in his place, enmeshed from head to foot in his unfolded kilt. The Highlander with his belted plaid, the Samoan with his *lavalava,* each sleep in their one vesture unfolded. One boy who slept in the open under the trees, had made his pillow of a smouldering brand, doubtless for the convenience of a midnight cigarette; all night the flame had crept nearer, and as he lay there, wrapped like an oriental woman, and still plunged in sleep, the redness was within two handbreadths of his frizzled hair.

I had scarce bathed, had scarce begun to enjoy the fineness and the precious colours of the morning, the golden glow along the edge of the high eastern woods, the clear light on the sugar-loaf of Maugalai, the woven blue and emerald of the cone, the chuckle of morning bird-song that filled the valley of the woods, when upon a sudden a draught of wind came from the leeward and the highlands of the isle, rain rattled on the tossing woods; the pride of the morning had come early, and from an unlooked-for side. I fled for refuge in the shed; but such of our boys as were awake stirred not in the least; they sat where they were, perched among the scattered boxes of our camp, and puffed at their stubborn cigarettes, and crouched a little in the slanting shower. So good a thing it is to wear few clothes. I, who was largely unclad—a pair of serge trousers, a singlet, woolen socks, and canvas shoes; think of it—envied them in their light array. Thursday.—The others withdrew to the next village. Meanwhile I had Virgil's bay all morning to myself, and feasted on solitude, and overhanging woods, and the retiring sea. The quiet was only broken by the hoarse cooing of wild pigeons up the valley, and certain inroads of capricious winds that found a way hence and thence down the hillside and set the palms clattering; my enjoyment only disturbed by clouds of dull, voracious, spotted, and not particularly envenomed mosquitoes. When I was still, I kept Buhac powder burning by me on a stone under the shed, and read Livy, and confused to-day and two thousand years ago, and wondered in which of these epochs I was flourishing at that moment; and then I would stroll out, and see the rocks and woods, and the arcs of beaches, curved like a whorl in a fair woman's ear, and huge ancient trees, jutting high overhead out of the hanging forest, and feel the place at least belonged to the age of fable, and waited Aeneas and his battered fleets.

Showers fell often in the night; some sounding from far off like a cataract, some striking the house, but not a drop came in. . . . At night a cry of a wild cat-like creature in the bush. Far up on the hill one golden tree; they say it is a wild coconut: I know it is not, they must know so too; and this leaves me free to think it sprang from the gold bough of Proserpine.[19]

Into these few brief paragraphs Louis packed only a hint of the ecstasy of thought and feeling which reach the heights of quiet exultation that come to one in solitude. We may call it communing with nature or any other poetic term, but it really is divesting one's self, for a precious and timeless hour, of the ego we call our personality and living in the naked self among the richest blessings of Demeter.

Back in Apia Louis wrote: "It is like a fairy-story that I should have recovered liberty and strength, and should go around among my fellow-men, boating, riding, bathing, toiling hard with a wood-knife in the forest."

And the Greek goddess scarcely could have given to the traveler in her fruitful land more strength of body and spirit than did those days of association with the eight bronze Herculeses who rowed sixteen or eighteen miles, out and return, around Tutuila's rocky coast; who cooked their meals, slept in the open, and sang and laughed and joked about the "wild coconut tree" and heaven knows what else, although never to the

19 *Ibid.*, 118–21.

point of impertinence. These young men would have been the crack oarsmen of Pago Pago, probably leaders of a rowing team who are trained for the annual *fautasi* races. With Louis's intense admiration of masculine strength and endurance, denied to him by his lung condition, and his sense of fun, these young gods of nature must have made, consciously or unconsciously, a lasting impression on his mind and lightened many an hour of work, as well as contributing to what later became ardent partisanship in the Samoan cause.

Graham Balfour, in his *Life of Robert Louis Stevenson,* says Louis and Mr. Sewall were twenty-eight hours in an open boat on their return trip from Pago Pago to Apia, a distance of only sixty-five miles, intimating the hardship of exposure and rough water. True, the sea is rough because of a peculiar meeting of north and south currents, but an open boat in the warmth of tropical night and the balmy Trades of day would be no hardship, and the schooner must have been slow indeed to take such a length of time for so short a distance.

However, Louis returned in one of his periods of excellent health and with a becoming increase in weight. Much has been written about his slender build. Mrs. Field said that his slimness was as much in his bones as in lack of flesh; that he never appeared gaunt except after an illness, and she never saw him walk across the broad slope of the Vailima lawn that she was not struck by the graceful swing of his stride and his easy, erect carriage.

In the "Skerryvore" days at Bournemouth, a newspaper assignment sent the English etcher and painter, William Strang of Dunbarton, to make a line portrait of R. L. S. He described Louis to Neil Munro:

"Funny looking fellow, Robert Louis!" he related; "long art-looking black hair hanging down to his shoulders—velveteen jacket, crimson shawl or muffler stretched loosely over his chest

—very big eyes with an extraordinary width between them—seemed to be on the outside of his temples, as it were, and as if they stood on stalks. Pale, pasty face, though not thin, yet his body was as thin as a match, and his legs looked like drumsticks inside his breeks."[20]

Then Morley Roberts once told about his visit in Samoa describing Stevenson tersely as so thin that his body "looked like a mere frame for holding up his eyes."

Louis had a definite degree of vanity. "Yet," Teuila added, "he was not vain—if this is not too paradoxical to be understandable. He derived considerable amusement from comments about his appearance, which humor did not extend to his mother and the Samoan houseboys. Yet when he would walk across the room with knees stiff and legs swinging from the hips as if he were walking on stilts, even they could not help laughing."

Samoans never see their *ali'i* in other than a dignified pose. Once elected to this high position, they are regarded in what might be termed beneficent awe, and how this *papalagi matai* Tusitala could swing from clowning to dignity, as he would change a *lavalava*, puzzled them thoroughly. To one held in lesser regard it could have meant forfeiture of esteem. However, in breaking down this exalted opinion of their rulers, Louis was unconsciously aiding the Samoans, for it was at this time that foreign powers were inflicting their worst possible punishment—humiliating their *ali'i* by robbing them of their traditional leadership. Once home from the day's work at Vailima, the boys related every detail as the evening's topic of conversation, to be told and retold to neighbors the next day.

Louis was ignorant of his influence, seeing rather the greater menace of traditions' being torn apart by commercial greed; but once he became sufficiently familiar with the language and secure against misunderstanding, he became imbued with the

[20] Neil Munro, *The Brave Days* (Edinburgh, The Porpoise Press, 1931).

desire to do what he could to right the wrongs brought by Western civilization and its attendant oppression. And his own work was heavy.

It was the close of 1892 before the big house, painted dark olive green with red corrugated iron roof, was finished to Louis's satisfaction. The addition gave the lower floor the great forty-by sixty-foot hall with its polished walls of California redwood, which still must be as beautiful as when they were first erected. There were five airy bedrooms and a library upstairs. But the library where Louis planned to work was darkened by the wide veranda, so he had half of the balcony enclosed, with wide windows on two sides, one French door opening into the library, another onto the veranda.

This was his bedroom as well, and here, in seclusion from the rest of the household, he spent the precious hours of early morning propped up in bed with his writing pad on his knees. He always had preferred a hard bed, but now the family persuaded him to have springs and mattress, and he admitted it was much more comfortable. Talolo brought tea and toast at daybreak, which within these few degrees south of the Equator varies only a few minutes before or after six o'clock the year round; then he remained undisturbed until luncheon time unless some matter came up for immediate decision that Fanny could not fend off.

However, if dictation had been decided upon as the order of the day, Teuila would go along at the appointed hour, never before the time set unless summoned. Louis did not dictate rapidly, for Teuila wrote in longhand, but he was sure and rarely made changes. She laughed as she recalled her reputation for bad spelling and how Louis spelled out words such as "seize" and "siege." There was never any other than bits of desultory conversation during work, although Louis wrote facetiously in a letter to J. M. Barrie: "The Amanuensis states that you are a lover of silence—and that ours is a noisy house—and she is a chatter-box. I am not answerable for these statements, though

I do think there is a touch of garrulity about my premises. We have so little to talk about, you see." This was when he was urging Barrie to make a visit to Vailima. "Come," he wrote, "it will broaden your mind, and be the making of me."[21]

But when Louis was lost in thought, the "chatter-box" sat silent on one of the two deal chairs, which with his bed and table comprised the whole of the furnishings of his room, and waited for the next low-spoken sentence. There is an expression in the South Seas that one learns to live a "thirty-minute hour"; Louis, unless in the heat of some new plot, learned to employ this moderation of time, to listen to the calls of birds, the sighing of wind through the heavy-leafed breadfruit trees and the crisp rattle of drying palm fronds, and always, always the ceaseless moaning of a tireless surf.

Along the wall beside his bed were shelves of books—poems, essays, and his favorite histories—and on the opposite wall three of his best-loved etchings. One window looked out across the wide slope of lawn and over the treetops to the sea; the other up the wooded steep of Mount Vaea, later conceded to be within the original boundary of the land he purchased. And contrary to reports that he wished his final resting place to be in his beloved homeland, Teuila said positively that he made the wish, as he gazed on the summit of Vaea, that this should be his burial place.

There were two rather serious drawbacks to this veranda room. The corrugated iron roof made it hot in the middle of the day, and it was within sight and hearing of arriving guests. Some member of the family always was available to entertain a visitor, giving Louis time to come downstairs if he could leave his work; if not, the guest was speeded on his way after a refreshing drink of beer or lemon squash. Occasionally, if Louis was reading and not yet dressed—callers come early in the tropics—a guest would be summoned to his room; then he would

21 *Letters of R. L. S.*, ed. by Colvin, II, 333.

close the book in hand and lay it aside at arm's length—the ultimate in listening courtesy, which he employed even when a member of the family dropped in.

Aside from *Footnote to History*, with its embroilment of Samoan difficulties and wrangling of the Three Powers, Louis's most serene periods were when he was deep in composition. He wrote with the air of having a perfectly grand time—with the possible exception of *Master of Ballantrae* which but for the lack of time might have been one of the most skillful stories he ever created—that is, from the point of plot and characters and the indulgence of licensed literary extravagance.

Such stories as "The Wrecker" and "Ebb Tide" lacked the thrill of composition since they were done in collaboration with Lloyd Osbourne and were more or less mechanical in working toward a logical climactic ending. *The Wrong Box* was entirely Lloyd's in the original draft written at Saranac when he was only nineteen. But following the completion of *Master of Ballantrae* in Honolulu, Louis put it in shape for publication. Edmund Gosse, in his introduction to this work in the Pentland edition, cites Lloyd's comment, "He breathed into it, of course, his own incomparable power, humour, and vivacity, and forced the thing to live as it had never lived before."

Perhaps this was a time when Louis preferred these lighter tasks, for the Samoan political pot was boiling ever more furiously. He was growing more and more proficient in the language and was endearing himself to the Samoans by his almost daily rides on Jack, the pony, out to their villages, where he would hold long conferences with the *ali'i;* sometimes remaining overnight and sleeping on a *laufala* rug on the floor of the *fale,* covered with a handsome piece of *siapo.*

This is not like sleeping on a hardwood floor. The rugs, or mats, are woven of the *laufala* and spread two or three thick on the floor of coral pebbles that give slightly to the contour of the body, and the covering of *siapo* is ideal because, unlike a linen sheet, it does not cling to the body and so provides for ventilation through the warm, often muggy, night, yet keeps out any errant breeze.

It was during these intimate visits that the Samoans began to use the name of "Tusi," or "Tala." The name was bestowed on Louis when Rev. J. E. Newell introduced him to his class in journalism at the Malua school of the London Missionary Society. The words are practically synonymous or, more properly, repetitious. Both are verbs as well as nouns. *Tusi* the noun is a writing or a letter; the verb is "to write." *Tala* the verb is "to tell" or relate; the noun, a tale or narration. *Tala'i* is to proclaim; *talaoso* is to gossip; *talaloa* is to talk quietly as friends stroll along the road; and *talafa'atupua* means to relate a legend or incident in history as the *Tu'ua* (old men of history) instruct the young men of the *'Aumaga*—the Society of Young Men— who function as a fraternity and are quite as smug as any college club. Old men proudly term them "the future of Samoa." For all its high place in the Samoan language, the word is reckoned to be of Malayan origin and was one of many picked up by the Polynesians during their centuries of migration across southern India.

It was these visits to the *faoa'a'ai*—villages, or estates of the *ali'i*—that prompted Louis's letters to the *London Times* and brought down upon his head the wrath of Judge Cedercrantz, Swedish chief justice, and the German president of the Council, Baron Senfft von Pilsach, when he accused their government of being only a "still-born child and except for some spasmodic movements, may be said to have done nothing but pay salaries" —these to themselves, which resulted in a depleted treasury. He challenged them by what powers of law they reversed a verbal public decision of the court of the year previous without a public hearing; he accused them of collusion, or the appearance of collusion, in handling public funds and of thwarting customs duties on their own imports, and of manipulating the affairs of the Council in secret sessions.

The letters to the *Times* began when Louis still was in Hawaii, and were written in general criticism of the government that was fastening its tentacles upon a helpless people. When he went to Apia and wrote *Footnote to History*, he honestly tried to speak for the Samoan people. Even the British consul called him an "eccentric meddler." When he appeared before the Municipal Council meetings, he was given only scant courtesy and his pleas for justice for the Samoans were ignored, even by men who professed to be his friends.

Angered and humiliated by these rebuffs, he wrote in one *Times* letter, "Surely in all Europe there must be two honest men who could be sent to administer the government of Samoa." And referring to the *Times* readers, he said in another letter, "This account [his letter regarding the *matai* and *faipule* (chiefs of lesser rank) who had been banished to the adjacent island of Manono] seems to have caused more amusement than concern. Well, it is not amusing to us here."

Then rumors began to circulate that official Apia would like to see this "eccentric meddler" out of the scene. Deportation was hinted. Suits for libel were threatened. Mrs. Field said that Louis apparently was not worried by these attempts at intimidation, and not even the family knew that he had taken the precaution—at least presumably a precaution—to transfer his title to the Vailima property to James Baxter, his business manager in Edinburgh. This was done by deed registered on March 28, 1892, in the Lands and Titles Office in Apia.

In the meantime the Municipal Council, in order to "protect" themselves, drafted a special ordinance requesting Louis's removal on the grounds that he was a disturbing element in Samoan affairs and dispatched it to London, where it was ignored by the British government as being illegal. Rid of these plaguing menaces, Louis turned the full blast of his denunciation upon the representatives of the Three Powers, the while continuing to ride his frisky Jack, who would prance and gallop along the slippery trails and "had a habit of shieing at everything along the road, even a bunch of bananas, and of sitting down on his tail."

Of Baron Senfft von Pilsach, he wrote, "He has shown that he neither understands nor yet is willing to be taught the condition of this country."[22] And further:

. . . but the cure of our troubles must come from home; it is from the Great Powers that we look for deliverance. They sent us the President. Let them either remove the man, or see that he is stringently instructed—instructed to respect public decency, so we will no longer be menaced with doings worthy of a revolutionary committee; and instructed to respect and administer the law, so if I be fined a dollar to-morrow for fast riding in Apia street, I may not awake next morning to find my sentence increased to one of banishment or death by dynamite.

P. S. I little expected further developments before the mail left. But the unresting President still mars the quiet of his neighbours. Even while I was writing the above lines, Apia was looking on in mere amazement on the continuation of his gambols. A white man had written to the King, and the King had answered the letter—crimes against Baron Senfft von Pilsach and (his private reading of) the Berlin Treaty. He offered to resign— I was about to say "accordingly," for the unexpected is here the normal—from the presidency of the municipal board, and to retain his position as the King's adviser. He was instructed that he must resign both, or neither; resigned both; fell out with the Consuls on details; and is now, as we are advised, seeking to resign from his resignations. Such an official I never remember to have read of, though I have seen the like, from across

22 *Letters from Samoa* (vol. XVII, Pentland ed. of *Works*), 352.

the footlights and the orchestra, evolving in similar figures to the strains of Offenbach.[23]

Still pounding away in his letters to the *Times*, Louis wrote on April 9, 1892:

Sirs,—A sketch of our latest difficulty in Samoa will be interesting, at least to lawyers. In the Berlin General Act there is one point on which, from the earliest moment, volunteer interpreters have been divided. The revenue arising from the customs was held by one party to belong to the Samoan Government, by another to the municipality; and the dispute was at last decided in favour of the municipality by Mr. Cedercrantz, Chief Justice. The decision was not given in writing; but it was reported by at least one of the Consuls to his Government, it was of public notoriety, it is not denied, and it was at once implicitly acted on by the parties.

Before that decision, the revenue from customs was suffered to accumulate; ever since, to the knowledge of the Chief Justice, and with the daily countenance of the President, it has been received, administered, and spent by the municipality. It is the function of the Chief Justice to interpret the Berlin Act; its sense was thus supposed to be established beyond cavil; those who were dissatisfied with the result conceived their only recourse lay in prayer to the Powers to have the treaty altered; and such a prayer was, but the other day, proposed, supported, and finally negatived, in a public meeting.

About a year has gone by since the decision, and the state of the Samoan government has been daily growing more precarious. Taxes have not been paid, and the Government has not ventured to enforce them. Fresh taxes have fallen due, and the Government has not ventured to call for them. Salaries were running on, and that of the Chief Justice alone amounts to a

[23] *Ibid.*, 354–55.

considerable figure for these islands; the coffers had fallen low, at last it was believed they were quite empty, no resource seemed left, and bystanders waited with a smiling curiosity for the wheels to stop. . . .

In this state of matters, on March 28th, the President of the Council, Baron Senfft von Pilsach, was suddenly and privately supplied by Mr. Cedercrantz with a written judgment, reversing the verbal and public decision of a year before. By what powers of law was this result attained? And how was the point brought again before his Honour? I feel I shall here strain the credulity of your readers, but our authority is the President in person. The suit was brought by himself in the capacity (perhaps an imaginary one) of King's adviser; it was defended by himself in his capacity of President of the Council, no notice had been given, the parties were not summoned, they were advised neither of the trial nor the judgment; so far as can be learned, two persons only met and parted—the first was the plaintiff and the defendant rolled in one, the other was a Judge who had decided black a year ago, and now intimated a modest willingness to decide white. But it is possible to follow more closely these original proceedings. Baron von Pilsach sat down (he told us) in his capacity of adviser to the King, and wrote to himself, in his capacity of President of the Council, an eloquent letter of reprimand three pages long; an unknown English artist clothed it for him in good language; and nothing remained but to have it signed by King Malietoa, to whom it was attributed. "So long as he knows how to sign!"—a white official is said thus to have summed up, with a shrug, the qualifications necessary in a Samoan king. It was signed accordingly, though whether the King knew what he was signing is matter of debate; and thus regularised, it was forwarded to the Chief Justice enclosed in a letter of adhesion from the President. Such as they were, they seem to have been the documents in this unusual cause.[24]

To Louis's inherent sense of fair play, this was shocking; to his legal training, the juggling with jurisprudence made oaths of office a travesty. It was revealed that the president of the Council and the chief justice had for the past year secretly spent the customs money; they themselves had paid no duties on their own imports. Citizens of Apia demanded an accounting, and Louis had no small part in this investigation. He comments, "The position of the President is thus extremely exposed." And speaking of the depleted treasury, he says further:

. . . who shall not in the hour of their destitution, seem to have diverted six hundred pounds of public money for the purchase of an inconsiderable sheet, or at a time when eight provinces of discontented natives threaten at any moment to sweep their ineffective Government into the sea to have sought safety and strength in gagging the local press of Apia. If it be otherwise—if we cannot be relieved, if the Powers are satisfied with the conduct of Mr. Cedercrantz and Baron Senfft von Pilsach; if these were sent here with the understanding that they should secretly purchase, perhaps privately edit, a little sheet of two pages, issued from a crazy wooden building at the mission gate; if it were, indeed, intended that, for this important end, they should divert (as it seems they have done) public funds and affront all the forms of law—we whites can only bow the head. We are here quite helpless. If we would complain of Baron Pilsach, it can only be to Mr. Cedercrantz, and the Powers will not hear us, the circle is complete. A nightly guard surrounds and protects their place of residence, while the house of the King is cynically left without the pickets. Secure from interference, one utters the voice of the law, the other moves the hands of authority; and now they seem to have sequestered in the course of a single week the only available funds and the only existing paper in the islands.

24 *Ibid.,* 360 ff.

But there is one thing they forgot. It is not the whites who menace the duration of their Government, and it is only the whites who read the newspaper. Mata'afa sits hard by in his armed camp and sees. He sees the weakness, he counts the scandals of their Government. He sees his rival and his "brother" sitting disconsidered at their doors, like Lazarus before the house of Dives, and, if he is not very fond of his "brother," he is very scrupulous of native dignities. He has seen his friends menaced with midnight destruction in the Government gaol, and deported without form of law.

He is not himself a talker, and his thoughts are hid from us; but what is said by his more hasty partisans we know. On March 29, the day after the Chief Justice signed the secret judgment, three days before it was made public, and while the purchase of the newspaper was yet in treaty, a native orator stood up in an assembly. "Who asked the Great Powers to make laws for us; to bring strangers here to rule us?" he cried. "We want no white officials to bind us in the bondage of taxation." Here is the changed spirit which these gentlemen have produced by a misgovernment of fifteen months. Here is their peril, which no purchase of newspapers and no subsequent editorial suppressions can avert.[25]

April, May, and most of June passed, for mail was slow in these days of the nineties; then on June 22, Louis wrote again to the *Times:*

Sir,—I read in a New Zealand paper that you published my last with misgiving. The writer then goes on to remind me that I am a novelist, and to bid me return to my romances and leave the affairs of Samoa to sub-editors in distant quarters of the world. "We, in common with other journals, have correspondents in Samoa," he complains, "and yet we have no news from

[25] *Ibid.,* 368 ff.

them of the curious conspiracy which Mr. Stevenson appears
to have unearthed, and which, if it had any real existence, would
be known to everybody on the island."

As this is the only voice which has yet reached me from beyond the seas, I am constrained to make some answer. But it
must not be supposed that, though you may perhaps have been
alone to publish, I have been alone to write. The same story is
now in the hands of the three Governments from their respective Consuls. Not only so, but the complaint of the municipal
council, drawn by two able solicitors, has been likewise laid
before them.

This at least is public, and I may say notorious. The solicitors
were authorised to proceed with their task at a public meeting.
The President (for I was there and heard him) approved the
step, though he refrained from voting. But he seems to have
entertained a hope of burking, or, at least indefinitely post-
poning, the whole business, and, when the meeting was over
and its proceedings had been approved (as is necessary) by the
Consular Board, he neglected to notify the two gentlemen
appointed of that approval. In a large city the trick might have
succeeded for a time; in a village like Apia, where all news
leaks out and the King meets the cobbler daily, it did no more
than to advertise his own artfulness. And the next he learned,
the case of the municipal council had been prepared, approved
by the Consuls, and despatched to the Great Powers.

I am accustomed to have my word doubted in this matter,
and must here look to have it doubted once again. But the
fact is certain. The two solicitors (Messrs. Carruthers and
Cooper) were actually cited to appear before the Chief Justice
in the Supreme Court. I have seen the summons, and the summons was the first and last of this State trial. The proceeding,
instituted in an hour of temper, was, in a moment of reaction,
allowed to drop.[26]

[26] *Ibid.*, 371.

It is a sad commentary on the so-called newspaper correspondents in Samoa that Louis was the only person with the forthrightness and courage to expose the chicanery of these officials in this and many other acts of double-dealing. And it took real courage and daring to expose fellow townsmen whom one met on every trip to town and at every social gathering. It is one thing to meet an arch enemy on a crowded thoroughfare, quite another for protagonists to meet on a wide, empty street with men standing in doorways watching for an untoward word or gesture. Louis never failed in a polite salutation. Small wonder that the Samoan *ali'i* came to look upon him as their one real friend. It was not until April 23, 1894, that he wrote of the departure of Baron Senfft von Pilsach and the demotion of Judge Cedercrantz to the status of a private citizen with the closing of his court. War between the forces of Mata'afa and those of Malietoa, reinforced by men from Savaii, had turned the whole island of Upolu into seething bush maneuvers, and all the European population of Apia were frightened into unaccustomed meekness by the contention.

The largest men in all Samoa—probably the largest in Polynesia—come from Savaii Island, westernmost of the Samoan group. Averaging well over six feet in height, erect, broad shouldered, lean flanked, with the stride of kings, they could strike terror to the bravest heart as, with faces painted, they rushed their enemy with war clubs swinging to their thunderous chant of battle. German plantation overseers fled for their lives, either to Apia or to the more secure shelter of British-owned plantations, leaving their livestock and their Solomon Island slaveboys to shift for themselves.

Even now, to see these men of magnificent stature on Savaii Island two and three hundred strong, gathered from every village from Sapalili on the east to Falialupo on the west, because to see them with drums and war chants and *sivas* that seem fairly to make the earth vibrate with the rhythmic stamping of bare feet on the hard ground of the *malie* in festive revival of their ancient "sports," is to watch fascinated while shivers ripple up one's spine in anticipatory headlessness from a savage-swinging war club.

Vailima, near the middle of the island of Upolu, was directly between the warring forces of Mata'afa and Malietoa. Mata'afa on the west end got the aid of these men from Savaii, but his district was not so populous and Malietoa had greater numbers of fighters. Yet the Stevensons saw only scattered guerrilla raiders who occasionally took a short cut across their property for a sneak attack on the enemy. Both chiefs had placed a tabu on the *fao'a'ai* of their friend, and any violation of this royal edict would have meant certain death and a disgrace to the whole village whence any offender came.

Louis did not know that this had been done, or would be done, and he had procured firearms for every member of the family in event of trouble; he often expressed anxiety because their house was wide open to attack. Yet throughout all the months of disturbance, he had communication by secret messengers with both Mata'afa and Malietoa camps, both men recognizing his fidelity to the Samoan people and his sympathy for the cause which had brought about this civil conflict.

Fighting was without pattern and consequently more dangerous to noncombatants. Firearms were limited in the Mata'afa ranks to the comparatively few that were smuggled in by daring boatmen who paid nightly visits to the customs dock at Apia. Even then they were often unable to get ammunition. Since there were no organized battle troops, each group of twenty, thirty, or forty would kill where and when they could and by whatever means was available. Ancient fighting with knives and clubs, which in former times was regarded by young men more as a sport than as warfare, was abandoned in favor of sniping from the hilltops or from hideaways in the thick undergrowth of the bush.

Heads of victims were brought in and displayed as trophies, having been cut from dead bodies and held as means of identification. The higher the victim's rank, the greater the glory of conquest. Louis cites the hysterical rumor in Apia that a *taupou's* head was brought in. No Samoan will verify this story, and Louis said, "There had never yet, in the history of Samoa, occurred an instance in which a man had taken a woman's head and kept it and laid it at his monarch's feet." Admitting that in the frenzy of battle when they would have stormed into a village where the dead had been abandoned, a woman's head might possibly have been taken in error, it would have been buried immediately to conceal the shame of inadvertence. To have exhibited it as a trophy would have cost a man his life; or if he had succeeded in escaping to another island, his *masiasi*, disgrace, would follow him all the days of his life, and his entire family would suffer equal humiliation. Of such sternness is the moral code of primitive people composed.

It is true that a *taupou*—beauty girl of the village—is always associated with war, although never outside the boundary of her father's domain. It is one of her duties to lead the men in an inspirational war *siva* as they assemble for departure, for she is cherished for her virginal purity, representing their ideal of femininity, and is strictly tabu to the amorous attention of any one man. She is constantly under the surveillance of a *tufale ta'i ta'i*, chaperone and teacher, and from early childhood has been carefully instructed in ceremonial *sivas*, and ranks next to the *ali'i sili* in entertaining guests and performing the ritualistic mixing of the *'ava* which is served at the opening of the chief's *fono*. Not even her mother outranks her in these royal formalities. And, on the most jubilant occasion of all, she leads thirty or forty gaily costumed girls in songs and *sivas* to celebrate the return of the warriors to their home villages. So Louis was right in putting the stamp of hysterical exaggeration on this story of the *taupou's* head as a trophy of war.

In the initial stages of this desultory bush fighting the consuls of the Three Powers stood supinely by, not even permitting
the famously eloquent and powerful Lauaki to mediate the differences between the warring factions. German, British, and
United States warships were anchored out in the Apia roadstead
like so many bullies. At last one German ship, with the excuse
of protecting its nationals' plantation properties, steamed along
the coast to the westward firing salvos into Mata'afa's territory.
Beyond frightening the whole countryside out of their collective
wits, little damage was done, since the coral reef, nearly two
miles wide, kept the warship well offshore.

But it did, as intended, send Mata'afa fleeing to Manono, the
little "garden island" two miles off the western point of Upolu.
From the village of Mulifanua eight men rowed him across in
a "long boat," as ten years previously Malietoa had been rowed
across to escape the warring followers of Tamasese, who was
a tool of the Germans under Theodor Weber of the D. H. & P. G.
Company. Weber had ordered Malietoa off his home site on
Mulinuu because he wanted it for his own house.

Manono is a tiny jewel-like island three miles around and
half a mile across. Villages planted with flowers—hibiscus and
tall stalks of red ginger—garland the shore line, flashing from
beneath trees that fairly touch the water; the air is sweet with
heavily scented frangipani and the delicately elusive *moisoi*.
It is rather densely populated, for the soil is rich, and taro fields
reach to the top of the one promontory which is less than two
hundred feet high. At night when darkness hides the flowers,
the island is rimmed with burning *tafuna'i*, fire-pits into which
the trash of the day has been dumped and lighted after the
wind has died down. They are beacons to warn sailors off the
reefs as well as to welcome tired fishermen home from sea.
Into this sanctuary Mata'afa fled. Only women and children
were there; their menfolk were fighting on Upolu.

But the Germans wanted Mata'afa so badly that they sent

three warships to this little defenseless island to capture him. When the gold-braided officer was rowed ashore, Mata'afa met him on the beach. With a quiet farewell to the people of the *faoa'a'ai* who had sheltered him, he went aboard the dark-hulled ship. His heart sank as he watched boats from other ships lowered and head for shore. It was mid-morning and there was little breeze, but he was ordered below in the stifling heat. Night was just approaching when the anchors were finally weighed and he was permitted to come on deck again.

One glance at the little island and he stood horrified. As far as he could see around the beach every beautiful thatched *fale* was in flames. Great bare spaces showed where breadfruit and coconut trees had been cut down; black places on the hillside marked the destruction of banana and taro patches. He turned to the captain to stop this wanton devastation; he pleaded for the safety of women and children; he met only stony-hearted insolence.

When Mata'afa followers heard of this outrage, especially the mistreatment of the women and girls, many of whom had been sent from Upolu to Manono for safety, the giants from Savaii went berserk. Forsaking all restraint, they burned all the buildings on German plantations, killed the horses and cattle and pigs, killed dogs and cats, and felled hundreds of coconut trees. They had the whole populace in terror. Many Germans fled to the safety of the warship anchored in the harbor. Both British and German ships began throwing shells into the hills.

Back in the harbor of Apia, Mata'afa was allowed, under guard, to go ashore to bid *tofa* to his people. He was to be exiled. A quiet taumafatoga (feast of love) was spread for him by friends and relatives and former foes, and he was formally served with the traditional *sau taute* (food of kings) by the young men of the 'Aumaga. The entire company were weeping as the *ali'i sili* asked the blessings of *Tagaloa* on their revered and beloved chief.

No more sorrowful scene is recorded in Samoan history than the farewell between the people and their *ali'i* as he was ordered aboard the warship with destination a mystery. Only Louis had the courage to protest. He went to Chief Justice Henry Clay Ide, lately raised to this position by President Cleveland from his former post as land commissioner, and even there he met with no hope of judicial co-operation. Louis, on the day previous, when he had heard of the lawless destruction of property and the outrages against women on Manono, had gone to the German commander to ask details and was met by an insulting shrug of uniformed shoulders and a casual admission that a few "huts" had been burned as an example to the people.

Then, as never before, the Samoans realized that Tusitala was their sole mediator. Mata'afa had embraced the Christian religion and for many years had been a staunch supporter of the London Missionary Church and its two schools. Now, accompanied by his brother, who had begged to be taken with him, Mata'afa asked the weeping crowd along the shore to pray for him in the name of their ancestral *tagaloa* of *Lagi* that their God of Heaven would in his mercy restore and heal their broken bonds of blood and fellowship. He implored them to abide in peace among themselves and obey the laws of the conquerors in order to avoid further bloodshed. With upraised hands he bade *tofa soifua* ("good-bye and my blessing") and with superb dignity turned to walk between his two guards to the rowboat that took him to the warship.

So was written one of the black pages of so-called Western civilization, staining hearts with hatred for generations to come.

Why the Germans took the old man first to New Zealand, then to England, then to Germany, as if peddling him out to some nation for incarceration is beyond comprehension. He was without the status of an acknowledged enemy of any country. Their act was a violation of international protocol and showed a disregard of humanitarian consideration for a royal personage. Finally, after months of unaccustomed living on shipboard and heretofore unknown rigors of cold weather, the old man was brought back to the South Pacific. Not to the home islands for which his heart was sick. Oh, no; not that!

They took him to Jaluit atoll in the Marshall group of Micronesia—low, sparsely wooded, and unattractive, with only brackish water from the wide central lagoon in place of the pure mountain water of home. Among people speaking a strange tongue, the now frail man was completely beaten. His daughter and several Samoan men of rank asked, and were permitted, to go to him. Louis asked the privilege of sending 'ava roots and tobacco, and was denied.

In a barbwire enclosure back of Apia there were imprisoned about fifty high chiefs, chiefs and *matai* who were followers of Mata'afa, but whose only crime was defiance of German orders to disperse. Their relatives were required to provide food, even water for bathing, and clean *lavalavas*. Louis asked the privilege of sending food and coconuts for drinking water from Vailima. His aid was declined. Therefore, he surreptitiously sent deep-sea fishermen for barracuda, and his own boys searched Vailima bush for bananas and papayas.

The family worried about his health, he was in such a state of continual rage. At last, grimly and without the usual family consultation, he announced a definite plan to restore the ravaged spirits of the prisoners. He asked the house boys to find twenty strong men for two days of hard work. No word was to be said about what they were to do, not even to their families to account for their absence. Then in pairs he set them to their tasks.

A large *umu* (ground oven) was to be dug in the bush at the rear of the kitchen; two men were to chop wood and gather porous stones for the *umu*. Skilled fishermen went to sea for barracuda and baby shark; the land was plundered for bananas, breadfruit, maume apple, mangoes, and papayas. Younger men climbed the trees for coconuts, green ones for vessels for drinking water and ripe ones for grating the meat and squeezing the cream; yams and taro were dug and cleaned. Two of Fanny's choicest young pigs were slaughtered and dressed; sheaves of *laufala* were cut and made into individual *laulaus* (trays) for serving the food; and baskets for carrying the food were made of strong palm fronds.

Louis had been hurrying from one sweating group to another until Fanny felt obliged to relinquish her self-imposed ban against scolding and remind him that if he didn't live to see this thing through, he would miss all the fun. Excitement such as he was suffering could easily bring on a hemorrhage.

At last, however, all the food was assembled, and in the dark of early night the fire in the *umu* was filling the air with the betraying fragrance of burning wood. Tired men took turns sleeping in the warmth of the fire. The Vailima house was dark. About midnight the stones shone red hot amid the ashes. The pigs, wrapped in plantain leaves with small stones inside for even roasting, were put in first; then fish, each wrapped separately, were placed at one end, with taro, yams, and green bananas at the other. Quickly the whole was covered with heavy *laufala* mats and sheets of *siapo*, then banked with clean earth. One man was left on watch while the others slept, each taking a brief turn of sleepy-eyed duty.

Shortly before daybreak a thin spiral of white smoke signaled that the heat was gone and the food cooked. By mid-morning baskets were filled, suspended on poles, and the men were ready to march single file, each pair with a bending pole from shoulder to shoulder. At the leader's signal each caught an easy rhythmic stride, and their voices rose in the chant of the march of the *sau taute*—sacred food of kings! Lloyd walked behind the men. Louis rode Jack. No women were permitted.

Louis was prepared to be halted as they passed through the street of Apia, but he vetoed the carrying of war clubs. The

Germans may have been too surprised to interfere, or perhaps they did not grasp the significance of the *sua taute*. Louis's triumph was complete.

The feast did exactly what Louis had hoped—roused public opinion against this flagrantly cruel indignity and shamed the Apia council into releasing the men. Within a week they were at home with their families, not as returning convicts but as heroes created by Louis with his gesture of esteem. They had thought of him as a good friend; now he was their god. And the faith that Mata'afa had in his opinions of Samoan political affairs is demonstrated by the letters he wrote from his refuge in Malie, a translation of one of which follows with Louis's reply:

GOVERNMENT OF SAMOA

Malie 8 June 1892

His Excellency Tusi Tala

Your Excellency!

I might be better if I sent you the copy of my overture which I just sent to Malietoa Laupepa of Mulinuu since I strongly desire the peace and reconciliation of Samoa. You may read and concentrate upon it.

May you ever live.
Your true friend
I. E. M. Mata'afa
King of Samoa[27]

Tanumaleko
9 June, 1892

His Majesty Malietoa Mata'afa,
   Malie.
Your Majesty:
   I am very glad to tell you that the British man-of-war *Curaçao*

[27] Translation by Maea'eofe.

arrived on Tuesday. The British chief justice, the British land judge and examiner in Tutuila, and I have talked over a problem concerning the examination of lands in those islands [Eastern Samoa—Tutuila, Aunuu, Tau, Ofu, and Olosega]. You have nothing to fear, for I have convinced the chief justice that the Three Powers [Germany, Great Britain, and the United States] should not hurt the Samoans.

I have read your well-written overture to Malietoa Laupepa. I congratulate you on your kindness and astuteness. May God fulfill your desire in peace.

There are two white men of Mulinu'u who have disagreed with Malietoa Laupepa because he never repented when the Chief Prince gave up his honor of advising the King; this honor is granted to Mepi, a land examiner. This is my opinion: Mepi is not to be suspected; he speaks frankly to you. If both of the white men in Mulinu'u are inconsistent, I know that I would rather not trust them.

May you ever live.

Your true friend,

Tusitala

P. S. A certain white man named Cabell wrote to Great Britain asking whether they needed the bark of the *u'a* tree for any purpose. We were told in a letter of Mr. Moors who had delivered the answer to Cabel.

Forgive me for my many mistakes.

Such correspondence, carried to and fro by foot messengers, reveals the role that Louis could have played in an amicable solution of native problems had the Powers possessed the prescience to recognize and use his friendly influence. Even Sir John Thurston of Fiji, at that time highest representative of British interests in the Pacific, brushed him off as a romantic idealist.

However, like a cyclone that whips up out of varying air pressures and blows itself out when the center calm is broken, the civil war died lingeringly after the deportation of Mata'afa. Malietoa was proclaimed king by the three consuls. But the opposing factions were not brought together in allegiance to a king who they knew would have no power; rather, they were welded by the fire of common hatred of the foreign conquerors. Plantation managers and overseers went about armed as they attempted to round up their black slave boys, and at night barricaded themselves against possible raiders in their hastily reconstructed houses. In Apia the consuls and other government officials found it much more pleasant to remain at home after dark than to gather at the Tivoli bar for drinks.

Only Louis went about in serene safety, again visiting villages, drinking 'ava with the ali'i and participating in the fono discussions. He liked best the single-file trails that led off into the dense forest. Jack, breaking into playful gallop and prancing impatiently when reined in, had, as Louis once said "a habit of shieing at everything," while Louis preferred a leisurely gait, with the pleasure of meeting countryside folks.

A young man with a stem of bananas on his shoulder would lower his burden as he came within sight, step aside, and with a smiling "Talofa," wait until the older man had passed. This courtesy of halting while an older person passes still prevails in areas away from Western influence. If two little fellows, most likely without a stitch of clothing on their straight-shouldered brown bodies, should come carrying a basket of coconuts swung between them on a slender pole, they, too, would step aside and wait in shy courtesy and eager smiles. Meeting older men, chiefs, and matai, Louis always dismounted for a few minutes of casual conversation.

Then riding on alone, he would set his mind on whatever story was in the making and commune with nature in the grandeur of solitude. It was but a matter of geography from the travels with the gentle mouse-colored donkey to the frisky former circus pony on the winding, moss-grown roads of Upolu, and in between were the glorious days of solitude as he tramped the heather-bordered highroads of Scotland.

It was solitude of a different variety, but solitude none the less, that gave him the plot and characters of "The Beach of Falesá." He tells Sidney Colvin of his experience, calling the bush a jungle:

My long, silent contests in the forest have had a strange effect on me. The unconcealed vitality of these vegetables, their exuberant number and strength, the attempts—I can use no other word—of lianas to enwrap and capture the intruder, the awful silence, the knowledge that all my efforts are only like the performance of an actor, the thing of a moment, and the wood will silently and swiftly heal them up with fresh effervescence; the cunning sense of the tuitui, suffering itself to be touched with wind-swayed grasses and not minding—but let the grass be moved by a man, and it shuts up; the whole silent battle, murder, and slow death of the contending forest; weigh upon my imagination.

My poem the *Woodman* stands; but I have taken refuge in a new story, which just shot through me like a bullet in one of my moments of awe, alone in that tragic jungle:—

The High Woods of Ulufanua.
1. A South Sea Bridal.
2. Under the Ban.
3. Savao and Faavao.
4. Cries in the High Wood.
5. Rumour full of Tongues.
6. The Hour of Peril.
7. The Day of Vengeance.

It is very strange, very extravagant, I dare say; but it's varied, and picturesque, and has a pretty love affair, and ends well. Ulufanu is a lovely Samoan word, ulu = grove; fanua = land; grove-land—"the tops of the high trees." Savao, "sacred to the wood," and Faavao, "wood-ways," are the names of two of the characters, Ulufanua the name of the supposed island.[28]

It is well that he designated the island as fictitious. Delightfully constructed in the telling, unpleasant as a story, peopled by characters so unattractive as not to be recognizable by those of us who know the South Pacific islands, it is strictly a man's yarn spun for masculine readers, portraying the cutthroat fight among traders for a fair share of copra. As for the morals depicted, many authors seem to have at least one such story that they have to get off their minds as scum off deeper and more beautiful human findings, and indeed, more truthful in presenting a people who have been morally maligned for so many years that the pattern of behavior has been universally accepted by those ignorant of the real facts.

But Louis liked this story and was surprised and disappointed when it was not well received by either publisher or readers. He maintained that Wiltshire was one of the best characters he had ever created. No one quarrels with that flat statement, and the execution in the first person testifies to the author's consummate skill. Without obtruding on the other characters, Wiltshire, the trader who is assigned to a new post from which his predecessors have mysteriously disappeared, is made the unforgettable hero of the story, revealing a gentleman's heart in his crude gallantries amid rough and lawless surroundings. It is conjecture that the publisher and not Louis changed the original title "Uma" to the more sensually suggestive "Beach of Falesá," the while viewing uneasily the effect on readers of the unconventional substance. However, the story first appeared in the *Illustrated London News* under the title of "Uma,"

[28] *Vailima Letters*, 14–15.

the name of a native girl in the tale, in the summer of 1892. It is a safe surmise that the names of people and places were from the Line Islands and the Micronesians, for Louis at that time had not become as well acquainted with the Samoans as he did later, and the cruises on the copra traders *Equator* and *Janet Nichol* were not long past. While the story had flashed through his mind "like a bullet" as he was pulling obnoxious weeds in the bush, the locale had been smoldering in his subconscious mind and the characters built from tall tales told by men of adventure on starlit tropic nights, for "The Beach of Falesá" is dedicated to "three old shipmates among the islands, Harry Henderson, Ben Hird, and Jack Buckland.

A poem born in the same weed patch where the unwholesome "Beach of Falesá" was conceived, and at the same time, is the rustically descriptive and wholesome "Woodman," illustrating Louis's versatility in musings and his characteristic and often impish way of elevating homely tasks above the sweat of labor. In this instance his mood fits with that of the Samoans, for weeding is everyone's work. It is pick-up work for the women, like knitting or crocheting, and killing-time work for old men; children are an uncertain quality in both behavior and efficiency.

But since it must be done, why not make it pleasant? Each person brings a small *fale-moe*, floor mat, seats himself comfortably, and works around the radius of his arm's length. Finishing this area, he moves on to the next, leaving in his wake neat plucks of iniquitous verdure to await the evening's *tafunaʻi* (burning pit). All this to singing, gossip, and gay banter by which the Samoans always turn work into play.

This is in the villages and around *fales* set in the bush where grounds have been tended for years. At Vailima, where land was virgin and seeds had accumulated for a thousand years, the task was naturally more arduous, and as Louis complained, "the weeds actually crowd upon one's heels." He scolded about the

225

fast growing *tuitui* and all the *lau lilïi*, small-leafed plants, and about their tentacled roots; but these roots are in soft damp earth, where five days without rain is a drought, and give a minimum of resistance to hoe or gloved fingers. It was such deep-rooted plants as the wild banana and lantana and the tough tangle of vines, some along the ground, some climbing trees and looping down to twist back on their own tendrils, necessitating a vigorous swing of a machete, that Louis could not undertake without risk of illness.

The "Woodman" poem did not flash through his mind like a bullet as did the story of Wiltshire. He confessed several times that he was stuck with it, and it was two years before it saw the printed page in *The New Review* of January, 1895—the month following his death.

THE WOODMAN

In all the grove, nor stream nor bird
Nor aught beside my blows was heard
And the woods wore their noonday dress—
The glory of their silentness.
From the island summit to the seas,
Trees mounted, and trees drooped, and trees
Groped upward in the gaps. The green
Inarboured talus and ravine
By fathoms. By the multitude,
The rugged columns of the wood
And bunches of the branches stood,
Thick as a mob, deep as a sea,
And silent as eternity.

With lowered axe, with backward head,
Late from this scene my labourer fled,
And with a ravelled tale to tell,
Returned. Some denizen of hell,

Samoa

Dead man or disinvested god,
Had close behind him peered and trod,
And triumphed when he turned to flee,
How different fell the lines with me!
Whose eye explored the dim arcade,
Impatient of the uncoming shade—
Shy elf, or dryad pale and cold,
Or mystic lingerer from of old:
Vainly. The fair and stately things,
Impassive as departed kings,
All still in the wood's stillness stood,
And dumb. The rooted multitude
Nodded and brooded, bloomed and dreamed,
Unmeaning, undivined. It seemed
No other art, no hope they knew,
Than clutch the earth and seek the blue.

Mid vegetable king and priest
And stripling, I (the only beast)
Was at the beast's work, killing; hewed
The stubborn roots across, bestrewed
The glebe with the dislustred leaves,
And bid the saplings fall in sheaves;
Bursting across the tangled math—
A ruin that I called a path:
A Golgotha, that, later on,
When rains had watered, and suns shone,
And seeds enriched the place, should bear
And be called garden. Here and there
I spied and plucked by the green hair
A foe more resolute to live—
The toothed and killing sensitive.
He, semi-conscious, fled the attack;
He shrank and tucked his branches back,

Last Witness for Robert Louis Stevenson

And, straining by his anchor strand,
Captured and scratched the rooting hand.
I saw him crouch, I felt him bite,
And straight my eyes were touched with sight.
I saw the wood for what it was—
The lost and the victorious cause;
The deadly battle pitched in line,
Saw silent weapons cross and shine;
Silent defeat, silent assault—
A battle and a burial vault.

Thick round me, in the teeming mud,
Briar and fern strove to the blood.
The hooked liana in his gin
Noosed his reluctant neighbours in;
There the green murderer throve and spread,
Upon his smothering victims fed,
And wantoned on his climbing coil.
Contending roots fought for the soil
Like frightened demons; with despair
Competing branches pushed for air.
Green conquerors from overhead
Bestrode the bodies of their dead;
The Cæsars of the sylvan field,
Unused to fail, foredoomed to yield;
For in the groins of branches, lo!
The cancers of the orchid grow.

Silent as in the listed ring,
Two chartered wrestlers strain and cling;
Dumb as by yellow Hooghly's side
The suffocating captives died:
So hushed the woodland warfare goes
Unceasing; and the silent foes
Grapple and smother, strain and clasp

Samoa

Without a cry, without a gasp.
Here also sound thy fans, O God,
Here, too, thy banners move abroad:
Forest and city, sea and shore,
And the whole earth thy threshing floor!
The drums of war, the drums of peace,
Roll through our cities without cease,
And all the iron halls of life
Ring with the unremitting strife.

The common lot we scarce perceive.
Crowds perish,—we nor mark nor grieve:
The bugle calls—we mourn a few!
What corporal's guard at Waterloo?
What scanty hundreds more or less
In the man-devouring wilderness?
What handful bled on Delhi ridge?—
See, rather, London, on thy bridge
The pale battalions trample by,
Resolved to slay, resigned to die.
Count, rather, all the maimed and dead
In the unbrotherly war of bread.
See, rather, under sultrier skies
What vegetable Londons rise,
And teem, and suffer without sound;
Or in your tranquil garden ground,
Contented, in the falling gloom,
Saunter and see the roses bloom.
That these might live, what thousands died!
All day the cruel hoe was plied;
The ambulance barrow rolled all day;
Your wife—the tender, kind and gay—
Donned her long gauntlets, caught the spud
And bathed in vegetable blood;

And the long massacre now at end,
See! where the lazy coils ascend,
See! where the bonfire sputters red
At even, for the innocent dead.

Why prate of peace? when, warriors all,
We clank in harness into hall,
And ever bare upon the board
Lies the necessary sword.
In the green field or quiet street,
Besieged we sleep, beleaguered eat;
Labour by day and wake o' nights,
In war with rival appetites.
The rose on roses feeds; the lark
On larks. The sedentary clerk
All morning with a diligent pen
Murders the babes of other men;
And like the beasts of wood and park,
Protects his whelps, defends his den.

Unshamed the narrow aim I hold;
I feed my sheep, patrol my fold;
Breathe war on wolves and rival flocks,
A pious outlaw on the rocks
Of God and morning; and when time
Shall bow, or rivals break me, climb
Where no undubbed civilian dares,
In my war harness, the loud stairs
Of honour; and my conqueror
Hail me a warrior fallen in war!

In this narrative poem Stevenson revealed all the many and varied facets of his character. If we had nothing more by which to judge the man, we could find here his complete pattern of life—adventure in fantasy, defiance and courage, supplication and pity, and the doom of materialism. Each line depicts a mood, and out of all the thought-whims comes the compact story of Vailima. Yet with all the work of the "Woodman" only 15 of the 314 acres of land were cleared during the Stevensons' four years of residence. The lagging endeavor is explained in the lines beginning *"By the multitude/ The rugged columns of the wood/ And bunches of the branches stood . . ."* and ending with *"And triumphed when he turned to flee."*

The *aitu,* or disembodied spirit, is very real to the Samoans, as it is to all Polynesians, Micronesians, and Melanesians. If not in the forest, these *aitu* are walking on the sea or hovering in the mist before dawn; or it may be the *agaga,* the voice, whispering through a soft swirl of night air that brushes a bare brown shoulder and sends shivers down the strongest spine.

As with all primitive people, and especially the island dwellers restricted to a relatively small area, the void is not wide between the physical and spiritual. The *aitu* bridges this empty space and creates a definite though eerie element in daily living, and in many instances wields a powerful disciplinary influence.

The *aoa* (banyan) tree is the eeriest of all. No one passes within a hundred feet of the sprawling tentacled giant after dark, nor much closer in the day. And no European or American, if he is wise, will defy this tabu. Among the branches and uncanny dangling roots are the permanent dwelling places of spirits who wait eternally to clutch or caress the living. Children who linger into dusk at play, forgetting they must pass an *aoa* tree on the way home, bunch up and run like all possessed, some screaming, others pop-eyed and grim.

Cut it down? Destroy the abode of the departed? Never! After all, the *aitu* is one of the dramatic essentials in primitive life. The celestial and terrestrial are not sharply divided by a pseudo-civilization that destroys as much as it builds.

By precept and example Louis tried to promote love of the forest when he continued in "The Woodman":

How different fell the lines with me!
Whose eye explored the dim arcade
Impatient of the oncoming shade—
Shy elf, or dryad pale and cold,
Or mystic lingerer from of old;
Vainly. The fair and stately things,
Impassive as departed kings,
All still in the wood's stillness stood,
And dumb. . . .
. . . It seemed
No other art, no hope, they knew,
Than clutch the earth and seek the blue.[29]

Louis never tired of adventuring into the mysteries of this virgin bush, rich in heavy-scented lantana and *moso'oi*—a tangle of vines concealing a clump of bananas or a fruiting papaya—and comparing it with the austere, prim-patterned forest of Fontainebleau which he used to love until he was "burned in horrid patches of red; my nose, I fear, is going to take the lead in color," prompting the rondel:

We'll walk the woods no more,
But stay beside the fire.
To weep for old desire
And things that are no more.
  The woods are spoiled and hoar,
The ways are full of mire;
We'll walk the woods no more,
But stay beside the fire.
  We loved the days of yore,
Love, laughter, and the lyre.
Ah, God, but death is dire,

---

[29] There were several corrections or changes in the manuscript sold in 1914 by the Stevenson heirs following Fanny's death.

And death is at the door—
We'll walk the woods no more.[30]

It worried neither Louis nor Fanny that their meager clearing of only about fifteen acres, with sloping lawn of vivid green, still sat like a nest in the circle of giant trees and thick bush. Mount Vailele made an imposing background, and Mount Vaea, forested so densely there was no hint of the land's contour, was a friendly sentinel in the foreground.

One fairly recent biographer states that Louis climbed to the summit of Mount Vaea. This would have been a physical impossibility. There was no trail at that time, and even had there been, the fact that it was impossible for Louis to breathe deeply in exertion, would have precluded any such venture.

Louis had tolerated Fanny's devotion to her "farm," as he called it, just a degree short of resentment; but as his home came to be acknowledged as the most attractive in the entire South Pacific, he became impishly conciliatory. "If only it were nearer Scotland," was his sad lament.

[30] *Letters of R. L. S.*, ed. by Colvin, I, 120.

10. Manners and Morals

ALTHOUGH LOUIS had attained what he fondly termed "high feather" in health and vigor, the Samoans, with their own robust physiques, always looked upon him as frail. When he first came, they would speak of him in hushed apprehension, " 'Ua vaivai le ma'i," that he was near death. They had not known him before the recent months at sea had heightened his usual ruddiness under a good coat of tan. It was his slender build that prompted their concern. In Apia he had but to appear at store or post office with a parcel and some stalwart would offer to carry it for him. Later it was a matter of inordinate pride with them that he was in better health during his residence in Samoa than at any previous time in his life.

This much for the merely physical.

If one is not prepared to live verily a fish-bowl existence, he should not take up a residence in Samoa, or any of the South Pacific islands. Upolu is forty miles long and averages about twenty miles in width, but news travels as fast as if it were three miles long and one mile wide. It is not essentially gossip. The papalagi is an oddity. What he does, and how, is a matter of interesting curiosity. Every movement is checked; every word weighed. Not with any degree of profundity, for the Samoans have no thought of setting a pattern for papalagi behavior, however strictly they may wish to adhere to their own conventions. They will not criticize, however silently they may condemn.

No one sets himself to spy upon the stranger; no one is inquisitively rude; observations are entirely casual and present a pleasant diversion, except when actions exceed the bounds of good conduct. A single misstep will catalog the errant one, and the word of disapprobation passes from one to another, spreading to other islands like a virus infection. There never is a thought of punishment, no obvious ostracism; but as time goes on, the erring one may find himself excluded from native social gatherings. The brand of the outcast has been laid. They say of him, *"Se a lou manoginogi"* (His conduct is no longer fragrant).

This is not to say that all Samoans are paragons of virtue. Weaknesses of the flesh prevail there as over all the earth; but they do average higher in the practices of moral rectitude than most races. How else could they have survived for countless centuries as a strong and virile people and maintained their high degree of culture except by observance of moral integrity? Such laxity of these attributes as exist today can be laid squarely upon the conscience (Heaven save the mark!) of European men of that branch of the Caucasian race presumed to have been bred in culture and refinement.

Many men writers, and some women, in order to be sensational, write vulgarities into Polynesian life which do not exist beyond isolated instances, as they exist in any society, civilized or primitive. They seek to portray the prevalence of baser qualities of character when nothing in primitive life can compare with the indecencies that were accepted as commonplace in the royal courts of Europe or the obscene practices of medieval "civilization."

It has been written and widely quoted that Samoan young people have promiscuous sexual relations before marriage. This is a serious error. The ruling *alii* have been outraged at such misstatements. True, sometimes a youth slips from the path of virtue, as youths do in any part of the world, our own no less than others. Samoans in remote sections who are unfamiliar with the conduct of European men—and some women—in such

235

island centers of commerce as Pago Pago and Apia, where a caress in public, however casual, is regarded as an insult, are shocked at the lack of respect shown by men toward women.

Interviews purported to appraise the virtue of young girls by asking them if they ever had "been with a boy" is the ultimate of injustice. These girls, shy and self-conscious, and embarrassed by being questioned by a stranger, say "yes" to queries they do not understand, without the slightest conception of the implication of the question. By saying "yes," they hope to finish the painful ordeal as quickly as possible.

"How many times have you been with a boy?"

The girl shakes her head, digs her bare toes in the sand, and blushes. Since boys and girls do not play together except in village *sivas* (dances), she thinks she may have spoken to the handsome boy who lives in the next village.

"Have you been with a boy four times, or maybe five?"

"Maybe."

And down it goes on the printed page to rob a race of virtue.

One has only to live in a village and experience the hushed shock of a rare instance of marital infidelity to realize the utter lack of foundation for any general statements about moral laxity. Interviews such as those cited should be conducted through an interpreter, properly through the *tufala ta'i ta'i* of the village, whose business as chaperone it is to know the conduct of every girl of the *Auluma* (society of girls), and it is very doubtful if she, a middle-aged or elderly woman, would understand our colloquialism, which has no place even in the English language.

These interviewers should more properly ask some of the married women to let them see the *'ie-sina* that they keep folded away under the rafters of the family *fale*. There are plenty of them. They would find out then the quiet pride each woman feels in this precious *'ie-sina*. It is the marriage mat of the virgin.

Sina is the mythological virgin goddess. The name represents the purity and chastity of womanhood.

Adventurers who return from the South Seas and tell with coy smirks of pseudo gallantry about some high chief's offering his daughter for the night, had better tell it to one who does not know that he has been given the local prostitute in order to save the daughter from the stranger's foul designs. And perhaps he did not know why she wore her hair cut short!

These observations are not the digression they may seem, but are meant primarily to establish the foundation for the Samoans' appraisal of their Tusitala; their simple verdict: *"Ali'i o amio lelei,"* a gentleman of good behavior. This was quite aside from their esteem of him as a friend and champion of the people. It was the man himself, watched by eyes he never saw, his goings and coming listened to by ears attuned to sounds carried across the sylvan quiet by day or night: the light-footed canter of Jack, the heavy cloppity-clop of Donald and Eadie, or the tugging tread of oxen laboring up the muddy Vailima road with cargo from yesterday's steamer.

They knew when he went to the Malua missionary school for a lesson in Samoan with Rev. S. J. Whitmee, when he dropped in for a chat with Mr. Sewell at the U.S. Consulate or at the home of Chief Justice Henry Ide, or to make a business call on Henry Moors. They knew, too, and stood aghast, when little Austin Strong and Lafaele of Vailima, riding Donald and Eadie, passed the Moors' store and tethered the two pack horses in front of the MacArthur Trading Company's store. Everyone gasped in wonder and astonishment. Although Austin was only nine, it was one of his regular jobs to ride down to market and see that the horses were not hurried beyond a walk on the homeward journey. He was too young to know, as did Lafaele, what a bomb they were dropping on the serene waterfront of Apia.

Teuila tells of the family conference at Vailima on the previous evening. Louis always had said to Mr. Moors, "Never mind about an itemized account. Just give me the total of my bill for the month."

But Fanny had asked for an itemized account and found that they were paying 25 and 50 per cent more than MacArthur charged for the same goods. Without question Louis sent a check for the bill as rendered by Mr. Moors. Hence the tethering of Donald and Eadie in front of MacArthur's store.

It was about these trips to markets at Apia that Louis in his "family poems" wrote to Austin:

> *What glory for a boy of ten,*
> *Who now must three gigantic men,*
> *And two enormous, dapple grey*
> *New Zealand pack-horses, array*
> *And lead, and wisely resolute*
> *Our day-long business execute*
> *In the far shore-side town. His soul*
> *Glows in his bosom like a coal;*
> *His innocent eyes glitter again,*
> *And his hand trembles on the rein.*
> *Once he reviews his whole command*
> *And chivalrously planting hand*
> *On hip—a borrowed attitude—*
> *Rides off downhill into the wood.*[1]

From their first acquaintance there had been a conspicuous lack of cordiality between Harry Moors and Fanny. Not particularly on Fanny's part, but Mr. Moors thought Louis was too ardently dominated by his wife, since he himself, with his Samoan wife, was free of any aspect of marital dominance.

While there never was any outward break in the friendship between the two families, meeting as they did at every social

[1] *The Complete Poems of R. L. S.* (New York, Scribner's, 1946), 455.

gathering, it was out of this feeling that the proposition came from Mr. Moors that Louis acquire the tiny island of Mothe and make a home in the wee village of Nassau as a refuge from what he termed the domestic irritations that were hindering his writing and retarding the full recovery of his health.

There was much banter in the Vailima household about Louis's prospective self-imposed exile to Mothe Island, and considerable speculation, wild and unfounded, by a few Stevenson biographers who have tried in vain for half a century to create in Fanny the characteristics of a martinet with the ruthless ambition to dictate and control every circumstance. Teuila shrugs these baseless comments off with a gesture of contempt, as does her brother in the following letter written in reply to one from Rev. Donald Macdonald-Millar regarding statements concerning Louis:

> 17 Dos de Mayo, Terreno
> Palma de Mallorca, Spain
> Feb. 20, 1936

Dear Mr. Macdonald-Millar,

Thank you for your very kind note of Jan 21, with the enclosure. I have already heard about that book of Hartman's—whoever he may be—from my sister. There is no truth in any of these statements except that R L S once considered buying an island. He did not seek the island; on the contrary an Apia trader was very eager to sell it to him at a bargain price of next to nothing. I remember we debated it for a while and finally abandoned the idea. But even if he had bought it there was no idea of giving up Vailima. The island had tumpty-tumpty cocoanut trees, and could be made to produce tempty-tempty tons, and the lagoon was "teeming with pearlshell." We had many a hearty laugh over "our island."

These other slanders are very odious and very unjust, but they seem to be the penalty that all greatness has to pay. R L S was essentially the man he revealed himself to be in his books. There was nothing hidden or base or mean about him. Your letter gave me the consoling feeling that real Stevensonians would never credit slanders about him.

I thank you again, and grasp your hand.

Sincerely yours,

Lloyd Osbourne

It is such frank statements as expressed in this letter, and the countless similar comments made by Teuila during an informal acquaintance of many years, plus the honest appraisal of the Samoans, that make it impossible to reckon other than a high Victorian gallantry in Louis's character and a sound foundation of Puritanism in Fanny's—this in spite of their mutual fondness for the unconventional so far as the strict social amenities in daily living were concerned. Never were moral decencies affronted. Why should going barefooted be shocking? Nothing is so invigorating as the feel of the good earth underfoot. Many of us remember our youth in the country when in the spring we were permitted to go barefooted in the soft wet grass. Fanny and Louis felt this same glee.

Trivial? Quite. Intended only as an illustration in thinking. As for analysis of character, each biographer must write into his account his own reaction in a specific circumstance. Let those hesitate who would fasten moral laxity upon the dead. The Samoans have an ancient proverb: "*E pala le ma‘a, a e le pala upu*" (Stones rot, but not words), and "*Ua lelea le laumea*" (Dry leaves—meaning worthless words—are carried away by the wind).

The absence of domination from any quarter was a prime principle in maintaining harmony at Vailima. From austere Aunt Maggie down to impish young Austin, each was a free agent. The only restraint imposed upon the latter was that the balcony room of "Uncle Louis" was strictly out of bounds. Yet there was no spiritless dawdling, for each had daily tasks—except Aunt Maggie, and when she innocently suggested morning prayers, it was because she never was up to see Fanny muster her "boys" at daybreak for work in the garden, gathering papayas and coconuts, milking and feeding the stock—all because no one works during the heat of midday.

Teuila said years ago in speaking of this morning prayers proposition that there was no controversy, the subject never was mentioned a second time, and the only resentment was Fanny's explosive comment in the privacy of her diary. With Fanny and Teuila as American as apple pie and Aunt Maggie and Louis as Scotch as Waughs' haggis, the two extremes set down with no conformity even to Polynesian background, constant adjustments were necessary.

Living in the serenity of nature's blessings brings out unusual complexities of character, and we function best under a degree of irascibility—just sufficient cantankerousness to maintain an emotional balance. The trivial splenetic outbursts in the Vailima household, usually credited to Fanny since she was the sole disciplinarian, amounted to this and nothing more. If they sent Fanny to the only outlet she permitted herself, it bore out her lifelong motto, "When in doubt, say nothing." A cautionary measure usually misinterpreted, but which left one free to enjoy the cheery table talk at the next mealtime without the need for apologies.

Fanny's abortive attempts to control her amateur gardeners always afforded Louis ample opportunity to indulge his playful penchant for teasing, and many of the mildly critical comments in his letters were written in this mood. Teuila says he teased only those of whom he was fond—never to mortify—and since he was fondest of Fanny, she received special attention, intending of course to bring a saucy response from her. In this he never was disappointed.

Gaiety of this type often set the tempo for dinner conversation, during which a whole gamut of subjects would be tossed across the table, from the absurdly silly to the serious question whether it was manly for men to shed tears.

There was, for instance, the time when little Austin in describing a funeral called the pallbearers, "pall-berries." And Louis asking in feigned amazement, "What would happen if some of the berries were green, or maybe rotten!"

Only one thing was tabu. This was stupidity. Teuila says with compassion, "Louis considered stupidity an ailment."

On the other extreme any attempt at pedantry was brushed aside as an affectation and made a subject for mild ridicule. Aunt Maggie was never sufficiently reckless in the use of words to take much part in this nonsense, but the type of teasing she received kept Fanny and Teuila constantly on tenterhooks, for just as sure as the laundress laid aside a nicely starched and ironed lace-trimmed cap, one of the houseboys would put it on his head and walk through the kitchen with a stately tread, his mouth set primly. It was too funny not to laugh, consequently scoldings were ineffectual. They even carried this form of clowning to their own villages, while Aunt Maggie wondered where her caps went.

This spirited *papalagi* household at Vailima, seeming always to be doing so many unnecessary things, presented grave and puzzling problems to the Samoans as far as social ethics were concerned. At his home they recognized Tusitala as a *matai*, the patriarchal head of his family; as they met him in Apia, he always was addressed as *"aliʾi,"* a gentleman; yet he was not a titled royal *aliʾi*, and in the *fonos* and public assemblies he had no designated position: he was not a *tulafale sili*, an official orator; he could not carry a *fue*, the stick of authority, nor the *toʾo toʾo*, the staff of an orator; yet they recognized him as a supreme adviser, and when he spoke by invitation, and in their own tongue, at their solemn *fonos* they listened to him as a prophet sent from *lagi* by Tagaloa.

For these occasions they gave him a chief's *'ula,* a necklace of highly polished brick-red pandanus seeds which is worn exclusively by *ali'i* of title. Came then the difficulty of proper seating, which in a *fono* carries the strictest formality of rank. Any deviation from traditional procedure would be challenged, and wars have been fought for less. Louis never would have been aware of the courtesy of some lesser ranking *ali'i* in relinquishing his place to the honored guest.

The way one sits cross-legged on the floor of the *fale* at a *fono,* or any other time, is an indication of good or bad taste. Knees must be flat, not sticking up like a half-opened jackknife. This was easy for Louis with his lean flanks, and he could rise without having to turn over on hands and knees and get up rump first, which action the Samoans liken to the bovine animal.

The womenfolk of Vailima worked even further confusion. In a royal Samoan household the wife ranks third in the formality of entertaining. The daughter, if she is a *taupou,* ranks first and officiates with her father in extending greetings to guests and mixing the *'ava* if he is entertaining dignitaries. The wife entertains the wives of dignitaries, should there be any; if not, she remains in the background. In political matters the eldest sister of the *ali'i* ranks ahead of the wife and sits as a consultant to her brother before the opening of the *fono.* The grandmother, although loved and respected in family life, remains one degree farther in the background than the wife. These are social forms adhered to for centuries. There is no question of feminine rivalry, no hint of slight.

The Samoans were not long in learning that "Aolele," Fanny, ranked next to Tusitala; that "Tamaitai Matua," Aunt Maggie, was the matriarch of the family and mentor of all social procedure by unanimous consent; and that Teuila, while she ranked first in their affections, was in third place at Vailima. Except for the fact that she was a married woman, Teuila might have been regarded in the position of a *taupou* since she always took the initiative in planning games and entertainment for all the festive occasions and because she was endowed with a natural gaiety of spirit, which attribute appeals mightily to the Samoans. But while a *taupou* may hold her rank after marriage if there is no younger sister or niece available, she cannot be made a *taupou* after marriage, even though she may have had the necessary years of training.

So for their love of Tusitala the Samoans gladly abrogated their strict forms of etiquette in their association with the Vailima family, and if any of their ethics of conduct were unconsciously ignored, the inadvertence would be quickly concealed. They had just as much enjoyment sitting higgilty-piggilty as if they had been punctiliously seated according to rank.

In riding along the roads, Louis never divided a *malaga* of men marching two or more abreast, as many careless *papalagi* have done and thus added one more brick to the wall of resentment steadily built up over a period of two centuries. He would rein Jack over to the side of the road to wait respectfully, and as quietly as Jack would permit, until the long procession had passed. These courtesies the Samoans never forgot.

He never walked in front of an *aliʻi* of high rank and he never failed to sit just slightly behind a ruling *aliʻi*, marks of deference still rigidly observed by those who would stand high in the good graces of Samoans who are fortunate enough to live remote from European influences.

In receiving the *ʻava* he took the *ipu* (polished half-shell of the coconut) with the grace of a Polynesian from the out-pointed palm of the young man who bowed low before him; he was careful to make the required libation, then raising the *ipu* to the elevation of his forehead, addressed his salutation, "*Ia manuʻa!*" to the highest ranking *aliʻi* present. These apparent trivialities mark the difference between gaining the genuine love and respect of the Samoans and mere tolerance. In "calling the *ʻava*," an orator never mentions the name of the one to be served but designates him by complimentary reference in highly poetical language. For their own people this could be some incident in a man's great-grandfather's history or an ancestor's exploit in their war for independence from Toga, which tests the knowledge of the young man serving the 'ava—usually the *manaia* of the village, son of either the ruling *ali'i* or the orator. Serving the *ipu* to the wrong man would be a disgrace he never would be able to live down.

In calling Louis's 'ava, which followed the serving of the highest ranking *ali'i* present, the orator would say something of this sort: "One who stands among us like a shining light to lead us in the darkness of our country's night; one who in a stormy sea quietly bids us to seek the still waters between two fishing boats; one upon whom we ask the blessings of Tagaloa, and offer to our gods the prayers that his roots may grow deep in the soil where he finds affections deeper than the waters of the sea and higher than the stars of heaven above the earth."

Spoken in eloquent Samoan phrasing, which Louis could understand, under a spell of solemnity comparable only to that of receiving the holy sacrament, such a speech cannot but be deeply touching. Louis may have penned his famous declaration, "I have chosen this land to be my land, and these people to be my people, to live and die with," after an 'ava ceremony away from European distractions.

As in most places in the world, food is the basis of Samoan social life. No opportunity for a feast is overlooked. The third aphorism of Brillat-Savarin, "The destiny of nations depends on the manner wherein they take their food," is applicable to the Samoans, and might be followed by number four: "Tell me what thou eatest, and I will tell thee what thou art." They are what we term "good feeders," and down through the centuries of their isolation they have maintained a strict form of serving their meals. Present-day importations of canned products had not broken down any of these formalities when Louis was there.

Sua is their plain food, served with no formality except the tabu imposed upon the food placed on the *laulau* (plaited tray) of the *ali'i sili; sua taumafa* is the food for the *taumafatoga* (feast of friendship) which carries the formality of traditional chants as the *umu* (ground oven) is opened, and blessings by the *tu'ua,* priests or old men of history, as selected portions of roast pig and fish are cut for the different ranks among the guests; and the height of ceremony comes with serving the *sua taute,* food of kings. Because of distracting political unrest during Louis's residence, this elaborate ceremony never took place. Although they esteemed him sufficiently for the bestowal of this honor, they could not defy sacred tradition.

But it was a high light in any village history when an *ali'i* could persuade Tusitala to join them in a *taumafatoga.* Participants in these feasts of friendship usually were exclusively men—*matai, ali'i,* and *ali'i sili*—with two or three villages combining to have thirty, forty, or fifty in attendance. Young men of the society of the *'Aumaga* prepared the food, cooked it, and served it. No *chefs de cuisine* could be prouder of their culinary ability than these twenty-five or thirty smiling bronze giants with hibiscus behind their ears and *'ulas* of ginger or frangipani around their necks. Decorations, however, are laid aside while food is being served as a gesture of respect for their elders.

Louis would have been served the same foods as the *ali'i.* At least half of a side of ribs and two or three pounds of the hind quarter of pork, and an equal poundage of the cuts next the head of barracuda and shark. With the latter they waived tradition, for these fish traditionally are served only to men who have been tattooed. If a man is in disfavor for the moment, he may find on his *laulau* a cut of fish near the tail. He cannot complain. He knows this is a royal reprimand. He swallows hard on that piece of fish. The *papalagi* of the merely tolerated class will be served the tail cut of any smaller fish. The difficulty is that only the Samoans themselves appreciate the significance.

In addition to the fish and pork, Louis would have had set before him a whole fowl, several yams, a breadfruit, a papaya, half a dozen baked bananas, a big yellow Chinese mango, and a large *pauli-sami*, which is the supreme delicacy of Samoan eating. This prodigious array might have awed him at first, but he would have learned that he was only to taste the various viands as a compliment to the men who prepared the feast, then compliment the village by passing the rest to the Vailima boy waiting behind him with a huge basket. No guest leaves a *taumafatoga* without food for those at home.

Had this custom of carrying away food in baskets prevailed in France, Louis could have avoided the minor crapulence he suffered after his breakfast at Puy. In a letter to William Ernest Henley, undated, and presented by Sir David Wallace's trustees to the Robert Louis Stevenson Society of Edinburgh in October, 1952, Louis wrote:

Dear Henley,

I hope to leave Monastier this day (Saturday) week; thence forward Poste Restante, Alais, Gard, is my address. Pronounce: Alesoz: Bad shot that: try again, Alez: Between the pair you have the elements. (*Travels with a donkey in the French Highlands.*) I was no good to-day. I cannot work, nor even write letters. A colossal breakfast yesterday at Puy has, I think, done for me forever: I certainly ate more than ever I ate before in my life: a big slice of melon, some ham and jelly, a filet, a helping of gudgeons, the breast and leg of a partridge, some green peas, three crayfish, some Mont d'or cheese, a peach and a handful of biscuits, macaroons and things. It sounds gargantuan; it cost 3 fr. a head. So that it was inexpensive to the pocket, although I fear it may prove extravagant to the fleshy tabernacle. I can't think how I did it or why. It is a new form of excess for me: but I think it pays less than any of them.

I hope a letter from you this evening, acknowledging Edinburgh. David is indeed a gone lunatic. I have a kind of savage pleasure when I think of my Rajah's Diamond: editor and edited, behold a handsome match!

R. L. S.[2]

Following the Samoan feast, which had begun before midday and lasted three or four hours, the young men of the 'Aumaga—'ulas now again around their necks and flowers behind their ears—would entertain with songs, chants, and *sivas* until dark. The Vailima boy would long ago have gone with the baskets of food for his village. Jack had been fed and watered. Those from neighboring villages would have departed according to the time it would take to walk home. As dusk settled, family prayers would be read and a hymn sung softly. By this time it would be too late for Louis to ride home over ten, fifteen, or twenty miles of rough trail. So he would be given a sleeping mat, a piece of *siapo* for covering, and a mosquito net if the village was back from the sea. And as he lay on the soft *laufala* rugs of the coral pebble floor and gazed into the night from the open *fale*, he must have thought with Henley of "Night with her train of stars and her great gift of sleep."

If this village happened to be far enough from European influence and Louis could have looked in on events of the previous evening, he would have witnessed one of the most stirring of age-old dramas of Samoan traditions in the summons for tomorrow's *fono* by the parade of the mace. My own priceless acquaintance with this ancient ritual was at Fitiuta on Tau Island in the Manua group of American Samoa, a village remote because of its inaccessibility and revered by the Samoans as the site of the creation of man when Tagaloa descended from heaven.

There is not the pomp that attends the carrying of the mace

[2] Letter reproduced through the courtesy of Mr. Charles Guthrie and Rev. Donald Macdonald-Millar.

in the British House of Commons, nor the quieting intent of the sergeant-at-arms as he marches down the aisle of the United States House of Representatives at the order of the Speaker of the House when debaters disregard the rap of the gavel. But for demonstration of ancient law there is nothing more awe inspiring than the slow and measured stride of the *manaia*, prince of the village, as he carries the mace the length of the single street.

This mace is without ornamentation. It has no iron-spiked tip designed to pierce a warrior's armor. It is only an inch-thick, highly polished stick of hard *poumuli* wood, about two feet in length and pointed at both ends. The majestic *manaia* holds it a few inches from his body, diagonally across his chest, and at intervals he cries in full resonant tones, "*Ta—e—ou le Fo—no! Ta—e—ou le fo—no!*" With an approximate pitch of middle *C*, ranging upward to *F*, dropping back to *E*, and again in a prolonged middle *C*, the powerful voice carries far into the hills and out to sea, echoing like responses of long-dead ancestors of countless generations. It is death to anyone in his path, friend or foe, man or child. One thinks with Milton of "Death with his mace petrific" as he scurries aside to stand motionless as if really petrified—not in fear of the actuality, but from the realization that in these few brief moments he is carried back by this simple demonstration of primeval law to an era of antiquity untimed by man.

It is impossible to say with what exaltation of mind and spirit Louis rode homeward the next morning through the dewy forest. Once, in defense of his fondness for the Samoans, he remarked to a critic that there was just the right degree between savagery and sophistication. Perhaps he wondered now which was found in the villages and which in the European-dominated offices in Apia.

Participation in these *fonos* inspired Louis to perfect himself in the Samoan tongue. Here was the best in royal dialect, not only in choice of words but in grace of phraseology and poetry of expression. Any direct statement was outside the area of their thinking. Simile and metaphor, imagery and extravagant hyperbole scintillated through their repartee, softened by ancient proverbs, of which there are hundreds, such as: *Amuia le masina, e alu ma sau* (Blessed is the moon which goes and returns; men die and return not); *Ia lafoia i le alo galo* (May you be thrown on the bosom of a wave); *Ia lafoia i le fogavaʻa tele* (Let it be thrown on the deck of a canoe [depreciating a speaker]); *Ia e vae a Vaeau* (Let your feet be those of Vaeau) —the god Vaeau went to heaven and back in a day, and this proverb is what kept the Vailima boys on the run. It is a subtle slur against dragging feet.

Always there would be laughing and singing. One or two starting a song would be joined in a chorus where full-throated voices in perfect harmony would lift the rafters of the fale.

> *E fataitai ma fale,*
> *Ma mauga loa ma Vaete,*
> *Ma utu a lau fau.*
> Chorus: *Aue mauga! Mauga o Sa aiʻi,*
> *E tuʻu fetaʻi*
> *E tiga mauga, mauga o Savaiʻi,*
> *E tuʻu fetaʻi.*

On and on for many verses.

Louis always returned happy and eager for work from these *fonos*. He felt he had touched the heights of an artistry that could lift the Western world out of its commercial greed. "Speech finely framed delighteth the ear" (Maccabees) was a favorite quotation, and now he was living this axiom.

Before the end of the day the news of Tusitala's visit might well have drifted the length and breadth of the island. Not by hurrying courier, just comments of interest: the village he honored by his presence, in whose royal *fale* he slept, with whom he talked, and what he said. Items of news in this fishbowl existence.

Those few—and there are but a comparative few—who would fasten laxity of moral fiber on Louis must have enjoyed a field day when in 1949 a Sydney, Australia, publication carried an old photograph of the Stevenson family taken in a local studio in 1891. The caption read: "R L S's sister, R L S himself, his Samoan wife, and R L S's mother." Many persons who were transient in Australia at this time and so failed to see the subsequent refutation appearing a month later in *Pacific Islands Monthly* are stubbornly unconvinced that it was a ridiculous error. R. L. S. never had a Samoan wife any more than he ever had a sister. Pictured were Fanny, Louis, Isobel Strong, and Louis's mother. Montaigne sagely observed that "nothing is so firmly believed as what we least know," and this is just another example of the difficulty of truth's catching up with the lie, even an innocent and wholly unintentional one. But the printed page carries a grave responsibility. Writers who indulge in surmise and conjecture should label their material as such.

A case in point is a book published in 1949, so filled with wantonly malicious misstatements as to rouse Isobel Field— the only living being who could speak with unimpeachable authority—to vehement denial of the statements made and irate condemnation of the author—this contrary to her practice of ignoring slanderous statements made by those ignorant of the facts.

With all the outward informality pervading every aspect of the house and premises at Vailima, life was circumspect to a degree beyond the comprehension of persons whose every detail of deportment is not a subject of notice and comment. One could no more escape notice than he could evade his own shadow.

Mrs. Field chided the author's "absurd story that R. L. S. was not the man the public had been taught to consider him—wise, kind, a devoted husband, adored by his friends and revered by his many readers . . . that he was a very common fellow with low tastes and vicious habits." She continued:

Now this is what Stevenson would have had to do, if the author's story were true that he sneaked out at night to hobnob with low characters in saloons on the Beach. R. L. S. would have had a difficult time. It would have been necessary to explain that he was retiring early, owing to fatigue; he wouldn't have dared to say that he was ill or his wife would have been in constant attendance. How could he have explained to Mrs. Stevenson that her usual evening visit to his bedside should be omitted and the door between their rooms be closed?

Then he would have to send for Sosimo to dress him in his riding-clothes and lace up his boots. Sosimo would then have had to go down to the field, capture Jack, Stevenson's frisky pony, and bring him to the lower veranda for his master to mount. The veranda doors were never closed, day or night, in the hot climate of Samoa, and as the family usually assembled in the evening in the hall, as the big room was called, playing games and telling stories, some one of us would have seen or heard what was going on.

The road from Vailima to town was then little more than a rocky, downhill stream, that R. L. S. has described as being "Highland burn, without the trout." Sosimo would then walk ahead with a lantern to light their way. About a mile down this hillside was a native village, where shouts of welcome would be called from various houses and invitations to stop and rest would be given. . . .

In my memory there were only two saloons in Apia, and the doors were always wide open; I never saw many customers, except on Steamer Day, when the men came in from the outlying plantations for their mail. These were mostly Germans.

Stevenson had no need to search for, as the author said, "tellers of tales of the wide and wonderful." When our favorite man-of-war, H. M. S. *Curaçao*, was in port, many British sailors on their liberty day ashore often took the three-mile walk to Vailima, and were cordially received. . . .

The really serious part of all this fantastic nonsense is the story that Stevenson received a blow from a native war club which "hurried him to his grave." No native in all Samoa would have raised a club against their beloved Tusitala. . . . I have often been advised not to worry about such fabrications; they are lightly read and forgotten . . . nor about any of the scandalous tales circulated about one of the best men I have ever known, my step-father, Robert Louis Stevenson.[3]

A vignette of the social life at Vailima is in this letter written in 1892 by Teuila, at Louis's request, to Will Low to be read at a meeting of the Saranac Stevenson Society, and her comments regarding guests points up an interesting preference:

The guests themselves are interesting to me and the different ways they are received is worth studying. Extra civility to the French priests, with a touch of Louis' best manner, the conversation carried on in French, the old brown sherry brought out and much courtesy on both sides. Some slight reluctance to meet the globe-trotter, who generally falls to me. I take him to see the waterfall, the kitchen garden, the view from Lloyd's bandstand, and returning to the veranda to dispense tea.

There was a happy time in days gone by when Germans used to ride this way—they were always liked, and a good deal of chaffing went on, and beer. The missionaries come *sans cere-monie* for they are all very pleasant and friendly; but the guest received with the most real interest and human joy is a stray trader from some unpronounceable island where Louis once

3 From *John o'London's Weekly*, November 24, 1950.

visited. They do not often appear, but when they do, then is the fatted calf killed and chocolate is brought out in the afternoon. . . . I wish you could hear the talk that goes on when these traders appear (who are sometimes accompanied by dusky brides in brand new shoes worn, very likely, for the first time); these my mother overwhelms with embraces and presents.

Louis listens with a languid ear to the globe-trotter's tidings of the outside world, but you should see his eye light up when he discusses the gossip of Appemama and the latest advices from Butaritari. They often bring messages and presents from mutual friends in these far off places—fine mats and carved coconuts, and one young trader in the fullness of his heart brought Louis a beautiful white felt hat with "Henry Heath, London," on the box, and a frying pan and a brick of mushroom-spawn for my mother. Tin Jack is this delightful creature's name—you will meet him again in some of Louis' stories.[4]

And Tin Jack became immortalized as Tommy Haddon in *The Wrecker,* a story written in collaboration with Lloyd Osbourne and plotted during the cruise of the *Janet Nichol* as they sat for long hours on a deck scented to high heaven with the sweet-sour smell of drying copra and listened to tales told in the terse, clipped phrases characteristic of men who dwell in lonely human areas. But the basis of *The Wrecker* plot was in a letter from his cousin of the Dale family of northern Scotland telling of a recent shipwreck near Smugglers' Cave on famous Bass Rock, offshore from the Dale property, which also figures in *Catriona* (in the United States titled *David Balfour*).

However, of all the South Sea characters, no one intrigued Louis's interest more than Captain Henry Hayes, better known —and feared—as "Bully" Hayes. Although he had been dead for a little more than a decade, those who had known him were

[4] From *This Life I've Loved,* by Isobel Field (New York and Toronto, 1948), 347–53.

always ready to recount his lawless exploits and contrast them with his virtues. Operating with a fast schooner, he roamed the Pacific from Rarotonga to the Solomons, smuggling and trading in contraband, even human lives. Then periodically, whether driven by weight of guilt or loneliness in a calling which has no cronies, he would put in at Apia for weeks, perhaps, and live quietly with his family as respected Captain Hayes, sharing the social life, contributing without ostentation to church and benevolences, and acting as big brother to many a stranded beachcomber.

Then, as silently as he had come, "Captain Hayes" would be gone. His schooner would have been beached, her hull painted and the bottom scraped, and who can say there was not a bargain with a plantation manager for fifty or sixty Solomon Islanders at ten or twenty dollars a head to be delivered at a remote rendezvous, slave labor, nothing less, to clear a virgin acreage for coconut planting. Or maybe a thousand cases of fine wines to be picked up from a hidden cache and delivered to a customer willing to pay a top price, plus whatever could be added.

Oddly enough, "Bully" Hayes based with others of his ilk in the little land-locked harbor of Levuka on Ovalau Island of Fiji, within shouting distance of *Treasure Island's* "stockade with the stream running through it," and literally under the flat-crested "shoulder mountain and the peak of spy-glass hill." Entering and leaving this harbor, he would pass directly under the "black cliff with the face on it" jutting like a sentinel from the thickly forested hills.

"Dundee Mike" based here, and "Pug-hat Ugu," and dried-up fuzzy-headed Koho. Bully regarded only Mike as a rival and wanted to get rid of him. Of the others he said contemptuously, "They're afraid of deep water." But Mike was six feet, four inches tall, every wicked inch of him reflected in a voice whose very tone was a curse. Mike's weakness was an uncontrollable temper, so Bully would taunt him with insults until he was angry enough to start a free-for-all fight—in which Bully never participated—and always someone would go overboard. At last Mike himself went over the rail.

But Bully failed to reckon with fate's retributive power, and he was not long to enjoy undisputed sway of lawlessness. A sudden tropical storm with no time to run for shelter, and his schooner was piled up on a reef in the Caroline Islands. There, on beautiful Kusaie Island, made famous by Louis Becke, he turned to the further crime of making an intoxicating drink from coconuts until the British deported him in ignominy.

Had he lived, Captain Hayes would have basked in parental pride when the wedding banns of his daughter, "Leonore Harriet Hayes, aged sixteen, born in Littelton, New Zealand," were posted on the courthouse door, proclaiming her marriage to Dr. Barnhard Ernest Frederic Charles Funk, aged thirty-six, of the German administrative staff.

Since snobbery was Louis's pet anathema—a veritable *bête noire*—and since this trait of human behavior had not at this time infested Samoan society, the Jekyll and Hyde character of the man gave him a status above the average. Teuila says that after these story-telling sessions Louis would remark wistfully, "I've missed it, not knowing the fellow."

To the provincially urbane critic this vicarious adventuring might seem to show in Louis a taste for what the biographer mentioned above referred to as his love for low companions. Rather, however, it boldly revealed the contempt he held for those in the conventional rut of sham and pretense, forced into a set mold of thinking, thus dwarfing both intellect and soul. It was freedom from this social bondage that he sought and found in Samoa.

Which did not interfere in the least with his keen enjoyment of an occasional party in Apia when the entire family would ride down the trail with their dress-up clothes packed in suit-

cases and remain for the night at the Tivoli Hotel. Many times
Fanny denied herself these rare pleasures and remained at home
with Aunt Maggie, who found them a trifle too frivolous for
her Calvinistic dignity.

Louis did not show off at these affairs. He was most brilliant
as a host in his own home, his keen qualities of conversation
always centering on the interests of his guests. Those in whom
he took the most genuine and uninhibited delight were the
bright and witty family of Judge and Mrs. Henry Clay Ide and
their three daughters, Annie,[5] Adelaide, and Marjorie. Within
the sacred walls of home these evenings were uproariously gay.
Judicial dignity and glass-house living were forgotten in dancing, singing, clowning, any impromptu fun built higher and
higher on a pinnacle of foolishness.

When time came for the Ide girls to return to their Vermont
home for schooling, Louis begged the parents to let Annie remain, volunteering to tutor her in French and provide books
for higher education. There was more than affection for the
girl in this request. Teuila, widowed by divorce, with Austin
away at school, had no companions of her own age, and he
knew there were times when she was wretchedly lonely, and
Annie's gay companionship was the answer he had been
hoping for.

But now, more than ever, careful deportment was necessary,
partly because of the vivacity of the two, and partly because
of Annie's exceptional beauty. Wherever they went, they were
accompanied by a Samoan girl, Sigua, who shared their *papalagi* fun and taught them Samoan games, songs, and *sivas*.

But the world remembers Annie as the recipient of Louis's
birthday—November 13—to replace her own, which fell on
Christmas Day. In the New York City Public Library one may

[5] Annie, Mrs. Bourke Cockran, became an internationally recognized
hostess who was known for her charm and beauty. She and Teuila remained close friends until Mrs. Cockran's death in 1939.

see the original of this unique document, and in the Public Library of St. Johnsbury, Vermont, the Ide family home, there is a facsimile:

I, Robert Louis Stevenson, Advocate of the Scots Bar, author of "The Master of Ballantrae" and "Moral Emblems," stuck civil engineer, sole owner and patentee of the Palace and Plantation known as Vailima in the island of Upolu, Samoa, a British subject, being in sound mind, and pretty well, I thank you, in body:

In consideration that Miss A. H. Ide, daughter of H. C. Ide, in the town of St. Johnsbury, in the county of Caledonia, in the state of Vermont, United States of America, was born, out of all reason, upon Christmas Day, and is therefore, out of all justice, denied the consolation and profit of a proper birthday;

And considering that I, the said Robert Louis Stevenson, have attained an age when, O, we never mention it, and that I have now no further use for a birthday of any description;

And in consideration that I have met H. C. Ide, the father of the said A. H. Ide, and found him about as white a land commissioner as I require:

Have transferred, and *do hereby transfer,* to the said A. H. Ide, *all and whole* my rights and privileges in the thirteenth day of November, formerly my birthday, now, hereby, and henceforth, the birthday of the said A. H. Ide, to have, hold, exercise, and enjoy the same in the customary manner, by the sporting of fine raiment, eating of rich meats, and receipt of gifts, compliments, and copies of verse, according to the manner of our ancestors;

And I direct the said A. H. Ide to add to her said name of A. H. Ide the name Louisa—at least in private; and I charge her to use my said birthday with moderation and humanity, et tamquam bona filia familia, the said birthday not being so young as it once was, and having carried me in a very satisfactory manner since I can remember;

And in case the said A. H. Ide shall neglect or contravene either of the above conditions, I hereby revoke the donation and transfer of my rights in the said birthday to the President of the United States of America for the time being:

In witness whereof I have here to set my hand and seal this nineteenth day of June in the year of grace eighteen hundred and ninety-one.

Robert Louis Stevenson

(seal)

I. P. D.

[*In Praesentia Dominorum:*
In the Presence of the Lords
of Session.]

Witness: Lloyd Osbourne
Witness: Harold Watts

The name Louisa was accepted readily by the Samoans, and Annie was known from then on as "Ah-nay Louisa" to her *papalagi* friends as well. To carry the fun farther, Louis began to wonder what relationship had been established by this bestowal of his birthday. In November he wrote to her in Vermont:

. . . I am now, I must be, one of your nearest relatives; exactly what we are to each other, I do not know, I doubt if the case has ever happened before—your papa ought to know, and I don't believe he does; but I think I ought to call you in the meanwhile, and until we get the advice of counsel learned in the law, my name-daughter. . . .

You are quite wrong as to the effect of the birthday on your age. From the moment the deed was registered (as it was in the public press with every solemnity), the thirteenth of November became your own and only birthday, and you ceased to have been born on Christmas Day. Ask your father; I am sure he will tell you this is sound law. You are thus become a month and twelve days younger than you were but will go on growing older for the future in the regular and human manner from one 13th November to the next. The effect on me is more doubtful; I may, as you suggest, live for ever; I might, on the other hand, come to pieces like the one-horse shay at a moment's notice; doubtless the step was risky, but I do not the least regret that which enables me to sign myself your revered and delighted name-father,

Robert Louis Stevenson

These and other whimsies—such as the autograph in a copy of *Treasure Island* made at Austin's request,

And now, little Austin, doff your hat,
For what a great grandpapa was that!

reveal poignantly what Teuila often said, "What a pity he never had a family of children of his own."

Much too much has been written in disparaging criticism of the evening prayers at Vailima, a prime statement being that Louis was not sincere in these prayer sessions and had merely assumed the role of piety for his mother's sake. No one can probe the heart of another, nor should we presume to do so. But there are phases in life, in mental development, which should be accepted as such, and nothing more. Whatever the obdurate and, at the time, impenitent sentiments of the young Edinburgh student were that so distressed both father and son, there is no indication that they prevailed for any length of time. Jousts which he experienced with the grim reaper when it was lance for lance during days of suffering, in which he gave no quarter to fear, could not have but softened his heart to the precepts of Calvinism. Even without these critical brushes with death, it is unlikely that his well-ordered mind could have cast aside the grounded traditions of his ancestors, or that he could have dissociated himself completely from his childhood training in principles of daily Christian living.

Yet, leaving all these surmises out of the question, Louis in Samoa was a *matai,* the lord of an estate, the patriarch of a *faoaʻaʻai.* Although without title, he was an *aliʻi,* a gentleman. He could not have maintained the dignity of this status had he failed to conform to the customary evening ceremony of the *lotu*[6]—the symbol of the new faith brought by the missionaries in 1830.

Down through the centuries of Samoan culture has come the *afiafi goto le la* (sacred hour of the setting sun), when at the close of day families assemble in their respective *fales* to harmonize the day's events in spiritual communion with their god, *Tagaloa;* a precious hour when the family bond was acknowledged in love and comradeship—when stories were told to record incidents of history by word of mouth, since they had no written language—when songs were sung to preserve myths and legends of folklore—when little children displayed new *siva* steps to admiring elders and received the usual kindly admonitions toward good behavior.

Following this hour, the boys attaining adolescence would be permitted to join the "Young Men of the *ʻAumaga*" in their clubhouse for further instruction by a venerable *tuʻua* (old man of history), and the girls of the same ages would be sent to the house of the *Aualuma* (society of girls) to be tutored by the *Tufale taʻi taʻi* (appointed chaperone of the village) in such graces as dancing and singing, ceremonial mixing of *ʻava* for girls of royal families, and general courtesies of entertaining. Before kerosene was available, illumination in these *fales* was by bowls of sputtering candlenuts.

During this time the lesser *aliʻi* from neighboring villages and oftentimes the *matai* would be congregating leisurely in the big royal *fale-tele* for a conference with the *aliʻi sili.* This

[6] Literally, to turn from heathenism.

was only a courtesy gathering unless some trouble had come up for adjustment, a dispute perhaps with a neighboring village. Each disputant in this event would present his case. The *ali'i sili* and his associates would listen attentively, searching out motives of ill will, rivalry, or fancied insult, which always is the Achilles heel of any Polynesian. If the *ali'i sili* should find himself completely baffled by different versions of the same incident, he does not say, "Take them away and lock them up"; he points quietly to an *ipu* (coconut half-shell highly polished) which hangs suspended in a woven mesh of sinnet from the apex of the rafters and asks who will touch it. No one who has even a shadow of a lie on his lips can rise and touch this sacred symbol of truth.

If no one is able to meet this challenge, the silence that settles on the gathering sends the culprits into cold sweats. There is no threat of punishment from the *ali'i sili*, no rebuke. He knows their punishment is in their own embarrassed suspense. He lets them wait. The surf pounds and thunders on the reef; dry palm fronds rattle lazily in the soft evening breeze. Then he asks in a low voice, "Are you little children quarreling over a handful of pretty shells from the sea, or are you grown men? Show me that you are not little boys. Apologize to each other, and to the *ali'i* assembled here, then go in peace and let the morrow's sun rise on the harmony of your thoughts. *Tofa, soifua* [good-night, and my blessing]!" That is a court trial at the hour of the setting sun.

Louis rarely was called upon to settle grievances. It was thoroughly understood that Fanny's word was supreme on the plantation, and Teuila's likewise in the house. Louis delivered but one edict, and that spoken sternly: if anyone should fail to work in harmony with the others, he must leave Vailima and never return. This forestalled complaints, for the shame of banishment would have been a brand of bad conduct which the complainant never would have been able to erase.

Louis was proud of his position as country squire, proud of the loyalty of those employed, and was well aware of the social and political influence this title of *matai* gave him. He was thankful for the quality of living that gave him peace of mind, for his health that enabled him to enjoy life as never before, for the material success that provided financial security; he was profoundly thankful for his friends. Why should he not spend a few moments each day in acknowledging these blessings?

Lord, behold our family here assembled. We thank Thee for this place in which we dwell; for the peace accorded us this day; for the hope with which we expect the morrow; for the health, the work, the food, and the bright skies that make our lives delightful; for our friends in all parts of the earth, and our friendly helpers in this foreign isle. Let peace abound in our small company. Purge out of every heart the lurking grudge.

Give us grace and strength to forbear and to persevere. Offenders, give us the grace to accept and to forgive offenders. Forgetful ourselves, help us to bear cheerfully the forgetfulness of others. Give us courage and gaiety and the quiet mind. Spare to us our friends, soften to us our enemies. Bless us, if it may be, in all our innocent endeavours. If it may not, give us the strength to encounter that which is to come, that we may be brave in peril, constant in tribulation, temperate in wrath, and in all changes of fortune, and, down to the gates of death, loyal and loving one to another. As the clay to the potter, as the windmill to the wind, as children of their sire, we beseech of Thee this help and mercy for Christ's sake.[7]

Pleasant and profitable as was the prayer hour with the assembled household, the really precious hour of the twenty-four was the intimate family conference at bed time in the rooms of Fanny and Louis at the end of the balcony. Not always,

[7] Vailima Prayers, in Balfour's *Life of R. L. S.*, II, Apendix C.

but frequently, this would include Teuila and occasionally Lloyd, and for this brief time they no longer dwelled in the glass house of continual observation. Here they could discuss family affairs freely and indulge in the small affectionate caresses denied them by Samoan etiquette.

Any caress in public, however slight, is to the Samoan an unseemly familiarity; an embrace or kiss is an insult. Husbands and wives never so much as clasp hands in public, never exchange glances that could be construed as amorous or use expressions of endearment. If at Vailima the family should be sitting with friends and the evening breeze happened to turn chilly, Fanny could never apparently carelessly throw a shawl across the back of Louis's chair. She had to signal some member of the circle to perform this ministration. While this was to conform to Samoan amenities, it was equally out of consideration for Louis's dignity and his aversion to any gesture that would suggest invalidism.

But in the privacy of this large airy suite of rooms it was different. Louis would have slipped into pajamas and dressing gown; Teuila might be brushing her mother's thick, wavy hair, or Fanny might be brushing her daughter's exceedingly long black tresses. Aunt Maggie never joined these sessions. Louis would have said his good-night to her as she retired to her own large and airy bedroom—the bit of Scotland she maintained for the privilege of living with her beloved son. In all the years at Vailima, Teuila never once entered that room, and Fanny only rarely upon specific invitation. Once in a query to Teuila regarding some especially beautiful pieces of furniture at Vailima mention was made of an immense solid walnut combination wardrobe and chest of drawers now in possession of a Samoan family. "I don't remember any such piece of furniture," she replied, adding quite casually, "It may have been in Aunt Maggie's room. I never was in there." Which did not necessarily imply a lack of friendliness, as was proved by the substantial legacy each received in Aunt Maggie's will.

Louis was a natural comic and could set a company into peals of laughter in the recital of an incident that might have passed as commonplace from another *raconteur*. Away from the dignified restraint of his mother he could enjoy whatever clownishness popped into his fertile brain. Especially was he fond of re-enacting the trials of his courtship with two children constantly underfoot, teasing his wife with ludicrous exaggerations, or twitting her about her present attempts at husbandry.

Most of this banter Fanny could laugh off if they were alone, but before guests she did not approve of the facetious recitals of his various hardships, one of which was his first arrival in New York in 1879 and his lodging for a night at Reunion House for the sum of twenty-five cents, of sharing the room with a ship's companion whom he hoped would act as bodyguard since other shipmates had solemnly warned him against thieves and cutthroats who inhabited the city.

He would describe in minutest detail the furniture of the room, a bed, a deal chair, and two clothes-pegs on the wall. There were two "borrowed windows," one opening into a hallway, the other into an adjoining room where three men were happily snoring in troubled and restless sleep. They could easily reach out and steal one's purse from under the pillow or stab him in the chest.

Magnanimously he gave his companion the exclusive use of the double bed and he lay on the uncarpeted floor—the easier to roll under the bed—and lay staring wide-eyed throughout the night waiting in terror for the cutthroats to come slinking in through the door that had no lock. In the morning he had to cross an open court in the pouring rain to the lavatories, chase small bits of soap on the dirty floor like a crane spearing fish, wipe his face on a slimy much-used towel . . . . At this juncture

Fanny would have disappeared. Never would she have expressed any disapproval, and no one would have seen her go. It was always as if she had vanished in thin air.

The one period of their lives that was sacrosant against Louis's levity were the weeks of poignant suspense at Monterey and the even harder and more bitter weeks in San Francisco and Oakland previous to their marriage. It was during this trying time that Fanny was elevated to sainthood in Louis's estimation, and for him she never fell from this canonization. In *Virginibus Puerisque* he wrote for youth: "Some one has written that love makes people believe in immortality, because there seems not to be room in life for so great a tenderness, and it is inconceivable that the most masterful of our emotions should have no more than the spare moments of a few years."

It is easy to see why Fanny never spoke sharply or criticized her husband. Yet, for one as spirited as we know Fanny to have been, repression may not always have been easy. Any woman's diary raises the curtain on her innermost thoughts, and Fanny's entry of July 24, 1893, is revealing:

. . . Louis looks much better again. He was in no condition for the fatigues and agitations consequent on the war, and certainly my savage attack concerning our conduct to *Mata'afa* could not have been good for him. He called me an "idiotic Enthusiast." . . . Well, he's another, and I insist upon his being consistent at least to his own ideals. It is not in him to be either a philosopher or a cynic.

The following day another entry:

Planted beans all morning with Simelo. . . . I had meant to plant all afternoon, but was persuaded to make calls instead, a poor substitute for the heavenly pastime of planting. . . . Belle and I called on Mrs. Blacklock, a very pleasant young native woman, then on Mrs. F——, a pretty young woman with a drunken husband, then on Mrs. Janney, another native wife of a white man, the latter a little mad, then Mrs. Schleuter, a most charming native woman with a very fat German husband; then Home where we met Mrs. Clarke at the gate, and a couple of new ship's officers who were drinking tea on the verandah. . . . The officers were pleasing enough. . . . First one of them mentioned casually that the chiefs imprisoned aboard the German ship had been put to menial labour. Belle gave a cry of indignation and looked as though she were about to strike the speaker with her fan or whip. I forget which she had in her hand. Soon after the other man said he thought it is a pity that Mata'afa had so persistently refused the vice-presidency.

"Who told you that he refused it?" asked Louis.

"Mr. Cusack-Smith," was the reply.

"Then he lied in his throat!" shouted Louis, springing to his feet in a hot fury. "They must think that Vailima is a sort of imitation Wuthering Heights."

The following day, the twenty-sixth, the Mata'afa incident seems closed in this peppery entry:

Lloyd went to Apia, took some 'ava and tobacco to Mata'afa, and learned on board that all the chiefs were to be deported instantly. The chiefs begged to know where they were to be sent; he was able to inform them that on account of the English ship being short of coal, the *Spurber* was to take them to the Tokalaus. . . . He hastened home to tell us the news, and found us just about ready to start to see Mata'afa. I felt very badly that I was not allowed to go before. It was thought to be "not convenable" that ladies should show any sympathy with their broken friends *until the Captain had called!*

What sort of a devil from hell is the British matron, and why should I, of all people in the world, take her for my pattern in conduct? It is like being a sham paralytic. I fear I shall carry away something yet. I always despised Mary Shelley, and here I am no whit better. I despise myself, and that's the fair truth. . . .

Laupepa did not go on board the man-of-war while Mata'afa was there. I presume he was not allowed lest the two high chiefs on meeting, should weep on each other's necks and become reconciled. If they had it would have been a comic incident indeed, and it is quite in keeping with the Samoan character and customs that they should have done so.

The edginess of tempers subsided abruptly with Mata'afa's departure and the "could haves" and "should haves" were sweetened in the zest of writing and planting. Just once in her diary (to which I had ready access over a period of years) does Fanny mention Louis's displeasure with her. This was an instance when they were all in Apia and she and Isobel defied his judgment (Louis was right according to Samoan etiquette) and went to the Mulinuu (headquarters of Malietoa) where Belle wanted to make sketches of war preparations. Fanny wrote: ". . . back to the hotel we started from. Here we found Louis still in the sulks. He stayed a little while and then went home saying he would send down our horses." But these fleecy clouds crossing the family purlieu were as fleeting and casual as tropic squalls—here, a splash—gone, and sunshine.

11. The Balcony Workroom

ASIDE FROM THE STRICT FORMALITY of dressing for seven o'clock dinner the only disciplinary edict at Vailima was for absolute quiet in that upper balcony where Louis, as he said, "roosted like an owl." No author could have taken greater pride than did Louis in making his talents pay generous dividends, and probably no author took greater pleasure in the actual work of writing, even under the handicap of illness and the cramping muscles of the hand. He played with words as a musician plays with the notes of his instrument. Success had not come too late to soften the adversities of earlier years, and he thoroughly enjoyed his prosperity, lacking only the personal contact with associates of the lean years with whom he had shared hopes and ambition.

No adventure is climaxed until one returns to family and friends and narrates the exploits. Louis himself was the adventure and the adventurer. He longed for Edmund Gosse and Sidney Colvin, for James Barrie and Bob Stevenson, Charles Baxter and Walter Simpson, and many others. He was happiest when he wrote of Scotland, yet ever mindful of the blessings of Vailima and the good fortune that had taken him away from the cruel Scottish cold.

The Samoans, outside his immediate household, never ceased to be astonished and slightly bewildered that the necessary money to maintain a rich man's family could be derived from merely putting words on paper. The London missionaries had given them a written language scarcely three generations earlier, and the accomplishment of writing was simply a pleasant pastime. If they wished to call on their good friend, Tusitala, the hour of the day and how many callers there were meant nothing, and their etiquette demanded a long visit as a matter of courtesy. At first Fanny and Teuila were put to the extremities of tactfulness to explain Louis's inability to see them if he was completely absorbed in a story. Then the venerable *ali'i* in departing would smile indulgently as if they had been asked not to disturb a child at play.

But when *The Bottle Imp* was translated by Rev. Newell for serial publication in *O Le Sulu Samoa*, a four-page monthly issued by the London Missionary Society, they understood where Tusitala's wealth was coming from. He possessed the *Aitu!* The writing was only a *tauvale*, a blind to deceive! Which was not at all what the good Reverend intended.

Under the title, *"O Le Faga Aitu,"* it was published in seven installments and was avidly read as the first story in fiction form to be printed in their own language. While their oral literature holds many stories and legends of the supernatural, these deal exclusively with nature—birds of fabulous proportions, fish with the power of speech, *aitus* who appear in thunder and lightning, wind and rain, and ancient gods with power to transform a man into an unseen emissary of good or evil. There are no quadrupeds in these stories, for four-footed creatures did not exist in Polynesia previous to European discovery and invasion.

And none of these stories had any reference to material gain. Even during Louis's time there was no ambition toward individually owned property. Each man shared not only with his family but with the village, and took pride in his contribution to the welfare of the *faoa'a'ai*. As recently as the turn of the present century, old men suffered the humiliation of watching their sons growing eager for financial gains, with a disinclination to share as had their forefathers. Not until the half-castes grew to manhood and followed their *papalagi* fathers in business did this matter of self-interest begin to influence the young Samoans of the same generation.

Since the story of *The Imp* presents personal gain as the work of Satan, Rev. Newell may have attempted to stem this tendency toward acquisition of wealth in emulation of the foreign traders. The example back-fired. Much as they loved Tusitala, much as they appreciated his kindnesses, the inquisitive always were looking for the *Aitu* at Vailima. They were not convinced when Louis tried to explain that the creature was of his imagination—a *fa'atagata*. All he received in reply were raised brows, a slow lowering of one eyelid, and a sly smile of incredulity. Whatever salutary effect Rev. Newell desired, the Samoan of pure blood has never, with rare exception, developed a sense of personal wealth and the *matai* and *ali'i* still regard the welfare of their village folk as a sacred trust. Title remains their coveted aggrandizement.

In an environment where fun had to be born of every small happening, *The Imp* afforded considerable amusement in the household. But it was cautiously mentioned outside. There were few Edmund Gosses or Will Lows in Apia who possessed a sense of humor to match the Vailima brand, that could parry with nonsense without being silly or play intelligently with extravagances. What little there was of Henley's humor had died in 1888, and Henry James and Sidney Colvin had slight traces of this grace-saving asset. Teuila says Louis was shocked when Sidney Colvin marked "The Swing" for deletion in the galleys of *A Child's Garden of Verses*, and Louis wrote *"stet"* in bold letters on the margin.

And speaking of deletions, it is universally presumed that Colvin was guilty of striking out the beautiful middle verse of "Requiem." Years ago I wrote to him at the British Museum Library asking him if he had deleted it and if so, why. His reply was: "The middle verse of 'Requiem' was probably deleted because the other two were happier without it." Just that, nothing more. He could not know what poignant prophecy had been written into those precious four lines:

> *Here may the winds about me blow;*
> *Here the clouds may come and go;*
> *Here may be rest for evermo',*
> *And the heart for aye shall be still.*

The first conception of the poem had three stanzas of eight lines each and was written in 1879—or at least published then—when Louis was critically ill in California. He once wrote to a friendly critic, "These are rhymes, jingles; I do not go in for eternity and the three unities." Yet he belied his own statement in writing and polishing "Requiem" for five years from this beginning, which Lloyd Osbourne, then living in London, found for me at the publishing house of Chatto and Windus:

> *Now when the number of my years*
> *Is all fulfilled, and I*
> *From sedentary life*
> *Shall rouse me up to die,*
> > *Bury me low and let me lie*
> > *Under the wide and starry sky.*
> > *Joying to live, I joyed to die,*
> > *Bury me low and let me lie.*

> *Clear was my soul, my deeds were free,*
> *Honour was called my name,*
> *I fell not back from fear*
> *Nor followed after fame.*
> > *Bury me low and let me lie*
> > *Under the wide and starry sky.*
> > *Joying to live, I joyed to die,*
> > *Bury me low and let me lie.*

The Balcony Workroom

Bury me low in valleys green
And where the milder breeze
Blows fresh along the stream,
Sings roundly in the trees—
  Bury me low and let me lie
  Under the wide and starry sky.
  Joying to live, I joyed to die,
  Bury me low and let me lie.

Stubbornly pursuing my quest of this middle verse so fraught with premonitory significance, I wrote to various literary men, whose replies reveal their sincere regard for the memory of the man, Louis, and his writings. Stephen Chalmers, for instance, said: ". . . less prejudiced than I have maintained that one of the major literary offenses is to dig up and print the odds and ends of condemned imperfection that were merely a master's experiments. These are the still-born children whose tomb, sealed by their own father, none should disturb."

It is interesting that when the William Harris Arnold collection was sold at auction in New York in 1925, Dr. A. S. W. Rosenbach purchased, together with some other Stevensoniana, the manuscript of "Requiem" for fifteen hundred dollars. It is now one of the prized possessions of the Huntington Library at San Marino, California.

Teuila said that Louis had no difficulty with cramps in his hand when he was relaxed and unhurried. Even through the confusion of building the big house, and later the remodeling, he wrote in the cottage or anywhere he could find a table or shelf or window sill where he could set a bottle of ink, and thoroughly enjoyed himself.

Fanny's sole ambition was to make the plantation support the household, and after the first few months she almost realized this goal by supplying vegetables and fruit, milk and butter, and eggs and chickens, with a pig ready for killing on feast

273

occasions. When Louis suffered severe cramps in his hands, she would say with vehement compassion as she rubbed with friar's balsam, "Just wait; there will come a time when this poor hand can rest!" In this, as in other instances, they failed to credit the Samoans with remedial knowledge. Any elderly woman could have given their Tusitala a *lomilomi,* a gentle kneading of muscles to relieve tension on nerves, even to dispel congestion.

A mad fever of writing seized the entire family with the imminence of "steamer days," often a month apart. And when the bulging mail sack would arrive on the back of one of the grays, there was a general convergence toward Louis's room. Here he distributed the contents to a hilariously eager circle as they sat cross-legged on the floor, calling out the names in tantalizing gravity. Then, like a calm following a storm, each would slip away to read his letters in privacy.

The next day, with sailing time posted for a certain hour, there would come from the balcony a frantic call for "Belle" to take dictation. Louis in nervous haste would have written letters until his hand would be stiff with pain. The household would find him trying all manner of ways to hold the pen in an attempt to relieve the strain. Writer's cramp had plagued him for years, and as early as 1874 he wrote to Colvin: "It is curious that I am almost unable to write at present; the reason is that I am gradually changing the attitude on my hand in writing; and at present both the old and the new position is intolerable to me for any length of time. Caligraphy is horrid to me."

A fat mailbag was always a delight, but it was when it brought disturbing messages from critics and publishers that Louis hurried to reply by the same steamer rather than wait perhaps a month for the next out-going mail. He was jealously loyal to his stories as conceived and, as in instance of *The Beach of Falesá* which he frankly regarded as a bit of bravado, was prepared to defend its boldly challenging characters. Critics had labeled it immoral, and publishers hesitated to give it a place with his other stories, fearing loss of prestige among his more discerning readers.

Of the effort put into telling the yarn he wrote: "Since I last laid down my pen, I have written and rewritten *The Beach of Falesá;* something like sixty thousand words of sterling domestic fiction (the story, you will understand, is only half that length); and now I don't want to write any more again for ever, or feel so; and I've got to overhaul it once again to my sorrow. I was all yesterday revising, and found a lot of slacknesses."[1] And in defense of the morals involved he wrote to Sidney Colvin:

It is the first realistic South Sea story; I mean with real South Sea character and details of life. Everybody else who has tried, that I have seen, got carried away by the romance, and ended in a kind of sugar-candy sham epic, and the whole effect was lost—there was no etching, no human grin, consequently no conviction. Now I have got the smell and look of the thing a good deal. You will know more about the South Seas after you have read my little tale than if you had read a library. As to whether any one else will read it I have no guess. I am in an off time, but there is just the possibility it might make a hit; for the yarn is good and melodramatic, and there is quite a love affair—for me.[2]

As for the absence of a marriage certificate, he said: "It is a poisoned bad world for the romancer, this Anglo-Saxon world."

While the story survived as written in the serial publication in 1892, Baxter and Colvin raised serious objections to the fake marriage certificate written by the depraved reprobate, Case:

[1] *Vailima Letters*, 80.
[2] *Ibid.*, 80–81.

This is to certify that Uma, daughter of Faʻavao of Falesa, Island of ——, is illegally married to Mr. John Wiltshire for one week and Mr. John Wiltshire is at liberty to send her to hell when he pleases.

John Blackamoar
Chaplain to the Hulks.

Extracted from the Register
by William T. Randall,
Master Mariner.

To which Wiltshire comments in the story: "A nice paper to put in a girl's hand and see her hide it away like gold."

Later, as Wiltshire's conscience is made to burn deeper and deeper and he conceives a tender and passsionate love for the girl, he anxiously seeks out the visiting missionary to perform a real marriage ceremony. Here again Louis hit a snag when he had Wiltshire declare, "I'm just a trader; I'm just a common, low-down, God-damned white man and a British subject, the sort you would like to wipe your boots on. I hope that's plain!"

This was what Louis admired in his character of Wiltshire, his appraisal of himself in his unwholesome role and his fight to retain some fragment of inherent gallantry, the sense of decency that characterizes the Britisher regardless of environment or circumstances. Louis's provincial friends could not comprehend this view and deplored it.

A paragraph from a Stevenson library catalog compiled by George L. McKay from the Edwin J. Beinecke collection of Stevensoniana is enlightening: "There are several textual variations in 'The Beach of Falesá' as between the copyright issue, the trial issue, and the first English published issue of *Island Nights' Entertainments*. For example the copyright issue lacks the text of the marriage certificate which is present in the other two issues (p. 18). A passage on p. 60 of the copyright issue

276

reads: 'I'm just a common, low white man and British subject.' In the trial issue (p. 66) this reads: 'I'm just a common, low God-d—ned white man and British subject." In the first English published issue of *Island Nights' Entertainments* (p. 66) this passage reads: 'I'm just a common, low-down, God-damned white man and British subject.'"

So in 1893 there appeared simultaneously with Cassell's English edition of the three stories, Scribner's American edition and Tauchnitz' German translations, *"Der Strand von Falesa," "Flaschenteufchen"* ("The Bottle Imp") and *"Die Stimmeninsel"* ("The Isle of Voices"). While "Falesá"'s previously deleted passages had been restored at Louis's insistence, it failed to lift "The Isle of Voices" (a tale of the supernatural at Molokai) and "The Bottle Imp" out of mediocrity and the book entitled *Island Nights' Entertainment* never attained popularity.

Louis was particularly pleased with the Tauchnitz editions of his stories—as with the French and Italian also—but a sorry end came to *Footnote to History*. Because it was harshly critical of German rule in Samoa, the German government ordered the entire edition destroyed. Louis was scarcely more surprised at this than he was when he received word that the book was being translated for German publication. He wrote immediately to Christian Karl von Tauchnitz that he would gladly share his loss and for him to draw upon Charles Baxter for whatever sum he deemed fair. Young Tauchnitz' reply is in the Beinecke collection.

My dear Mr. Stevenson,

Your kind letter of the 6th December and the generous proposal contained in it, have really touched us, and we thank you heartily for both. On the other hand, we consider it merely our duty to bear the loss in question quite alone, and request you kindly to give your assent to these our views of the matter.

I have, accordingly, written to our common friend Mr. Baxter not to place any amount to our credit.

With my father's and my own kindest regards

> I beg to believe me
> Yours very truly
> Tauchnitz

Leipzig,
the 9th of January,
1894.

Aside from speaking out in self-defense, criticism and minor setbacks had little effect on Louis's spirits. In one less modest such a casual attitude might have been construed as conceit. Teuila spoke often of his love of being alone. Whether walking in the forest or riding the bush trails on Jack, he lived in a world apart, and when he would return to his balcony room, it was as if he had not been away.

Living in remote places does this to one. The mail comes, or a friend arrives. For the moment you are of the world. Then the world recedes, and you stand theoretically aloof from the rest of mankind. Nature's compensation, perhaps, to those who live in far-away places.

One day when I was reading with Teuila the laudatory comments of Cope Cornford written the year after Louis's death in praise of the story, "Will o' the Mill," she said sadly, "Oh, what that would have meant to Louis! He thought people did not care for the story that he himself loved so dearly."

The story was written in 1872, when he was groping for literary style, but not published until 1878, when it received little notice. Then in 1895 Cornford acclaimed it "his greatest achievement in literature":

To me, at least, that melancholy and beautiful fable is the best of Stevenson, and resumes his whole ideal pholosophy of life.

. . . the whole is informed with a sort of fatalism, hopeless yet courageous, which the English mind sets to the account of the Celtic temperament.

Had Stevenson been untimely taken by death when he had written *Virginibus Puerisque* and *Will o' the Mill,* and of all his works only these two gone down to posterity, he would still have earned the reputation of a refined and admirable artist. . . .

Style and treatment exactly accord with the subject; and the scenes, succeeding each other in natural progression, remain like pictures in the memory . . . above all, the night when Will o' the Mill goes at last upon his travels, which I venture to characterise as one of the finest pieces of pictorial narration in English literature.[3]

The dramatic chapter, "Death," must through the years have been a solace to millions of readers, picturing as it does the Reaper coming as a friend who invites Will o' the Mill to come with him on a journey, offering him his arm as they walk out of the courtyard. Still a law student and already having experienced critical illnesses, the young author is putting into words his serene comradeship with Death. He has Will philosophize, "When I was a boy I was a bit puzzled, and hardly knew whether it was myself or the world that was curious and worth looking into. Now I know it is myself, and stick to that."

Cornford says further: "Stevenson was forever exploring his consciousness; and, with a sort of naïve egoism, has made the whole reading world partaker in the fruits of that fantastic country. . . . 'Will o' the Mill' is the Stevensonian 'pattern in the heavens'; the story of a sojourn in the country of the ideal. . . . There is no moral to this fable, but the Celtic moral of fatalism; a fatalism which Stevenson sometimes tacitly disavows, and sometimes poignantly presents to you."[4]

[3] (New York, Dodd, Mead, 1900), 89–90.
[4] *Ibid.,* 90.

And Louis himself once wrote: "Life is not designed to minister to a man's vanity . . . when the time comes that he should go, there need be few illusions left about himself. Here lies one who meant well, tried a little, failed much. . . . surely that may be his epitaph, of which he need not be ashamed."[5]

Considering everything, Louis had during his lifetime more praise for his work than many writers of that time, and came nearer to personifying romance by accepting the unconventional without defying fundamentals, so that he himself was the story. At Vailima, where he literally was lord of all he surveyed, he was happier than at any other time in his life and able to do more work. When he was cutting double capers and applying himself more arduously to writing than Fanny deemed safe, she used to call him Mr. Fastidious Brisk, a nickname he enjoyed.

There were restless periods when he longed desperately to get away for visits to other places. Vicarious adventure became an irritant. Characters dawdled across the page. The sea's call was a cruel taunt. Fanny and Teuila would quickly arrange a *malaga* with a dozen men rowing a "long boat" for a picnic at some coast village with singing and *sivas,* swimming and diving, searching the reef for shrimp and clams, and home by torchlight.

But Louis's illnesses in Sydney and on his return visit to Honolulu warned him against leaving the balminess of Vailima, where good food, cheerful companionship, and regular hours of rest and sleep kept him in better health than he had ever dreamed he would enjoy.

His brain had never been so active. Story plots and characters crowded upon him faster than he could write. Teuila scoffed at the reports that he feared the time was near when he should be written out. There were times when he was tired and writ-

---

[5] "Christmas Sermon," *Records, etc.* (vol. XV, Pentland ed. of *Works*), 347.

ing would be laid aside for a few days for the pleasure of correspondence. At these times there would be gay dinner parties with guests from Apia, or a *taumafatoga* (feast of friendship) spread on the veranda with all their Samoan friends invited. Following these diversions, it was back to work in the quiet of that balcony room.

Teuila herself was the model for Catriona, with all sorts of arguments ensuing over such momentous questions as the position of dimples on the elbow and whether the heroine should wear white or pink stockings with a pink dress. Louis held out stubbornly for the pink hosiery. There was no arduous application in the writing of Catriona. David Balfour and Alan Breck were well-established characters, and only James Drummond and Catriona had to be brought forward from their places in *Kidnapped.* It was the cramp in the hand, defying all efforts at relaxation, that would call Teuila to take dictation for a few hours, or a few days in stubborn attacks.

Louis enjoyed telling his stories in the first person. He himself was David Balfour, and there was considerable boyish glee in working the young hero into and out of tight situations. *Kidnapped* was originally published as a serial in *Young Folks* magazine with the idea of making it a companion story to *Treasure Island,* which had been such a surprising success. Later in the same year, 1886, it was published as a book. But it lacked the swift-moving adventure of the earlier work, and when Louis had David fleeing the Red Coats with Alan Breck, he juggled Scotland's geography, to the consternation of the Highlanders. Since this yarn was written at Bournemouth, there seems little excuse for misplacing dells and burns, especially when he had been provided with a detailed map; also with a parcel of accounts of historical trials sent from London as a source of entertainment for the Skerryvore family, in which there was included, writes Edmund Gosse, "The trial of James Stewart in Aucharn in Duror of Appin for the murder of Colin Campbell of Glenure."

Edmund Gosse comments further:

"Kidnapped" had the honour of being read and eagerly discussed in the Appin country itself. For several years after his first residence in America, Stevenson frequently received "letters of expostulation or commendation from members of the Campbell and Stewart clans," and one enthusiastic Highlander presented him with a M S. pedigree of the family of Appin, which differed in several particulars from the facts as laid down in Stevenson's romance. The worthy clansman seemed to think that the least the novelist could do was to re-write his romance. But by that time the guilty historian was starting a fresh tissue of biographical inexactitudes, the story of "Catriona," and the honour of the house of Appin was never avenged.[6]

In Louis's dedication of the story to Charles Baxter he wrote:

I might go on for long to justify one point and own another indefensible; it is more honest to confess at once how little I am touched by the desire for accuracy. This is no furniture for the scholar's library, but a book for the evening schoolroom when the tasks are over, and the hour for bed draws near; and honest Alan, who was a grim old fire-eater in his day, has in this new avatar no more desperate purpose than to steal some young gentleman's attention from his "Ovid," carry him a while into the Highlands and the last century, and pack him to bed with some engaging images to mingle with his dreams.

Such trivial inaccuracies as David's resolve to purchase a new wardrobe for Catriona and returning in a few hours with ready-made dresses, etc., complete, would not have worried a *man* in writing of the seventeenth century!

[6] Introduction to vol X of Pentland ed. of *Works* (*Kidnapped, Catriona,* Part One), 6.

Catriona (*David Balfour*) was not designed for youth's reading. David was now a grown man, and Louis, grown richer in thought by five years of writing, was dipping deeper into a hitherto restrained portrayal of conventional amorousness. He was making a "bold pitch" of a love affair which was to motivate the story instead of being incidental to adventure and thus calling down criticism for his inability to handle feminine characters. And for that period the romance of David and Catriona might have been considered as risqué to Victorian readers as was the innocently unconventional affair of Uma and Wiltshire.

As amanuensis for *Catriona,* Teuila confesses that the Scottish words had to be spelled—as always did the words with *ie* and *ei,* and she adds with a chuckle, "many others of three syllables and over!" Sometimes in his dictating Louis would make an excuse to stop for a while; then when work was resumed, Teuila would find that he had written through a touching or emotional scene. At first he used to apologize for this, what he termed, weakness; later the procedure was rather taken for granted and nothing was said about it.

"Louis never used a dictionary or thesaurus," says Teuila. "There was a dictionary in the library downstairs for use by the rest of the family—most often to settle disputes—but Louis seldom hesitated for the right word from his rich vocabulary. Occasionally he might change a phrase or an entire sentence in the final copy, but the original words would be the same.

"And he never discussed stories, as such, with the family. Occasionally some bit of local color or historical incident might be mentioned casually as a holdover from the day's work, and rarely a character whom he liked might be mentioned; but plots, never—they were not divulged until the denouement was approached, not even to me as I would be writing for him.

"If ever he did read portions of a story to the family, it was most probably to clear a phrase or situation that was puzzling him. I know he did discuss sales values and reader reaction with my mother in those cordially intimate evening visits, for he had sincere respect for my mother's judgment and often laughingly deplored his own business acumen.

"But I'm afraid my brother got a trifle overdramatic when he told of Louis's following him out into the night and begging his praise for a story he'd just finished reading. Lloyd, bless his heart, was adding his own act to Louis's drama."

Louis's frank appraisal of his own work shows not only his zest in writing but confidence in his creative ability. In September of 1892 when *Catriona,* which he himself first titled *David Balfour,* was finished, he wrote to Sidney Colvin:

David Balfour done, and its author along with it, or nearly so. Strange to think of even our doctor here repeating his nonsense about debilitating climate. Why, the work I have been doing the last twelve months, in one continuous spate, mostly with annoying interruptions and without any collapse to mention, would be incredible in Norway. But I *have* broken down now, and will do nothing as long as I possibly can. With David Balfour I am very well pleased; in fact these labours of the last year—I mean *Falesá* and *D. B.,* not Samoa of course—seem to me to be nearer what I mean than anything I have ever done; nearer what I mean by fiction; the nearest thing before was *Kidnapped.* I am not forgetting the *Master of Ballantrae,* but that lacked all pleasurableness, and hence was imperfect in essence. So you see, if I am a little tired, I do not repent.[7]

In this same letter he writes of Emil Zola's novel of the Franco-Prussian war:

The third part of the *Débâcle* may be all very fine; but I cannot read it. It suffers from *impaired vitality,* and *uncertain aim;* two deadly sicknesses.

[7] *Vailima Letters,* 193.

Vital—that's what I am, at first: wholly vital, with a buoyancy of life. Then lyrical, if it may be, and picturesque, always with an epic value of scenes, so that the figures remain in the mind's eye for ever.[8]

This criticism of *Débâcle* followed praise of parts one and two in a previous letter:

I am now well on with the third part of the *Débâcle*. The first two I liked much; the second completely knocking me; so far as it has gone, this third part appears the ramblings of a dull man who has forgotten what he has to say—he reminds me of an M.P. But Sedan was really great, and I will pick no holes. The batteries under fire, the red-cross folk, the county charge—perhaps, above all, Major Bouroche and the operations, all beyond discussion; and every word about the Emperor splendid.[9]

Which shows a zest in reading quite equal to that of writing.

It is difficult to say whether Louis enjoyed more the social interlude between stories or the long periods of work. Teuila smiled cryptically at his "and will do nothing as long as I possibly can." Even though he was the most gregarious of men, writing was his life—a consuming part of his very existence. Idleness begat restlessness, then followed nervousness, overexertion in helping about the premises or overexcitement in social affairs at Apia, and consequent fever and irritability.

Of one of these interludes of idleness he writes to Colvin in October, 1892:

This is very late to begin the monthly budget, but I have a good excuse this time, for I have had a very annoying fever

[8] *Ibid.*
[9] *Ibid.*, 192.

with symptoms of sore arm, and in the midst of it a very annoying piece of business which suffered no delay or idleness. . . .
The consequence of all this was that my fever got very much
worse. . . . But, my dear fellow, do compare these little larky
fevers with the fine, healthy, prostrating colds of the dear old
dead days at home. Here was I, in the middle of a pretty bad
one, and I was able to put it in my pocket, and go down day
after day, and attend to and put my strength into this beastly
business. Do you see me doing that with a catarrh? And if I had
done so, what would have been the result?

Last night, about four o'clock, Belle and I set off to Apia,
whither my mother had preceded us. She was at the Mission;
we went to Haggard's. There we had to wait the most uncon-
scionable time for dinner. I do not wish to speak lightly of the
Amanuensis, who is unavoidably present, but I may at least say
for myself that I was as cross as two sticks. Dinner came at last,
we had the tinned soup which is usually the *pièce de résistance*
in the halls of Haggard and we pitched into it. Followed an
excellent salad of tomatoes and crayfish, a good Indian curry,
a tender joint of beef, a dish of pigeons, a pudding, cheese and
coffee. I was so over-eaten after this "hunger and burst" that
I could scarcely move; and it was my sad fate that night in
the character of the local author to eloqute before the public
—"Mr. Stevenson will read a selection from his own works"—
a degrading picture. I had determined to read them the account
of the hurricane, I do not know if I told you that my book has
never turned up here, or rather only one copy has, and that in
the unfriendly hands of ———. It has therefore only been seen
by enemies; and this combination of mystery and evil report
has been greatly envenomed by some ill-judged newspaper
articles from the States. Altogether this specimen was listened
to with a good deal of uncomfortable expectation on the part
of the Germans, and when it was over was applauded with un-
mistakable relief. . . . Belle, my mother and I rode home about

midnight in a fine display of lightning and witch-fires. My mother is absent, so that I may dare to say that she struck me as voluble. The Amanuensis did not strike me the same way, she was probably thinking, but it was really rather a weird business, and I saw what I have never seen before, the witch-fires gathered into little bright blue points almost as bright as a night-light.[10]

The "beastly business" he refers to, into which he had to put his strength, was, of course, the continuing drive against the corrupt German government of Samoa. With the land title of Vailima safely transferred to James Baxter in late April of that year, he could fight with a freer hand; and knowing law, he could not be bluffed into silence, even though others who might have supported him did remain silent in order to save their business and professional interests.

Later, on a storm-threatening evening after an interview in Apia that he had expected to be not too pleasant, but in which he had vowed to say all that he had to say, he writes: "I got home to a silent house of sleepers, only Fanny awaiting me; we talked a while, in whispers, on the interview." Diminutive Fanny sitting at the top of the veranda steps, anxiously watching the approaching storm, listening intently for Jack's quick nervous hoof-beats on the soft earth road, in the great hall a single lamp burning low—we cannot wonder that through all the subsequent years of loneliness she never used the word "widow."

Scarcely a month had passed since the completion of *Catriona,* yet there was the chaos of interviews during which he spoke his mind without reserve, the days of beastly business at Apia, of dancing parties and dinners, of seeing Austin off to school in San Francisco, upon which occasion he observed, "There is always something touching in a mite's first launch." And in addition the persistent rumor of possible deportation, which

[10] *Ibid.,* 196–97.

stirred the Samoans to greater anxiety than it did Louis himself, since he practically had dared them to do their worst and he knew he had called their hand—out of all this was born *Weir of Hermiston.*

Unlike "Falesá," it was not conceived as a coruscation. Rather, the drama of such a story had been brewing in his brain ever since his law student days when he pored over the infamously cruel verdicts of Robert MacQueen, Lord Braxfield, of the Scottish bench, which had earned for him the unsavory cognomen of the "Jeffreys of Scotland." No other jurist in history has equaled the judicial barbarities of that English judge, Baron George Jeffreys, born a Welshman, whose name for a hundred years—and ever after—has been a synonym for inhumanity. The only difference between him and Braxfield was the latter's narrower confines of judicial authority.

Louis wanted to use the single name, Braxfield, for the title of the novel, but ruled it out as impossible, even though the man had been dead for nearly a century and the details of the story were laid twenty years or so after his time. Consequently he chose one of the commonest names in Scotland, Adam Weir, and put him in the role of Lord-Justice Clerk, Lord of Hermiston. The locale was the village of Hermiston, one and one-half miles north of Currie in Midlothian. Time: about 1812.

The first cast of his characters included, besides the title name, Adam's son, Archie; Aunt Kirstie Elliott, housekeeper at Hermiston; her brother Elliott, of Cauldstaneslap; Kirstie Elliott, his daughter; and four Elliott sons—Jim, Gib, Hob, and Dandie; then there was Patrick Innes, a young advocate, and the Lord-Justice General. The character missing in this early enumeration was Adam's wife, Archie's sanctimonious mother. Yet, when he actually got down to writing the story, it opens with this woman, Jean, daughter of the "riding Rutherfords of Hermiston," in the role of foil in depicting the innate cruelty of Adam as her suitor. He was exuberantly happy with this prospect and wrote immediately to Edinburgh for all available records and documents of Braxfield's reign of terror.

Had Louis been able to devote himself entirely to *Hermiston* when it was first conceived, he undoubtedly would have made it among the best of his many stories. But work on *Ebb Tide* kept hitting snags. There was too much discrepancy in the talents of the collaborators. Louis would straighten mediocre passages, and Lloyd immediately would work the characters into another dead end, from which they again had to be extricated and set on a proper course. Rewriting for literary perfection was one of Louis's chief enjoyments, but the manual labor entailed in this type of rewriting irritated him to the point of profanity. Yet he was too generous and kind to refuse aid to Lloyd's meager talents in story construction. Months passed, and in May, 1893, Louis wrote:

We call it *The Ebb Tide*. . . . The book, however, falls in two halves, when the fourth chapter appears. I am on p. 82 . . . and expect to finish on I suppose 110 or so; but it goes slowly, as you may judge from the fact that this three weeks past, I have only struggled from p. 58 to p. 82: twenty-four pages, *et encore* sure to be rewritten, in twenty-one days. This is no prize-taker; not much Waverley Novels about this! . . .

I can't think what to say about the tale, but it seems to me to go off with a considerable bang. . . . Attwater is a no end of a courageous attempt . . . how far successful is another affair. If my island ain't a thing of beauty, I'll be damned. Please observe Wiseman and Wishart; for incidental grimness, they strike me as in it. Also, kindly observe the Captain and *Adar;* I think that knocks spots. In short, as you see, I'm a trifle vainglorious. But oh, it has been such a grind! The devil himself would allow a man to brag a little after such a crucifixion! And indeed I'm only bragging for a change before I return to . . . p. 88, where I last broke down. I break down at every paragraph, I may observe; and lie here and sweat, till I can get one sentence wrung out after another. Strange doom; after having worked so easily for so long! Did ever anybody see such a story of four characters?

It may interest you to know that I am entirely *tapu,* and live apart in my chambers like a caged beast. Lloyd has a bad cold, and Graham and Belle are getting it. Accordingly, I dwell here without the light of any human countenance or voice, and strap away at *The Ebb Tide* until (as now) I can no more. Fanny can still come, but is gone to glory now, or to her garden. Page 88 is done, and must be done over again to-morrow, and I confess myself exhausted. Pity a man who can't work on along when he has nothing else on earth to do! But I have ordered Jack, and am going for a ride in the bush presently to refresh the machine; then back to a lonely dinner and durance vile.

[*Two days later:*]

My progress is crabwise, and I fear only IX. chapters will be ready for the mail. I am on p. 88 again, and with half an idea of going back again to 85. We shall see when we come to read: I used to regard reading as a pleasure in my old light days. All the house are down with the influenza in a body, except Fanny and me. The influenza appears to become endemic here, but it has always been a scourge in the islands. Witness the beginning of *The Ebb Tide,* which was observed long before the Iffle had distinguished himself at home by such Napoleonic conquests. I am now of course "quite a recluse," and it is very stale, and there is no amanuensis to carry me over my mail, to which I shall have to devote many hours that would have been more usefully devoted to *The Ebb Tide.* For you know you can dictate at all hours of the day and at any odd moment; but to sit down and write with your red right hand is a very different matter.

[*Again two days later:*]

Well, I believe I've about finished the thing, I mean as far as the mail is to take it. Chapter X. is now in Lloyd's hands for remarks, and extends in its present form to p. 93 incl. On the 12th of May, I see by looking back, I was on p. 82, not for the first time; so that I have made 11 pages in nine livelong days.

[*The following day:*]

And here I am back again on p. 85! the last chapter demanding an entire revision, which accordingly it is to get. And where my mail is to come in, God knows! This forced, violent, alembicated style is most abhorrent to me; it can't be helped; the note was struck years ago on the *Janet Nicoll*, and has to be maintained somehow; and I can only hope the intrinsic horror and pathos, and a kind of fierce glow of colour there is to it, and the surely remarkable wealth of striking incident, may guide our little shallop into port. If Gordon Browne is to get it, he should see the Brassey photographs of Papeete. But mind, the three waifs were never in the town; only on the beach and in the calaboose. By George, but it's a good thing to illustrate for a man like that! Fanny is all right again. False alarm!

23rd. Mail day.

The Ebb Tide, all but (I take it) fifteen pages, is now in your hands—possibly only about eleven pp. It is hard to say. But there it is, and you can do your best with it. Personally, I believe I would in this case make even a sacrifice to get Gordon Browne and copious illustration. I guess in ten days I shall have finished with it; then I go next to D. Balfour, and get the proofs ready: a nasty job for me, as you know. And then? Well, perhaps I'll take a go at the family history. I think that will be wise, as I am so much off work. And then, I suppose, *Weir of Hermiston,* but it may be anything. I am discontented with *The Ebb Tide,* naturally; there seems such a veil of words over it; and I like more and more naked writing; and yet sometimes one has a longing for full colour and there comes the veil again. *The Young Chevalier* is in very full colour, and I fear it for that reason.

[*The 29th of May:*]

Still grinding at Chap. xi. I began many days ago on p. 93, and am still on p. 93, which is exhilarating, but the thing takes shape all the same and should make a pretty lively chapter for an end of it. For xii, is only a footnote *ad explicandum*.

[*June 1:*]

Back on p. 93. I was on 100 yesterday, but read it over and condemned it.

[*10 A.M.:*]

I have worked up again to 97, but how? The deuce fly away with literature, for the basest sport in creation. But it's got to come straight! and if possible, so that I may finish *D. Balfour* in time for the same mail. What a getting upstairs! This is Flaubert outdone. Belle, Graham, and Lloyd leave to-day on a malaga down the coast; to be absent a week or so: this leaves Fanny, me, and —— who seems a nice, kindly fellow.

[*June 2:*]

I am nearly dead with dyspepsia, oversmoking, and unre-munerative overwork. Last night, I went to bed by seven; woke up again about ten for a minute to find myself light-headed and altogether off my legs; went to sleep again, and woke this morning fairly fit. I have crippled on to p. 101, but I haven't read it yet, so do not boast. What kills me is the frame of mind of one of the characters; I cannot get it through. Of course that does not interfere with my total inability to write; so that yes-terday I was a living half-hour upon a single clause and have a gallery of variants that would surprise you. And this sort of trouble (which I cannot avoid) unfortunately produces nothing when done but alembication and the far-fetched. Well, read it with mercy!

The Balcony Workroom

[8 A.M.:]

Going to bed. Have read it, and believe the chapter practically done at last. But lord! it has been a business.

[*June 3, 8:15:*]

The draft is finished, the end of Chapter XII. and the tale, and I have only eight pages *wiederzuarbeiten.* This is just a cry of joy in passing.

[*10:30:*]

Knocked out of time. Did 101 and 102. Alas, no more to-day, as I have to go down town to a meeting. Just as well though, as my thumb is about done up.

[*Monday, June 5:*]

I have to-day written 103 and 104, all perfectly wrong, and shall have to rewrite them. This tale is devilish, and Chapter XI. the worst of the lot. The truth is of course that I am wholly worked out; but it's nearly done, and shall go somehow according to promise. I go against all my gods, and say it is *not worth while* to massacre yourself over the last few pages of a rancid yarn, that the reviewers will quite justly tear to bits. As for D. B., no hope, I fear, this mail, but we'll see what the afternoon does for me.

[*4:15:*]

Well, it's done. Those tragic 16 pp. are at last finished, and I have put away thirty-two pages of chips, and I have spent thirteen days about as nearly in Hell as a man could expect to live through. It's done, and of course it ain't worth while, and who cares? There it is, and about as grim a tale as was ever written, and as grimy, and as hateful.

[*Tuesday, 6th of June:*]

I am exulting to do nothing. It pours with rain from the westward, very unusual kind of weather; I was standing out on the little verandah in front of my room this morning, and there went through me or over me a wave of extraordinary and apparently baseless emotion. I literally staggered. And then the explanation came, and I knew I had found a frame of mind and body that belonged to Scotland, and particularly to the neighbourhood of Callander. Very odd these identities of sensation, and the world of connotations implied; highland huts, and peat smoke, and the brown, swirling rivers, and wet clothes, and whiskey, and the romance of the past, and that indescribable bite of the whole thing at a man's heart, which is—or rather lies at the bottom of—a story.[11]

He pays glowing tribute to Jules Barbey d'Aurevilly, French *littérateur* who had died only in 1889, for his stories of Norman life; then he resumes a moody lookingglass analysis: "I wonder exceedingly if I have done anything at all good; and who can tell me? and why should I wish to know? In so little a while, I, and the English language, and the bones of my descendants, will have ceased to be a memory! And yet—and yet—one would like to leave an image for a few years upon men's minds—for fun. This a very dark frame of mind, consequent on overwork and the conclusion of the excruciating *Ebb Tide*. Adieu."

A few days later the mail came bringing some adverse criticism of *Island Nights' Entertainments*, upon which Louis commented: "Very amusing how the reviews pick out one story and damn the rest! . . . I know I ought to rewrite the end of this bluidy *Ebb Tide:* well, I can't. *C'est plus fort que moi;* it has to go the way it is, and be jowned to it!"

Here he turned with relief to a family history:

11 *Ibid.*, 228–38.

I propose to call the book: *Northern Lights: Memoirs of a Family of Engineers.* I tell you, it is going to be a good book. . . . come on with criticism! But I'll have to see. . . .

I shall put in this envelope the end of the ever-to-be-execrated *Ebb Tide,* or Stevenson's Blooming Error. Also, a paper apart for *David Balfour.* . . . Anyway, there are two pieces of work off my mind, and though I could wish I had rewritten a little more of *David,* yet it was plainly to be seen it was impossible. All the points indicated by you have been brought out; but to rewrite the end, in my present state of over-exhaustion and fiction-phobia, would have been madness; and I let it go as it stood. My grandfather is good enough for me, these days. I do not work any less; on the whole, if anything, a little more. But it is different.

. . . I am at a pitch of discontent with fiction in all its form— or *my* forms—that prevents me being able to be even interested. I have had to stop all drink; smoking I am trying to stop also. It annoys me dreadfully: and yet if I take a glass of claret, I have a headache the next day! Oh, and a good headache too; none of your trifles.[12]

A week later, after a day of absolute temperance, he wakened with one of the worst headaches he had ever had, so his high resolve went out the window and quinine was resorted to with apparently good results. It was now the latter part of June. Through July and into August there was little writing done. Civil war, mentioned previously, which Louis worked so hard to prevent, was on with all its ugly aspects of intrigue and deception. On one occasion Louis speaks of his being "in a crispation of energy and ill-temper. . . . It is a hateful business, waiting for the news; it may come to a fearful massacre yet."

Teuila remembered these off-writing days as filled with constant anxiety for her mother, who feared Louis's restlessness

[12] *Ibid.,* 241–42.

would tempt him to overexertion of some sort, yet hesitated, as always, to offend him by admonitions of caution. Sure enough, he foolishly joined his cousin Graham in a game of tennis and suffered a hemorrhage, which, he acknowledged, was to be expected. The swinging of the racket and the resulting deep breathing caused a rupture of the inelastic supportive tissue of the lungs, probably a break in the tender area of a former wound.

There was no pain—there rarely is in tissue hemorrhages—but it meant three or four days flat on his back in bed with absolute quiet; for another three or four days he could gradually be raised with an additional pillow from time to time. There was none of the pallor of former days. His skin was so ruddy and brown he could have passed for a light-complected Samoan. More than once he wished he could walk into the Saville Club and show off his coat of tan.

Out of that fortnight of inactivity came the recasting of the beginning of *Weir of Hermiston,* and as he called it, "cobbling on my grandfather,"

whose last chapter (there are only to be four) is in the form of pieces of paper, a huge welter of inconsequence, and that glimmer of faith (or hope) which one learns at this trade, that somehow and some time, by perpetual staring and glowering and re-writing, order will emerge. It is indeed a queer hope; there is one piece for instance that I want in—I cannot put it one place for a good reason—I cannot put it another for a better—and every time I look at it, I turn sick and put the MS. away. . . .

. . . I have a strange feeling of responsibility, as if I had my ancestors' *souls* in my charge, and might miscarry with them.

There's a lot of work gone into it, and a lot more is needed. Still, Chapter I. seems about right to me, and much of Chapter II. Chapter III. I know nothing of, as I told you. And Chapter IV. is at present all ends and beginnings; but it can be pulled together.

This is all I have been able to screw up to you for this month, and I may add that it is not only more than you deserve, but just about more than I was equal to. I have been and am entirely useless; just able to tinker at my Grandfather. . . .

All our wars are over in the meantime, to begin again as soon as the war-ships leave.[13]

Days of downright illness were accepted with a modicum of grace. Convalescence, no. Never outwardly unpleasant, Louis was drearily impatient with the infirmity that reduced him to idleness. In this instance he was stuck with the fourth chapter on his grandfather, dissatisfied with the progress of recasting *Weir of Hermiston,* and so turned to "Anne," which was the first title for "Viscount Ives," later named "St. Ives."

Deprecatingly he labels it a light story, "unintellectual, and except for adventure, a dull story"; but with the zest of composition, of seeing words materialize on paper, his spirits were restored like magic. He wrote to Colvin that he didn't promise anything and might "throw in your face the very last thing you expect—or I expect." He dictated fourteen chapters to Teuila; then began the long, tedious process of copying for the final draft.

Breaking into this writing and demonstrating his generosity was a manuscript received from W. H. Triggs, a young reporter on the *Christchurch Press,* New Zealand, to whom he had granted an interview in Auckland as he was en route home from Sydney. Louis was surprised and delighted that the young man had the grace to submit what he had written for criticism before publication instead of afterward, as was the general practice. He made annotations of errors and dictated corrections in a letter which is now in the files of Stevensoniana in the Turnbull Library at Wellington:

[13] *Ibid.,* 257–58.

[Triggs wrote a rather disparaging description of Apia, stressing its small inducement for a popular author who had to keep in touch with the English reading public all over the world to make it his home. The "bright spots in the picture" were the arrival of a mail steamer once a month and a small public library, started by an appeal from the British consul, Mr. Cusack-Smith. With Mr. Stevenson, it was added, "it was purely a question of health"; he had tried previously nearly every part of the world reputed to favor recovery from his disease. Louis commented:]

Certainly if this were all I would prefer to go to hell. Nor was it purely an affair of health. Honolulu suited me equally well. The high Alps probably better. I chose Samoa instead of Honolulu, for instance, for the simple and eminently satisfactory reason that it was less civilized. . . . As for the library, it was begun to a not inconsiderable extent from duplicates and discards from my own overflowing one. My own library was brought out from England. [Mr. Stevenson's own library fills shelves of two large rooms from floor to ceiling.—Note by amanuensis.]

[On several topographical inaccuracies:]

My dear Sir, you seem to have got into such a devil of a tangle about the way to my house that I have difficulty in knowing how to put you right. One part of the road which you seem to have ridden, *is* good, and it *does* lie through the plantations although not thick ones. Get past that and you will come to a road that is not a road at all and to bush that is only now (this year) being cleared in patches. You will best understand the position when I tell you that all the wood to build my house was carried about a third of the way on men's shoulders, and that all the stores and parcels were brought by pack-saddle.

The Balcony Workroom

We have a couple of old Auckland tram-car horses, a most excellent selection, the biggest and handsomest horses on the island. You should see them coming up through the forest with its tall trees, lianas, wild pineapples etc. The Sydney Civil Service Co-operative Society—our universal provider—are always most attentive to Donald and Edie whose tonnage they have accurately gauged and pack accordingly.

[About a statement quoted from one of Stevenson's writings that he gave four hundred pounds for his land; the writer adding that it was considered in the district that he gave a good price for it, but that he must "have spent that sum greatly magnified, upon it since":]

My house alone has cost me not less at least than two thousand pounds, so you may conceive how far you underrate the cost of things in this happy island. I bought about three hundred and fifty acres at about one pound an acre; it was thought extravagant at the time even by myself but nobody could buy land so cheap now. There are other seventy-three acres in dispute.

[The Samoans, notwithstanding their natural antipathy to work, did work for Stevenson, "from whom they are sure of good wages and good treatment":]

It may surprise you to learn that I pay lower wages than anyone in Samoa and it is my boast that I get better served, visitors have frequently said that Vailima is the only place where you can see Samoans run. People always tell you that Samoans will not work, or even if they do will not stay with you beyond a few months. Such seems to be the general experience; it is not mine. The reason of this is neither high wages nor indulgent treatment. Samoans rather enjoy discipline, they like however to be used like gentle-folk. They like to be used with scrupulous justice—they like a service of which they can be proud. This we try to give them by "trying" all cases of misdemeanour in the most serious manner with interpreters, forms of oath, etc., and by giving them a particular dress on great occasions.

If during your visit to Apia you saw a few handsome smart fellows in a striped jacket and a Royal Stewart tartan native lavalava, which as you are aware is a kind of kilt and *not* a loin cloth, they were Vailima boys. We have a tree at Christmas for all hands, a great native feast upon my birthday, and try in other ways to make them feel themselves of the family. Of course no Samoan works except for his family. The chief is the master; to serve another clan may be possible for a short time, and to get money for a specific purpose. Accordingly to insure permanent service in Samoa I have tried to play the native chief with necessary European variations. Just now it looks as if I was succeeding. Our last triumph was at the annual missionary feast. Up to now our boys had gone home and marched into the show with their own individual village. This time of their own accord they marched in a body by themselves to the meeting clad in the Vailima uniforms, and on their entrance were saluted as "Tama Ona" which may be literally translated into Scotch "Mac Richies" (children of the rich man).

We have a child on the place, a small fellow of eight or thereabouts; my daughter has amused herself in dressing him out in fine lavalava, white linen coat, and straw hat. In this guise he was strutting about in the Tivoli Hotel when the proprietor noticed him. "Hi Youngster," he asked in Samoan, "who may you be?" Feloaʻi replied with pride, "I am one of the Vailima men!"

Of course this almost involves discharging nobody; they must learn to count upon this house as a permanent refuge and I am rather hopeful that I may be able to carry it out upon these lines. Cases of misconduct must be met with some sort of pun-

ishment. At first I always discharged; now that we are beginning to take so much the character of a clan, and that, by the
previous process of discharges, as by survival of the fittest we
have so good a class together, I'm trying to substitute fines upon
a large scale. The other day I cut down the wages of one de-
faulter by one-half, this was cheerfully accepted and the man
is still with us. In fines, if the boy is Catholic the amount is
taken by the culprit to the Catholic Mission, if Protestant to
the Protestant Mission.

If you had come up about five o'clock you would have found
Mr. Osbourne and Mrs. Strong playing lawn tennis with some
of the boys who take it *a tour de role*, and sometimes go on
with the game by themselves after the bosses go in to dinner—
bosses I cannot say they are with regard to the game, for some
of the Samoans are capital players.

It is particularly pleasant, too, to hear them singing in their
houses at night, shouting with laughter and speechifying. At
my last birthday feast there were great doings, one or two of
which illustrate the feeling of the boys. (When I say "boys"
I mean men). You must know that every chief who respects
himself in Samoa must have an officer called a Tulafale, usually
Englished "Speaking Man." It is a part and perhaps the most
momentous of this officer's attributes to cry out the names at
the 'ava drinking. This is done in a peculiar howl or song very
difficult to acquire and I may say to understand. He must also
be fairly well versed in the science of Samoan names, as no
chief above a certain rank is ever "called" under his own name.
He has another, an " 'ava" name for the purpose. Well, I had
no Tulafale, and Mr. Osbourne held a competition in which
three or four of them howled against each other. The judgment
of Apollo fell upon one boy who was instantly a foot taller. I
am sorry to make such confessions of my disrespectability but
I must continue. I had not only no Tulafale—I had no *'ava name.*
I was "called" plain bald Tusitala or "Ona" which is only a sou-

briquet at the best. On this coming to the knowledge of a high chief who was present he paid me the graceful attention of giving me one of his own, and I was kindly warned before the event that I must look out and recognize the new name of Au-Mai-Taua-Ma-Le-Manuvao. The feast was laid on the floor of the hall; fifty feet by eight of solid provisions, fifteen pigs cooked whole underground, two hundred pounds of beef, ditto of pork, two hundred pineapples, over four hundred head of taro, together with fish, chickens, Samoan prepared dishes, shrimp, oranges, sugar cane, bananas, biscuit and tinned salmon in a proportion. The biscuit and tinned salmon, though not exactly to our taste, are a favorite luxury of the Samoan.

By night, and we sat down at four P.M., there was nothing left barring a few oranges and a single bunch of bananas. This is not to say of course that it was all eaten, the Samoans are comparatively dainty at a feast; but so soon as we rose, the arduous and difficult task of dividing what remained between the different guests was at once entered into, and the retainers of our guests, white and Samoan, departed laden to the sea. The wretched giver of a feast thus wakens on the morrow with a clean house, but it is not all loss. All gifts or favours in Samoa are to be repaid in kind and in a proportion, and to my feast nobody had come empty-handed. It was rather strange to look out next morning and see my courtyard alive with cocks, hens, and chickens.

[Concerning a statement that the white population was about four hundred and "the majority of these are Germans":]

No. An ignorant error continually repeated. There are only ninety Germans. The Americans less than twenty—and the rest English.

[On a description of the Stevenson "menage" and the zeal and efficiency with which Mrs. Stevenson directed and controlled the native staff:]

Here is the correct hierarchy at Vailima. Mr. Osbourne is the bookkeeper, general business manager and looks after the overseer and his gang of outside boys; Mrs. Stevenson—Agriculturist in correspondence with Kew Gardens, Honolulu, Brisbane, Florida, etc. Is general referee on all matters of science. Special charge of her own two experimental gardens. General supervisor of all the additions and improvements; for example, has just engineered a court of cement between the house and the kitchen, working with her hands, when her tongue failed her. Also doctor. Mrs. Strong acts as my amanuensis and has charge of the household and the house and kitchen boys. Thanks to her training, whereas we began with an Australian table-maid, German cook etc., we are now equally well served and better by a set of Samoan boys. Mr. Stevenson may be discredited as playing the part of veiled prophet and general. He rarely appears upon the scene unless someone has misbehaved; you must not be led into the idea that these are frequent occasions or the misdemeanours serious. The boys are awfully good on the whole. They are more like a set of well-behaved young ladies. They are perfectly honest people. Nothing of value has ever been taken from our house, where doors and windows are always left open, and upon one occasion when white ants attacked the silver chest, the whole of my family plate lay spread upon the floor of the hall for two days, unguarded. The hall is on the ground floor; we all sleep upstairs.

[Of the description of Mrs. Stevenson's dress in the house as "a single, loose flowing dress, such as Samoan women wear"; and "not infrequently going barefoot":]

No such things as shoes and stockings are ever worn by any

of us at Vailima. At home my costume consists invariably of an undershirt and a pair of trousers, *all told*. You seem to have got the notion of my Apia costume, which is perfectly correct consisting, if you please, not of a flannel but a fine linen shirt, and proper corduroy riding breeches and elegant half boots. [Mr. Stevenson's riding suits are made by Chorley, the tailor, in Sydney; and his boots by Abbey of the same place and that's as much as to say they are perfect.—Note added by the amanuensis.]

[On the statement that Mr. Stevenson is an early riser. For the sake of change he not infrequently takes a run to Sydney, or Honolulu by the mail steamer, and on board ship has been known to turn out at two o'clock in the morning to start writing:]

I rise with the sun, neither before nor after. I have never "put in" more than eight hours, and that I consider about three too many. I generally begin about six and finish when luncheon is ready at twelve.

[Local opponents of Stevenson's policy in espousing the cause of the "Arch Rebel," Mata'afa, declared that "he had mistaken his vocation when he set up as a politician." They concluded that "the romantic in Mata'afa's character and career appealed to the element of romance and chivalry in Stevenson himself," but they contended that he was "backing the wrong horse":]

I think I have been able to identify the source of your account of my political views in general. I shall content myself by saying that it is not yet proved that I "am sometimes" or indeed ever have been "mistaken in my political views." Indeed it looks very like as if I were to be proved right. If you had asked about a year ago you would have been told that I was out of my element, "had mistaken my vocation" and was "romantic" in my opposition to the Chief Justice and President, it would scarcely do to say so now. In other questions where I have not been so fortunate as to have my own way, you are told something of the same thing; at least I am entitled to the benefit of the doubt.

Dear Sir, These are the main criticisms I have to make and I have been led in making them into much more detail than I had anticipated. You will of course understand that I have been led into that detail solely for the purpose of clearness, but I think by vigorous selection and rejection you will have here the bones of a very interesting article, with the somewhat unusual quality of being true. It has been a pleasure to me to place at your disposal any facts which appeared needful to enable you to attain your purpose. I am little accustomed among newspaper men to be used with so much courtesy and consideration. So far all was plain sailing, I had merely to annotate those points in which you were led in error. It is a very different question when you ask me to volunteer information on my own book. I am very anxious to please you for the reason above stated but I own I do not like the task.

About reading: I can tell you what I have been reading in the last month. *Wodrow's Analecta, The Cloud of Witnesses, The Life of James Renwick, Fountainhall's Decisions. The Cruise of the Alert, Rob Roy* by Walter Scott for the eight-hundred-and-fiftieth time, a month's file of *Figaro* and the *Saturday Review*— and I have still the daily *Times* before me. There is a full confession and it does not seem to me very interesting; neither you nor your readers will probably know one half the books mentioned. About my life: I rise at six, work till twelve, lunch then, and either write or read again, or walk or ride or receive an occasional guest, or if my company are Samoans, I may sit down to a solemn 'ava drinking with the correct libations and salutations. This is a thing in which I consider myself a past master, and there are perhaps not twenty whites in the world who could say as much. At six I dine on fish and claret, and go to bed at eight. It seems to me the main defect of your paper is to hold me up as a helpless invalid. Although the routine of my life is so sedentary I often make considerable excursions on horseback or otherwise.

Yours very truly

Robert Louis Stevenson[14]

When in 1931 Mr. Triggs presented this letter to the Alexander Turnbull Library at Wellington, he wrote to Johannes Andersen:

In 1893, when I was a young journalist on the staff of the *Christchurch Press*, I was introduced to Stevenson in Auckland, and he gave me an interesting interview. A few months afterwards, when on a tour of the South Sea Islands, I called at Apia, hoping to see the great author in his island home. To my sore disappointment, I found he had gone on a visit to Honolulu. However, I got enough material on the spot, as I thought, to furnish an article on "R. L. Stevenson in Samoa" for an English magazine for which I was an occasional contributor. I thought it due to "R. L. S.," especially after his kindness in the Auckland interview, to let him see the article before publication, and did so with a request that he would strike out any inaccuracies, or any details which he thought should not be published. By return mail my draft came back with these twelve closely written pages of "Annotations" and supplementary information, dictated by Stevenson to his Amanuensis, Mrs. Strong, and signed by him. The great author was then in the full tide of success, with

14 This material is used here by permission of the Turnbull Library and Helen Hardwick-Smith, of Wellington, Mr. Triggs' daughter. See appendix for additional information about it.

Arrival of goods from Civil Service Co-operative Society
of New South Wales at Vailima, Upolu, Samoa, in 1892.
From left are Lloyd Osbourne, R. L. S., and Joe Strong.
Later Louis cut Joe Strong out of this picture and carefully
matched the foliage of the trees so that the omission
would be unnoticed.

Supreme Chief Mataʻafa-Iosefa of Upolu, with the *fue*,
emblem of authority, across his knees. It was of no avail
against German cannon fire.

R. L. S. with High Chief Tuimaleali'ifano. This photograph
was taken by a young Lutheran missionary who had
stopped at Apia on her way home from work in Melanesia.
This aristocratic Samoan orator spoke no English.

Teuila taking dictation in the cool downstairs sitting
room at Vailima.

Fanua, with Fanny, making *'ava* for the men of the
household in the breakfast room, 1893.

Robert Louis Stevenson in his final sleep in the
great hall at Vailima.

Last prayers beside the grave on the summit of Mount Vaea. Teuila is at the far right, Austin Strong and Lloyd Osbourne at her right.

XXXI   Requiem.
Under the wide and starry sky,
Dig the grave and let me lie.
Glad did I live and gladly die
   And I laid me down with a will.

Here may the winds about me blow;
Here the clouds may come and go;
Here shall be rest for evermo,
   And the heart for aye shall be still

This be the verse you grave for me:
Here he lies where he longed to be;
Home is the sailor, home from sea,
   And the hunter home from the hill

Original manuscript of R. L. S.'s "Requiem," showing
the "lost" second stanza.

Courtesy Henry E. Huntington Library

editors and publishers eager to take anything from his pen; yet he could put himself to all this trouble for a young colonial journalist, who had no claim whatever on his indulgence.

When the story was published in the London *Bookman,* Mr. Triggs sent a copy of the magazine to Vailima. Louis replied that he often had been interviewed by "beasts of the field," and it was a treat to find what he actually said faithfully reproduced. And added: "But why, O why, my dear Mr. Triggs, did you say I had long hair? It is years since I wore my hair long." Mr. Triggs says that in the interview he remembered only Louis's kindly brown eyes and the pleasant Scottish burr in his cultured voice, and the long hair came from an earlier photograph.

When they first went to Vailima, Teuila persuaded Louis to have his hair cut short, and she did the cutting, having gained his reluctant consent after watching the "barber's" work on Lloyd and Austin. He granted it neatened their appearance. Then, given a mirror after the work was done on his own locks, he remarked wryly that it didn't make him look any worse.

Louis's fleeting periods of impatience because of his lack of strength were minor irritants in the day's work at Vailima as compared with his petulant despair during the Davos days a decade and more ago. It was about the same time that he wrote the poem criticizing the course of "a river that from morn to night down all the valley plays the fool," that he read William Hurrell Mallock's book *Is Life Worth Living?,* published in London in 1879.

William Mallock was only a year older than Louis. Educated privately and at Balliol College, Oxford, he became entangled in Positivist theories and wrote *The New Paul and Virginia.* The following year there emerged from this mental tangle *Is Life Worth Living?,* dedicated to John Ruskin. Whether it was both books or merely the latter that inspired Louis's poem, we do not know, or whether or not it was published at that time or

307

merely sent to W. E. Henley, in whose handwriting we find the masterpiece of satire at the Huntington Library.[15]

To William Hurrell Mallock
By R. L. Stevenson

I am kind of a farthing dip,
Unfriendly to the nose and eyes;
A blue-behinded ape, I skip
Upon the trees of Paradise.

Now naked, now intent on ale—
Ensconced in a monastic cowl,
The angel lawns of life I still
With great activity befoul.

At mankind's feast, I take my place
In solemn, sanctimonious state,
And have the air of saying grace
While I defile my dinner-plate.

I am "the smiler with the knife,"
The battener upon garbage, I—
Dear Heaven, with such a rancid life,
Were it not better far to die?

Yet still, about the human pale,
I love to scamper, love to race,
To swing my irreverent tail
All over the most holy place;

And when at length, some golden day,
The unfailing sportsman, aiming at,
Shall bag me—all the world shall say:
Thank God, and there's an end to that!

[15] A gift from Phillip Gosse.

EPIGRAM

By the Same, on the Same

I saw him reach with several other birds
The isle of the Eternal sages who
On being pertly questioned in these words,
"Is life worth living?" answered, "Not for you!"[16]

If Louis knew Mallock personally, it would have required a well-fortified friendship to withstand the blast of this barrage of unconventional verbiage. Otherwise, if it had got to Mallock through publication, there must surely have been the challenge of "coffee and pistols at nine." Certainly they must have had friends in common among the self-styled literati of that day.

The poem is mentioned here because it probably represents the richest source of anything that Louis wrote for the ribbing that constantly went on at Vailima. Within that closely knit circle speech was daring and reckless, and no opening for a playful jab was overlooked. The merrier the better, and risibilities were easily tapped. Occasionally Fanny was anxious about Graham Balfour. He had not the mercurial qualities of the Vailima family, to say nothing of the temperamentally erupting Samoan help whom he never could quite understand, and his silences were puzzling. Fanny and Teuila were both relieved when Aunt Maggie returned from her visit to Scotland and resumed her post as hostess-in-general. Teuila spoke often of the high regard the entire family had for her, although her serene presence was the only contribution she made to the work of the household.

One afternoon when Louis was watching his mother paste

16 A notation signed "E. G." reads: "Given to me by R. L. S. in 1882. They are in Henley's writing." In *The Complete Poems of Robert Louis Stevenson* (1946), the second stanza and the epigram are omitted and the title is merely "A Portrait."

his press notices in her huge scrapbook, Teuila leaned over his shoulder and whispered, "Is fame all that it's cracked up to be?"

"It is," he replied, "when I see my mother's face."

"When he was ill and could not write, we'd all have given our eye-teeth to have been able to help a little," declared Teuila. "Our playing at deaf and dumb symbols was just an amusement. I used to read to him by the hour."

She had an excellent voice for the task—rich and deep, which in later years would have been described as almost masculine except for its color and modulation; her enunciation was precise, and always there was the infectious throaty laugh. This was in contrast to Fanny's rather high-pitched voice and high girlish laughter. The few Samoan women left who as young girls knew the Vailima family still speak of Teuila's laugh.

Reading was to Louis a solemn obligation to one's intelligence, and, strangely, fiction rated fifth in his taste. Taking precedence in the order named were history, poetry, articles on world affairs, and essays on every and any subject. Exceptions were the Bible, especially the Gospel according to St. Matthew, and Montaigne's essays. For poetry he always had within easy reach Walt Whitman's *Leaves of Grass,* and so often had he read and re-read "The Song of the Open Road" that the book opened at these pages. He expressed the effect of this volume on him in the *British Weekly,* London: ". . . a book of singular service, a book which tumbled the world upside down for me, blew into space a thousand cobwebs of genteel and ethical illusion, and, having shaken my tabernacle of lies, set me back again upon a strong foundation of all the original and manly virtues. But it is, once more, only a book for those who have the gift of reading. I will be frank—I believe it is so with all good books, except perhaps, fiction." This was written in 1887, yet *Leaves of Grass* remained within arm's length in that balcony workroom, and Teuila says he put infinite fire and vibrancy in his carefully measured reading:

The Balcony Workroom

Afoot and light-hearted I take to the open road,
Healthy, free, the world before me,
The long brown path before me leading wherever I choose. . . .

Coming at a time when Whitman was being derided by American critics for failure to conform to their conception of poetic form, this praise from Louis must have been heartening to the man who had had more than his share of adversity. And Louis may still have been thinking of him when he wrote:

Not all men can read all books; it is only in a chosen few that any man will find his appointed food; and the fittest lessons are the most palatable, and make themselves welcome to the mind. A writer learns this early, and it is his chief support; he goes on unafraid, laying down the law; and he is sure at heart that most of what he says is demonstrably false, and much of a mingled strain, and some hurtful, and very little good for service; but he is sure besides that when his words fall into the hands of any genuine reader, they will be weighed and winnowed, and only that which suits will be assimilated; and when they fall into the hands of one who cannot intelligently read, they come there quite silent and inarticulate, falling upon deaf ears, and his secret is kept as if he had not written.

The gift of reading, as I have called it, is not very common, nor very generally understood. It consists, first of all, in a vast intellectual endowment—a free grace, I find I must call it—by which a man rises to understand that he is not punctually right, nor those from whom he differs absolutely wrong. He may hold dogmas; he may hold them passionately; and he may know that others hold them but coldly, or hold them differently, or hold them not at all.

Well, if he has the gift of reading, these others will be full of meat for him. They will see the other side of propositions and the other side of virtues. He need not change his dogma for that, but he may change his reading of that dogma, and he must supplement and correct his deductions from it. . . . If he tries to see what it means, what truth excuses it, he has the gift, and let him read. If he is merely hurt, or offended, or exclaims upon his author's folly, he had better take to the daily papers; he will never be a reader.[17]

In his prodigious amount of reading, Louis promptly discarded books he did not care for; those he liked he regarded as new-found friends and zealously championed them as such in event of family criticism. Striking passages were brought to the dinner or luncheon table to be read and discussed, and an inspiring thought or neatly worded phrase was figuratively caressed for its beauty. On occasion, though not too often, he wrote to authors whose works he especially liked, as he did to David Christie Murray from Honolulu:

Dear Mr. Christie Murray,
Here is a strange place for me to date a letter from, to, a Brother Britain, a Brother artist, and (unless your three names belie you strangely) a Brother Scot. But the truth is I am committed to the South Seas (where I find everything to interest me and more health than I am used to have for some time) and I must do that by letter which I had rather do by word of mouth.

"By the Gates of the Sea" was my first introduction to your work; since then I have had a great deal of pleasure from your pages; and this last week I have been working up leeway with "Aunt Rachel," "Hearts," "The Weaker Vessel," and "First Person Singular," which I lay down to write to you. I wish to thank you, and congratulate you; setting aside George Meredith, our elder and better, I read more of my contemporaries with the same delight, and whatever you may think of my own produc-

[17] *Later Essays* (vol. XV, Pentland ed. of *Works*), 309.

tions, I think you will be like me in this, that you will set a value on the admiration of any fellow craftsman. I should not say what I meant if I did not add my thanks for the tone of your writing; several times you have encouraged me—and several times rebuked.

Take this very stupid scrawl from a worked out man, who is reduced to the level of writing blank verse when he tries to write prose (do you know the stage?) and take it for a little more than it is worth; for had I been my own man, and could I express adequately what I feel at this moment, you should have had a charming letter. Mrs. Stevenson sends her compliments to Mrs. Murray, which I do more humbly; for the result of a prolonged course of your novels is to make us inclined not only to like yourself, but your wife; a man's wife gets into his fiction, for better, for worse. Some day I hope we may meet, and—*For heaven's sake,* don't answer this; I know what a business it is; only when you hear [?] and have a chance, be as kindly as your books and come to see me.

R. L. S.[18]

It was at Sydney following the *Janet Nichol* cruise that Louis found the first writings of Rudyard Kipling—two or three pocket-sized paper-bound books, as Teuila remembered, and a few issues of the Allahabad *Pioneer,* one of the leading publications of the East, to which the young journalist contributed as a staff writer. Louis was charmed. He had a very extensive library of books on India—which he had always wanted to visit —but here was a writer, virile, daring, and brilliant, bringing India to him as no other writer had, and depicting characters even more sinister than the Secundra Dass he had created for his *Master of Ballantrae.*

Louis probably purchased *Plain Tales from the Hills, Departmental Ditties,* and *Letters of Marque,* the last containing

[18] In the Henry E. Huntington Library.

the three stories, "Dead City of Amber," "Chitor," and "Palace of Boondi," later surpressed at the author's request because he considered them amateurish. All had been published in *The Pioneer* and afterward reprinted by Wheeler's Railway Library at Allahabad, designed for sale on the railway trains and at news depots at one rupee each. Only a few fragments of Kipling's work had found their way to London, and it was the wealthy *Pioneer* editor and publishers who sent the young writer on a trip to England via Australia and the United States. But for the tricks that fate often plays in human destiny the two writers might have met in Sydney in 1889.

Louis left an open order with a bookdealer in Sydney to send everything that Kipling wrote to Samoa. Then he wrote one of his characteristic letters of sincere appreciation to his fellow craftsman. When Kipling's *Soldiers Three* was published, the story of Black Jack began: "There is a writer called Robert Louis Stevenson, who makes most delicate inlay-work in black and white, and files out to the fraction of a hair. He has written a story about a suicide club, wherein men gambled for death, because other amusements did not bite sufficiently. My friend Private Mulvaney knows nothing about Mr. Stevenson, but he once assisted informally at a meeting of almost such a club as that gentleman has described; and his words are true."

Louis wrote in reply: "Well and indeed, Mr. Mulvaney, but it's good as meat to meet in with you, sir. They tell me it was a man of the name of Kipling made ye; but indeed and they can't fool me; it was the Lord God Almighty that made you."

Later Louis wrote to Henry James:

Kipling is by far the most promising young man who has appeared since—ahem—I appeared. He amazes me by his precocity and various endowment. But he alarms me by his copiousness and haste. He should shield his fire with both hands "and draw up all his strength and sweetness in one ball." ("Draw all his strength and all His sweetness up into one ball"? I cannot remember Marvell's words.) So the critics have been saying of me; but I was never capable of—and surely never guilty of— such a debauch of production. At this rate his works will soon fill the habitable globe; and surely he was armed for better conflicts than these succinct sketches and flying leaves of verse? I look on, I admire, I rejoice for myself; but in a kind of ambition we all have for our tongue and literature I am wounded. If I had this man's fertility and courage, it seems to me I could heave a pyramid.

Well, we begin to be old fogies now; and it was high time *something* rose to take our places. Certainly Kipling has the gifts; the fairy godmothers were all tipsy at his christening: what will he do with them?[19]

Thus there was always keen delight when a Kipling book or story appeared in the mail sack for Vailima, and the family gathered round after dinner to hear Louis "burr" his way through the roll and tumble of cockney dialect.

These vicarious visits gave zest and vigor to the nesiote working alone and far off in that upper balcony room. Teuila remembers the brighter eye, the cheerier voice, the more resolute qualities of dictation. And when the mail sack brought also the long-awaited legal material for *Weir of Hermiston,* Louis laid aside temporarily the lighter work on "Anne of St. Ives" and delved into the historical phases of the story he meant to be his best.

But mail sacks bring unpleasant messages, too. Some time previous Sidney Colvin had asked for money. Louis, presuming the request to be in the nature of reasonable commissions for criticisms and marketing, informed Charles Baxter to give him whatever he asked. Now came word from Charles Baxter that Colvin was drawing too much and that he, Louis, should pro-

[19] *Letters of R. L. S.,* ed. by Colvin, II, 256.

test. So Louis had the distasteful task of detailing to his friend the heavy expenses involved in maintaining the Vailima estate, that he had been advised of his diminishing funds in Edinburgh, and for the present it would be impossible to make further advances.

On the other hand, Louis had made specific provision that Henley, not in comparable financial circumstances with Colvin and never in good health, was to be given money if and when he needed it. The source of the funds was not to be revealed since their relationship had not been cordial after the flare-up in Saranac, which Louis certainly had gone more than halfway to overcome.

By this time the Viscount Anne had grown into a character much too interesting to be brushed aside, and Louis was continually turning back to dictate the daredevil through another perilous escape from his own foolhardiness. Then "Heathercat," a grim story of Scotland's tragic years, stepped into the author's versatile mind. The amanuensis never knew from one day to the next what story, or even stories, Louis would be dictating as she drew up her chair to the plain deal table with a cheery "*Saunia*" (Ready). There was no hurry about work, and some mornings would be given over entirely to correspondence—a pastime which was Louis's especial delight.

Months went by. A siege of influenza hit the household, and Louis was hustled off to Sydney. He escaped with only a light attack and worked a little on *St. Ives*. Back in the balcony workroom he found that the brief interlude had sharpened the characters of *Hermiston*, and Teuila remembered taking dictation only once or twice after that.

In order to avoid the long sessions of writing, he had taken to making the final draft after each episode. As a consequence, there is scarcely any evidence of the change in handwriting that appears in other manuscripts.

The manuscript of *St. Ives*, exquisitely boxed, is in the ar-

chives of Stevensoniana at the Huntington Library. To look
through these 312 legal-sized pages of finely written copy of
precisely even lines, with little marginal correction and little
interlineation, is a lesson in painstaking care in preparing a
manuscript. Only in Chapter XXVII does the handwriting of
the amanuensis appear. One's eyes dim with the last paragraph:
"I looked about the room, the goggling Rowley, the extinguished
fire; my mind reviewed the laughable incidents of the day and
night; and I laughed out loud to myself—lonely and cheerless
laughter! . . ."

Fortunately Louis had laughingly outlined to Teuila further
madcap escapades he had planned for the daring "Mr. Anne,"
so when Arthur Thomas Quiller-Couch, English critic and
novelist, accepted the assignment to complete his friend's unfinished story, he fulfilled his task with so much sympathy and
understanding that the casual reader might not be aware of the
change in authorship.

As for "Heathercat," this fragment of a few pages must ever
remain a mystery profoundly tantalizing. It should not be read
by the impressionable person, for he must forever after swing
above the eerie void of conjecture and supposition. Characters
drawn in this meager sketch are among the author's strongest,
and the theme is so gripping that no substitute writer could
evaluate and carry on the principal motivation, dealing as it
does with that tumultuous period of Scottish religious history
in the seventeenth century, out of which was born the tragically determined movement of nonconformists.

Louis wrote to his cousin, R. A. M. Stevenson, in June, 1894:

My work goes along but slowly. I have got to a crossing-place,
I suppose; the present book, *Saint Ives*, is nothing; it is in no
style in particular, a tissue of adventures, the central character
not very well done, no philosophic pith under the yarn; and,
in short, if people will read it, that's all I ask; and if they won't,

damn them! I like doing it, though; and if you ask me, why!—
After that I am on *Weir of Hermiston* and *Heathercat,* two
Scotch stories, which will either be something different, or I
shall have failed. The first is generally designed, and is a private
story of two or three characters in a very grim vein. The second
—alas! the thought—is an attempt at a real historical novel, to
present a whole field of time; the race—our own race—the west
land and Clydesdale bluebonnets, under the influence of their
last trial, when they got to a pitch of organisation in madness
that no other peasantry has ever made an offer at. I was going
to call it *The Killing Time,* but this man Crockett[20] has forestalled me in that. Well, it'll be a big smash if I fail in it; but
a gallant attempt. All my weary reading as a boy, which you
remember well enough, will come to bear on it; and if my mind
will keep up to the point it was in a while back, perhaps I can
pull it through.[21]

But Teuila declares it was the boy character, Archie, who began
to dominate Louis's mind, and all through the summer months
she would find him ready for dictation on *Weir of Hermiston.*
He loved the boy, and the pathetic scenes left him deeply
moved and probably built up his hate for the "Hanging Judge."
Louis loved boys, and in his books they were the happiest creatures of his imagination as they struggled up and out of their
young miseries of circumstances.

The embroilments of Samoan politics had leveled off into
the murkiness of distrust and resentment. The proud, light-
hearted young men who used to sing and laugh their swagger-
ing early morning way down Siumu Road, walked now in
silence, their bare feet treading their own land half in fear,
half in haughty defiance. Their *"talofas,"* no longer spoken with

[20] Samuel Rutherford Crockett, Scottish clergyman and novelist, just
Louis's age.
[21] *Letters of R. L. S.,* ed. by Colvin, II, 401.

a wide smile and gracious bow, were crisply flung with imperceptible lift to the chin.

Offending officials had concluded the climate was not conducive to their good health and had been replaced by others only slightly less arrogant towards the Samoans and Europeans who were outside the administrative radius. Louis commented to his cousin, R. A. M. Stevenson:

My great recent interruptions have (as you know) come from politics; not much in my line you will say. But it is impossible to live here and not feel very sorely the consequences of the horrid white mismanagement. I tried standing by and looking on, and it became too much for me. They are such illogical fools; a logical fool in an office, with a lot of red tape, is conceivable. Furthermore, he is as much as we have any reason to expect of officials—a thoroughly commonplace, unintellectual lot. . . . I observe in the official class mostly an insane jealousy of the smallest kind . . . . Sometimes, when I see one of these little kings strutting over one of his victories—wholly illegal, perhaps, and certain to be reversed to his shame if his superiors ever heard of it—I could weep. . . . *Tenez,* you know what a French post-office or railway official is? That is the diplomatic card to the life. Dickens is not in it; caricature fails.[22]

But with all the aggravating setbacks, Louis kept pounding away in the interests of common decency and consideration for the Samoans, especially dignity and respect for the Samoans of high rank. Occasionally there was still the deep boom of intimidating cannon shots and the shrill ping of rifle fire in reply. Germany did not want peace in Samoa. It was to her political advantage to maintain a semblance of war and thus extend her powers of government. Louis saw through this ruse, and the officials hated him for his discerning appraisal of their roguery.

[22] *Ibid.,* 399–400.

Not until August of this year were the imprisoned chiefs released from the crude open enclosure called a gaol. And in the month following they graded and built the rutty bit of road that led from the main highway to Vailima, calling it the "Road of Gratitude" for all that Louis had done in their behalf. Roadwork in Samoa usually is done as punishment for delinquent taxes or to work out a fine, but in this instance, when the officials at Apia sought to appraise the value of their work, the Samoans told them flatly to keep hands off, that this was their *alofa* to a beloved friend.

Yet all Louis's hammering away could not induce the stubborn officials to bring Mata'afa back from his exile on barren Jaluit Island in the Marshalls. At every opportunity Louis sent 'ava root and tobacco to the old man and the five lesser chiefs who had volunteered to share his banishment, along with his devoted daughter. Once Graham Balfour went personally to report on how the venerable high chief was faring. Louis was furious when Graham said it seemed as if the old man's spirit was completely broken—furious and utterly helpless.

In the meantime, though writing suffered, Louis worked unhurriedly on *Weir of Hermiston*. He was enjoying better health than he had ever known and was happy except for worry over the fate of the Samoans. It was during this August that he organized the famous, or infamous, paper chase on Sunday. On Monday he wrote to James Barrie:

Well sir, I have escaped the dangerous conjunction of the widow's only son and the Sabbath Day. We had a most enjoyable time, and Lloyd and I were 3 and 4 to arrive. I will not tell here what interval had elapsed between our arrival and the arrival of 1 and 2; the question, sir, is otiose and malign; it deserves, it shall have no answer. . . . The whole head is useless, and the whole sitting part painful: reason, the recent Paper Chase.

The Balcony Workroom

There was racing and chasing in Vailile plantation,
And vastly we enjoyed it,
But, alas! for the state of my foundation,
For it wholly has destroyed it.

Come, my mind is looking up. The above is wholly impromptu.—On oath,[23]

The thing of it was that they got lost in those rolling bush-
covered hills where the harriers had made too many feints
with the scattered paper, and frisky little Jack galloped over
half of the island of Upolu before they found their way home.
This, together with his "wholly destroyed foundation," cost
Louis considerable ribbing. The family never neglected to make
the most of such events, and this occasion afforded Aunt Maggie
the opportunity for some caustic remarks about his breaking
the Sabbath to frolic with the devil.

Each day during the making of the road Louis strolled down
to visit with the men, usually following luncheon, when they
would be resting from the midday heat. From these visits he
would return strangely serene. With driving nervousness gone,
he might loiter with the three womenfolk who, seeking the
coolest place, would have brought their needlework to the
great hall.

One afternoon when Teuila was putting a button-hole edging
on a saddle blanket, Louis wanted to try his hand at what he
thought was easy work. After wrestling with three or four snarls
of thread and surveying a couple of inches of drunken stitches,
he handed the task back. "Somehow," he admitted ruefully, "I
don't get the woman's bite-your-thread effect."

Sometimes he would just sit quietly, as if he had forgotten
the pettinesses of petty officials in Apia; sometimes he would
ask Fanny to go for a walk in the deep forest where he was

[23] *Ibid.,* 418.

fond of quoting Darwin's observation: "No one can stand in these solitudes unmoved, and not feel that there is more in man than the mere breath of his body."

If, with a quiet *"Tofa o tama'ita'i,"* (Good-bye, ladies), he went upstairs, Teuila knew that at any moment she might be summoned for dictation.

Question and answer programs might have originated at Vailima, for one of the pastimes of evening was what they called "Answer my question." All sorts of penalties and forfeitures were imposed if the person to whom the query was directed was not able to answer before someone else in the circle did. One evening Louis directed a question to Teuila. "What would you say to a person whom you did not remember, and who didn't remember you?" "Should I?" she shot back, and lifted her forfeitures for the session. All the family, including Aunt Maggie, tried in vain to confuse Louis by misleading questions on Scottish history. There was a heavy penalty for asking a question you yourself could not answer; as a consequence, erudition could not prevail against nonsense and sharp-wittedness.

While Fanny always was apprehensive of Aunt Maggie's acceptance of the family's clowning, she was doubly concerned about Graham Balfour's judgment of these antics. He had not lived in isolation where self-made entertainment of the froth-and-bubble type was an antidote for mental lethargy and he had shown little inclination to participate in creating nonsensical amusement.

One evening at dinner he innocently paid serious tribute to Louis's character of Will o' the Mill, saying he had made a deep impression upon his mind and, in a way, had molded his thinking on the problems of life.

Louis replied facetiously and rudely, "Will's sentiments about life are cat's meat!"

The entire family blushed with Graham as he replied stubbornly, "It's the best thing on life that has been written in this age."

Then Fanny, in one of her rare reprimands, said sharply, "Edmund Gosse has told Louis that if he'd never written another thing, Will o' the Mill would have made his literary fame."

Louis merely grimaced. To him it was simply not dinner-table talk—although secretly he always was a bit puzzled about what it was he had written into this character, a character created in the adolescence of his career and one he intentionally kept in the background.

However, nothing pleased Louis more in all his Pacific years than this visit from his cousin. He wanted Graham to tell those critics in London that he had not gone to "live among savages." And no better opportunity could have been afforded than to watch the building of *Ala loto alofa* (road of a loving heart). Here were a hundred men working—the strongest young men from the ranks of the *'Aumaga* and the *matai*. No *ali'i* (chief) did any actual work beyond the token gesture of swinging an axe or breaking a stone. His high office forbade it, however willing he might be.

These powerful men, naked except for tight loin-cloths, felled trees, grubbed stumps, carried crushed coral to level a roadbed, searched for stones as large as coconuts or larger, and drove them into the soft earth, then fitted the surface with smooth rocks. They worked from the first hint of dawn to the last flicker of daylight, many walking eight or ten miles from their homes, with only a brief rest for their midday meal, which was brought by the women of different villages as designated by the *ali'i*. Louis had offered to furnish food, but the Samoans would not have it.

These were no quiet, grim workers, sweating at their task through drenching showers and muggy tropical heat. They laughed and sang and kept up a continual reckless banter about the excellence of each group's work—who could fell a tree with the fewest strokes, which group could pull a stump with the fewest men, which two could carry away a felled tree, who could break the largest rock with a single blow of the sledge-hammer, anything and everything that presented competition, each for the approbation of their own *ali'i*. It is proverbial that Samoans play at their work and work at their play.

It was into the fifth week before they covered the road with thick slabs of sod and cleared away the debris, when the *ali'i* declared the work *fa'amu* (finished). Louis was invited to be the first to travel over it. So he rode Jack, who pranced side-ways, champed his bit, and nodded his head at the double row of men who sat cross-legged and stiff-backed on either side of the road, many with tears filling their eyes. Louis walked slowly back over this *Ala loto alofa* as he delivered feelingly in Samoan one of his best speeches, over which, as Teuila related, he had spent many hours of thoughtful study.

Then followed the grand climax—the *taumafatoga*. Again Louis's offer to furnish food was declined. Before dawn on that memorable September morning members of the 'Aumaga came in pairs, poles from shoulder to shoulder, chanting softly as they swung single-file in briskly measured strides up the rutted trail to the foot of the new road. Many had walked ten or twelve miles to get there, and many had been up the entire night pre-paring the food. From the poles were suspended whole roast pigs, baskets of cooked chickens, and lengths of barracuda and swordfish, each wrapped tightly in plantain leaves, baskets of cooked taro, yams, and breadfruit, fresh crayfish and shrimp, pineapples, papaya, maumé apples and mangoes, dozens of stems of bananas and literally mountains of coconuts—this feast of *sua taumafa* is second only to *sua taute* (food for royalty). It was the ultimate in their adoration.

Freshly cut saplings were stuck on either side of the lower portion of the road and awnings fashioned of palm leaves. Clean and polished banana leaves were spread for a table on the newly placed sod, and others were cut for plates to be used on the *laulaus*.

Later and with leisurely dignity came the *ali'i* wearing ceremonial *lavalavas* of *siapo* in shades of brilliant brown, each in his own traditional design, belted with fine old *fusi* of black *siapo*, each with his royal *'ula* (necklace of dull red pandanus seeds), and each carrying his *fue* (short stick with tassel of sinnet, which is his insigne of authority) over his shoulder.

Flocks of bright plumaged paroquets darting among the trees were no more colorful than the women in their gaily flowered *lavalavas*, who came with dozens of baskets of flowers—hibiscus, frangipani, delicate *pua* flowers, sweet-scented *moso'oi* and *laumaile*, fragrant-leafed vine. In addition to the *'ulas* woven for each member of the Stevenson family, they decorated the table with these and the lacy mountain fern. There were no children, so the quiet was broken only by the impudent notes of the saucy Polynesian blackbird and the half-sad cooing of the *manu-tagi* (Indian turtle dove or wild pigeon).

When the food had been spread down the length of the "table," the Vailima family was summoned; and when they were seated on the *laufala* mats, the *ali'i sili* asked a blessing in all the quiet eloquence characteristic of a Samoan orator. Although all are nominally Christian, upon occasions of deep emotion it is to their god Tagaloa that supplication is made. Even a stranger who is totally unfamiliar with the language cannot listen unmoved by the musical full-throated half-chanting tones of a man who has been trained from boyhood in oratory.

During a moment of silence a whole roast pig was placed before the highest ranking *ali'i*, who carved the hind quarter, and Louis was served with the ceremonial cut of pork—the *alaga-vae*, reserved usually for royalty. With this the feast was under way, to last until nightfall, with songs, competitive *sivas*

325

from different groups of the *'Aumaga,* and all sorts of competitive sports for groups and individuals.[24]

Louis was feeling so well at this time that he was toying with the idea of a lecture tour in the United States, then a quick visit to Scotland in midsummer. Fanny listened to these plans, but Louis knew by her silence that she did not approve. Finally he insisted upon having her opinion.

"Louis, you are strong only because we live here quietly. We don't need more money than we have. The plantation is almost keeping the house. Our heavy expenses are over . . ."

"Yes, yes, dear," he interrupted, "it's only that I'd like to strut a bit." They both laughed as he continued, "You remember the good time I had in Sydney, speaking to all the clubs and societies. I'd have walked ten miles to speak to an infants' school!"

"Wait until next springtime north of the equator, May or June," she cautioned patiently, "Then if you still are feeling as well as you do now, we'll go merely for a visit. But there must be no scheduled speaking tour. *That is out.* O-U-T, *OUT!*

"Thus spake the oracle!" he said with an exaggerated bow, kissed her good-night, and went to his own room.

Fanny had worried about his not having the companionship of those of his own ilk, and now this uneasiness was intensified by his apparent determination to try again to get back to Scotland. He had urged James Barrie to come to Samoa on a honeymoon trip; he had urged William Low to come for painting; most of all he wanted Edmund Gosse, just for the companionship of the friend he loved perhaps above all others.

She would have to see that there were more guests at Vailima. Yet many of the local personalities irritated him. They simply did not speak his language. Their topics of conversation were the "bread and gravy" type, and she knew a good book would be preferable. Songs and *sivas* of the Samoans he enjoyed for

[24] The feast was described to me in 1927 by an elderly *ali'i* who had been a *matai* at the time.

an hour or two every fortnight or so, but since it was an affront to stop a group of performers before all had practically reached the point of exhaustion, that diversion could not be employed too often.

However, in that quick way that time rolls along in a lively household, October passed, and it was Louis's November 13 birthday. For weeks Fanny, Teuila, and Lloyd had planned a great celebration. He would be forty-four. Only forty-four, yet he had accomplished through years of ill health a prodigious amount of writing. With flesh on his bones, tanned skin, hair cut short, and erect, easy carriage he might have passed for thirty-five. There was youth in his graciousness.

The day previous to the celebration men worked straight through the twenty-four hours killing and dressing four young pigs, fifty chickens, and hundreds of fish, digging yams and taro that stacked higher than a man's head, making hundreds of *pauli-sami* with the crisp fresh taro tops, cutting pineapple and banana stalks, and in general stripping the plantation. Women and girls gathered flowers from the forest in addition to denuding their own gardens, and wove at least a hundred *'ulas* and made half as many *sisi* (wide belts of flowers) for both the girls and the young men who would participate in the *sivas*.

Improvised arbors of palm fronds were erected over a wide spread of the grassy lawn, and from mid-morning guests arrived from distant villages. Early in the afternoon the *umus* were opened and the *tu'ua*, old men of history, gathered to chant their ancient blessing on the food as it was lifted out, steaming hot and fragrant with the spicy tang of plantain leaves. Carving of the pigs was done strictly according to traditional cuts for those of highest rank, and serving was strictly according to rank. As was their custom, Louis was rated an *ali'i sili*, high orator of his estate.

Teuila declares that there was not a single awkward moment during the entire day. The house boys were everywhere at once, playing the gracious host with the family. Louis was supremely happy, supremely proud. And when in the cool of early night, after hours of singing and dancing, the guests took their departure with baskets heavy with food, he found himself with scarcely a morsel for a late snack.

But the next morning when at daybreak he looked down from his balcony, he saw pigs tethered by a hind leg, chickens clucking in frightened choruses, bananas freshly cut from the forest, and yams and taro stacked in a circle of yellow papayas.

Thanksgiving Day that year fell on November 29. Fanny and Teuila planned a real American dinner—traditional turkey and cranberry sauce, chestnut dressing and brown gravy, creamed pearl onions and pumpkin pies—with all the Americans in Apia as guests. The table with satin napery, gleaming silver, and dazzling glassware presented a picture seldom seen in those days. Louis in the white dress jacket of the tropics at the head of the table, Fanny opposite in the black velvet evening dress with duchess lace which Louis had insisted upon buying when she had insisted she would never have occasion to wear it, Teuila and all the other ladies in a daring expanse of bosom and shoulders, men in white, with a dress-uniform or two— it is a picture that hallows the great hall at Vailima, November 29, 1894.

12. Last Days in the Balcony Workroom

"On Friday following Thanksgiving," said Teuila,[1] "Louis dictated with unusual precision. Relaxed and confident he paced the balcony room, or stopped before open windows to gaze at nothing in particular, or occasionally sat down at the deal table where I was writing to thumb through notes made on scraps of yellow paper, some going into the wastebasket, others stacked neatly and laid to one side.

"Among these discards were several trials of what he wished to say in dedicating *Weir of Hermiston* to my mother, although he was not wholly pleased with what he did write:

> *I saw rain falling and the rainbow drawn*
> *On Lammermuir. Hearkening I heard again*
> *In my precipitous city beaten bells*
> *Winnow the keen sea wind. And here afar,*
> *Intent on my own race and place, I wrote.*
> *   Take thou the writing: thine it is, For who*
> *Burnished the sword, blew the drowsy coal,*
> *Held still the target higher, chary of praise*
> *And prodigal of counsel—who but thou?*
> *So now, in the end, if this the least be good,*
> *If any deed be done, if any fire*
> *Burn in the imperfect page, the praise be thine.*

"Saturday was a hard day. The air was humid and still and

[1] The first part of this chapter is written wholly from Isobel Field's personal recounting to me.

sticky as it can be only in the tropics. We began work earlier than usual. Much of the time Louis stood with his back to the open window, resting against the sill, seeing nothing except the Scotland of his story as it unrolled before him. He made me think of an artist at his easel—a bold stroke of dark color here, a delicate pastel tint there, a background filled in with description . . . Yet Louis had said once that writing was like music. It should have rhythm and key. And once when I asked him if it were good for young writers to wade in emotions, he replied sharply, 'Good God, No! First make his words go sweet, and if he can't spend an afternoon turning a single phrase he'd better give up the profession of literature.'

"It was a mid-morning break when Sosimo brought a pitcher of limeade and Louis revealed the versatility of his temperament when he bowed low and addressed him as the statue of Forbes of Culloden. This nonsense dated back to Louis's beginning of *Hermiston*. Some form of drollery, even buffoonery, always set the tenor of our dinners, and this evening Louis came downstairs, folded his table napkin lengthwise, and put it on his head in imitation of a barrister's wig, then announced as he strode down the hall, 'I am walking in Parliament Hall in Edinburgh town. Here is the portrait of Lord Justice-Clerk, here is Lord Braxfield, and down here is Archie!' waving dramatically toward the end of the room.

"At that moment Sosimo appeared with a platter of hot food. Louis turned solemnly toward him, bowed low and said in his best Scotch brogue, 'And this is the statue of Forbes of Culloden!'

"Our house boys long ago had ceased to be surprised at the antics of this *papalagi* family, and poor Sosimo stood gaping for a few seconds before we all burst out laughing—that is, all except Aunt Maggie, who was scandalized—and Sosimo's mirth nearly cost us our platter of roast beef and yams. The pitcher of limeade was similarly endangered before the tray could be set down.

"The following morning Louis resumed dictation as if there had been no interruption, and we worked steadily until the gong sounded for luncheon. He had just finished the paragraph so poignant with emotion that no writer has been able to carry on: 'Archie ran to her. He took the poor child in his arms, and she nestled to his breast as to a mother's, and clasped him in hands that were strong like vises. He felt her whole body shaken by the throes of distress, and had pity upon her beyond speech. Pity, and at the same time a bewildered fear that this explosive engine in his arms, whose works he did not understand, and yet had been tampering with. There arose from before him the curtains of boyhood, and he saw for the first time the ambiguous face of woman as she is. In vain he looked back over the interview; he saw not where he had offended. It seemed unprovoked, a wilful convulsion of brute nature.'

"He reached across the table and with the exclamation, '*soia!*' (enough), closed the folio. With luminous brown eyes shining, he said, 'I see it all—right to the finish. Every phrase and paragraph is as plain as if written. I honestly believe it will be the best thing I've done.'

"But no one was to know what it was he saw. If only he had given me a hint—if only I had asked him, although at that time I would not have presumed to do so. Certainly it would not have been the happy ending which others made for him, since he once wrote to James Barrie deploring the happy ending he had given his *Little Minister*—that it was illogical and a lie."

A quiet Sunday was given over to letter writing. The mail steamer was due on Monday. It was summer holiday, and Austin was home from school in New Zealand, so there was more than a hint of boisterousness around the premises. But when Teuila tried impatiently to quiet him, Louis declared he liked the boyish exuberance. "I like the puppy-dog fun he gets out of wrestling with life."

And presently it was Louis chasing Austin out through the house and across the lawn, his long legs flying as he shouted to the laughing youngster, "Wait 'til I catch you and you'll get a sound spanking!"

"Austin called up to me, 'Uncle Louis says for you to come out and play ball,' related Teuila. "I replied to my eternal regret that I was busy writing letters, and I didn't go."

Monday morning saw the usual flurry of mail day, the start of the day's work receiving secondary consideration to the arrival of Sosimo with the waterproof bag hung across Donald's saddle. As always the bag was carried straight to Louis's room, the entire family following. Louis emptied the bag as usual on the floor and dealt out the letters and parcels. Snitching out of the pile was strictly tabu, although unless he was in a teasing mood, he made decent haste to conform to squeals of delight at a recognized handwriting on envelope or package wrapper. All the picture papers were tossed to Austin to open. From his own mail Louis gave letters and cards from strangers to Teuila—anywhere from a dozen to twenty of these.

Most were from autograph seekers, but some asked how to become a successful writer; a few asked for money with which to start a commercial venture with quick returns on a loan of fifty or a hundred pounds. Louis never neglected answering letters from children or sick people, and he always was deeply touched when invalids wrote of having had pleasure from his writings. He kept a supply of cards for the autograph hunters, some with only his name, others with a sentiment or rhyme. It was Teuila's task to send these. In reply to the ordinary request she sent a "penny plain," while the person who sent a self-addressed envelope with a Samoan stamp would receive a "tuppence colored" with a rhyme such as:

How jolly 'tis to sit and laugh
In gay green-wood,

Last Days in the Balcony Workroom

And write the merry autograph
For other people's good.

Letters or cards on which his name was spelled with a "ph," or
"Step Henson" as he called it, were thrown in the wastebasket.

On this particular morning of December 2 his eyes fell on
a small parcel. With quick movements of long slender fingers
he ripped the wrappings off a book bound in russet and silver.
He opened it, closed it reverently and laid it on a chair behind
him. Preoccupied and silent, he finished sorting the mail.

"That evening," continued Teuila, "he brought the book,
Russet and Silver, by Edmund Gosse, downstairs, and after
dinner he read the poem, 'Dedication to Tusitala in Vailima'
to us as we sat in the great hall—read it as only a poet can read
poetry, with the emotion of a man who would clasp the hand
of a long-absent friend":

> *Clearest voice in Britain's chorus,*
> > *Tusitala!*
> *Years ago, years four and twenty,*
> *Grey the cloudland drifted o'er us,*
> *When these ears first heard you talking,*
> *When these eyes first saw you smiling.*
>
> *Years of famine, years of plenty,*
> *Years of beckoning and beguiling,*
> *Years of yielding, shifting, baulking,—*
> *When the good ship "Clansman" bore us*
> *Round the spits of Tobermory,*
> *Glens of Voulin like a vision,*
> *Crags of Knoidart, huge and hoary,—*
> *We had laughed in light derision,*
> *Had they told us, told the daring*
> > *Tusitala,*

Last Witness for Robert Louis Stevenson

What the years' pale hands were bearing,—
Years in stately dim division.

Now the skies are pure above you,
                    Tusitala;
Feather'd trees bow down to love you;
Perfum'd winds from shining waters
Stir the sanguine-leav'd hibiscus
That your kingdom's dusk-ey'd daughters
Weave about their shining tresses;
Dew-fed guavas drop their viscous
Honey at the sun's caresses,
Where eternal summer blesses
Your ethereal musky highlands;—
Ah! but does your heart remember,
                    Tusitala,
Westward in our Scotch September,
Blue against the pale sun's ember,—
That low rim of faint long islands,
Barren granite-snouted nesses,
Plunging in the dull'd Atlantic,
Where beyond Tiree one guesses
At the full tide, loud and frantic?

By strange pathways God hath brought you,
                    Tusitala,
In strange webs of fortune caught you,
Led you by strange moods and measures
To this paradise of pleasures!
And the body-guard that fought you
To conduct you home to glory,—
Dark the oriflammes they carried,
In the mist their cohort tarried,—
They were Languor, Pain, and Sorrow,
                    Tusitala!

Last Days in the Balcony Workroom

Scarcely we endured their story
Frailing on from morn to morrow,
Such the devious road they led you,
Such the error, such the vastness,
Such the cloud that overspread you,
Under exile bow'd and banish'd,
Lost, like Moses in the fastness,
Till we almost deem'd you vanish'd.

Vanish'd ay, that's still the trouble,
             Tusitala!
Though your tropic isle rejoices,
'Tis to us an Isle of Voices
Hollow like the elfin double
Cry of disembodied echoes,
Or an owlet's wicked laughter,
Or the cold and horned grecko's
Croaking from a ruined rafter,—
Voices these of things existing,
Yet incessantly resisting
Eyes and hands that follow after;
You are circled, as by magic,
In a surf-built palmy bubble,
             Tusitala;
Fate hath chosen, but the choice is
Half delectable, half tragic,
For we hear you speak, like Moses,
And we greet you back, enchanted,
Then the rifted cloud-land closes.

September, 1894.

In the dewy-eyed silence that followed Louis said solemnly, "It is the most beautiful thing I've ever received." With a gesture of mingled pain and pleasure he clasped the small volume to his breast, happy to have shared this moment with those he loved so dearly and held in such high esteem as would prompt this emotional communion. Teuila did not recall that an acknowledgment was made—if so, it must have been written in his own hand and not dictated, the better perhaps to express his deep sentiment. A letter may have been in the "out-going" mail sack to "Dear old Gosse, one of the world's finest!"

It was a peculiarly quiet evening—that evening of December 2. The family circle broke early. Each had letters to re-read. Mail to the nesiote stirs strangely.

The morning of December 3 began as usual, the family deploying to routine tasks following breakfast. Graham Balfour had gone on a small copra-trading schooner, one of those hazardous trips where anything can happen and usually does. With household duties finished, Teuila presented herself ready for dictation. But Louis was in an idling mood. A few business letters were written before Fanny came in saying she had an overpowering premonition that something had happened to Graham—at least he was the only one of the family unaccounted for, so it must be he, and she had sent one of the boys to Apia to see if there was any news of a disaster to the schooner.

Louis dismissed the idea lightly, and at luncheon when word had come from Apia that there was no report of any shipwreck he chided her rather sharply for her imagined fears. Fanny did one of her casual disappearing acts and slipped away on some trivial excuse, leaving her plate of food untouched. Louis found her in the garden, and as they returned to the house Teuila heard her mother say, "I can't help it. I know something dreadful has happened. There's a load on my mind that I cannot lift. Just let me gloom it out, and if we find nothing has happened, I'll take a dose of calomel for my liver!" Both gave a subdued chuckle. After talking for an hour or so, Louis went to his room for his afternoon rest. Fanny went back to her flowers. Teuila denied vehemently the rumor spread by one biographer that there was a violent quarrel between the two which might have contributed to Louis's tragic death. They differed often, high-spirited as they were, but each had too much regard for the other to stoop to a quarrel.

It was early, the lamps not yet lighted, when Louis came down for dinner. Fanny was at the sideboard assembling the ingredients for mayonnaise, which for lack of refrigeration had to be mixed fresh every evening.

"Don't you want a big strong man to drop the oil for you?" Louis asked mischievously.

Talolo brought a small bowl of the jellylike passion fruit that he had spooned out of the shells and smiled knowingly as he set it on the sideboard in front of Louis, who always wanted the exact amount to flavor the salad of pineapple, guava, papaya, banana, persimmon, mango, or whatever was ripe at the time. Then just a sprinkle of grated *vi* apple when this acid fruit was in season made a dish which Louis boasted no chef in the world could match.

Fanny and Louis stood there, heads bowed to their trivial task, one smiling, the other grim under the unreasoning yet persistent shadow of impending calamity. No one knows their spoken words—whispered nothings—vows of devotion—tender scoldings—or perhaps no words at all—lovers have so little need. If words were spoken, Fanny kept them sacrosanct within the memory chambers of her heart.

Then abruptly, though not in panic, Louis set the cruet down. "Look at me," he said sharply, "do I look strange?"

"No, dear, you look all right." But it was not so. He was deathly pale. In another instant his body began to sag. Sosimo was passing. He leaped forward, caught Louis in his strong arms, and carried the inert form, tenderly as he would a child, to Louis's big chair in the hall.

Fanny's frantic cry, *"Louis!"* brought Talolo and Aunt Maggie on the run. Hot water for his feet and cold cloths on his head were all they could think of. Teuila came flying downstairs.

"Find Lloyd and tell him to go for a doctor," Fanny said in a voice scarcely audible. Yet as she spoke she knew only a miracle could save him. Intuition had prepared her for this ordeal.

When there was no more pulse beat, Sosimo and Talolo laid him on a couch. He looked quietly serene, as if he had just dropped into a sound sleep. Holding his hand, Fanny had felt his pulse slowly ebbing, ebbing, ebbing—. In these moments of supreme anguish her face was as ashen as that of the man she loved with all a woman's passion of tenderness and adoration.

Talolo and Sosimo sat half-crouching at Louis's feet, alert still to do whatever could be done. The other household boys came to sit just inside the door. Any one of them gladly would have given his life for their beloved *ali'i* Tusitala. News of the tragedy spread throughout the countryside even before darkness had settled. Lloyd had given the doctor at Apia the horse he was leading, and he himself rode on to the mission to tell Mr. Clarke, the good London missionary friend.

High Chief Tuimaleali'ifano was the first to arrive. He stood outside for some time, until Teuila motioned him to come in. Slowly he advanced, bowing low from the waist. With consummate grace of reverence he sank cross-legged on the floor beside Louis's head. In tense emotion he addressed him: *"Tatou moni Tusitala! Ua tagi le fatu ma le eleele!"* (Our beloved Tusitala! The stones and the earth weep!) The words spoken slowly in measured rhythm, in the full-throated pitch of the trained orator, resounded through the great hall like the tolling of a bell.

The doctor had come. He shook his head. There was no life.

Tuimaleali'ifano rose. *"Tofa, Tusitala; tofa soifua,"* he whispered softly, laid his gift of a fine mat across the body, and slipped out into the night.

Other chiefs began to arrive each bringing his most precious *'ie toga* as an *alofa* (fine mat as a gift). Each greeted Louis as if he still lived, and upon leaving bade him an affectionate *"Tofa soifua."* Fanny and Aunt Maggie sat silent.

It was commonly understood, however lightly considered, that Louis wished to be buried on the summit of Mount Vaea[2] on his own estate instead of (his own words) "being shipped back to Scotland in a box." Now there was no hesitancy in the family's decision to carry out this wish, even though it might have been lightly made.

The chiefs who had built the Road of Gratitude were summoned by Tuimaleali'ifano to meet along the creek below the Vailima gateway. Each chief brought with him his strongest young men. Stores and warehouses in Apia had been opened to furnish axes and bush knives. Maleali'ifano, by the weirdly flaring light of dried coconut-leaf torches, counted the chiefs and their men as they hurried up out of the dark crooked road— Chiefs Tupuola, Poè Lelei, and Poè Teleso, the recently elected new Mata'afa, Solevao, Tupuola Lotofaga, Tupuola Amaile, Muliaiga, Ifopo, Fatialofa, and Lemusu answered the roll call, each giving the number of his men—more than two hundred in all.

It was a night of the new moon, which had already set. There was no light except the Milky Way and kindred stars. These are nearer in the Southern Hemisphere and much brighter where there is no dust in the atmosphere. Each man was assigned to his length on the mountainside, each chief overseeing his own group. Volunteers competed for places farthest up the precipitous ascent and silently breasted their way into the apparently stygian density of the dank forest.

It is a surprising fact that a person unaccustomed to artificial lighting has a strangely superior vision. It is remarkable

[2] Mount Vaea is approximately 1,200 feet above sea level. It is about 600 feet from summit to base, with a gentle slope seaward from the Vailima residence.

that these men worked all through the night swinging their axes and knives with as much precision as in daylight, cutting away the shin-tangle of centuries and felling giant trees forty and fifty feet in height and two feet and more in diameter.

But to those who sat in stunned silence in the great hall the night hours were harassed to the point of near anguish by the continual chopping-chop, chop-chopping, chop-chop—with the sharp ping of axes biting into hard wood, the duller thud of blades against softer wood, the minor rasp of ripping bush knives; the sickening wait for the hushed cry of warning—the half-second of bated breath—then the splintering, smothering crash of another fallen tree, reverberations bouncing back from taller Mount Vailele. The cows lowed uneasily. Jack's high-pitched whinney came coaxingly from his corral. A rooster's raucous crow sent nerves jangling. The whole dissonant confusion constituted a maddening cacophony. Who knows, but a disguised blessing.

Fanny, tearless and with features like sculptured marble, never took her eyes off the face of her beloved.

Morning broke hot and still. Air hung in the narrow path where sweating men still labored at their back-breaking job like a chatoyant prism of a great emerald. Mist rolled in across the treetops and sank into the pathway. Breathing became difficult, and the heat was stifling until the sun rose high enough to draw the heavy air up from the forest canyon.

As men finished clearing their allotted space, some went on to the summit to dig the comparatively shallow grave, others to the beach to gather coral pebbles and crushed lava rock for the *fanua loto,* the bed for the body; although for Louis a coffin was made by the local carpenter instead of the many layers of *laufala* rugs and *siapo* that the Samoans use. The *fanua loto* is only for royal burial. The thick bed of stones, slightly mounded in the center, assures drainage of water seeping in from the torrential tropical rains.

Last Days in the Balcony Workroom

There was no mortician in Apia. Sosimo and Talolo prepared the body of their beloved *ali'i* for burial by rubbing it tenderly with fresh sun-rendered coconut oil scented with the elusively fragrant flowers of the *moso'oi* tree (*Cananga odorata*)—rubbing for an hour or more until the skin would absorb no more. They dressed him just as he would have come down to dinner, with the addition of the velvet jacket, and brought him on a cot into the great hall. Hands on his chest, fingers interlaced, he looked as if he were peacefully sleeping. At Fanny's suggestion the Union Jack was spread across the slender form. As fine mats arrived, presented by sorrowing chiefs, they were laid across the body or draped over chairs. Flowers were banked everywhere. Samoan house boys sat through the night at either side of the low cot, sometimes softly chanting their own ancient laments of death, other times repeating the prayers they had learned at the mission. Fanny sat quietly hour after hour as if completely numbed.

The sun had been up for two or three hours on a lovely morning before the tardy start of the funeral procession from the house. Fanny and Aunt Maggie were advised not to attempt the exhausting trip to the summit, so Teuila, Lloyd, and Austin made up the family. The Samoan chiefs wore traditional dark *lavalavas* with sashes of black *siapo*. A venerable high chief led the way accompanied by a younger man who blew long, low mournful notes on a conch shell. Some distance behind them slowly walked the four chiefs bearing the coffin. Together with Mr. Clarke, the three of the family followed down the quarter-mile slope to the foot of Vaea, where a great crowd waited. Only a few were attempting the climb.

From the first steep ascent men in groups of four were stationed along the pathway, each group taking the coffin and passing it on to the next, on to the next, on to the next, until it was gently deposited at the summit. In the same way helping hands were extended to Teuila and to the older Samoan women.

341

With the sea breeze blowing through the clearing that had been cut, it was delightfully cool at the summit. Mr. Clarke read the Presbyterian burial service and paid eloquent tribute to his friend. Several Samoan *ali'i sili* paid their final respects to the dead in such poetic eloquence as can be expressed only by the sincerely stirred orator.

At the conclusion of Rev. Clarke's final prayer,[3] four men stepped down into the wide cradlelike grave to receive the hardwood coffin. With exquisite care they made it steady and firm on the raised level of lava stones and rock. Then several pieces of heavy *siapo* and as many *laufala* rugs were laid over the coffin and tightly tucked in along the sides before dirt was filled in and built up to a smooth mound. Immediately this was covered with wreaths and *u'las* of flowers. A canopy was erected and hung with *siapo*, and the outline of the grave was marked with black stones, indicative of royalty.

The ceremonies, except for words spoken, had been in reverent silence but for the chattering calls and musical cadences of the many birds disturbed in their sanctuary—a forest symphony by the wild life Louis so much enjoyed.

After the departure of the family and their few *papalagi* friends, the Samoans remained at the grave. When they knew they were quite alone, they began softly their ancient chant to a departed chief, "*O le fatu ia Suluga.*" A piece of rolled siapo served as a drum and supple fingers provided the rhythm:

> *Imoaaimanu e, i logologo 'ua a'u sau.*
> *Na a'u sailia mai Sepupuelogonaivao.*
> *Soufuna Faufauiatane ma Le'aunofoitalau,*
> *Na a'au sailia mai Sepupuelogonaivao . . . .*

It carries on for more than thirty lines, ending with the poignantly touching lament:

[3] Rev. Clarke, first to greet Louis upon his arrival at Apia, last of the *papalagi* to say farewell.

Last Days in the Balcony Workroom

Le usoilei 'ua tagi mai ala—
Fagumau ia o leutuu'amea,
Ma Samoa 'ua fa'atautala.

[*The brother of our ali'i who died in our far land—*
Locked in our hearts you shall never be forgotten,
And Samoans will mourn as long as we have words to speak.]

With whispered *"Tofa, Tusitala,"* many blinded with tears, they went down the mountainside for their first rest in more than thirty-six hours. Older men knew that their bright star of hope had set and the light he had held high for their future, like a flaming torch carried in a dark forest, was gone forever.

These men are gone now, called by their god Tagaloa. High Chief Tuimaleali'ifano died on October 14, 1937, well past ninety years of age, and is buried on the Mulinuu. Selu To'omata Ma'atusi Le'au'anae died on December 26, 1935, at eighty-five years of age, and is buried at his home village of Paputa near Vailima. On my first visit to Samoa in 1927 he was assigned by Administrator Major General Sir George Richardson to be my mentor. He had been only a *matai* during Louis's life time, had worked on construction of the Road of Gratitude, had helped cut the trail to the summit of Mount Vaea, and helped pass the coffin from man to man on that memorable morning of December 4, 1894. Now he held the title of *To'omata Ma'atusi* from the royal line of Malietoa of Savaii and the orator's title of *Le'au-'anae*, making him the most important *tulafale* (ruler of a village) in Samoa. Courteous, soft spoken, using fluent English, he related to me many incidents of Louis's life, and from him also I learned for the first time that their Tusitala did not suffer from tuberculosis, although just what his lung ailment was he did not know.

To have heard his fervent words of praise is to place still higher values on the power and charm of Louis's personality.

343

That an alien people should thus esteem him, in an acquaintance of four brief years when he left them not a heritage of literary achievement but only the memory of high principles and good deeds, testifies to a character that had earned a hallowed place in their minds and hearts—*la matou pele moni* (our dearly beloved)!

For us of the Western world no tribute can excel that of Edmund Gosse when he heard of his friend's death:

> *Rest, oh thou restless angel, rest at last*
> > *High on thy mountain peak that caps the waves;*
> > *Anguish no more thy delicate soul enslaves,*
> *Dream-clouds no more thy slumber overcast.*
>
> *Adventurous angel, fold thy wings! The vast*
> > *Pacific Forest, with its architraves,*
> > *The stillness of its long liana'd naves,*
> *Involves thee in a silence of times past.*
>
> *Thou whom we loved, a child of sportive whim,*
> > *So fair to play with, comfort, thrill or chide,*
> > > *Art grown as ancient as thine island gods,*
>
> *As mystic as the menacing seraphim,*
> > *As grim as priests upon a red hill-side,*
> > > *Or lictors shouldering high their sheaves of rods.*

Fanny could no longer stay at Vailima, where every room in the house, every piece of furniture, every book, and every painting on the walls spoke of Louis. There was no solace in the garden, where every flower and tree spoke of him. She purchased three acres of land about halfway down the slope toward Apia, expecting to build a small house where she, with Teuila and Lloyd and young Austin, might live quietly—Aunt Maggie having gone back to Scotland. But there was poor heart in this plan, and the family left for San Francisco. The three acres is still there in her name with only a Samoan *fale* in the pretty setting.

Vailima is little changed. A wider sweep of lawn; an addition to the house, affording extra living rooms upstairs and a ballroom on the ground floor. Inside one steps into the great hall and sees through memory's eyes and listening ears the oft told stories of gay and happy life. Hanging above the fireplace in the upstairs sitting room is a large oil painting of Louis, made from the portrait painted by Count Girolamo Nerli at Vailima in 1892. This is a gift to Vailima from Mr. Edwin J. Beinecke, who deems it "almost better than the original," which is one of the many treasures in his great collection of Stevensoniana. A cement foundation under the original part of the building has recently replaced the redwood sills. Long ago white paint replaced the original azure blue, which Louis called Swiss blue, and which with the deep red roof gave a striking effect against the varied greens of the forest.

When Louis died, the property still was recorded in the name of James Baxter, but on March 3, 1895, he granted the deed to Fanny; then because no court grant had been issued either to Louis or to Baxter, the Tripartite Land and Titles Commission granted one to Fanny Matilda Stevenson. Fanny sold the property to Gustav Kunst through her attorney in San Francisco in 1899, reserving an acre of ground at the summit of Mount Vaea and the road leading up the mountainside.

Mr. Kunst did not live at Vailima, but rented it to the German government for the administrator's residence. Then in 1911 the heirs of Mr. Kunst sold the property to the German government for 150,000 marks, approximately $30,000. During World War I, on August 29, 1914, New Zealand troops, a strength of 1,365, occupied Western Samoa without opposition. Colonel Robert Logan became military administrator. German Governor E. Schultz-Ewerth with various officials and other German residents were sent to New Zealand for internment. Two Germans, married to Samoan women of rank, each with several children, were permitted to remain.

Military government continued until 1920 when a mandate from Allied and Associated Powers of the League of Nations Council delegated the government of Western Samoa to New Zealand, where it functions under the Minister of External Affairs. Vailima, of course, was included in lands confiscated by New Zealand as war reparations, and the famous home was made the official residence of each high commissioner sent from New Zealand to administer island affairs.

The new government cleared the zigzag trail to the summit of Vaea and has kept the narrow path free of clogging undergrowth and maintained the tomb site, cutting the rank grass and pruning trees to keep open vistas of Vailima and the port of Apia. On three sides the land drops precipitously from a plot no larger than a drawing room. On the north, the sea; on the east and west, impenetrable forests downgrade the mountain from summit to base; while to the south, a spinelike ridge leads to the higher, densely forested hills of the center of Upolu Island.

Before leaving Samoa, Fanny wanted a sarcophagus for Louis's grave. The Samoan chiefs begged to be permitted to build one of their ancient cairnlike sarcophagi of black basaltic stones designating the grade of royalty. These are built of sea-worn stones of all shapes and sizes, rounded smooth and polished from the surging surf of centuries, and fitted so precisely that once placed the stones can not be removed, yet it is done without use of cement. This would have made a tomb of incomparable beauty, an art seldom seen. But Fanny preferred the traditional white of the European and commissioned Gelett Burgess to design a fitting memorial. He quickly recognized that any ornamentation would be incongruous in this setting of nature's magnificence, hence the severely plain tomb familiar to the world. Solid blocks of finely mixed cement, each weighing approximately one hundred pounds, were carried up the steep path by Samoans to be fitted so neatly as to give the impression of stone. The whole of this exacting work was done by Samoans under the supervision of George Stowers, an American-Samoan.[4]

Considerable searching through old German and English records in Apia by the Director of Land and Surveys in 1950 revealed the burial site still in the name of "Fanny Matilda Stevenson, known also as Fanny Van de Grift Stevenson (deceased)." I brought this to the attention of Isobel Field, and while she was aware of the title as it stood, she realized the value of perpetuity. She first thought of the Samoan government, but sentiment prompted granting this honor to the society of Louis's birthplace. The Edinburgh Stevenson Society declined the offer, saying they were too remote, as did the London Society. Then began correspondence with High Commissioner Richard Powles, New Zealand administrator at Apia. Under date of May 29, 1953, he wrote:

Dear Mrs. Field:

. . . about the site of Robert Louis Stevenson's tomb . . . . It is my great pleasure to offer on behalf of the Government of Western Samoa to accept both title and responsibility. Your step-father is still remembered in Samoa and the Executive Council in advising me to make this offer spoke with unanimous voice. . . .

With your consent the Government of Western Samoa could,

[4] Unfortunately this shrine is constantly desecrated by the callously unsentimental tourist who writes his name on the concrete base and chips off a corner for a souvenir. One ambitious despoiler tried to pick away the cement and pry out the bronze plate. What a rich memento to carry home! These defacements are constantly being repaired, while the miscreant goes his way to be the fool eternally

by Ordinance passed in the Legislative Assembly, assume ownership of the site. This would simplify proceedings for you and would give to the transfer the dignity which would be fitting for the most satisfying transaction.

I hope you will be able to accept this offer, made, as it is, with deep feeling of appreciation for the services rendered to Samoa by the most famous of those who have dwelt in this Territory, and for the sympathy with which he approached the problems he discovered here.

Mrs. Caldwell tells me you have not been very well recently; I hope this letter finds you recovered.

Yours faithfully,
G. R. Powles
High Commissioner

Although Teuila was too ill to reply to this letter and died just a month later, on June 26, she did express a fervent wish for its fulfillment and a deep gratitude to Mr. Powles. However, legal technicalities now became necessary, and further negotiations were delayed until her estate was settled and consent given by her only heir, the widow of her son, Austin Strong, who had died in 1952. Even though it was made as an outright gift to the Samoan government, there ran like the smooth flowing current of a quiet river the formalities and judicial decisions essential to proper transfer of property. Thus in the year of our Lord 1956 title of the tomb site was dedicated in perpetuity.

Perpetual care means nothing more than that assumed by the New Zealand government when they first took over the islands of Western Samoa from the Germans during World War I and Major William Bell of the New Zealand Land Commission surveyed and cut the zigzag trail to the summit of Vaea. Even on my first visit to Samoa in 1927 the straight-up track cut by the

Samoans in a single night and up which they had carried the body of their beloved Tusitala had become almost obliterated and was discernible only through the lighter green of the foliage and a shorter growth of the thick forest.

Besides the acre of ground at the summit the title provides for "the track leading thereto," but when Mr. Kunst purchased Vailima from Fanny Stevenson, he graciously tendered to her all the Mount Vaea area. Fanny then declared it a bird sanctuary, and such it remains in an effort to preserve the brightly plumaged birds very nearly annihilated by the Samoans in their love of multicolored feathers for their fine mats.

The rumor first circulated upon Louis's death that he was not buried on his own land was set right later when Mr. Kunst had a survey made for the purchase of additional acreage and found the stakes of the original survey made for Louis by Mr. Trood (spelled this way in the land record, but sometimes spelled "Trude"), from whom he bought the 314 acres in 1890.

Not until 1960 will New Zealand relinquish to the Samoans the government of their four islands—Upolu, upon which Apia is located, Savaii, the big island unfortunately devastated extensively by lava flow, and the small jewel-like islands of Apolima and Manono. New Zealand administration has been signally successful in promoting economic and cultural values. Reparation estates have been brought into productive plantations of varied crops in addition to the vast world-famous plantings of coconuts left by the Germans.

The name "Road of Loving Hearts" is now given to the wide grassy lane that leads from the entrance of Vailima's grounds to the foot of the Mount Vaea trail. The ground is spongy with the constant rains, and the trees on either side drip with the dew of daybreak, for one must start early for this climb. It is only six hundred feet, but with the constant slipping backwards and sideways on the moist moss-grown track the distance easily becomes seven hundred plus, and the effort of pulling the humid air into one's lungs further reduces one's upward push.

Halfway up, at the turning of a sharp curve, one spies a welcome bench and drops down to reduce the panting. An inquisitive lizard pops out from somewhere, stares for a fleeting second and pops back to somewhere. Instinctively one turns to see if he might have companions and is shocked and amused to see carved on the back of the bench, "Why didn't they bury him at sea?"

Although no rays of the sun can penetrate the forest, dawn is brief in the tropics, and one feels the air becoming steamy, like turning on the heat in a Finnish bath—a warning against further loitering. The final hundred feet, almost perpendicular, leave one dripping with perspiration as he emerges suddenly into the cleared area like entering a reception room through a door left ajar, and a bench is here to receive the half-exhausted guest. Such are the purely physical aspects.

Presently in the quiet aloneness it seems as if the body like a chrysalis were slipping away, and one realizes he is here where for so many years he has dreamed of being. The heart and mind fairly leap to that roll call of the drums and bugle of time, and I rise to stand with exalted soul in God's great cathedral. Giant trees, symmetrically pillared, arch majestically overhead like a St. Peter's ceiling with the glorious dome of azure sky seen through the lacework of spreading boughs to rival the art of a Michelangelo.

Intensity of unseen companionship whelms through one's being. The lonely shrine is peopled by those who have loved, and still love, the valiant soul whose body lies beneath the plain sarcophagus. Clouds of morning mist, white as angels' skirts, float along the treetops and a blessed breeze cools the humid air. The middle verse of "Requiem" sings through my thoughts:

> *Here may the winds about me blow;*
> *Here the clouds may come and go;*

Last Days in the Balcony Workroom

Here may he rest for evermo',
And the heart for aye shall be still.

In the immortal lines carved on the tomb there is a small but regrettable error. The last line but one reads; "Home is the sailor home from *the* sea." And though both American and Scottish Stevenson Societies have requested permission to delete the offending article, no arrangement has been made to rectify the inadvertence in copying. Although the operation would be exceedingly simple, some Stevenson lovers think the error should be preserved as unique. In this, others do not concur. Louis, the perfectionist, most surely would be among the latter.

Sitting there in the eerie half-world of unreality, imagination like a spirit with outflung wings soaring in the cerulean heavens, the timeless morning has the earthy emptiness of sublimity. A pale gray cloud bends too low and the treetops brush out the rain—soft rain like a priest sprinkling water with an aspergillum to sanctify my morning in hallowed memory.

Appendices

A. *Letters from Teuila*

WITH HER previously distinctive handwriting reduced to only finger movements because her right arm never wholly revived after the stroke, Teuila used to write long letters, maybe just a paragraph at a time, about the life at Vailima which we would have discussed on my most recent visit. The following is typical:

El Mirasol, Santa Barbara,
June 4, 1951

Dear Esi,

In answer to your questions—when I was a girl in East Oakland and my grandmother Osbourne came to visit us, she thought I should be taught sewing, cooking and housework. We had a cook who didn't want to be bothered with me—and it was much easier for her to do the housework herself than trail me. My grandmother finally settled on lamps and taught me to care for them. To keep the chimneys sparkling clear—to put in enough, but not too much kerosene—and most important of all to trim the wicks evenly, which made a great difference in the light. She also taught me to darn stockings exquisitely. Also my father's socks.

I went to Honolulu much later and though the streets and the King's palace were lit by electricity the people all used old-fashioned kerosene lamps. Then later when we lived in Samoa all our lights were from lamps. In the "hall," as Stevenson called the big room where we dined, there were two large lamps, with shades that hung over the table and gave a fine light—there may have been three lamps over the table—and there were others hung from the ceiling. [Here she made a drawing.]

Every morning I had all the lamps of the house set out for me on a small porch back of the "hall," and there I personally trimmed the wicks, polished the lamp chimneys, filling with kerosene, etc. I could teach my Samoan helpers to do some things but I always had to trim the wicks.

There were smaller lamps for the breakfast room—for Aunt Maggie's—my own room, the one Louis and my mother had, one in the library—in a big house of eleven rooms we needed many. The back porch was a large one with wide stairs that led to the upper storey. The breakfast room opened on to this, so did a wide pantry and a locked store-room. On the floor was the entrance to the cellar where the wine was kept. R. L. S. imported his father's fine cellar of wines. And it was there that we kept the milk from three Jersey cows. It was cool in the cellar and we had fine cream for the best coffee in the world—grown at Utumapu. We had bags of it and every morning it was freshly roasted and ground by the cook, Talolo. On a shelf in the pantry was a row of candles in their candle-sticks. When any of the family returned home from a trip Louis gave orders to place a candle in every window.

When Austin came back from school in Monterey, stopping with my mother's sister, Mrs. Sanchez, the house was illumined on his arrival. For my mother when she came back from Fiji—for me on returning from New Zealand, and of course for Louis who was taken on an island cruise by the man-of-war, Curaçoa. . . .

Floor rugs. My mother received many presents of Oriental rugs when the new home, "Skerryvore," was given her and her husband. Mr. Thomas Stevenson furnished it for them and he and his pretty American daughter-in-law had grand visits to London shops. In Mr. Thomas Stevenson's own house in Edinburgh there were many fine Oriental rugs. So with everything out of both houses there were many handsome rugs for Vailima.

The hall was lined with redwood, polished, and the floor waxed and covered with several large rugs. With some very fine paintings—a lovely sideboard with silver trays, goblets and vase, a carved sideboard, the table, chairs and the two East Indian idols the room was very handsome.

The large double doors were never shut even at night. On all the veranda doors there were mosquito gauze doors. In my memory we were not bothered much by mosquitoes. Our rooms were kept free of them and we did not sit on the veranda at night. We'd have an occasional bad night of mosquitoes, but that meant that something like a coconut half-shell with water in it was attracting them. We'd have the place cleared and— no biters!

About cooking—our "cook-house" was a separate building and you know about our fine chef, Talolo. My brother introduces him beautifully in the book we wrote together, *Memories of Vailima.*

Flowers—my mother had a garden and I confess I was more interested in her kitchen garden. We had all the flowers we wanted—gardenias, jasmine, hibiscus—others the whole names I can't remember—and we had the loveliest ferns I ever saw, and there were wild flowers that looked like French candy. I was afraid to eat it but it was pretty to decorate the table with for a dinner party.

Whoops I'm tired—I wish I knew more about the flowers. Send me some more questions. Alofa mai [Love from] Teuila.

Dear Esi, There are a lot of your questions I did not answer, but I will now, though I want to tell you how lucky you are to have a young friend like Dorothy. When I was thirty my best friend was sixteen year old Anne Ide! We considered ourselves the only white women in Samoa, not counting missionaries and traders' wives. We were fast friends as long as she lived. When I was taken ill she sent me the wheel-chair I still use, and in her will she left me a lovely brooch of diamonds and pearls. We two studied the Samoan language and Samoan good manners. I could write a book about Samoa and tell a lot that isn't known—but now I'll answer your questions for I am deeply interested in your book.

Do you remember the sounds of Samoa? The never-ending roar of the surf beating against the rocks that protect the island? At Vailima besides that sound was the waterfall, a much higher sweeter note. Then the notes of the pu, a big shell Lloyd blew into waking the household at six A.M. rousing workmen who were clearing a path to the forest. Only a few trees were cut down to make way for the house, the flower garden and the vegetable one. It was a story-book forest of enormous trees, vines draped over and between them and thick underbrush of the loveliest fern you ever saw. There were five streams of water—Vai, and Lima is number five. No snakes, no venomous insects. We, Anne and I, saw some Samoans cut a notch in a tree, hold a folded leaf under it and drink. The trees were so large that the forest was dark and I was always afraid there. The land was slanting upwards for the forest was on the side of the mountain that forms the middle of Samoa, sloping down on the other side.

I could fill pages telling you of the strange trees and curious objects we found in the forest. The same great trees cover the side of Mt. Vaea to the summit where the land comprising Vailima ends.

Alofa tele,   Teuila.

Dear Esi, did you know that no birds are allowed to be shot anywhere on Vaea mountain? It was the Samoans themselves who made that law.   Teuila.

January 21, 1950

Dear Esi:

Your photograph has come. We didn't open the parcel, knowing what it is, but we'll keep it for you. This time, my dear, come comfortably. You have been like Mrs. Santa Claus on your previous visits. They were very nice but don't make it a habit. The last time you fairly staggered in my room laden down with food and clothing. To be sure I gobbled down the food and wear the clothing with pride, but after all you are a hardworking busy dame and now I am staggering under a load of obligations, so let up and we'll both be happy. What I like best of all is *you* and our talks.

I had a very nice letter from Mr. Bush from Samoa and he sent me an article he wrote about R. L. S. that he read over the Samoan radio, and my dear it is good—true, every word and well expressed. I'm always afraid to read an article about Mr. Stevenson for it hurts me terribly to read ugly untruthful slanders about a man I respected and admired. I've done a lot of good though. You don't see those horrid sickly pictures of him that he called "watermelon seed portraits." The writers (who never saw him) all made up different yarns about him—and lately I read one where he was described as a lean pale cadaverous creature riding on a lean bony horse! He had a fine horse, Jack. All our horses, and we had seven or more, were good-looking well fed, well groomed animals—why should R. L. S. —a rich man—buy an "old bony beast" at all?

We also had three cows and a bull. We sent a man down to Apia every morning with milk for sick and old people. There were no other cows on the island. I never knew where the animals came from that supplied us with fresh meat every other day. No choice. We took what was sent us. I know for it was my business to run the house, train the servants, and make out the menu. Oh, what a letter! Forgive me, dear Esi, and believe me, yours affectionately, Teuila.

[*No date*]

Dear Esi,

I like your MS very much—and oh, how I appreciate your help in saving my mother and R. L. S. from empty-headed malicious scandal mongers! There is only one paragraph I'd like omitted, for it looks as though you were describing a quarrel. I knew R. L. S. from the time Fanny Osbourne first met him at Grez. I was with her on every summer she spent there—two or three, I can't remember.

Aunt Maggie and Lloyd were at Tautira with R. L. S. waiting for the Casco to be made ready for the homeward trip. I even remember the native language for "no ship" when they were waiting—No, it's gone. They loved the chief at Tautira, Ori a Ori, and later when a tidal wave damaged his village Louis sent him three hundred dollars and Aunt Maggie sent a whole family silver tea set!

They made many friends at the various islands of their voyage whose names are familiar to me.

My mother had gall-stones and I remember she suffered from them on our visit to Sydney in the Spring of 1894, but then only occasionally. They weren't bad enough for an operation till we went to London after Louis' death. Louis was very well off then with not only his own fortune but that of his father and mother as well. Did I tell you that he left me $30,000.00? In the will it was a fraction of what was left when certain sums were given to his cousin Bob [R. A. M. Stevenson]. I think it is wise not to repeat ——'s vile accusations. Just mention them only as "false" and "discredited."

Stress that Fanny Osbourne married Louis at the lowest ebb of his fame and fortune. Her Husband—my father—loved her but had no influence over her. No one knew of his infidelities and the divorce was a complete surprise to their acquaintances.

The wire recorder—I'm not up to making another one. My doctor brought a recorder here for me to record for the Stevenson House and I told of the death and burial of R. L. S. I was a week recovering from the ordeal though Angel directed it and took care of me. Angel says "perhaps later." It depends on her decision. I'd like to fill another page with thanks for the good work you are doing, clearing the name of a good man.

Alofa, Teuila.

April 1951

Dear Esi,

There is so much I want to say to you and questions I want to answer but my mind is a blank. I've had a bad time fighting off a cold, then Ferrell was sick and could not come for some time, and Angel has not only been taking care of me but her husband too who as you know, has been ill—but it is against my principles to hand on my troubles so I'll only tell you enough to explain why I haven't answered your dear good letters— for I do appreciate with a full and grateful heart all you have done for me and for the help you have given and are giving to clear the good name of the best man I ever knew—my stepfather.

Oh, my dear, I know your book about him will be a great help. Did you tell me, or was it Austin, that numbers of letters have been found and will soon be published that tell the story of his youth.

In Samoa we had no radio, or even a gramophone or telephone, so we naturally did a lot of talking and very naturally we talked about ourselves. I'm sure if those stories about him were true he would have made some mention of them.

Oh, my dear, I promised my cousin Ned that he would be my next visitor. I think I'm well enough to telephone him now. I'll add more to this letter later on. I will telephone my cousin now—I did, and he said he'd let me know when he was coming and I'll let you know—and when you come please be my very welcome guest. Alofa lomi mai, Teuila.

Later: My mother came to California to make arrangements to hire a yacht for a trip on the South Seas. I had a house-keeping flat on the first floor of a building on Hyde street. My mother, Aunt Maggie, and Lloyd took rooms in the same building and took their meals with me. Louis stayed at the Occidental Hotel on Montgomery street.

I went with my mother when she called on the owner of the Casco to make final arrangements. I remember my surprise at her levity when Dr. Merritt said finally, "Now that's settled and I'm glad, Little One!" and she answered. "So am I, Big One!"

Louis was in bed at the Occidental where we stopped to tell him. Neither he nor my mother had seen the yacht which was on the bay near San Francisco. Of course Louis wanted to see it. It wasn't long before they had a cook and sailor and Louis went on board to live. Every friend we had, but especially Charley Stoddard and Frank Unger accompanied by Lloyd scoured the town, my mother giving them lists of the articles needed.

I remember Frank Unger saying desperately, "What is a barger? A yachtsman I know said we must have a barger and I didn't like to show my ignorance by asking what it was."— Even now I can't be certain but it was some kind of a flag that a visiting yacht must fly when entering a foreign port.

The man they finally got Louis put in a book and called him *Nares*.

Now I'm tired. I will send more later but my cousin Col. Orr is coming to see me soon and I may not have time. Is this what you want? Tell me frankly for I'm not sensitive about my writing. Don't work too hard and get too tired. My warmest alofa, from

Teuila.

May 6 1951

Dear Esi,

Oh, my dear! Mr. Moors wrote a hateful book about the Stevensons—especially vindictive against my mother. With three enemies against her it is small wonder that few knew her as the one person every lover of Stevenson's works should venerate.

Mr. Moors kept a grocery store in Apia and was very cordial and kind to both the Stevensons when they arrived there. He was an American and knew all the details—after a year or more Louis discovered that he had been overcharged in nearly all his dealings with Mr. Moors and as he was a "friend," he did not like to quarrel with him but from then on dealt with the big German store in Apia called, on account of its long name—"The Long-handled Firm." Moors was furious at losing such a good customer and blamed my mother. In his book he described her as a termagant and R. L. S. as a weakling mentally.

It is a stupid book but was much read and quoted on account of the subject. . . .

May 7

Mr. Moors was originally a good friend of the Stevensons. I mean they were all very friendly, even intimate. We all liked his Samoan wife and his half-caste children. We went to a Christmas party at his house. I remember all his nice little girls recited verses.

I told you that Aunt Maggie taught Austin poetry. Well after the Moors children had recited Austin amazed us (he was nine then) by saying, "I will now give you The Lay of the Last Minstrel by Sir Walter Scott," and I was proud of him, at first, I mean. But he went on and on remembering every word! I don't know how we stopped him but he hadn't finished when he sat down! Aunt Maggie was a grand teacher!

Once much later when Austin and I were in England we

were walking on the moor and heard a lovely note of music.
We stopped, looking around, and then saw it was a bird! Austin
threw out his arms and recited Shelly's Ode to the Skylark! He
hadn't though of it till that moment—and he wasn't ten when
he was her pupil! One night he came to my flat in New York
to keep me company while Ned was away and recited Bobby
Burns to me—yards of it—Oh, dear, I'm writing too much! But
it's to *you!*

Oh, my dear, I'm getting vain! I look at that wonderful picture Dorothy took and smirk with vanity! It is beautiful! And
everybody who sees it says so! Like the old woman whose petticoats reached her knee and she said, "Lawks can this be I?" I
look at that lovely lady in the photograph and gasp!

I'm expecting Angel every minute. It is early morning and
I've had two days with this letter—but oh, my dear, it is exciting
to find a friend—a real one—but now I want to write more pages!
But you know, and I know—and Dorothy knows!

Alofa pea mai,   Teuila.

B. *About the Triggs Letter*

Mr. Triggs, then editor of the *Christchurch Press,* wrote to
Lloyd Osbourne in 1929 concerning Stevenson's letter and
acknowledging the copyright as his (Osbourne's), stating his
intention of giving the manuscript to the Turnbull Library in
Wellington, where it now is. Mr. Osbourne replied from Cap
d'Antibes, France:

I thank you for your exceedingly kind letter; Indeed, I was
greatly touched to receive it, and to be reminded with so much
graciousness and cordiality of those long departed days . . . of
"those diamond mornings of long ago."

I cannot imagine a better disposition of the little MS than

to present it to the Alexander Turnbull Library of Wellington; it will save it from the collector and from being buried out of sight. If a few people copy it, and thus bring it into print, it does not seem to me a matter of great concern. To me at least it is pleasant to have New Zealanders associating R L S with their part of the world. However, I do think it would be a good idea for you to write a little account of how you received it originally and print it in some good magazine. If you will kindly send me a copy I shall be very happy to advise you as to the disposition of such an article.

Formal permission came from the Incorporated Society of Authors, Playwrights, and Composers, dated April 4, 1930, on behalf of Mr. Lloyd Osbourne. It read:

11 Gower Street, London, W. C. 1.

The Hon. W. H. Triggs
The Legislative Council of New Zealand,
Wellington, N. Z.

Dear Sir,
With reference to your request contained in your communication to Mr. Lloyd Osbourne for permission to publish a letter addressed to you by Mr. Robert Louis Stevenson from Vailima, and dated December 6th, '93, acting on behalf of Mr. Lloyd Osbourne, we will permit such publication by yourself in one issue of *Scribner's Magazine* or any magazine of the same literary status which enjoys copyright protection in the United States and throughout the British Empire. In submitting the letter to magazines, you must grant nothing more than a license to the magazine to publish it in one issue of the magazine and must not assign copyright or grant any license other than the one specified in this letter. The condition respecting the enjoyment of copyright in the United States and the British Empire

is essential owing to the fact that publication in a magazine enjoying copyright protection only in the United States would mean that the copyright in the British Empire would be lost and vice versa. No payment is asked by Mr. Lloyd Osbourne for the permission granted, but acknowledgment to Mr. Lloyd Osbourne must be printed with the letter.

Yours faithfully,

D. Kilharry Roberts.

C. *Stevenson Memorial Reserve and Mount Vaea Scenic Reserve*

I. *COPY OF PROCEEDINGS OF THE SAMOAN LEGISLATURE:*

Attorney General's Office,
Apia, Western Samoa,
29th April, 1958.

ROBERT LOUIS STEVENSON'S TOMB
DESCRIPTION OF LAND

Parcel 113/79. Flur VIII Upolu (1 acre) together with right-of-way delineated in Grund buch IV–415 Folio 5.

1. The title to this land is recorded in Volume 1 Folio 122 of the Land Register of Western Samoa, and records that title was vested in Fanny Van de Grift Shevenson deceased. The Samoan Public Trustee acquired title in the estate of Fanny Van de Grift Stevenson by virtue of transmission No. 209z. Transmission No. 210z purports to transfer the land to the Samoan Public Trustee as Administrator of the estate of Isobel Field.

2. There is a gap in the title between the two transmissions

363

which should be bridged by a conveyance from the Public Trustee (re Stevenson) to Isobel Field (Strong). This conveyance has been prepared and registration of transmission 210z will be amended to take effect subsequent to registration of the conveyance. The Public Trustee will then be registered owner as trustee of the estate in Western Samoa of Isobel Field.

3. By the will of Fanny Stevenson a burden of 300 dollars per month is charged on the real estate to secure the payment of an annuity to testator's son Lloyd Osbourne during his lifetime. While there is no proof of Lloyd Osbourne's death, I am prepared to accept that he is dead because of a reference to his death in an enclosure to a letter from Mr. Wood, Secretary of the Robert Louis Stevenson Club (London) to the High Commissioner of 28. 7. 53. The enclosure is a copy of a letter to Mr. Wood from Mrs. Caldwell advising of the death of Mrs. Field, and saying that she gave up her home at "Serena" "after Lloyd Osbourne died."

4. Accordingly, Isobel Strong the residuary beneficiary of Fanny Stevenson's will was at the time of her death entitled to the land at Mount Vaea free of the charge in favour of Lloyd Osbourne.

5. On the file of Fanny Stevenson is a letter to A. S. Meredith (acting for the Samoan Public Trustee) dated 25. 9. 46 signed "Isobel Field" and containing the passage—" . . . I don't know whether my name was on the deed or not. Isobel Strong it was then—before I married Mr. Field." I accept this as evidence that Isobel Strong and Isobel Field were the same person.

6. The next steps are Conveyances—
   (a) from Samoan Public Trustee (re Isobel Field) to the residuary beneficiary of her estate, Mary Strong.
   (b) from Mary Strong to the Government.

These can be combined into a Deed of Conveyance from the Public Trustee (re Field) to the Government by direction of Mary Strong (from whom the Samoan Public Trustee holds a power of attorney). The deed has been prepared accordingly.

7. The land over which the right of way is granted is owned by the Crown and on the transfer to the Crown of the Mount Vaea property on which the tomb is sited the right of way will be merged in the fee simple title. This is of no consequence so long as care is taken to see that the land which was previously given by the right of way is not alienated without providing proper access to the tomb.

8. Both sections, namely, the land previously owned by the Crown which was subject to the right of way and the section now conveyed to the Crown from the estate of Isobel Field, are declared to be reserves either by a Warrant under the hand of the High Commissioner or by Ordinance. The Chief Surveyor is of the opinion that both sections should be set aside to constitute a single reserve in respect of the tomb of Robert Louis Stevenson. This will probably be done by Ordinance as it is desired to take power to control access to the tomb by regulation so that if at any future time the Government so desires it can prevent unauthorized people acting as guides and could deal with any other problem that might arise with regard to mis-use of the reserve.

9. Although the foregoing steps have been approved, it should be placed on record that a number of facts which would normally require to be verified have been accepted as having been established in order to avoid any delay in completion of the transaction. One of these, of course, is verification that Austin Strong predeceased Isobel Field so that Mary Strong was in fact the residuary beneficiary in Isobel Field's estate.

10. According to a Codicil made on 28. 3.52 Austin Strong must then have been alive because he was named in the codicil as an executor.[1] Testatrix died on 26. 6.53.

11. A letter dated 12. 4.56 to the Public Trustee from the Assistant Trust Officer of the First Western Bank (executors of Mrs. Field's will) refer to Mrs. Austin Strong as the residuary beneficiary. There is also a letter dated 4. 8.53 from Francis Price, to the High Commissioner which refers to Mrs. Austin Strong as residuary devisee.

12. A letter dated 2. 7.53 from Francis Price, Councillor at Law, Santa Barbara to the Samoan Public Trustee contains the following passage: "Under her will, the residuary estate is bequeathed to Mary Strong (widow of Austin Strong, the late son of Mrs. Field) who resides in New York City."

II. *DEED*

THIS DEED made the 29th day of April 1958 between the Samoan Public Trustee (hereinafter called the Administrator) of the first part and MARY STRONG of Massachusetts in the United States of America, Widow, (hereinafter called the donor) of the second part and HER MAJESTY THE QUEEN IN RIGHT of the Government of Western Samoa (hereinafter called the donee) of the third part

WHEREAS the Administrator is seised of an estate in fee simple in the land described in the Schedule hereto as administrator in Western Samoa of the estate of ISOBEL FIELD (hereinafter called the deceased) and

WHEREAS the Donor is the residuary devisee under the will of the said deceased and is entitled to have convevey to her *all that* the said land described in the Schedule hereto and

WHEREAS the said land in the site of the tomb of Robert Louis Stevenson formerly of Vailima, Author, and of Fanny Van De Grift Stevenson his widow and

[1] Austin Strong died on September 18, 1952.

WHEREAS the said Fanny Van de Grift Stevenson at the time of her death was seised of an estate in fee simple in the said land and did by her last will and testament devise the said land to her daughter ISOBEL FIELD and

WHEREAS the said Isobel Field by her last will and testament devised the said land to her daughter-in-law the Donor and

WHEREAS the Donor believes that it was the wish and desire of her mother-in-law the said ISOBEL FIELD that the said land should be given to the Government of Western Samoa to be kept in perpetuity as the site of the tomb of Robert Louis Stevenson and of Fanny Van deGrift Stevenson his widow and the mother of said ISOBEL FIELD and

WHEREAS the donor is of like mind and

WHEREAS the Government of Western Samoa has agreed to accept the gift of the said land and to have it declared to be reserve to be kept for all time as a memorial to Robert Louis Stevenson and his widow Fanny Van de Grift Stevenson and

WHEREAS the donor being of full age has directed the Administrator to give and convey to the Donee all that the estate and interest in the said land to which the donor is beneficially entitled under the will of the said ISOBEL FIELD and

WHEREAS all duties debts and funeral and testamentary expenses in the estate of the deceased have been duly paid or discharged or otherwise provided for *NOW THIS DEED WITNESSETH* that in consideration of the premises and at the request and by the direction of the Donor (testified to by her execution of these presents) the Administrator *DOTH HEREBY GIVE AND CONVEY* unto Her Majesty the Queen in right of the Government of Western Samoa all that the parcel of land described in the Schedule hereto together with all appurtenances thereunto belonging or thereto pertaining to hold the same in fee simple as a reserve in perpetuity as a memorial to Robert Louis Stevenson and his widow Fanny Van deGrift Stevenson and the Donee hereby accepts the gift on the terms hereinbefore reited.

SCHEDULE

ALL that piece or parcel of land containing an area of one acre (1a. Or. Op.) more or less, situated on Vaea Mountain near Alia, in the district of Tuamasaga described as Parcel 113/79, Flur VIII, Upolu being part of Court Grant 174 and being all of the land registered in Volume 1 Folio 122 of the Land Register of Western Samoa together with a right of way appurtenant thereto, over portions of Parcels 115/83 and 114/79 Flur VIII, such right of way being more particularly delineated in Grund buch IV-415 Folio 5.

IN WITNESS WHEREOF these presents have been executed the day and year first hereinbefore written.

SIGNED by the SAMOAN PUBLIC TRUS-
TEE (as administrator of the estate of Isobel   B. L. Clare
Field) by BERNARD LEWIS CLARE and   (L. S.)
sealed with his seal of office in the presence of:

         E. R. Winkel
         Attorney-General
         Apia.

SIGNED by MARY STRONG as Donor by her
Attorney the Samoan Public Trustee by Ber-   B. L. Clare
nard Lewis Clare and sealed with his seal of   (L. S.)
office in the presence of:

         E. R. Winkel
         Attorney-General
         Apia.

SIGNED by THE HIGH COMMISSIONER
OF WESTERN SAMOA for and on behalf of   G. R. Powles
HER MAJESTY THE QUEEN as Donee and   (L. S.)
sealed with his seal of office in the presence of:

         E. R. Winkel
         Attorney-General
         Apia.

III. *DECLARATION OF NON REVOCATION*

I, BERNARD LEWIS CLARE, of Apia in Western Samoa, Samoan Public Trustee do solemnly and sincerely declare as follows:

1. ... THAT I have executed the foregoing Conveyance as the Attorney and in the name of the therein described MARY STRONG under and by virtue of a certain Power of Attorney bearing date the 25th day of June, 1956.
2. ... THAT I have received no notice or information of the revocation of the said Power of Attorney by death or otherwise and I do verily believe the same to be in full force and effect.

AND I make this solemn declaration conscientiously believing the same to be true and by virtue of an act of the General Assembly of New Zealand entitled the Samoan Act, 1921.

DECLARED at Apia this 29th day

of April 1958 before me: } (signed) B. L. Clare

(signed)   E. R. Winkel

A Solicitor of the Supreme Court of New Zealand.

IV. *STEVENSON MEMORIAL RESERVE AND MOUNT VAEA*
Scenic Reserve

1958, No. 10

An Ordinance to set aside certain lands as a reserve in memory of Robert Louis Stevenson and certain other lands as a scenic reserve   (22 September 1958

WHEREAS certain land on Mount Vaea which is the resting place of Robert Louis Stevenson formerly of Vailima (known to the people of Western Samoa as Tusitala), and of Fanny Stevenson, his wife, has been given to the Government of Western Samoa by the heir of said Fanny Stevenson as a memorial to Robert Louis Stevenson.

And whereas certain adjoining land which is also owned by the Government of Western Samoa has an intrinsic scenic value.

And whereas it is desirable that provision be made for the maintenance and control of such lands.

Now Therefore be it enacted by the Legislative Assembly of Western Samoa as follows:

1. Short Title—This Ordinance may be cited as the Stevenson Memorial Reserve and Mount Vaea Scenic Reserve Ordinance 1958.

2. Land set aside as Reserve—(1) The lands described in the First and Second Schedules to this Ordinance are hereby set aside as reserves.

(2) The land described in the First Schedule shall be known as the Stevenson Memorial Reserve and shall be maintained in perpetuity by the Government of Western Samoa in memory of Robert Louis Stevenson and his love for the people of Samoa.

(3) The land described in the Second Schedule shall be known as the Mount Vaea Scenic Reserve and shall be maintained in perpetuity by the Government of Western Samoa as a scenic reserve.

3. Adding land to Mount Vaea Reserve—The High Commissioner may by warrant under his hand and under the Seal of Western Samoa add any contiguous area of Crown land to the Mount Vaea Scenic Reserve and such land shall thereupon be deemed to be part of the Mount Vaea Scenic Reserve for the purposes of this Ordinance.

4. Regulations—(1) The High Commissioner may from time to time make all such regulations as he considers necessary or expedient for giving full effect to the provisions of this Ordinance or for the due administration thereof.

(2) Without limiting the general power to make regulations conferred by subsection one of this section it is hereby declared that regulations may be made under that subsection for all or any of the following purposes:

(a) Prescribing the conditions under which public access may be granted to the reserves hereby declared, or either of them;

(b) Prescribing the charge (if any) which may be imposed for admission to the reserves, or either of them;

(c) Prescribing the conditions under which persons may be authorised to act as guides on the reserves, or either of them;

(d) Prescribing the maximum fee that may be charged by any authorised guide for his service as a guide;

(e) Making it an offence for any authorised guide to charge a fee for his services as a guide in excess of the maximum fee prescribed;

(f) Making it an offence for any person other than an authorised guide to charge a fee for any services as a guide offered or rendered by him in respect of the reserves, or either of them;

(g) Making it an offence for any person without prior authority of the High Commissioner or other person having control of the reserves or either of them to fell any tree on either reserve or to remove any tree therefrom or in any way wilfully cause damage to either reserve;

(h) Delegating control of the reserves or either of them to any person or body of persons;

(i) Prescribing fines not exceeding twenty pounds for any breach of the regulations.

(3) Any person who commits a breach of any regulation made under this Ordinance commits an offence.

(4) Every person who commits an offence under any regu-

371

lations made under this Ordinance for which no other penalty is prescribed shall be liable to a fine not exceeding twenty pounds.

SCHEDULES

First Schedule

All that piece or parcel of land containing an area of one acre (1 acre), more or less, situated at Vaea Mountain, near Apia, in the District of Tuamasaga, described as Parcel 113/79, Flur VIII, Upolu, being part of Court Grant 174 and being all the land registered in Volume 1, Folio 122, of the Land Register of Western Samoa.

Second Schedule

Firstly, all that piece or parcel of land containing an area of sixty-nine acres two roods and thirty perches (69 acres 2 roods 30 perches), more or less, situated at Vaea Mountain, near Apia, in the District of Tuamasaga, described as Parcel 280, Flur VIII, Upolu, being part of Court Grant 156 and part of the land registered in Volume 2, Folio 107, of the Land Register of Western Samoa and more particularly delineated on plan 18 u/viii L deposited at the office of the Chief Surveyor at Apia.

Secondly, all that piece or parcel of land containing an area of forty-nine acres and thirteen perches (49 acres 13 perches), more or less, situated at Vaea Mountain, near Apia, in the District of Tuamasaga, described as Parcel 114/79, Flur VIII, Upolu, being part of Court Grant 174 and part of the land registered in Volume 1, Folio 121, of the Land Register of Western Samoa and more particularly delineated on a plan in Grund buch IV, Number 415, Folio 6, deposited at the office of the Land Register of Western Samoa.

Index

Index

Keen, John: 3
King, Arthur Aris: 164, 165
Kipling, Rudyard: 313-15
Koho (South Sea trader): 255
Kussaie Island (Caroline group): 256
Kunst, Gustav: 345, 349

La Farge, John: 166
La Solitude (R. L. S.'s home at Hyères): 15, 18
Lauaki (Samoan chief): 215
Lemusu (Samoan chief): 339
Lepers: 123 ff.; *see also* Molokai
Levuka harbor, Ovalau Island (Fiji Is.): 255
Libel: R. L. S. threatened for, 144, 205
Liliuokalani, Princess (later Queen), Hawaii: 101, 105, 112
Line Islands: 148, 225
Logan, Col. Robert: 345
London Missionary Society: 49 n., 154, 156, 204, 217, 269, 270
Long-boat, Samoan: 195
Low, Will: 25, 26, 326; description of last walk with R. L. S., 28-30; letter to, 113 n., 253-54
Low Archipelago: 54
Lubeck (steamer): 159, 167, 180
Ludgate Hill (freighter): 24
Lundie, Rev. George Archibald: 176
Lupe (pigeons): 167

McCallum, Mr. (on Hiva Oa Island): 50
MacCallum, Thomas Murray: on *Equator* voyage, 146-47, 148
McClure, Mr. (publisher): 25
McClure's magazine: 82
Macdonald-Millar, Rev. Donald: 239
Mackaness, George: 144
McKay, George L.: 276
Madison Island (Marquesas Is.): 46
Makanalua Peninsula, Molokai Island: 123, 124
Makin, Greater (*or* Taritari,

Gilbert Is.): described, 48-50; R. L. S.'s visit to, 149-51
Malietoa Laupepa (High Chief of Upolu): 171, 172, 173, 208, 213, 215, 268; forces war with Mata'afa, 212, 220
Mallock, William Hurrell: 307-309
Malua missionary school, Apia: 237
Manasquan, N. J.: 26-27
Manono Island (Samoa): 172, 205, 215; village burned by Germans, 216
Manua group of islands of Samoa: 171
"Manuia Lanai" (R. L. S.'s cottage on Waikiki Beach): 106
Maota tree: 167
Marchand Island: *see* Nuku Hiva
Marquesans: history and habits, 45 ff.; food, 46; etiquette of, 46-47, 48; manners and morals, 51-53; *see also* Polynesians
Marquesas Islands: 42 ff., 103-104; history of, 46
Marshall, George: 4
Mata'afa (High Chief of Upolu): 171, 173, 212, 304; reaction to foreign rule, 210; war with Malietoa, 212; as prisoner of Germans, 215 ff.; letter to R. L. S., 220; in exile, 320
Maume apples (papayas): 168
Mauna Kea, Island of Hawaii: 112
Mauna Loa, Island of Hawaii: 112
Melanesians: 164
Melville, Herman: locale of *Typee*, 49
Mepi (Samoan land examiner): 221
Merritt, Dr. (owner of *Casco*): 31, 32, 359
Meyer, Mr., of Molokai: 139
Michel, Brother: 50
Micronesians (Gilbertese): 150-51, 225
Missionaries: 103-104, 253; in Marquesas, 48-49; in Hawaii, 103-104, 106; in Gilberts, 150-51; R. L. S. comments on, 151;

377

give Polynesians a written language, 175–76; in Samoa, 177–78
Moé, Matea of Tautira: 71, 85, 87, 103; gives feast for R. L. S., 90
Molokai Island (Hawaii): description of, 124–25; R. L. S. visits, 111, 123–27
Mooréa Channel: 68
Mooréa Island (Tahitian Is.): 44, 98
Moors, Harry J.: 221, 237; identified, 157; opinion of Fanny Stevenson, 158, 238–40; Stevensons break with, 237–38; writes book about Stevensons, 360
Mormons (at Tautira): 85
Morning Star (missionary ship): 110, 111
Morris, Hedstrom (trading company): 192
Mosher, Thomas B. (Portland, Me., publisher): 144
Motane Island (Marquesas Is.): 51, 239
Mothe Island (Samoa): 161, 239
Mount Pioa, Pago Pago: 194–95
Mount Tohivea, (Mooréa Island: 44
Mount Vaea, Upolu (Samoa): 154, 233, 339, 345; R. L. S.'s choice for burial, 202; bird refuge, 355
Mount Vailele, Upolu (Samoa): 233, 340
Mu, Lost Continent of: 54, 147, 177
Muliaiga (Samoan chief): 339
Mulifanua Beach, Upolu (Samoa): 154
Mulinuu, Upolu (Samoa): 154
Murray, David Christie: letter to, 312–13
Murrays, the, Earls of Tullibardine: 75–76

Nassau, Mothe Island: 161
Nerli, Count Girolamo: portrait of R. L. S., 345
Newell, Rev. J. E.: 204, 270, 271
The New Review (periodical): 226
New Zealand: takes over government of Samoa, 346; accepts tomb site, 347–49
"North, Capt. George" (R. L. S.'s pseudonym in writing *Treasure Island*): 14
Noumea, New Caledonia: 164
Nuku Hiva (*or* Marchand Island): R. L. S. at 42 ff.; smallpox epidemic on, 45
Nuuanu Pali: 10

Oa, Bay of (Aoa Bay, Tutuila Island): 195
Oahu Island (Hawaii): 10
Oahu Pali: 106
Oakland, Calif.: 5
Ofu Island (Samoa): 171, 221
O Le Sulu Samoa (monthly Polynesian paper): 270
Olosega Island (Samoa): 171, 221; *see also* Swain's Island
Ori, Arii (Tautira noble): 71, 85, 87, 103, 357; characterized, 84; to Papeete for supplies, 90–91; farewell letter to R. L. S., 96–97
Orsmond, Rev. John Muggridge: 87
Osbourne, Fanny: *see* Fanny Stevenson
Osbourne, Hervey: 5, 6
Osbourne, Isobel: *see* Isobel Field
Osbourne, Samuel: 4, 5, 8, 9
Osbourne, (Samuel) Lloyd: 4, 6, 33, 35, 145, 160, 161, 180, 187, 291, 301, 338, 341, 344; writes *The Wrong Box* with R. L. S., 26; R. L. S.'s regard for, 108–109, 165; to Skerryvore, 164–65; defends mother against slanderous remarks, 239–40; collaborates with R. L. S. on *The Wrecker*, 254; letter to Triggs, 361–63
Otis, Capt. (of *Casco*): 31, 34, 35, 56, 66, 67, 101; opinion of R. L. S., 32, 38; agrees to sail to Fakarava, 54; discovers rotten mainmast, 72; on voyage to Honolulu

Pacific Islands Monthly: 251

Index

Vailima prayer: 263
Virginibus Puerisque: 266, 279
Weir of Hermiston: 288–89, 291, 296–97, 315, 318, 320; dedication of, 320
"Will o' the Mill": 278–80, 322–23
"Woodman, The": 223–24, 225–33
Wrecker, The: (with Lloyd Osbourne): 99, 170, 203, 254
Wrong Box, The (with Lloyd Osbourne): 26, 109, 145
Young Chevalier, The: 291

Stevenson Society, Edinburgh: 347
Stevenson, Thomas (R. L. S.'s father): 24, 353
Stevenson tomb: site, 346, 347 ff.; error on, 351
Stirling, Scotland: 74, 75
Stoddard, Charles: 31, 49, 359
Stowers, George: 347
Strang, William: describes R. L. S., 199–200
Strong, Austin: 145, 180, 184, 186, 237, 238, 260, 287, 331, 332, 341, 344, 353, 360–61
Strong, Mrs. Austin: 348
Strong, Joe: 10, 100, 145, 157, 180, 184; in Hawaii, 106; on *Equator*, 146; marital difficulties, 185–87
Stuart, A. V.: poem quoted, 20–24
Stuebel, Dr. (German consul at Apia): 158
Submissive Islands: *see* Paumotus
Swain's Island: 162–63
Swanston Cottage: 56–58
Sydney, Australia: 164, 313, 316; climate of, 159
Sydney Civil Service Co-operative Society: 299
Symonds, John Addington: letter to, 93–95

Taa Huku Bay, Hiva Oa Is.: 50
Tafuna'i (pit for burning rubbish): 168, 215
Tagaloa (Samoan god): 248, 261, 325
Tahiti: 68, 69

Tahitian food: 71, 84, 85, 86
Tahitian houses: 70–71
Tahitians: 58; manners and customs, 65, 69–70, 71, 85–86, 97–98; character of, 66; description of, 69 ff.; response to R. L. S., 84 ff.
Taiarapu, Tahiti: 68
Taiohae Bay, Nuku Hiva: 49
Talolo (Vailima boy): 201, 337, 338, 354
Tamafaiga (Samoan chief): 172, 178
Tamasese (Samoan chief): 171
"Tamate": *see* James Chalmers
Taniera (Tuamotuan leader): 60–61, 62, 63
Taravao, Tahiti: 68
Tarawa (Gilbert Is.): 150
Taritari Island: *see* Makin Island
Tattooing: 47
Tauchnitz, Christian Karl von (German publisher): 277–78
Tau Island (Manua group, Samoa): 171, 189–91, 221
Taumafatoga (Samoan feast of friendship): 246–47, 324–26
Taupou (Samoan beauty girl): 214–15, 244
Tautira, Tahiti: 357; trip to, 68 ff.; description of, 70, 84; R. L. S.'s work at, 83; life in, 83 ff.; R. L. S.'s feast at, 85–86; comment on, 91, 93–95, 96
Taylor, Griffiths: 177
Taylor, Sir Henry and Lady: 20
Tebureimoa, Chief (Greater Makin): 149
Teriitera, "Splendor of the Sky": Ori's nickname for R. L. S., 98
Thomson, Johnstone, W. S.: 78
Thornhill, Scotland: 75
Three Powers (England, Germany, U. S.): 172, 206, 207, 209, 210, 211; in Samoan civil war, 214–18
Thurston, Sir John: 221
Tikei Island (Pernicious group): 54
"Tin Jack" (trader): 254

383

Last Witness for Robert Louis Stevenson

is set on the Linotype in 10 point Caledonia with 3 points of spacing between the lines. Caledonia is an original design by W. A. Dwiggins, cut for the Linotype in 1940. While it has the feeling of the original Scotch faces on which it was based, Caledonia is lighter and better suited to modern tastes. For this reason, as well as for its many other noteworthy qualities, it was chosen for this book.

UNIVERSITY OF OKLAHOMA PRESS : NORMAN